G000139486

As a Director of Saatchi & Saatchi, ALEX FYNN helped produce the first advertising campaign for a football club featuring Tottenham Hotspur back in the '80s. He wrote the commercial section in the FA's Blueprint for the future of football which led directly to the formation of the Premier League and the BSkyB television contract. Now a consultant to clubs at home and abroad, he also writes and broadcasts on football.

H. DAVIDSON is a Tottenham supporter of 29 years standing (and more recently sitting). He has contributed to a variety of supporter publications and has written on other sports for general interest magazines.

'Every once in a while a football book comes along that completely forgets what it's supposed to be and applies the same sort of values you'd expect in, you know, a proper book. *Dream On* is that book. A book with a sense of drama, a strong narrative driven by more than purely the subject, room for intelligent opinion and a point to it other than paying homage to a particular individual or institution'
Lloyd Bradley, *Sky Sports Magazine*

'A football classic – the *Glory Game* of its time. Don't be put off if you're not a Spurs fan. So cleverly do the authors use the ups and downs of Spurs' season to launch a series of debates and arguments concerning football as a whole, it's more the story of the year in the life of an English League club'
Olivia Blair, *FourFourTwo*

'Make no mistake, this book is not just of interest to Tottenham fans. Anyone who wants a fascinating, intelligent analysis of the modern game should look no further than this superb tome that demands to be bought and read'
Chas Newkey-Burden, *90 Minutes*

'From the viewpoint of London N17, *Dream On* plays a blinder – cogent, entertaining, penetrating, unafraid to tackle Bosman and Sky. But wherever your loyalties lie, *Dream On* expertly maps the Premiership turf'
Mat Snow, *Total Sport*

'Insights, infighting...revealing interviews...Fynn and Davidson don't pull many punches'
Nick Szczepanik, *Total Football*

'Alex Fynn has once again done us fans proud with an armoury of inside knowledge that scarcely anyone else has the ability to unearth'
Mark Perryman, *New Times*

'It satisfies our train-spotting cravings for knowledge of the esoteric and arcane happenings behind the scenes in professional football...fascinating portraits of Terry Venables, Alan Sugar and Gerry Francis...I thoroughly enjoyed *Dream On*'
The Absolute Game (Scottish fanzine)

Also by Alex Fynn (and Lynton Guest)

Out of Time:
Why football isn't working

Heroes and Villains:
*The inside story of the 1990/91 season at Arsenal
and Tottenham Hotspur*

The Secret Life of Football

By Alex Fynn and Eric Cantona

Cantona on Cantona

DREAM ON

A Year in the Life of a Premier League Club

ALEX FYNN
AND
H. DAVIDSON

POCKET BOOKS

LONDON · SYDNEY · NEW YORK · TOKYO · SINGAPORE · TORONTO

First published in Great Britain by Simon & Schuster, 1996
This edition published by Pocket Books, 1997
An imprint of Simon & Schuster Ltd
A Viacom Company

Copyright © Alex Fynn and H. Davidson, 1996

This book is copyright under the Berne Convention
No reproduction without permission
All rights reserved

The right of Alex Fynn and H. Davidson to be identified as author of this
work has been asserted in accordance with sections 77 and 78 of the
Copyright Designs and Patents Act 1988

Simon & Schuster
West Garden Place
Kendal Street
London W2 2AQ

Simon & Schuster Australia
Sydney

A CIP catalogue record for this book is available
from the British Library.

0-671-85509-3

Printed and bound in Great Britain by Caledonian International Book
Manufacturing, Glasgow

To Daniel Stern

Contents

Introduction   xiii

Prologue   Hello, I Must Be Going . . .   1

1 The Greed-Is-Good League   17

2 Carry on Intertoto   37

3 The Way We Were   69

4 Tomorrow Belongs to Me   99

5 Mind The Gap   133

6 Love Thy Neighbour   163

7 Sky's The Limit   209

8 Top Gear   237

9 Walking Alone   269

10 Wholesale/Retail/Import/Export . . . ish   299

11 Yesterdays Gone   339

12 Survival of the Fittest   373

13 The End of the Beginning   397

Postscript   423

14 1996–97: What's Glory Got To Do With It?   427

Acknowledgements

It will be obvious that without the considerable assistance
of many people this book would not have been produced.
When Tottenham were approached for privileged access,
they refused. Indeed, why should they go out of their way
to give assistance to a project that, by its very nature,
was bound to be critical? Nevertheless they were not
obstructive. Far from it – they allowed us to make our own
contacts. Thus we were able to talk to everyone we wanted.
So special thanks go to Claude Littner, the Managing
Director, and to John Fennelly, John Moulding and Ashley
Weller – the best press office in the Premier League.

In addition to those people directly quoted in the book,
largely the result of specific interviews, we would especially
like to thank Philip Cornwall, Harry Lansdown, and
Greville Waterman who were kind enough to read the
manuscript. Similarly, Douglas Alexiou, Mark Jacob, Bernie
Kingsley and Gerard Tyrell who cast their professional eyes
over the proofs. Also Rob Bagchi, James Freedman and
Mark Burton who read some of the early drafts. Without

Dream On

exception all were constructively critical and substantially improved the book.

Chris Belt, Gary Briggs, Brian Collinson and Barry Neville verified some important facts, while Pam Kemmey, Katie Camy, Aruna Bansal, Andra Morrison, Sonia Medin and Beverley Palmer from Saatchi and Saatchi provided invaluable background information.

Contributing to the acclaimed *Alive and Kicking* brought a double bonus as we were privy to so much material. Some of it concerning the Spurs heroes of yesterday has found its way into Chapter Four. Our gratitude goes to series producer, Jean Claude Braggard, and his assistant Brenda Hollingsworth.

Discussions with Greg Dyke, David Lacey, Myles Palmer and Martin Thorpe were always an enormous help. Thanks also to Sue Mott, we have drawn liberally from her *Daily Telegraph* interview with Alan Sugar, particularly in Chapter Thirteen. Similarly, many of Gerry Francis' comments in the same chapter were acquired during the course of our session with him for the Tottenham fanzine *Cock-a-Doodle-Doo*.

Photographs, taken by Frank Baron, Michael Steel and Tom Jenkins are by kind permission of the *Guardian* and the *Observer*. Special thanks to Eamonn McCabe and Mark Bygraves.

Football fans come in all shapes and sizes. There is undoubtedly a John Harris, a Morris Keston and an Amy Lawrence at every club. Being the beneficiaries of their commitment and enthusiasm convinced us that their isolation from the decision-making process is their club's loss. Many have been quoted at length. Others such as Steve Mono and Kevin Millichip have not. Either way, thanks for the insights.

Acknowledgements

Over at Simon & Schuster, Gillian Holmes was an inde-
fatigably skilled and knowledgeable editor, Martin Fletcher
supervised the project with cool assurance, Bob Kelly was
an understanding sales director and Aniz Damani an always
helpful production manager.

With the adding of another chapter for the paperback
edition, more thanks are in order; to Alan and Daniel
Sugar for their interviews; to John Sinnott of *Match of
the Day Magazine* who provided some of Gerry Francis'
observations and to Julie Davies and Keith Barnes at Simon
& Schuster.

Introduction

In the four years since the formation of the Premier League, football in England has undergone a greater change than at any time in its history. With the influence of BSkyB, and club chairmen at last given the free rein they craved, the game has been reincarnated. A fan returning to these shores after a four-year absence would not recognise the game he left behind. The players, their strip, their wages, their agents, the tactics, the stadia, the TV coverage, the transfer fees, the media attention, the club owners, the admission prices, the crowd make-up and the merchandising would perplex anyone who hadn't actually lived through the changes.

This book is about one year in the life of one club. If you are a Spurs fan, it is your club. But the dramas could equally apply to followers of Arsenal, Manchester United or any of the other clubs that make up the top division. In telling the story of one club, we are really telling the story of English Premier League football today.

Why Spurs? Simply because of the author's great

Dream On

affection for the club, gained by working for it, supporting it, living nearby and through the privilege of knowing some of the key characters both on and off the pitch.

It is a legacy of *The Glory Game* that any subsequent book following Spurs through a season draws comparison with Hunter Davies' wonderful 1973 volume. Would that any author received such cooperation from the club today. Although we were not actively hindered in our progress, we should make it clear that all insights and access gained were due to initiatives by the authors.

Written as the season unfolded, we were sometimes overtaken by events that left us looking either mistaken, or occasionally prescient. However, a decision was taken at the outset not to be masters of hindsight. We hope that the reader will acknowledge our policy not to re-write each chapter, but instead view each as a snapshot of the situation at that moment in time.

This is not a match-by-match account of the season, rather a journey through the issues that shape today's game, using the chronology of a season to lead from one event to the next. We have tried to offer solutions rather than snipe, although we fear most criticism may be unwelcome by the recipients, but we hope our words can be accepted in the constructive vein in which they are offered.

Even as this book goes to press, breaking stories suggest season number five of the Premiership will be every bit as dramatic as its predecessors. We hope this story represents an accurate picture of what life in the Premiership is actually like.

Alex Fynn & H. Davidson
July 1996

Prologue

Hello, I Must Be Going . . .

For the home fans who had resisted their usual urge to shoot off early and miss the North Circular bottlenecks, the final whistle came as blessed relief.

Two peeps from referee Paul Durkin concluded the match, and closed the 1994–95 season for both Spurs and their visitors, Leeds United. The travelling Yorkshire support could now give full vent to their joy. The scruffy 1-1 draw had ensured that Howard Wilkinson's side got the single point needed to guarantee automatic entry into next season's UEFA Cup.

Being a Sunday afternoon, there was little chance of those fans being able to toast their team's achievement before the long trip home. For that they could thank Sky Sports and its flunkies at the Premier League. With the entire Premiership programme put back 24 hours to accommodate satellite TV's insatiable appetite for live drama, it would take a good driver to negotiate almost the entire length of the M1 in time to enjoy a pint of Tetley's before the pubs closed at ten-thirty. Still, as news

_____

Dream On

leaked out, to further riotous celebration, that Manchester United had just lost their Premiership crown to Blackburn Rovers, you could indeed conceive, as so many of the visitors would have you believe, that 'God is a Yorkshireman'. The t-shirt merchants would be busy during the coming summer.

Nobody outside Newcastle, whom they had overhauled for the final automatic qualifying position, could really begrudge Leeds their reward nor their supporters the day-dreams of forthcoming trips to Paris, Milan or Barcelona. A string of fine performances and, in particular, late winning goals, had propelled Leeds into the top five and must have had fans and management alike pondering what could have been if this late charge had begun at Christmas instead of at Easter.

But what the heck; as if Spurs fans didn't have concerns of their own at a time like this. Dreams of exotic destinations were far from the thoughts of the home crowd who had swelled the gate to a best-of-season 33,040.

As captain for the day Jurgen Klinsmann took his bows and waved his farewells from the centre circle, it was difficult for most, and particularly those wearing 'Klinsmann 18' replica shirts, not to feel a twinge of envy for Leeds and those of their supporters in 'Yeboah 21' shirts. Leeds had amply demonstrated that they had the makings of a fine, well balanced side. There was much for them to look forward to next season. In particular, Tony Yeboah, their expensive foreign import, had turned into a goal-scoring sensation and one who was happy to pledge his immediate future to the club.

Not so Jurgen. His lawyers had demonstrated how a 'two-year contract', could expire after twelve months and now Klinsmann was, for sure, off to Bayern Munich.

Hello, I Must Be Going. . .

So Leeds had a rosy future, and Jurgen thought he had too. But what of Spurs?

It is difficult to relate any part of Tottenham's recent history without a deep sigh, the ensuing pause acting as a warning that here begins a tale of self-inflicted woe and lost opportunities. A season of transition, it would appear, is the permanent status quo at White Hart Lane. By default.

There always seems to be a good reason why 'next year' will be the one when the team really clicks, when the new signings will gel, when the football will flow, when the wins will come and the trophies will be collected. *Audere est Facere* is the club's motto, which could be translated as *Free Beer Tomorrow*.

Terry Venables arrived as Messiah in November 1987. Given a free hand by chairman Irving Scholar to do whatever was necessary to bring back the glory days, Venables failed miserably. The triumphant 1991 FA Cup campaign stands alone in marked contrast to a six-year reign that highlighted a roller-coaster transfer market business. For every sensational Gazza, Lineker, Anderton or Sheringham he bought, there is a commensurately awful folly who should never have been allowed anywhere near a Spurs shirt.

Even as he brushed Sugar's bootmark from his rump in May 1993, Venables was still spouting about the foundations for a successful future that he had supposedly laid for his successor. That successor, Ossie Ardiles, fared even worse.

The likeable Argentinian at least had the decency to cram his failings into just fifteen memorable months. A record of Played 65, Won 21, Drew 16 and Lost 28 does scant justice to the depths of despair felt by fans who witnessed just four

Dream On

home league wins in the whole of his first season, including none at all between October '93 and April '94. As money was thrown at the problem of impending relegation, Ossie entered the transfer market and brought in six staggeringly ordinary journeymen for the thick end of £4 million.

Amazingly, relegation was avoided by a whisker and, against all odds, Ardiles kept his job. In fact, not only was he given a second chance to sink Spurs (and thereby emulate his record at Newcastle; somebody wasn't paying attention), he was also handed a further £7 million by his chairman to splash out on three World Cup stars. But even nine new players and an outlay of £11 million could only produce two home wins before Sugar's boot swung again and two months into the new season, Ardiles once again became part of Tottenham's history rather than its future.

In an attempt to go back to the future, Alan Sugar tried to prise David Pleat away from Luton Town, just as his predecessor Irving Scholar had successfully done in 1986. Pleat's stay at White Hart Lane had been as sweet – FA Cup finalists, Littlewoods Cup semi-finalists and third in the league – as it was short. Tabloid allegations of an unseemly side to his private life brought proceedings to a premature conclusion after just eighteen months. The sudden availability of Terry Venables, freed by Barcelona, did nothing to help Pleat's long term job prospects. Now, as negotiations became stuck in job definitions, David Pleat was again rebuffed by Tottenham when Alan Sugar was presented with an unexpected chance to change his mind.

Enter Gerry Francis.

QPR chairman Richard Thompson, in a manoeuvre born of good intentions but horribly executed, had lost one of the highly regarded breed of younger managers, following a blundered attempt to bring in Rodney Marsh

Hello, I Must Be Going. . .

as the chief executive at Loftus Road. Apparently neglecting to tell Gerry Francis of his plan was an oversight he never got the chance to rectify. The very next day, Gerry walked on principle, and Alan Sugar wasted no time in offering the vacant Spurs position to him. So keen was Sugar to get his man that, as with the Klinsmann signing earlier that summer, he made the extraordinary concession of waiving the watertight contracts that would traditionally mark any deal of this magnitude. For a quarter of a million a year, and an agreement that he could walk away the moment he so chose, Gerry Francis took over the hot seat at White Hart Lane on 15th November, 1994.

The turnaround in form and results was greater than anyone could have predicted. Once again, the fans talked of a glorious tomorrow. Once again, their dreams were cruelly dashed.

Within a week of the season ending, two of the three World Cup stars were gone. Klinsmann to Bayern and Popescu to Barcelona. The third, Dumitrescu, was talking to anyone who would listen. A grim-faced Gerry Francis meanwhile faced the media and admitted he was prepared to 'give it another year' at Spurs. Still no contract. The fans, and the chairman it seems, were in for another season of transition.

Free beer tomorrow.

To compound Ardiles' first catastrophic season in charge, the summer of 1994 saw the FA impose swingeing penalties on Tottenham for supposed financial irregularities over a period of years prior to chairman Alan Sugar's arrival. It had been Sugar himself who had exposed the bulk of these irregularities – which mainly took the form of undeclared 'loans' to players. Sugar co-operated in the Premier League

Dream On

and FA investigations, in the belief that such co-operation would result in lenient treatment when the question of punishment arose. This proved to be wishful thinking.

The FA clobbered Tottenham to a degree without precedent among the so-called big clubs: a fine of £600,000; a docking of twelve points for the next season, and a total ban from the 1994/95 FA Cup competition. If it was any consolation to the club, compulsory relegation was not enforced. But in truth, the twelve-point deduction made that fate an inevitability.

Sugar took the matter as a personal slight, and his legal team set about getting the penalties overturned. Success was partial with a halving of the points deficit from twelve to six, which at least lifted the threat of almost certain relegation for the year ahead. But the fine was increased to a whopping £1.5 million, and the FA Cup ban stood.

While two sets of lawyers locked horns before eventually agreeing to abide by the findings of an independent tribunal, Sugar snapped into action. No way was he going to allow the FA to scupper his season as punishment for crimes committed by others. They could take away his points, but they couldn't take away his money – well only a fraction of it. Ossie was given a budget for new players and promptly scooped two of the genuine superstars of world football. First in, for two-and-a-half million pounds, came Ilie Dumitrescu, a hero of Romania's World Cup campaign and in particular their victory over Argentina. Next, word reached Sugar that Jurgen Klinsmann – a striker so famous that even Sugar had heard of him – was out of contract and up for grabs. Another two million quid.

Sugar knew that signing the German World Cup star, to go with Dumitrescu, would be a massive boost to the club and also to his own personal standing with the fans and

Hello, I Must Be Going. . .

within the game. If it also told the FA where they could stick their fine, points deduction and FA Cup ban, then so much the better.

Although foreign imports were now an accepted part of the English league's make-up, Klinsmann would represent, without doubt, the biggest coup yet. For possibly the first time ever, England's top division was able to compete with the Continental giants for the superstars of world football. Not only was the money available in never-before seen amounts (through sponsorship, TV and merchandising), but also the Premiership had gained international credibility, helped in no small measure by the increasing number of countries who were taking live television feeds of the weekly action. When players like Klinsmann, Dumitrescu, Stefan Schwartz, and Daniel Amokachi were offered the chance to come to England, the cons no longer outweighed the pros.

The experience might even prove to be instructive for the glamorous imports, as a competitive edge would have to be added to even a virtuoso's repertoire as a prerequisite to Premiership survival. Wages for short term contracts could be spectacular. Hefty signing-on fees could provide a tolerable cushion against a lifestyle that might compare unfavourably with those in more hedonistic Barcelona, Milan or Monaco.

Prospective signings could be assured of favourable media attention and lucrative commercial opportunities. A year or two in London (or Manchester) wasn't that bad a prospect and any on-field success would be on a stage closely monitored throughout the football world.

Klinsmann had in fact been wooed by Bayern Munich during and after the 1994 USA World Cup. However, his

Dream On

opinion of his own worth proved an insurmountable barrier to the fallen German giants. 'He had', according to Franz Beckenbauer, the Bayern President, 'salary demands that we could not meet.' Most clubs in Europe would have gladly signed Klinsmann, but very few were prepared to compromise their prevailing wage structure by accepting terms that so demonstrably favoured the player. Besides, to return to Bayern for the 1994/95 season would once again mean working under Italian coach Giovanni Trapattoni, with whom Klinsmann had already fallen out during their spell together at Inter Milan.

The contract that formed the agreement between Jurgen Klinsmann and Spurs was a testament to the relative positions of both parties. Spurs wanted Klinsmann badly. Klinsmann could afford to dictate outrageous take-it-or-leave-it terms knowing that sooner or later, he would get exactly what he was asking from someone.

For a start, he proposed no more than a two-year contract. This was born from his bitter experience at Monaco where he clashed with the tactical approach of coach Arsene Wenger to the extent that the German striker felt he had wasted a valuable final year there, merely going through the motions. Although he felt that Spurs manager Ossie Ardiles would be a kindred spirit on the way the game should be played, Klinsmann could not allow himself to become trapped again. Any contract would have an earlier 'get out' clause to exercise should he feel the need. A further clause favoured by Klinsmann stipulated that any club that sold him would have to do so for no more than their initial purchase price; a ploy that enabled Klinsmann to move on continually at increasingly favourable terms.

Sugar was surely mindful of the potential for disruption that anyone earning a million pounds a year could wreak on

Hello, I Must Be Going. . .

his existing squad. Nevertheless he was adamant he would get his man. A compromise deal was thrashed out where Klinsmann's wages were a relatively modest £7,000 per week, but a 'London living' allowance and a hefty signing-on fee brought the total annual remuneration to around £1 million and hence led to the widely reported £23,000 per week figure. Klinsmann was happy for the media to perpetuate the myth of his superstar salary, while Sugar was honour bound to preserve his player's ego.

And so Jurgen Klinsmann signed for Sugar and for Spurs.

And the move was everything Sugar could have hoped (and even dreamed). The media went crazy, and amid a flurry of bad puns (Jurg-er King! Herr-iffic! Jurgen Klinical! Klin the money! Our Herr-o! Now Jurgen-a believe us! I've stuka one in! Klin with a shout!), Klinsmania was born. Jurgen's easy going attitude, perfect English and non-clichéd soundbites had the media over the moon and eating out of his hand. Home fans queued to have his name spelled across the back of their replica shirts, while Klinsmann Hotspur on the road became the country's all-ticket top draw (Spurs at Elland Road in October attracted a bigger crowd than the FA Cup semi-final at the same ground six months later).

On the pitch, Jurgen smashed a personal best of 29 goals that season (and was hugely instrumental in Teddy Sheringham's not inconsiderable tally of 23). Bar one game at Goodison which clashed with international duty, he was ever-present in the Spurs line-up throughout the season, despite two horrific accidents that saw him stretchered off bloodied and unconscious, at Hillsborough and at Villa Park, respectively. His award as Player of the Year from the Football Writers' Association was virtually unchallenged.

Dream On

The neutrals loved him, and the worst that Arsenal fans could feel was jealousy.

Although the team itself suffered its ups and downs, Klinsmann's continued good form ensured Sugar's personal stock remained high. However, as the 1994–95 season drew to its close, Jurgen was increasingly pressed to confirm his intention of seeing out the remaining year of his contract. Worryingly, he would not do so, amid speculation, and soon confirmation, that Franz Beckenbauer had earmarked his countryman to become the final piece in the restructured Bayern Munich jigsaw.

Since his accession to Bayern's presidency in November 1994, Beckenbauer had instilled a realistic appreciation of the cost of assembling a team capable of challenging for major honours. He was determined to leave a presidential imprint on the club; adamant that Bayern should no longer live in the shadow of the side he had captained to three successive European Cup wins between 1974–76. His objective was simply stated: that 'Bayern should resume its position among the Euro mega clubs on a regular basis'.

Beckenbauer offered the 30-year-old Klinsmann a three-year contract worth £1 million a year, with a further £1.6 million signing-on fee; terms that almost doubled the German's earnings from White Hart Lane. Perhaps more important (after all, Jurgen had already accumulated a personal fortune from three previous big-money moves – he may have driven the streets of London in a Beetle but the Porsche was garaged in his villa at Lake Como) was that Bayern, under Beckenbauer, had determined to do exactly what Alan Sugar wanted to do at Tottenham – build a championship side. However, unlike Tottenham, Bayern were not prepared to sacrifice a transitional season. With a new coach, Otto Rehhagel – who had failed to win by one

Hello, I Must Be Going. . .

point the title for Werder Bremen when his new club beat them in the last game of the season (mixed emotions, eh, Otto?) – the signals were clear: a revitalised Bayern with Klinsmann in attack, alongside new signings Strunz, Sforza and Herzog, together with Jean Pierre Papin and Lothar Matthäus returning after injury, going all out for the German championship in year one, followed by an assault on the Champions League in year two.

Klinsmann had always been polite when commenting on Tottenham and the fans, but there was no denying that Bayern, playing in Munich's Olympic Stadium and commanding home crowds twice the 27,258 that Spurs had averaged, really were in a different league. The German Bundesliga was enjoying a resurgence that saw average crowds exceed 30,000 and boast a strength in depth that surpassed the Premiership's league-within-a-league hierarchy. Just about every member of the German national side was now back playing league football in Germany after their dalliances with overseas clubs. Add the attraction of finishing his career on home ground, plus the thinly veiled assurances given by Beckenbauer that Jurgen would have a coaching career with Bayern when his playing days were over, and you couldn't really argue with Klinsmann's decision to jump ship.

Against all those Fatherland comforts, the debits of staying at Tottenham were beginning to mount. Spurs had failed to qualify for Europe again and were far from being potential title chasers. The side was heavily weighed down with footballing journeymen; there was still no midfield genius who could appreciate and reward Klinsmann's runs and feints (as previously Gascoigne had with Lineker). Gerry Francis had indeed turned his team into a functioning unit, but the consequence of this was that Klinsmann was

Dream On

expected to play his full part in defensive duties – a chore few strikers relish. Klinsmann was also concerned at the number of games he was expected to play – the previous Christmas and New Year period had come as a shock to his system, as had the myopic referees who had consistently refused to protect him despite some serious penalty area butchery. No wonder thoughts of his second nightmare season at Monaco returned. Klinsmann had to ask himself why he should play a second year for Spurs when he could play fewer games in a better team for more money in his own country.

The adoration he had received from the Spurs fans had been touching, but was really only an extension of what he had already experienced in France and Italy. The north London fans proved unusually philosophical about his proposed departure. No riots, no protests, no campaigns. Just a grateful acknowledgement that they had been lucky to have Jurgen even for a year; a world class player who got his hands dirty in the interests of his team mates. In Jurgen's home town of Stuttgart where he had spent the first eight years of his career, news of the proposed move was received with more than a few raised eyebrows. To return 'home' and yet sign for deadly rivals Bayern Munich was akin to Gazza returning from Lazio to sign for Arsenal.

If the Spurs fans were philosophical about Jurgen's decision, then Sugar most certainly was not. He believed that he had an agreement, that Jurgen – his signing Jurgen – would be at the club for the full two years. In a nutshell, Sugar saw the contract as being for two years, with a possible get-out option after one. Klinsmann, however, saw it as a one-year contract with an option for a second year. Moreover, Beckenbauer's unauthorised approaches to Klinsmann infuriated the Tottenham chairman, who was more aware than most about correct protocol in such matters. As the

Hello, I Must Be Going. . .

season dragged to its anti-climactic conclusion, and Spurs blew their chances of UEFA Cup qualification, Sugar and manager Gerry Francis still believed they had done enough to win over their key asset.

On the afternoon of Thursday 11 May, 1995, the media were summoned to The Comedy Cafe in London's unfashionable East End, where Jurgen announced his decision to leave Spurs in just three days' time.

'It takes time to build a championship winning side,' he said, 'and Gerry and Alan will do that. But I don't have that much time.'

Alan Sugar had already received a phone call in his car that morning from Franz Beckenbauer, telling him of Jurgen's decision, and consoling him with the advice 'not to be too angry, because these things happen in football.' Sugar was furious. After all, you can hardly imagine Sugar himself acting in a similar manner, can you? But he had sufficiently regained his composure by four-thirty that afternoon when it was his turn to host a press conference, at White Hart Lane. Sugar expressed regret at losing Klinsmann, the manner in which the decision had been announced, and the manner in which the player had been wooed by Bayern.

'If anyone's to blame,' confessed Sugar, 'it's me. I signed Jurgen to solve a problem, and I've created another one. Maybe that's part of the learning process for me. Gerry looks more deeply into things.'

His tempered calm betrayed his true emotions. Sugar was to later take up the matter with FIFA who instigated their own investigation into both Bayern's approach and the meagre fee received by Spurs – at just £1.2 million it was exactly what Monaco had received after Klinsmann's signing-off fee had been deducted.

It could however be suggested that Sugar was trying it on,

Dream On

as it was understood by all parties involved that a proportion of the fee paid to Monaco would in turn be passed on to the player. Klinsmann could therefore somewhat justifiably take the line, 'What is all the fuss about? You're getting back what you paid for me'. Indeed, FIFA came to much the same conclusion: that there was nothing contractually amiss with the fee that Spurs received. However they did call into question the validity of the approach made by the man Sugar called 'Arch vice-Duke Beckenbauer of Munich'. It was a pyrrhic victory for the Tottenham chairman – just the sort he despises.

Certainly Sugar felt he had been betrayed by Jurgen, who after all had admitted back in August, 'There is a tingle of excitement running down my spine whenever I think of playing for a great club like Spurs. I don't think I have felt this excited for a long while. Signing for Tottenham has given me an immense lift and virtually saved my career.'

For the present, though, Sugar had been stitched up. He had committed the sin of entering into a contract prioritising trust rather than fully exploring the implications of the small print. The contract had two escape clauses; one was relegation and the other was if Jurgen could not settle in London. Tottenham of course didn't get relegated and from his luxury apartment in fashionable Hampstead, Jurgen enjoyed the delights of the capital. As he told BBC Radio 5, he found London 'Cosmopolitan ... tolerant, never so aggressive like big cities on the Continent ... it [was] just a wonderful experience to discover a place like London.'

Thus to invoke this clause as a reason for leaving was, in Alan Sugar's eyes, sheer hypocrisy and clearly broke the spirit if not the letter of the agreement. The Spurs chairman had previously demonstrated that his legal eagles

Hello, I Must Be Going...

were more than a match for their counterparts at the FA. However, it would appear that they still had much to learn from their Teutonic rivals. *Vorsprung durch Technik*, or So Long, Suckers, as they can be heard to say in Munich.

And Spurs were faced with yet another transitional season. Jurgen's departure had left the team in a worse state than when he had arrived; he was an impossible act to follow.

Jurgen's final game for Spurs, that Sunday afternoon against Leeds, was a very low key affair indeed. A goal from him would have been nice, but instead it was yesterday's man, Teddy Sheringham, who scored to give Spurs their 1-1 draw. Teddy had taken a back seat all season to Klinsmania, forced to play in an unfamiliar position behind the German striker; more provider than taker of goals. But Teddy to his credit had stuck at it, playing in every game bar one and scoring a highly respectable 23 goals.

It may have been an unfamiliar position for Sheringham, so used to being the main striker himself. But he would later acknowledge that the experience made him a better player, and his adaptability made a strong impression on Klinsmann himself who would fondly recall his time playing alongside the England striker.

As the 22 players completed their farewell lap and disappeared back down the tunnel, it was Sheringham who remained on the pitch as the crowd chanted his name with increased vigour. With Klinsmann gone, Sheringham would be expected to return to centre stage and provide those valuable goals that would get Spurs through the coming season. The crowd knew this, and Teddy knew this. And Teddy knew the crowd knew this. It was as if both parties in a marriage had acknowledged that Klinsmann – the mistress

Dream On

– had driven a wedge between them. But now that wedge had been removed. The crowd's distraction by Klinsmann's flirtatious behaviour had been wanton but understandable. But as with many affairs, it had ended in tears. Now the marriage could resume, stronger for the challenge it had beaten off.

The ground emptied, and the tannoy announced further match results that no one was there to hear. And then it fell quiet, as if the PA announcer had been the last person to realise the season had finished.

As always, it was difficult to believe that the disillusionment and utter exhaustion felt with football at that moment would be gone when August came around. To be replaced with that ridiculous optimism that fans (and players?) feel on the first day of a new season when everybody starts with a clean sheet, and nobody's crap and nobody's bottom and everybody just knows that this is going to be *their* year.

If the fans could avoid their TV screens and newspapers for three months, then they could conceivably forget football for the summer. But not so the club chairmen. For them, the planning and preparation would start immediately. The name of the game in 1995/96 would be the price of success. For others it would be the fear of failure; the fear of falling off the Premiership gravy train. To get a competitive edge, the rules would go out of the window. Up and down the country, the boardrooms were full of super fans. Super fans who would not sit idle while rival clubs drained the players pool of all the big fish.

Blackburn Rovers had proven once again that money, vast quantities of money, can buy happiness and success. And that's what every club wanted for next season: money and happiness and success.

Chapter 1

The Greed-Is-Good League

For a few wealthy clubs the name of the game is the price of success. For the rest it is the cost of avoiding relegation into the division time forgot. Whatever the objective – success or avoiding failure – market forces are effecting an escalating price for both glory and survival. The word was out: buy star players.

During the summer break, Gerry Francis had been facing up to the challenge of strengthening his squad for the season ahead. The absence of Klinsmann was the squad's most obvious depletion, but not Francis's biggest headache. In Teddy Sheringham, he already had the kind of frontman for whom most Premiership clubs would go seriously into debt. With Jurgen now gone, Teddy relished the thought of resuming his role as undisputed frontman, with perhaps young Nicky Barmby alongside, as Robin to his Batman.

But Gerry Francis had other ideas. He was an unashamed fan of QPR striker Les Ferdinand, a player whom he had adopted almost as a personal protégé during their time together at Loftus Road. With QPR manager Ray

Dream On

Wilkins under pressure to raise money before he could himself play the transfer market, the temptation to cash in on 28-year-old Ferdinand before his contract expired was too great. A string of top clubs were expected to move for Ferdinand, but the renewed speculation of a link with Francis coupled with a perceived desire by the player to remain in London would seem to have tipped the balance in Tottenham's favour.

Not so. It was Newcastle's money and Kevin Keegan's charm that clinched the deal. In addition, QPR chairman Richard Thompson had weighed the dice heavily against any move to a fellow London club, particularly one managed by a former employee with whom he had spectacularly fallen out. Besides, Spurs may have been the previous big-money kings, but under Alan Sugar they were simply out of this spending league.

Undeterred, Francis knew his priority remained to land a new striker to replace Klinsmann and provide cover in case of injury to his current squad. He turned his attention to a player who had been grabbing the headlines at Crystal Palace, but for all the wrong reasons.

If Jurgen Klinsmann was the role model who exemplified the Premiership's ideal, then Chris Armstrong was an unlikely successor. Born in Newcastle to a Nigerian mother and an Irish father, Chris was given for adoption at the age of three and raised as an orphan in south London. Chris and his adoptive parents then moved to Wales when he was aged ten.

'My childhood and upbringing were tough,' noted Armstrong, 'and I don't like to talk about it.' Although still in touch with his natural mother (now back in Africa), Chris has no contact with his father.

When he left school at sixteen, his football playing days

The Greed-Is-Good League

seemed over. 'I still loved the game, but I just didn't have time to play. I needed the money so I started work in this burger factory. [Presumably not the same sausage factory that had previously employed Chris Waddle.]

'Anyway, I never really felt I was good enough to play at the highest level.' His friends, however, thought otherwise, and persuaded him to turn out for a local Sunday league side. It was a logical progression for Wrexham to take an interest in the promising seventeen-year-old on their doorstep, and he signed for them in March 1989. Seventy games and sixteen goals later, Millwall manager Bruce Rioch paid £75,000 in August 1991 to bring Armstrong back to south London. 'When I signed for Wrexham, it was the big time for me. I thought they would be as far as I would get. Before then a professional career had never crossed my mind.'

Within a year, Armstrong was taking on the Premier League's top defences after a £1 million move to Crystal Palace in September 1992. But despite Armstrong's fifteen goals in 35 matches, the Eagles were relegated on goal-difference the following May. However, thanks in no small measure to 25 Chris Armstrong goals, Palace bounced back immediately as Division One champions in May 1994. That kind of scoring record from a 22-year-old caused the big clubs to take note, and prompted Palace chairman Ron Noades to slap a deterring £6 million price tag on his star asset.

So Palace and Armstrong were back in the top flight for 1994–95, but Armstrong's goals dried up and the Palace fans began to get on his back. Manager Alan Smith, himself under pressure, became frustrated at Armstrong's scoring drought, and accused him of letting himself and the club down, and even of 'not trying'. Armstrong's personal total of ten cup goals took Palace to semi-finals in both the FA

Dream On

and Coca-Cola Cups, but his meagre total of just eight league goals help doom Palace to relegation yet again which in turn cost Alan Smith his job.

Said Armstrong at the time, 'It is totally wrong to accuse me of not trying or caring. The finger is being pointed at me because of Palace's position. If we go down the blame will be heaped on me.'

What certainly didn't help Palace's cause was the uproar following the disclosure that Chris Armstrong had failed a routine drugs test. The Sports Council have a drugs-detection hit-squad (operating under FA directives) which descends unannounced on a club's training ground to take urine samples from players. This initiative is part of a general crackdown in 50 British sports that netted 67 failures in over 4,000 random tests. Thirteen footballers tested positive during the course of the '94–'95 season – a remarkably low number given the widespread use of soft and recreational drugs in the population as a whole, and amongst youngsters in particular. Eight of those players were found to contain traces of marijuana, two had been users of speed, while the remainder tested positive for stimulants commonly found in routine medication.

FA policy is to conceal the identity of those players who test positive, preferring to make the guilty parties attend a four-week rehabilitation course where they receive counselling for the substance abuse. Chris Armstrong became the first high profile victim of the crackdown when manager Alan Smith went public in response to media rumours about the player's 'mysterious' absence from the first team.

Armstrong held his hands up, admitted that he had smoked a joint, and received a four-match ban for his sins. But that surely wasn't the end of the problem for football. The too-much, too-soon syndrome that has blighted the

The Greed-Is-Good League

career of many a young music star will surely be repeated as young, cash-rich footballers increasingly find themselves moving in social circles where drugs are not only available but actively promoted and (for someone earning perhaps £5,000 per week) eminently affordable.

Given Paul Merson's widely publicised problems with cocaine and alcohol, and now Armstrong's admission, it would appear that these two cases were simply the tip of an iceberg. To assume that the only two players in the Premiership using drugs had both now been identified, caught and punished would seem a trifle presumptuous. Still, Armstrong completed his ban, returned to the Palace side, but was unable to give them the goals they needed to avoid the drop.

For Gerry Francis, there was a lot of the young Les Ferdinand in Armstrong. Gerry had a limited budget for new players. Not enough for Ferdinand – even if he could get him. But enough to make a substantial bid for Armstrong. Francis told his board he wanted to make a move, and got the nod. Newcastle, having secured Ferdinand, were no longer interested, which left only Tottenham and Everton as serious candidates for Armstrong's signature.

Both Joe Royle and Gerry Francis had seen something in Armstrong that had thus far eluded their clubs' fans. Both sets of supporters were less than enthusiastic about the prospect of their club paying millions for a potential 'problem' player and were openly voicing hopes that their team would be the one unsuccessful in this particular hunt. Tottenham's manager certainly had no such misgivings. He told his board that Armstrong was quick, raw, good in the air, had a good goal-scoring record and although he had 'no idea where to run' he could be coached. Francis wanted him,

Dream On

and on 20 June he got him. Following Palace's refusal of a player-plus-cash deal, Spurs paid a club record £4.5 million for the 24-year-old.

As the *Sun* headline put it, '8 GOALS AND ONE JOINT, NOW HE'S GONE FOR £4.5 MILLION'.

'I've made a mistake,' said Armstrong on signing, 'and there seems to be a lot of people who don't ever want me to forget it. Tottenham manager Gerry Francis has given me a great chance and I'll take it with both hands.

'I can't promise goals. I can't promise spectacular performances, but I can guarantee 100% effort 100% of the time and that's what Tottenham will get from me.'

According to many Palace fans, that's exactly what he didn't give to his former club, which is why so many were pleased to see the back of him. Arthur Greenway has been a Palace fan for more than 35 years. He has eight season tickets; one each for wife, son, daughter, brother-in-law and two nephews, plus a spare which, on occasions, he couldn't even give away last season. Arthur spoke for many when he said, 'I'm glad he left Crystal Palace even if we haven't got a replacement, because you know someone is going to come in and give it 100%. If a player doesn't want to play, there is no point in him being out there. No one is good enough to only give 50%. Armstrong gives 100% . . . for about four minutes.'

Everton manager Joe Royle was disappointed at losing out, saying, 'He has told me that he doesn't want to leave London, and so I wish him all the best,' but adding cryptically that 'I have admired him for some time – he is a player of great potential.' The thought that £4.5 million only buys a player with potential boggles the mind. It certainly boggles Arthur's mind that Messrs Keegan, Royle and Francis could see something when, in his opinion,

The Greed-Is-Good League

'He [Armstrong] is always going to be one of those players everyone thinks is going to be great but who never quite makes it'.

Chris Armstrong signed a four-year deal with Spurs, reckoned to be worth around £6,000 a week. The deal seemed typical of a Premier League that had suddenly gone transfer crazy. Since its creation in 1992, membership had granted a licence to print money; money that gushed in from advertising, sponsorship, merchandising, gate receipts and of course television. The £40 million a season that BSkyB dished out was a tidy sum, but not enough in itself to fund much more than one decent player per club. No, the television deal was more important for creating a platform upon which the clubs could make a quantum leap in their commercial activities. Manchester United, for example, now had a merchandising turnover that was greater than the entire trading turnover of most other clubs.

The money that the Taylor Report had forced clubs to spend on improving their grounds was also beginning to pay dividends (not least because it gave clubs an excuse to hike prices). Fans were coming to realise that all-seater stadia were no longer the cattle-pens of recent memory, but also that the only way to secure a guaranteed place for a game was to buy an annual season ticket. Several clubs – Chelsea, Arsenal, Manchester United, Newcastle – were anticipating complete sell-outs for every one of their forthcoming home games, although Arsenal and Manchester United, refused to turn the whole of their grounds over to season ticket holders.

Arsenal's season ticket sales topped £8 million for the summer, and vice-chairman David Dein commented, 'We have put 50% of our tickets up for season tickets and have done record business this summer. We could sell more, but we don't want to make Highbury into a closed shop. I know

Dream On

clubs like Newcastle sell all their tickets in advance, but they are one club in a city. We do not want the next generation of Arsenal fans to go to another London club because they can never get a seat at Highbury.'

Admission prices remained high, despite a reduction in size of the Premiership meaning two fewer home games for 1995–96. Predictably there was an uproar from supporter organisations who were concerned – justifiably so – that short term revenue would break long term loyalty. Many potential fans would be excluded from their local club by their inability to afford seat prices, or by the unavailability of admission to non-season ticket holders. 'Let them watch our reserves then,' was the insensitive response from a Manchester United director when confronted with the dilemma of the many thousands who would no longer be able to gain access to his club's sell-out first team matches.

Figures supplied by the Sir Norman Chester Centre for Football Research illustrated the average cost of a season ticket at each Premiership ground for 1995–96. The cheapest deal was at Hillsborough, where Sheffield Wednesday season ticket holders were paying on average just £200 for the year. Newly promoted Bolton were next lowest at £208, followed by QPR (£210), Nottingham Forest (£211), Everton (£216), Manchester City (£218) and Liverpool (£228).

At the wrong end of the scale were Newcastle (£302), Manchester United (£323), Chelsea (£363), Arsenal (£380) and weighing in with the heftiest average prices in the whole league, Tottenham Hotspur at £425. The fact that Spurs' prices were only marginally up from the previous season hardly seemed a consolation, particularly taking into account the fact there were two fewer home games.

*   *   *

The Greed-Is-Good League

The Premier League gravy train rolled on, with a momentum that was self-perpetuating and a direction that suggested no one was at the footplate. The consequences of dropping out of the Premier League were just too horrible to contemplate. Not that there wasn't life outside of the top flight, just that it was 'Life, Jim, but not as we know it'. No club in the Football League could reasonably hope to compete with the Premiership giants when it came to signing new players. Who outside the Premier League could afford (or risk) £4.5 million for an unproven 24-year-old striker with one England B cap?

And so the summer of 1995 saw a transfer frenzy as each player to move set a precedent for the next deal. Andy Cole's earlier move from Newcastle United to Manchester United was the opening push in football's own domino theory. The transfer fee was widely reported at being £7 million, although the cash that passed hands was £6.25 million and the balance was the assumed value of make-weight Keith Gillespie. Bucking the trend, Manchester United became high sellers so Paul Ince (value £7 million), Andrei Kanchelskis (£5.5 million) and Mark Hughes (£1.5 million) left Old Trafford. Newcastle found themselves cash rich, and so splashed out £6 million on Les Ferdinand, £4 million on Warren Barton and £2.5 million on Paris St. Germain's David Ginola.

QPR took the Ferdinand cash and bought Aussie Ned Zelic for a club record £1.25 million. Meanwhile Forest put the money received from Liverpool for Stan Collymore (a British record of £8.5 million) back into circulation by signing Italian Andrea Silenzi for £1.8 million, Chris Bart Williams for £2.5 million and Arsenal's Kevin Campbell for another £2.5 million.

Operating like a party game where each team was afraid

Dream On

of being left holding cash when the music stopped (or when the season started), the money filtered down through the Premiership in ever decreasing amounts as the loose change bought lesser players at frighteningly high prices by 1994 standards.

Although the Collymore figure was a new record between British clubs, it is still below sums paid in Spain or Italy. The crucial difference is that in those countries, regional and local authorities see their clubs as community assets, subsidise them, build them state-of-the-art stadia and give rent rebates. In addition gates of 50–60,000 are commonplace for the top sides. The revenue generated by such numbers, not to mention ticket prices far in excess of Liverpool's average £12, ensure that clubs can conceivably justify their outlays. In contrast, the new all-seater Anfield holds a tad over 40,000. Assuming a healthy average of 37,000 for their 19 home games, their whole season's gate revenue would only meet the sum they paid for one player, Stan Collymore. Nevertheless, the biggest transfers abroad involved players of international quality. By what stretch of the imagination could Stan Collymore be worth substantially more than Hristo Stoichkov and the same as Roberto Baggio? It was crazy business.

And the madness certainly would not end at Arsenal, for a long time a byword for financial stability and prudence. The Gunners had thrown off the self-imposed wage shackles of George Graham (who it is believed wouldn't allow any player at the club to earn more than he did), and were now making up for lost time with new manager Bruce Rioch.

The legendary Highbury cash reserves – and compliant bank manager – were severely tested when supporter pressure demanded that the Gunners join the spiralling transfer free-for-all. 'We want a star!' demanded their fans, and

The Greed-Is-Good League

the club duly obliged with one of the biggest, Dutchman
Dennis Bergkamp from Inter Milan. Not only was the fee a
whopper (£7.5 million, or nearly four times what Klinsmann
had cost Spurs twelve months earlier), but the wages were
reckoned to amount to £4 million over a four-year contract.
With another super-fan – David Dein – in the boardroom,
as keen as the average North Bank Gooner to see the club
throw off its 'boring, boring' tag, the opportunity to secure
Bergkamp was too good to miss.

A further shock was in store for Highbury regulars who
had already splashed out their £37.99 for a 'Bergkamp 10'
replica shirt. England captain David Platt made it known
that he was seeking to leave Sampdoria and return home.
Before anyone had time to realise the implications, Bruce
Rioch had swooped again and 29-year-old Platt was a £4.75
million Gunner.

Three weeks before the season got under way, Dein's
gamble looked to have paid dividends. The Gunners had
taken £8 million in pre-season ticket sales, moving Dein to
comment, 'To use a City term, we have realised you have
to speculate to accumulate. We had to invest in players this
season. It was very important to the club and the chequebook is still open if needed.' Bruce Rioch was left in no
doubt that there was a price to pay for his shopping spree.
'These are very exciting times for Arsenal', noted Dein,
'with new players and a new manager. Now all we need
are some trophies to show for it . . .'

'It's crazy money. I must be mad,' said Arsenal chairman
Peter Hill Wood after the Bergkamp signing. 'But . . . you
either get involved or you opt out. You have a responsibility
to stay in the game. How can a football club spend half
its season's gate receipts on one player? It is madness,
I know that. But others are doing it, so you either join

Dream On

them or get beaten. Thank God we have a friendly bank manager.'

'It has got to stop after Bergkamp. I hope we've reached the end of this lunacy in transfer prices,' chipped in Alan Sugar as he unveiled new signing Chris Armstrong. 'It's total madness. It has got out of all proportion and can only bring trouble down the line. In any other business in the world you cannot trade if you are insolvent. But in football they just seem to get on with it. I won't be intimidated into plugging a gap to solve a problem – and if the chairman of Arsenal said he had to do it to appease people, it's a sorry world.'

A Dutchman who had only scored two league goals last season for Inter Milan for £7.5 million? £8.5 million on Stan Collymore? – a player who couldn't command a regular place in the England team, and who only two years previous had been a Southend United player. And how come it was only the Southend manager, Colin Murphy, who had seen anything in Collymore when Crystal Place were trying to give him away in 1992? Where were the Premiership's scouts then?

What kind of long-term strategy persuaded Arsenal to pay £4.75 million for a 29-year-old David Platt? And did Chelsea really have nothing better to do with their funds than promise Ruud Gullit £2.5 million for two years' work? And how come Tottenham's reserves and youth teams can both win their respective championships in 1995, and yet the club has to spend £4.5 million on a centre forward and sign a 34-year-old defender (Clive Wilson) from QPR? Did they really have no players capable of coming through the ranks?

Anyone who has ever driven on a motorway in dense fog will know the terror that is 'motorway madness', and will

The Greed-Is-Good League

recognise its similarities with the transfer market during the summer of 1995. You are in a twilight zone. You can see nothing. Divisions are blurred. You're not sure where you are, nor where you are going. All familiar signposts and indicators have vanished. You wish you had never started out in the first place. All you know is that the bloke behind is zooming right up your back-side, and everyone else is whizzing by at breath-taking speed. They're all doing it. It's madness. But what can you do? You just have to keep going foot to the floor at the same crazy speed as everyone else, because pulling over and saying 'Enough. This is madness!' just isn't an option. You console yourself with the thought that maybe everyone bar you really can see quite clearly, or just maybe, somebody up ahead knows what they are doing and where you are all being led.

Only when the fog lifts do you get a chance to see where you've ended up; to pull over and mop your brow and thank your lucky stars for a safe deliverance. Only then do you see if you've ended up where you thought you would.

Or else the fog doesn't lift. And you, and the maniacs behind and the maniacs in front and all the maniacs whizzing alongside you, go *Crash!* Because the guy up in front didn't know where he was going after all. He was just racing to keep ahead of you lot.

And on the news that night, everyone looks at the footage of the carnage on their motorway, and shakes their head when they hear of the speed everyone was doing, and asks the same question: 'What on earth were they thinking of?'

It's all very well the Premier League negotiating deals which leave its member clubs with cash beyond their dreams. But unless those clubs can show a degree of sanity in the disposal of that money, then maybe the Premier League

Dream On

management must think about playing Nanny – for the good of its members, and for the good of English football as a whole.

It was socialist principles like these from the Football League that caused the top clubs to run away screaming *'Market forces!'* and form the Premier League. But for all its shortcomings, the Football League had at least got most of its members through 107 years, which rather vindicated its actions. The worrying development now was that the big money transfers were excluding Football League clubs. Not only had the Football League lost its top clubs, but those clubs were now starving the smaller clubs of much-needed transfer income. The trickle-down was drying up.

The Bergkamp money was equivalent to the total gate receipts from 250 third division matches, all lost to the English game. Add the Platt, Ginola, Silenzi, Kinkladze (Manchester City) and Milosevic (Aston Villa) transfers and that figure trebles. Each week, Ruud Gullit is earning as much as a third division club can expect to take at the turnstiles. It cannot be in the best interests of the game as a whole when the money paid to overseas players in one season, in transfers and in wages, is equal to the total gate revenue of the English third division for a whole season.

A crucial source of income for the smaller clubs is being diverted, making the big clubs richer and the small clubs poorer. Both Leicester and Crystal Palace had to sell their star players when relegation tumbled them from the Premier League. These two clubs notwithstanding, there were simply no major deals that redistributed wealth from the top flight to its Endsleigh counterparts. An increase in so-called 'free transfers' means simply that no cash moves between clubs, but wages and signing-on fees go instead into the pockets of players and agents. Smaller clubs are

The Greed-Is-Good League

denied funds essential to their continued role as nurseries for football's young talent.

It wasn't Liverpool or Juventus that found Ian Rush, it was Chester; Peter Beardsley can thank Carlisle United for his big chance after being rejected by Manchester United; Chris Armstrong would have disappeared from football if Wrexham had not spotted his potential; Steve Bruce can thank Gillingham; Lee Sharpe owes his big break to Torquay United; Teddy Sheringham started out at Millwall, as did Neil Ruddock. These clubs aren't there just to make up the numbers on a pools coupon; they find players; they rehabilitate players; they hold a key position in the football food chain. And these clubs in return rely on the likes of Hayes, Stafford Rangers, Tow Law Town and Maidstone Utd as feeder clubs.

Football is our national game not because of the twenty clubs that comprise the top division, but because of the thousands of lesser clubs that provide a far more accessible entry level for fans and players alike. This vast pool of footballing activity should be every bit as much part of the system as is the Premier League, and should be nurtured and valued.

It is true that smaller clubs have a diminishing appeal, and the focus is increasingly put upon those glamour clubs that have cornered the market in star players and TV appearences. Youngsters increasingly feel no allegiance to their local sides, and instead 'support' a club based maybe hundreds of miles away. A look at any school playground or playing field will show this by the vast diversity of replica shirts being worn.

As smaller clubs become marginalised, the system needs to respond sympathetically so that those clubs can continue to function, continue to exist. If this means that the lower

Dream On

divisions become regionalised then so be it. If some clubs have to operate on a part-time basis, then so be it. That is preferable to going under completely.

Of course there should be an elitist showcase for the big clubs, but that is no reason why small clubs shouldn't still be seen and treated as part of the system. At this lower level, football is nothing if it is not parochial. With the right support and funding there should be no reason why a club cannot rise – like Wimbledon – all the way to the top. But it can only do so if it is part of the system.

In Germany, Italy, Spain and France, there is one unified league system for club football. Of course, each has an elitist top division, but smaller clubs are kept in the system, which may indeed be regionalised or even part-time at the lower end of the pyramid. Those smaller clubs acknowledge that the odds are stacked against them and in the favour of the top flight teams. But because money flows down from that top division, the lower divisions are not cut adrift and do not see the big clubs as existence-threatening. Such smaller clubs cling to the belief that with the aid of a skilled coach, a wealthy patron, homegrown players and a two-way escalator (both up and down the divisions) for old pros and young hopefuls, they have a role to play. Deportivo La Coruna (Spain) and Freiburg (Germany) have both astounded their national critics by proving that minnows can qualify for Europe, while French clubs Gueugnon and Guingamp and Italian upstarts Piacenza have won promotion to their respective premier divisions, causing the kind of stir we would expect should Milton Keynes haul their way into the FA Carling Premiership.

Two years ago, in the loo at Wembley's banqueting suite, the former Tottenham chairman Irving Scholar suggested to Graham Kelly that he should look ahead five years and

The Greed-Is-Good League

note where – in an ideal world – he would like to be. Kelly was taken aback by the notion of a five-year plan. Certainly there have since been beneficial changes in FA youth policies, but it is BSkyB's five-year plan that is the only one in operation with the consequent marginalisation of the national team. Such a proposed five-year plan should attempt to control players' wages and transfers at the highest level and therefore contain proposals for a transfer cap, a salary cap, and a limited window when all transfer movement must take place.

The transfer cap could be fixed at a figure that would permit every Premiership club to afford any player who becomes available. If this figure was to be set at say, £3 million (or its index linked equivalent), then no club would realistically be excluded from the bidding. Coupled with a salary cap, again set at a level where players could be amply rewarded for their skills without forcing clubs to jeopardise their future existence to secure their services, then a player would choose where to move based not just upon some crude financial auction for his services, but upon a club's likelihood of providing the player with success.

Of course a club could top up the salary with bonuses based on the usual win/crowd/trophy basis, or on the attainment of personal targets where a striker for example could be rewarded for scoring twenty goals in a season, and of course there would also be the non-footballing opportunities for players to supplement their income through commercial endorsements. These would remain unaffected because they do not operate to the detriment of the league system.

This concept has a proven precedent in America, where a partnership formed between players and authorities in America's National Basketball Association (NBA) has worked to the benefit of both sides. The players accept

Dream On

a salary cap, but in return have a say in their league's marketing strategies including TV deals, and take a cut from the success of those strategies.

The upshot of these proposals would be a game where the top stars earned a very good wage indeed, but not as much as they do now. If the salary cap was brought in overnight, there would of course be uproar as the top 5% of Premiership players would find their wages reduced. But if the cap were phased in over a five-year period, then all new contracts would have to take this impending rule into account. When the five years are up, everyone will have contracts in line with the regulation, and the transition should be seamless.

If any player felt that he wasn't prepared to work under those conditions, then he would of course be free to move overseas where no such financial restrictions apply. In reality, there would be no exodus from England because there are only a limited number of overseas clubs prepared to pay big money for English players. On the other hand, with no transfer fee limit on overseas players, the true stars of world football could still be enticed. Their scarcity value would enhance the Premiership and their fellow professionals would welcome them.

The third proposal would be for fixed transfer 'windows' during which all transactions must take place. This could be an eight-week spell pre-season, with perhaps another fortnight over Christmas/New Year. This limitation would return the emphasis to coaching as a means to success, rather than simply allowing clubs to buy stop-gap solutions to a mid-season crisis. Clubs would increasingly look to their own reserve and youth setups for first team replacements, rather than simply being able to get out the chequebook.

These three proposals – caps on transfers and salaries, and

The Greed-Is-Good League

a transfer window – would help bridge the gulf between clubs in the Premier League. There would of course still be rich clubs; non-transfer revenue would remain unaffected. But those riches would not have the same buying power for their clubs, and so a levelling up would take place as Manchester United or Blackburn found they were no longer just competing with each other in the transfer market, but with every other Premiership club who may want that player.

The 1995–96 season was to be Year Four for the division that had begun life officially as the FA Premier League and unofficially as the 'greed-is-good league' according to the indefatigable Brian 'voice of the *People*' Glanville. For those twenty clubs who enjoy membership of what is currently the FA Carling Premiership, there could be no question that for all its shortcomings and compromises, life is better in than out.

To one of the chief architects of the system, Arsenal vice-chairman David Dein, it is much more than this. 'The monetary aspect doesn't come into it, because as a sport the Premier League has achieved something unparalleled in English football; we have managed to turn the corner, to increase spectator interest.' To Dein, this is the bottom line. 'So how do you judge a success? Simply by saying *are people prepared to accept the product that is being delivered?* And the answer is yes, yes and yes again.'

The English Football League can be congratulated that it has overseen such rags-to-riches success stories many times in its 100-year history. Cognizant of this responsibility, it is now up to the Premier League to set plans in motion to secure the future of England's national league hierarchy for the next 100 years. By definition this means caring about

Dream On

more than twenty clubs. The Football League can't; the FA won't. While the Premier League may be coming round to the realisation that it cannot survive as a self-contained unit of twenty clubs it does not believe that the alternative is an all-inclusive league of 90-plus clubs. The compromise that will probably emerge is a Premier League of two divisions with 44 full-time professional clubs. This at least will concentrate resources and provide more depth than at present, but it will also sound the death knell for the second and third divisions as we now know them. Bye-bye Fulham, bye-bye Rochdale. Shameful.

Chapter 2

Carry on Intertoto

For a sharp trader with an eye to the main chance, it was a spectacular blunder by Alan Sugar to miss out on UEFA's special summer offer.

Having watched Tottenham stumble through the previous season in the manner of an athlete with both legs tied together, it must have been acutely painful for Sugar to see his team at last burst free from its shackles only to trip within sight of the May finishing tape.

The FA Cup semi-final defeat by Everton was a major blow to Tottenham's hopes of qualifying for Europe, but their consolation was the strong belief that a top six league placing would serve the same purpose. When a string of poor results also scuppered that ambition, Sugar needed no reminding of the dire financial implications. Not only would he and manager Gerry Francis have their work cut out through the summer keeping their existing squad together, but it would be that much harder to attract potential recruits to White Hart Lane. Another season of domestic toil loomed.

Dream On

Until that is, an unexpected gift from Switzerland.

In the autumn of 1994, the FA had given an assurance to their masters at UEFA (having secured – or so they thought – the acquiescence of the Premier League), that three English clubs could be counted on for the new 'improved' Intertoto Cup scheduled for the summer of 1995. Although a new name to these shores, the competition in one guise or another had been around for 35 years and was a familiar fixture to Continental fans, particularly those who fancy a flutter.

It had survived for two reasons. First, it was a handy device for introducing competitive European football to those teams who otherwise may not get the opportunity (Partick Thistle – Scotland's representative in this year's competition – was able to play in Europe for the first time in 23 years). Second, for the opportunity it brought for punters to continue to gamble via the football pools throughout the summer.

Gambling via football pools and associated lottery/bingo (lotto) variations is big business across Europe, so big in fact that in most countries the state now has a monopoly on this form of betting. Along with a national lottery, such pools – or toto – are great generators of revenue for governments via betting levies, as well as providing the funding for perceived good causes, including many sports stadia. Intertoto is the world's foremost toto/lotto organisation.

Such is the money to be earned from football-based betting that the summer siesta – as most European leagues took a break – became too tempting a target and a competition was launched to provide toto junkies with their regular fix of betting on football results. So successful did this prove that football clubs were in turn paid a handsome

Carry on Intertoto

fee for participating – a clear indication of how much the pools companies themselves were raking in. Periodical fine-tuning has seen fixtures and formats juggled around to suit the paymasters, but most invited clubs have been happy for the 'privilege' to play overseas opposition and to make a bob or two during the dead months of summer.

UEFA was already committed to a series of initiatives to help integrate the fledgling football associations in countries like Belarus, Estonia, Latvia, Moldovia and Azerbaijan. This was through a department set up in 1994 within UEFA called the East European Assistance Bureau (EEAB). UEFA funds were diverted to get grassroots football up and running in these ink blot outposts of the new Europe. The problem was how to involve these new members in competitive action without diluting the value of UEFA's three main cup competitions.

UEFA's brainwave was to 'adopt' the hitherto marginalised Intertoto Cup competition, slap on a UEFA prefix, increase the number of participating clubs to include those screaming for representation, pat itself on the back for its contribution to furthering European unity, and count the cash flowing in from sponsors Intertoto.

It was also no secret that UEFA was becoming increasingly jittery at the power of the big clubs. Central control became their modus operandi (hence the destruction of the old style European Cup and its replacement by the Champions' League), and thus it was no suprise to find the Intertoto Cup being given increased status to provide another centralised UEFA competition.

The summer of 1995 therefore witnessed the revamped competition enlarged to 60 clubs and grandly renamed the UEFA Intertoto Cup. Twelve groups of five teams leading to a knockout format for the sixteen qualifiers, with UEFA's

Dream On

direct involvement meaning a crucial sweetener, could now be added to the Intertoto recipe; all four semi-finalists would gain automatic qualification to the UEFA Cup proper. (There would be no actual Intertoto cup to be presented as the competition ended at the semi-final stage.) This really was an extraordinary concession from UEFA, one which makes it all the more astounding that the three English club representatives saw fit to treat the whole exercise with such scorn.

When the Premier League agreed to nominate three participants, it knew it had six months in which to sell the idea to its members. Unfortunately, the Premier League failed to give most clubs ample warning of their potential commitments, and as a result the FA had to go back to UEFA in May with a sick note asking, please sir, could it be excused from this year's competition?

UEFA was not amused, and told the FA in no uncertain terms to get its act together or face a substantial punishment. The whole competition had been planned around 60 competitors, and an awkward 57 simply wouldn't do. Spain and Italy had both declined to enter, but their decision had come early in the year and had been taken into account. Thus the Premier League had to exercise a three-line whip to get the necessary 'volunteers'. Inducements to the value of around £250,000 were offered to each of the three clubs, together with assurances that no team would have to actually field its strongest line-up nor even play its home matches 'at home'. And so it came to pass that the seventeen non-participating Premiership clubs were forced to stump up £50,000 each to underwrite the costs anticipated by the reluctant participants – now confirmed as Tottenham and (following the stubborn refusals from Newcastle and QPR) Sheffield Wednesday and Wimbledon.

Carry on Intertoto

The utter contempt that was shown for the competition shamed all three participants, their league and English football as a whole. The uniformly negative attitude to the competition spread to the national media who rubbished the concept, stigmatised the participants, and failed to recognise that here was a chance to qualify for a major European competition simply by performing well through six preliminary matches. Surely this was preferable to the 'conventional' rout of slogging out a 38-match season, or stringing together a minimum eight-match League Cup winning sequence.

The reported response from the clubs was that after a long tiring season, the last thing they needed was more games and more travelling. Well, that's what they said. The truth was that games against Slovenian no-hopers and Swiss part-timers were never going to pull in the crowds. Players had already made their summer plans for family holidays or lucrative coaching tours, and many grounds were utilising the summer recess for essential maintenance. The logistics of staging these games was a problem that most clubs were happy to allow to defeat them.

At Wimbledon, owner Sam Hammam's attitude was that Wimbledon simply couldn't afford *not* to take part if invited. However, mindful of the need to rest first team players prior to August's Premiership kick-off, manager Joe Kinnear's compromise strategy was to play the preliminary rounds with those players who hadn't burnt themselves out during the previous season – those coming back from injury and those reserves on the fringe of the first team. Subject to progressing to the later stages, Joe then planned to bring back his first team big guns for the final matches at the end of July – a time when those players would expect to be playing competitive pre-season friendlies anyway.

Dream On

Sheffield Wednesday had other distractions following the summer sacking of manager Trevor Francis, so it is no surprise they failed to perform to potential. Wednesday in addition were unable to use Hillsborough for their home games and so played at nearby Rotherham. When David Pleat was appointed as new manager, the club suddenly started to take the competition seriously, but by then it was too late and elimination was inevitable.

But it was at Tottenham that the apathetic attitude was hardest to understand. The reasons why Gerry Francis was allowed to ridicule and virtually ostracise the competition were an open secret. It has been 'custom and practice' for players to become free agents during the summer months, working or resting at their discretion. Football contracts in England do not cover pre- and post-season games, whereas on the Continent year-round commitment is expected and received. Once the league season has ended in England, the rush to the beach begins. Tottenham itself had arranged an end-of-season tour to the Far East, departing within days of the club's 51-match season ending. This is easy money for the club, but makes a mockery of its supposed concern for reducing the number of competitive games played. For players, the only redeeming factor on these trips is that a large percentage of tour revenues goes straight to the players' pool. Such are the concessions that English clubs must make in order to secure the services of staff who, let us not forget, continue to draw their not-inconsiderable wages throughout the summer months. The problem was that the timing of the Intertoto Cup would encroach on the players' mandatory holiday period of at least four weeks.

Gerry Francis was dismissive of obligations to put out a strong Intertoto team. He maintained that he wanted his players hungry for action when they reported back for pre-season training, not jaded – or worse injured – from a tournament that would run into early August for the successful clubs.

'I will not make anyone play,' said Francis. 'The players are entitled to their holiday.' His support for the players was touching, but surely misguided. Sure, you can understand why footballers want a two-month break between mid-May and mid-July. But apart from being a historical precedent, is it an inalienable right? Wouldn't everyone like a two-month holiday every summer? Do Premiership footballers really have the right to complain of fatigue and jaded appetites when even mediocre players demand and get wages of up to £300,000 per year, offering the perceived justification that their careers are short and earning potential correspondingly limited? When even a 'hectic' week means playing two 90-minute games in seven days, with perhaps training a further three mornings a week – unlike their Continental colleagues who although playing fewer games regularly spend full days at the training ground – players seem to want all the trappings and status conferred with the title 'professional', but with few of the responsibilities or obligations it brings.

Whatever the arguments, the fact is that Gerry Francis defended his players' rights to an extended break, and thus the honour of defending the club's name in the four opening group matches fell largely to Tottenham's youth team, bolstered by some on-loan signings from Northampton and Barnet. Gerry Francis distanced himself from the competition delegating the managerial role to Messrs Cross and Hughton.

A gathering of just 2,497 watched Spurs lose their opening game to Swiss side Lucerne, a 'home' fixture played – because of a new pitch being laid at White Hart Lane –

---

at the nearest available football stadium to north London: Brighton. A win away at Rudar Velenje (in sunny Slovenia) raised hopes momentarily, until another south coast setback – a 1-2 defeat by Oesters (Sweden) – sealed Tottenham's fate. It had been literally men against boys, never better illustrated than in the final group match that saw reserve team manager Chris Hughton take a raggle-taggle bag of waifs and strays to mighty Cologne in Germany. The Londoners' 8-0 defeat was a fair reflection on the approach to the competition adopted by the two sides. The Glory, Glory Nights it was not.

Elsewhere, both Wimbledon and Sheffield Wednesday failed to make it past the preliminary round; Wimbledon failing to win a single game and Wednesday finishing group runners up to the Germans of Karlsruhe.

To the football authorities in France or Germany, the attitude adopted by the English clubs must have seemed plain crazy. Both their national leagues ended after the Premiership, and were scheduled to recommence before the Premiership. Yet despite having a shorter summer break, their representatives still managed to treat the Intertoto with a degree of professionalism – there was never any question that the first team would not represent the club – and that professionalism brought its own rewards. Overseas TV companies gave extensive coverage to the Intertoto games, with live transmission on TF1, the major French channel, of a key Bordeaux game drawing a 5 million armchair audience. Similar exposure in Germany and Austria compared dramatically with the 'InterTwo-Bob Cup' jibes hurled by the tabloids and the total lack of interest shown by terrestrial and satellite TV in the UK.

The bottom line was that those teams that took the competition seriously enough were rewarded both financially

Carry on Intertoto

(surpluses generated by the competition were paid directly to participating clubs) and with a place in the 1995/96 UEFA Cup competition going to the lucky foursome. Strasbourg and Bordeaux (France) both qualified, bringing to eight the number of French clubs in Europe this season (one each for the Champions League and the Cup Winners Cup, and a whopping six in the UEFA Cup). Karlsruhe (Germany) and Tirol Innsbruck (Austria) made up the successful Intertoto quartet.

As the country sweltered through the hottest summer since records began – records that go back even further than Tottenham's last championship win – it was no wonder that enthusiasm was at a low as the Spurs squad reported back for pre-season training on Monday 17 July.

Teddy Sheringham was heard to complain, 'I don't feel fresh at all. I've only had five weeks off [Tough! That's the penalty for being an England international beholden to an FA, who always seem to want to go on a summer tour] and now face, all being well, another twelve months of football. I asked Gerry [Francis] for more time to rest but he said that was impossible as we're going on tour to Norway and Sweden soon. I've never known anything like this summer.' That Sheringham made these comments at the launch of his Adidas Predator boot deal did not go unnoticed.

Tottenham had lined themselves up with a somewhat punishing pre-season schedule. Four games in Scandinavia were to be followed by an appearance in the Ibrox International Tournament in Glasgow. Then came friendlies against Watford, Derby and Luton, before preparations were completed with the Gary Mabbutt testimonial game against Newcastle on 12 August. A hectic schedule, but one that would allow manager Gerry Francis to determine his

Dream On

strongest side for the coming season's challenge. Alas, as is often the case, things didn't go at all to plan.

Spurs captain Gary Mabbutt tells the story.

'Normally for pre-season training, we have two sessions: perhaps a two-hour session in the morning and a one-hour running session in the afternoon. The mornings would cover a good warm-up, followed by some ball work. There would be an hour's break at lunchtime for a light lunch.

'Under Gerry, however, we don't have a break. We start at about eleven, then train right the way through, for maybe three and a half hours. As well as ball work – we need to get the feel again after not having kicked a ball for perhaps five weeks – we also do fitness circuits and more running to help build up that important stamina.

'That lasted for the first week, and then we went out to Sweden for a tour. On this tour we were training as well as playing games. We trained on the morning of our first game; in fact we had three games to play in three days. It was quite a stiff programme but we had a squad of 23 players who travelled with us. However, we picked up a number of injuries and so the manager wasn't always able to play the side he would have liked. For the first match we all got half a game each; for the second game, the team that started played three-quarters of the match and for the third game, the starting line-up played the full 90 minutes. We were just building gently.'

So did Gerry Francis have in mind his preferred first team line-up at that early stage?

'No, I don't think so. I think that no matter how the last season has gone, every player starts on the same level. If one of the younger players has a good end to the previous season, and has a good pre-season also, then his prospects are excellent. For example young Gerard

Carry on Intertoto

McMahon was turning out to be one of our best players in those pre-season games, until he got an injury playing in the Ibrox Tournament. Of course the manager will have an idea of the players who can do the job he wants, but if other players come through then he will give those players a chance.

'Anyway, in the fourth and final game of the Scandinavia tour, the manager played all those players who hadn't yet played a full game. That final game was on a Wednesday. We flew back to England on the Thursday, and on the Friday morning we trained at White Hart Lane before travelling up to Scotland for that weekend's Ibrox Tournament.

'On the Saturday we trained in the morning and then played against Sampdoria in the afternoon. Then on the Sunday we played Steaua Bucharest. Those players who never got a game against Sampdoria were given a game against Steaua. However there were again a number of injuries – we didn't even have enough players to fill the subs' spots. So I came on as centre-forward and played up front in the second half.

'Every player dreads pre-season. It is the hardest time of year from a physically demanding point of view. Even back at our post-season Hong Kong tour, the players were already dreading pre-season training. Even though we may only have had five weeks off, I would say that every player would do some fitness work during those five weeks. You may want to have a rest because you have been playing perhaps two, three games a week and training virtually every day for 47 weeks. You know your body needs to recuperate, but you know that if you don't do some kind of training, when you come back it will be even harder to get back that fitness.

Dream On

'I was going running perhaps three times a week on holiday. In fact when I was staying in Barbados, Erik Thorstvedt was also there on holiday and the two of us went out running at 7am.

'Of course, as I'm getting older, I'm not sure whether the training is getting harder or if I'm just feeling it more. It's a difficult one to judge. Touch wood I've stayed fit for the pre-season period and played in all the games so far. You don't actually enjoy it at the time – there are players actually being physically sick at the end of our training sessions. After all the years I've been doing it, I think I just switch on to autopilot now.

'Because of my diabetes, I take a blood test before, during and after training. Cans of Lucozade or Diet Coke are put by the pitch-side in case I have a problem but thankfully that hasn't been the case this pre-season. I've sometimes had a problem in training where my blood sugars get too low. When it first happened, there was some concern and the physio would come rushing over. But now if I start stumbling a bit or acting vague and falling over, they just say "Oh for goodness sake get him some Lucozade!" The players can tell if I'm having a problem. It doesn't happen too often, but occasionally it does.

'So I feel that I have enjoyed this pre-season. You don't feel that way at the time, but after you have finished for the day, you know you have got it in the bag. All you do is train, eat, sleep. Train, eat, sleep. There's no time to do anything else. You come home absolutely wiped out. You have a bite to eat then go to bed, knowing that the moment you wake up from that sleep, you're going again. It really is a tough period.

'But I have never known a pre-season like this. The first team squad have played eight games and we've won just

Carry on Intertoto

two – against Gothenberg and Watford. But not once has the manager been able to choose from his full squad. This is very unusual for a pre-season period. Back on the first day of training, Darren Anderton, Teddy Sheringham and Clive Wilson all got injured and since then we have always had three or four players missing.

'It makes it very difficult for Gerry, particularly as I feel we are short on top quality within our squad. I feel we need to add another two or three top quality players at least to have a realistic chance of challenging for major honours. We need players in the wide midfield area; we are still short of strength in depth. If we have two or three injuries once the season starts, I think we will be found to be wanting in the Premiership.'

The results in Scandinavia were disappointing for those fans looking for early indicators, but secondary to the task of easing players back to match fitness. The Ibrox Tournament would mean changing up a gear.

Tottenham have a long history of playing pre-season games at Ibrox, although the fixture is rarely reciprocated because of police opposition to the prospect of tartan hoards laying waste to vast tracts of Soho and N17. For 1995, a four-team tournament had been organised by Dennis Roach, arguably the most successful football agent in the country and a man who had been involved in many of the British game's major transfers. It was the second year in succession that Roach had made the arrangements for his friend David Murray, the Rangers chairman. For the first time in nearly ten years there was no Makita tournament – Roach's baby was no more – so he was free to devote his energies to Glasgow. (That is, until an even older friend, Martin Edwards the Manchester United chairman, decided

Dream On

it wasn't fair for Roach to miss out on a Far East jaunt and thus forced the agent to forgo the delights of Glasgow for those of Kuala Lumpur. Other agents should have his problems . . .)

Rangers (as hosts) and Sampdoria were obvious candidates to fit the top half of the bill. Roach had brokered several big transfers to Ibrox including those of Trevor Steven, Basile Boli and Mark Hateley. Tottenham had been invited to attend when Klinsmann was still on their books. Without him they were somewhat less of an attraction, but Roach was nevertheless keen to improve his relations with the Tottenham board, relations which had never regained the intimacy that existed in the days of Irving Scholar's reign.

So it was really no great surprise when the Spurs board treated the Ibrox weekend as an extension of their half-hearted Intertoto experience. No directors bothered to attend, except club architect Igal Yawetz who has family in the city. In contrast, Rangers and Sampdoria were fully represented at board level, including three members of the Mantovani family who own the Italian club. Even at staff level, no Spurs management were present in the directors' box when Rangers played Steaua, despite the fact that one of those two teams would provide Tottenham's opposition the next day. Unlike the Sampdoria coach, Sven Goran Eriksson, and his assistant who sat attentively throughout the match making copious notes on their future opponents.

Spurs lost 2-0 to Sampdoria on the Saturday, and 3-2 to Steaua Bucharest on the Sunday. Two dull and dismal performances that moved one Rangers director to sigh ruefully about the good Spurs sides he could recall. Glenn Gibbons in the *Observer* seemed to sum up the tournament for Spurs in one telling sentence when he wrote that, 'Barmby was one of the few Spurs players who appeared to have any fundamental knowledge of how the game should be played, but the unsettled youngster also seemed to be part of a general lethargy which settled on the Premiership side and never lifted'.

At both post-match press conferences, Gerry made much of his injury woes, and could offer little optimism for the new season that was now just three weeks away. Gerry was not a happy man.

'There are so many things you want to work on in the summer. So much you want to try. This injury crisis is easily the worst in my ten years as a manager,' he said at the end of the Ibrox games.

Was there any consolation?

'I don't think we've seen the real Spurs yet, not by a long way.'

William Hill responded by making Gerry Francis 5/4-on second favourite to be sacked during the coming season. Everyone likes a bet during the summer.

For Spurs captain Gary Mabbutt, the indicators were that this wasn't going to be the graceful and dignified glide into retirement that he may have hoped for.

Beginning his 14th season with the club and with a 34th birthday imminent, Gary's ambition was to continue playing at the highest level for as long as his fitness would allow – a further two or three years in his estimation. Mabbutt had one year left on his contract at White Hart Lane, and his hope was that there would be further one-year extensions on offer.

Known affectionately to his fans and friend as 'Mabbs', Gary Mabbutt is a model professional who enjoys a rare

Dream On

distinction in today's game – respect from fans wherever Spurs may play. It's no secret that Tottenham have few friends outside their north London base, and their players are easy targets for fan abuse at away games. High-profile stars like Sheringham and Armstrong will be jeered as England flops or as a 'waste of money', while Anderton will be wolf-whistled for being a 'pretty boy'. Even a world-class player like Klinsmann was often greeted at grounds with the *Dam Busters* theme and *heil* Hitler salutes. In Mabbutt's case, however, there seems to be an unspoken but acknowledged acceptance among fans that he is 'all right'. Like Gary Lineker before him, Mabbutt has transcended his Spurs ties and earned the right to be judged on his playing record, not by the shirt he wears. When Lineker ended his career playing a league game for Spurs at Old Trafford, he headed an 87th minute consolation goal in a 1-3 defeat. It took a moment for the incident to register with the capacity crowd, who then rose as one to give the England hero a standing ovation for what was obviously going to be his farewell goal. Such spontaneous displays of sportsmanship are as rare as they are moving. Based on nothing more tangible than gut feeling, this supporter empathy has a value beyond medals and trophies and is a far greater gauge of true achievement.

Because of his age and experience, Gary Mabbutt can have very little in common with his Spurs team-mates. In his time at White Hart Lane he has seen out, in his own words, 'eight different managers, about seven different teams and three different boardroom regimes'.

In an era of change at Tottenham, Gary Mabbutt has been the one constant. He played for the team back in the days of Graham Roberts, Steve Perryman, Ricky Villa, Glenn Hoddle, Steve Archibald and Ray Clemence – most of whom have long since hung up their boots and tackled management. Mabbutt joined the club pre-Irving Scholar and before the Stock Exchange share flotation. Before the first live league match was shown on ITV, and when White Hart Lane still held 48,000. It cost £2 to stand on the Shelf when Mabbutt arrived and a terrace ticket for that year's Spurs v QPR FA Cup final cost £4. You feel like you have to consult a history book to see if ration cards were still in use.

After Steve Perryman and Pat Jennings, Gary Mabbutt has played more league games for Tottenham than any other player – over 430 as the season began. Together with thirteen years of cup activity and friendlies, his total appearances for Spurs approach 600.

Such a career must have been far from the player's mind when he found himself out of contract with Bristol Rovers back in 1982. The Millwall manager, Peter Anderson, received a routine circular announcing the player's availability, but, unable to afford the fee being asked, tipped off his mentor Bill Nicholson about the 'terrific player' he'd just been offered by Bobby Gould. Nicholson, in his consultancy capacity at Spurs, knew of Mabbutt and rated him highly. The news that he was available for a knock-down price was a surprise, and Nicholson quickly informed team manager Keith Burkinshaw,

And yet when Keith Burkinshaw offered £105,000 to Bristol Rovers in July 1982, it was made perfectly clear to the player that he was being bought for his potential (compare and contrast with the purchase of Chris Armstrong for £4.5 million for the same reason), and that Mabbutt's immediate role was to be that of a squad player. Despite being warned that it could be two or three years before he made it into the first team (Burkinshaw kidology?) and despite interest

Dream On

from Birmingham City (who were also in the First Division and offering a better financial deal) Mabbutt signed for Tottenham.

'Joining Tottenham seemed my best chance of achieving what I wanted from my career.'

The contract paid him the same wages he had been getting at Bristol, together with a massive signing-on fee of £1,500.

Following injuries to key players during the pre-season games, Mabbutt found himself drafted into the first team and playing Glasgow Rangers at Ibrox. Mabbutt scored the only goal in a 1-0 win.

Two weeks later he played for Spurs against Liverpool in front of 82,500 at Wembley in the Charity Shield game, and a week after that he made his First Division debut against Luton – scoring within five minutes from a Glenn Hoddle cross. Six weeks later, he made his England debut at right back against West Germany at Wembley – the first of sixteen caps. By the end of his first season he had played 49 league and cup games for Spurs and with 11 goals was their second highest scorer after Steve Archibald. Keith Burkinshaw had surely made the most inspired signing of his managerial career.

At the end of that season, Gary Mabbutt was summoned into his manager's office and given an improved four-year deal.

His first trophy came as part of the UEFA Cup winning side in 1984, and a second should have followed but for a below par team performance that saw Spurs lose the 1987 FA Cup final with an own goal by Mabbutt giving victory to Coventry City. That team, managed by David Pleat, was as exciting as any in Tottenham's history, but the Wembley defeat was its nemesis. Within a year, Clive Allen, Glenn

Carry on Intertoto

Hoddle, Ray Clemence, Ossie Ardiles, Nico Claesen, Steve Hodge, Richard Gough and even manager Pleat had all moved on.

Mabbutt himself was out of contract, and was entitled to listen to offers.

'The day after the Coventry defeat, I got a phone call from [Liverpool manager] Kenny Dalglish saying he wanted to sign three players that summer: Peter Beardsley, John Barnes and me. I also had the opportunity to go to Athletico Madrid in Spain, to Lyon in France, as well as interest from Manchester United, Everton and Arsenal.

'In the end, it was down to a choice of staying at Tottenham or going to Liverpool. At that stage of course, Liverpool were the team of the decade. They were going to fly me out to Spain to meet Kenny who was on holiday with his family. But I was going out to Spain for a holiday anyway, so we met up and Kenny made me an offer. I think the fee at the time was going to be about £1 million. It was very enticing and I was very honoured they had come in for me.

'I sat down and thought over my options, but in the end decided that I'd had five very enjoyable years at Tottenham; that I was enjoying my football, enjoying going to work every day, enjoying training and playing. My main concern was compromising my happiness. Would I be as happy at Liverpool? Tottenham at that stage had just played in the FA Cup final, they had finished third in the league and had got to the League Cup semi-finals and I felt we could be as good as Liverpool over the next couple of years. And so I renewed my contract with Tottenham.'

Former chairman Irving Scholar takes great delight in telling how Mabbutt re-signed for Spurs even while Dalglish was parked outside the player's house.

Dream On

Promoted to club captain, Mabbutt presided over a new era. In came Terry Venables, followed by Paul Gascoigne, Gary Lineker, Nayim, Paul Walsh, Paul Stewart and Erik Thorstvedt, followed by the high point of his playing career to date, the FA Cup win of 1991.

In 1994, Gary Vincent Mabbutt was awarded the MBE in the New Year's Honours List. On the international scene, sixteen full England caps is no mean achievement.

'If someone had told me when I was a schoolboy, that I would win sixteen caps for my country, I wouldn't have believed them. But on the other hand, a big disappointment is that I've never played in a major international tournament – a World Cup or a European Championship.

'Back in 1986, it looked as though I could be going to the World Cup in Mexico, but that never happened. I was told afterwards, by David Pleat, that discreet enquiries had been made about my condition and the conclusion was reached that my diabetes could pose problems in the extreme heat. If that was the reason for my non-selection, that is a huge disappointment because I've played all around the world with no problems at all.'

Mabbutt is stoical about the demands that diabetes makes on him.

'The year before I signed for Tottenham, Ipswich manager Bobby Robson wanted to sign me, but was advised against it by the Ipswich medical officer. Then I had to have a complete medical by a diabetes specialist before joining Tottenham.

'Of course people are going to be concerned, and managers are going to have people warning them about the hypotheticals of what could happen with me. But I think my record speaks for itself. I've always played over thirty games every season. The facts of my career speak for themselves and the diabetes hasn't been a hindrance.'

He is equally philosophical about praise of his loyalty to Tottenham.

'People tell me I've been really loyal to the club, but I think real loyalty is when someone isn't enjoying their work yet still stays with that company. But I've always been really happy here. Of course it has been a bit of a roller-coaster at times, and yet through it all I have enjoyed being part of it. If I hadn't enjoyed it I am sure I would have been enticed to leave. But that wasn't the case. It still isn't.'

That loyalty hasn't always been reciprocated. Irving Scholar tells of being shocked when manager Terry Venables would hand him a list of players he wanted to sell, and top of that list would be Mabbutt's name. Popular opinion has it that Venables had earmarked Terry Fenwick for the captain's role, but Mabbutt remains unconvinced.

'Terry Venables is very loyal to people, and Terry Fenwick had done well for him both at Crystal Palace and at QPR. I can only say that in all the time that Terry Venables was at Tottenham, I was captain all the way through. He never dropped me once.'

When Mabbutt's ten years with the club were up, in 1992, he was granted a testimonial. These games are viewed with some suspicion by many fans, who feel they are an anachronism from the days of the maximum wage and flat caps. Certainly it is difficult to argue the case for any player who may have spent ten or more years at the top of his profession, in doing so earning wages well in excess of those the average supporter could hope to attain in a lifetime. If such a player then decides to set himself up for retirement at 35 by asking his club's supporters to dig deep into their pockets to provide a tax-free lump sum

Dream On

from a moneyspinning testimonial match ... well it's no wonder those supporters may not fall over themselves to support the cause.

Not that supporters in general are mean, nor heartless nor unsympathetic. When genuine cases of hardship have been highlighted, the response has often been overwhelmingly generous. Long-time Tottenham fan Morris ('I haven't missed a home match since 1951') Keston has served on many a testiminial committee: Jimmy Greaves, Geoff Hurst and Bobby Moore to name three.

The sudden and unexpected death of former Tottenham player Cyril Knowles in August 1991 saw him hastily arrange a benefit fixture between Spurs and Arsenal teams of yore. Huge (and largely unsung) generosity by then Arsenal manager George Graham, his 1971 team-mates and three generations of players ensured that Morris could offer a cheque for over £100,000 to Cyril's widow and three children.

Not all was sweetness and light however as a former Tottenham stalwart charged Morris exorbitant expenses when all the other participants simply played for free. Similarly, in order to get the League Cup to White Hart Lane to complete the trio of trophies on display – Arsenal and Tottenham being respective holders of the Championship and FA Cup – Morris was presented with a bill for a couple of hundred quid for transporting the trophy from its then northern residence.

In such cases, few could argue that the cause is deserving and the efforts worthwhile. In Mabbutt's case the testimonial was to be a chance for the fans to recognise the (relative) financial sacrifices made by those players who choose not to hop from one club to another throughout their career.

'Hopefully,' said Mabbutt, 'it will be a celebration day

Carry on Intertoto

after thirteen years. The big money in football is made these days by being transferred quite often. If a player moves and receives a £500,000 "signing-on fee" the fans don't perceive that money as having come from their pocket, but of course it has.

'Signing-on fees and transfer fees are spiralling. Being at one club for thirteen years means I haven't made those moves and I haven't made those sums.

'So clubs give players the opportunity of a testimonial as a thank you for service and a chance to make up for a move that didn't happen. On the day, if you have attractive opposition and the crowd decide that you're not a bad person who hasn't given bad service, then they may turn up. But you never know. If the fans think they don't want to support me because they think I've earned enough, that's their decision and that's fair enough. It's their choice.'

The signing-on fees to be made on a multi-million-pound transfer can set a player up for life. With many players making several such moves during a career, and particularly if such a move takes them overseas, a one-club man like Gary Mabbutt can find himself questioning whether his loyalty has benefited everyone bar himself.

As an example, Darren Anderton is a very exciting young player with a great career ahead of him. However, when he moved from Portsmouth to Spurs for a fee of £2 million in 1992, his personal deal would have been a very tidy sum indeed, particularly for a 20-year-old. When interest in Darren grew as a result of his sparkling performances, efforts were made by Tottenham to secure his long term future. When he became a fixture in Terry Venables' England team and was strongly linked with Manchester United during the summer of 1995, Tottenham rushed to offer a new four-year contract which the player was more

Dream On

than happy to accept. (According to Manchester United he made the 'wrong' decision for an extra £100,000 – but then they would say that, wouldn't they?)

It would be no surprise to discover now that 23-year-old Anderton is earning considerably more than his 34-year-old club captain. When Anderton's contract expires in 1999, he will still be young enough to command a further big money move with the very real expectation of pocketing several million pounds. A look into the club car park where Darren's sparkling new Mercedes sits in contrast to his own somewhat older model provides Gary Mabbutt with a daily reminder of the downside to his loyalty.

Clubs themselves have usually adopted an attitude to testimonials that sees them tolerated but never encouraged. When a current or former player applies for a testimonial match, most clubs will provide their ground for a nominal fee of £1, more in the interests of avoiding bad PR than any act of inherent generosity. The visiting team will usually offer its services at a price. Graeme Souness brought Glasgow Rangers to White Hart Lane in 1986 as a personal favour to Paul Miller's then father-in-law, Morris Keston. Moreover, as a result of that friendship no fee was charged and thus the majority of the income from a crowd of 16,365 went directly to the testimonee.

On the other hand, long-time Spurs fans will recall how Phil Beal lost heavily on his testimonial in 1973 when receipts from a modest crowd of 19,150 failed to cover the cost of bringing over Bayern Munich as glamour opposition. The attitude with most players and managers, when invited to take part in a testimonial, is akin to that which sees so many people buy a copy of *The Big Issue*: 'there but for the grace of God, go I'. It's like an insurance policy in the event that someday they too may find themselves having to call on benevolence.

Testimonial games, as spectacles, are rarely more than a half-paced workout between two below-strength teams. Nobody wants to risk an injury or compromise fitness, and so 22 players, augmented by umpteen youth-team substitutes plus physio and the odd turnstile operator, stroll around the park going through the motions in an embarrassing parody of a football match. When attending such a game, the thought does occur that it would be less painful all round if it were possible to simply donate £10 to the cause in question and stay at home.

In the current climate of economic recession, high unemployment and negative equity mortgages, the prevailing attitude from fans seems to be that players earn quite enough as it is, thank you very much. If they hang up their boots only to find that society doesn't want the limited skills they now have to offer, or if they haven't been sufficiently diligent to salt away enough for a decent pension, then tough luck matey and welcome to the real world where the rest of us have been living for all these years. The incessant hype given to the surreal wage packets earned by the likes of Gullit, Bergkamp, Platt, Klinsmann and Collymore has simply promoted the impression that all Premiership footballers are millionaires many times over. In summary, sympathy is in short supply.

What compassion can be spared is reserved for those players whose careers ended before the modern wages boom, and who can usually be found eking out a living by running a pub in the roughest part of town or compelled to act as match-day hosts at Legends in Tottenham's East Stand.

It's a shame that a twenty-year playing career apparently proves such a poor apprenticeship for post-football careers.

Dream On

In England it would appear that for the 99% of ex-pros who are unable to cut it as football managers, the choice narrows to, in descending order: publican, minicab driver, milkman, window cleaner or a life in the former colonies where the sun shines all the time and ex-players are in great demand for coaching kiddies.

Embarrassing 'Where are they now?' features in the tabloids regularly turn up stars from the 1970s who are pitifully down on their luck and showing no signs of any apparent wealth derived from their playing days. It can only be hoped that the Professional Footballers Association (PFA) have a more charitable attitude to their former members than the clubs that earned so much from their stars but paid back so little.

So it was in this climate that Gary Mabbutt was granted a testimonial by the Terry Venables regime in 1992. Because of the stringent Inland Revenue rules that must be adhered to if tax is to be avoided, the whole testimonial subject is a minefield for the unwary. The PFA have even issued a series of guidelines on the subject. All negotiations and transactions have to be handled by an independent 'testimonial committee' which generally comprises of fans whose occupational expertise will facilitate fund raising: solicitors, accountants and a smattering of showbiz names. It usually follows that those same fans like Morris Keston are called upon again and again by long-serving players.

Mabbutt's testimonial year, 1992, saw a succession of events where the public were invited to join him for a day out or an evening's entertainment. There was 'Rabbit with Mabbutt' featuring those Cockney icons Chas'n'Dave; there was a golf day and a dinner at a top London Hotel. However, the actual testimonial football match never got played. Securing a firm date and suitable opposition proved

Carry on Intertoto

a problem as a succession of managers came and went at White Hart Lane. Provisional dates were booked and then cancelled as pre-season tournaments like the Makita took priority. Eventually, Mabbutt was able to sit down with Gerry Francis in March of 1995 and fix a firm date. Saturday 12 August was selected, and the player was told – that's your day.

Initially, it looked as if Jurgen Klinsmann would be able to pull a few strings. He had spoken to Franz Beckenbauer about bringing over Bayern Munich as opposition. However, Jurgen had to tell his ex-colleague that the earlier start planned for the German Bundesliga meant this was no longer feasible.

It was then that an approach was made to Kevin Keegan's revitalised Newcastle United. It would be a cynical person who said this approach was made because of Newcastle's huge away following, but then fund raising can be a cynical business. Certainly the last two Premiership games between Spurs and Newcastle had both been crackers (finishing 4-2 and 3-3), but would the fans turn up pre-season to watch a side who would be back in north London within a few weeks for a league game?

A request was sent to Kevin Keegan who personally responded the very same day, telling Gary it would be a pleasure to bring his side down for him. 'It made me feel really humble', said Gary afterwards, 'for Kevin Keegan to say that to me. When I was growing up, Keegan was up there on a pedestal as captain of England.'

However, any relief Mabbutt may have felt from this news was tempered by the growing realisation that he would in fact have two opponents for his testimonial game: not only Newcastle United but also the chief executive of Tottenham Hotspur.

Dream On

Claude Littner is not a popular man at White Hart Lane, but then troubleshooters rarely are. Appointed by Alan Sugar following the departure of the previous incumbent (T. Venables), Littner's job was to run the company on a day-to-day basis, as a tight and efficient business. Many of Littner's decisions were unpopular. The story about cancelling the club's milk delivery to save 2p a pint at the supermarket made good tabloid headlines, but also hinted at the club's new found devotion to good housekeeping.

To stage a match at White Hart lane costs money, no matter whether that match be a vital cup tie or Gary Mabbutt's testimonial. It could be predicted therefore that Littner, allegedly recipient of compassion bypass surgery, would ensure that the club was recompensed for each and every expense incurred in staging the game. And so it proved.

'This is a business and we are not prepared to lose a farthing over this match,' was the quote attributed to Littner that indeed summed up his attitude. Although, to his credit, Gary Mabbutt refused to comment on the stories of Littner's parsimonious stance, there remained plenty of disgruntled employees at the club who were more than happy to dish the dirt. Word got out that every employee was being asked to keep a log of all worktime and phone calls spent on the project, so that a suitable bill could be prepared. The club insisted that Mabbutt's testimonial committee lodge with it a £30,000 deposit in anticipation of expenses that would be incurred. In the event, by the time the deposit became due, advance takings exceeded £30,000 so the demand was rendered academic. Tickets for the game were charged at Premier League fixture prices, and a 50p handling charge was levied by the club. A fee was also demanded for the match-day

Carry on Intertoto

watering of the playing surface, together with a subsequent bill for repairing damage to the turf incurred during the game. Even the directors' buffet was allegedly going to be billed to the player.

What Mabbutt – or more precisely Mabbutt's testimonial committee – had failed to take into account, was that this current regime at Tottenham were businessmen running a football club. They had no previous experience of testimonials, and were unfamiliar with what was expected of them. The club was particularly keen to avoid any financial concessions that could return to embarrass them in the future. And so when the club granted the testimonial game to Mabbutt, Claude Littner insisted that a proper contract be drawn up, to make quite clear where the obligations lay.

Mabbutt's testimonial representitives duly signed the contract, perhaps without giving too much thought to the terms and conditions listed therein. Thus when the club, quite within its rights, started making charges for services and facilities – down to the match day pennants at £4.50 – the testimonial committee were horrified, but powerless. They were victims of their own naïvity. The club in turn was astounded that it was being cast as a villain when it believed it had acted by the book.

Through it all, Mabbutt retained a dignified silence. Whatever thoughts he may have harboured about such affronts to the club's longest serving professional were not for public consumption. A feature in London's *Time Out* magazine let slip details of how Mabbutt would donate £1 from every seat which was sold to diabetic associations, who ran a special promotion for one of their favourite sons. Unfortunately, a piece also appeared in the *News of The World* after the match highlighting Mabbutt's treatment

Dream On

by the club and telling of his disappointment. The news item was probably originated by a disgruntled member of the testimonial committee, but it didn't prevent Mabbutt from receiving an almighty dressing down from the club which was enraged at seeing its dirty laundry aired, yet again, in a national newpaper.

The day itself dawned bright, sunny and hot. A healthy crowd conformed to testimonial traditions by looking much bigger that the announced figure of 17,200. Spurs were once again injury-ridden and their weakened team proved no more than cannon-fodder in a 2-0 Newcastle victory. Chris Armstrong still had not scored his first goal for Spurs, and fears were raised when he was stretchered from the pitch with a head injury after just 25 minutes. Manager Gerry Francis was not at the game, preferring to scout elsewhere for reinforcements.

It must be assumed that Mabbutt was disappointed with the turnout; it is only human to hope that such loyalty would be better rewarded. Of course nothing to that effect was ever spoken, an indicator why a very healthy travelling contingent of 3,500 Geordies had been the first to lead the chanting in Mabbutt's praise – another spontaneous gesture that spoke volumes about the quality of support that Newcastle engenders and for the general esteem in which the player is held. It is also perhaps worth pointing out that pre-season testimonials have traditionally been poorly attended and that the crowd figure compares favourably with others in Tottenham's history. Steve Perryman played seventeen seasons at White Hart Lane and would figure in most fans' Greatest XI, but he drew just 17,702 to his testimonial in 1979. Glenn Hoddle chose a wretched wet evening for his testimonial and drew just 13,567 to a game against Arsenal in 1985. Another ten-season man, defender Terry Naylor, saw just 6,363 attend his benefit match against Crystal Palace in 1980.

Only Jimmy Greaves, who drew 45,799 to his benefit game against Feyenoord in 1972 (two years after he'd left the club), could really be said to have received a bumper turnout. And even on that night, many will recall that when the attendance was announced over the PA, the ground rang to boos as fans made known their displeasure at the stayaways who had prevented the 55,000 capacity from being attained.

Mabbutt would do well to also note the case of Joe Kinnear, whose ten-year career at Tottenham was cut short by injury. Joe played in four victorious cup finals for Spurs and yet his departure to Brighton was a shabby affair whereby the player received a derisory cash settlement and the promise of a testimonial. That game took place a year later, when Spurs took a representative XI to Brighton, refusing Kinnear his plea for a game at White Hart Lane as he had understood the agreement to be.

So although it was perhaps poor timing that saw Mabbutt's game take place under the current boardroom regime, history indicates that Tottenham as a club have never really come to grips with the concept of rewarding loyalty. If he is looking for consolation, it should come from the fact that he has at least been permitted a full career in which to ply his trade, unlike former team-mate Danny Thomas whose severe injury forced him into retirement aged 26 after just 103 games for Spurs.

A week earlier at Stamford Bridge, Paul Elliot had seen the other side of Lady Luck's coin when his testimonial, granted by Chelsea after only five years' injury-interrupted service, had coincided with the home debuts for new signings Ruud Gullit and Mark Hughes. The crowd figure

Dream On

that evening had been little more than Mabbutt's, but the degree of co-operation afforded by Chelsea ensured that all proceeds went solely to the player as the public would have wanted.

Like weddings, funerals and family visits, testimonials appear to be an unavoidable embarrassment to be endured as infrequently as possible. The positive aspect from Tottenham's point of view is that ten-year careers are increasingly an anachronism and thus testimonial matches will surely go the same way as wooden stands, half-time Bovril, trainers with sponges and managers in sheepskin coats. Of the current squad, only Erik Thorstvedt and David Howells have the potential to embarrass the club with their loyalty, and with the kind of season most fans were now anticipating, there was no betting on either player still being on the books in twelve months' time.

Chapter 3

The Way We Were

At the opening of Stanley Kubrick's epic film, *2001: A Space Odyssey*, there is a scene set in pre-Neanderthal times. A mysterious black monolith appears on Earth; a marker to record a critical stage in man's development. As the dawn sun rises above the giant monument, a long shadow is cast and primitive man cowers in the presence of a supernatural force.

Some years later, in 1961, a similar thing happened.

The problem facing every Spurs side, every Spurs manager and indeed every Spurs fan is that its future cannot possibly hold a candle to its past. The club is saddled with a history that, rather than serving to inspire future generations, instead seems to emphasise the futility of their efforts. If The Tottenham Hotspur Story had been a Hollywood movie, then the scriptwriters would have been tempted to write in a disaster to wipe out the entire cast on 16 May, 1963.

A generation of players, officials and supporters survive to this day, whose contribution to and memories of a golden

Dream On

era between 1949 and 1963 will forever deny them the undiluted pleasure of contemporary football. For many, it was a watershed in their lives. They are the Push and Run generation.

On a glorious autumnal afternoon in late August 1995, a big White Hart Lane crowd were thrilling to a display of Push and Run football at its finest. Skilled ball players were pinging passes between one another with pin-point accuracy. There was a readiness by each player to work for one another, to give a pass then move into space to create the option for a return. Veteran internationals were working as hard as the crop-haired youngsters: making runs, finding space, creating choices, befuddling the opposition. Defenders were left chasing shadows, just like the good old days. A two-goal lead was a fair reflection of the disparity between the teams, but the best was yet to come as another plodding attack was effortlessly stifled and defence turned to attack in a flurry of one-touch interchanges.

The ball was worked out to the full-back. He skipped down the inside right channel before releasing his overlapping colleague whose burst of speed left defenders exposed and out of position. A hard low cross was met by a waif in baggy shorts who swept the ball into the back of the net with an instinctive flourish reminiscent of the great Jimmy Greaves; three-nil. Applause thundered from all sides; this surely was how football was meant to be played.

But the appreciation was grudging, for it was the Reds of Liverpool who were giving the footballing lesson. And it was the Whites of Tottenham Hotspur who were finding out just how much had changed in the six months since their FA Cup quarter-final win at Anfield. Spurs had won a famous and deserved victory that day, but had undoubtedly regressed since. Gone were

The Way We Were

Popescu, Klinsmann and now Nicky Barmby. Long term injuries to Campbell and Anderton had further weakened the manager's hand. In had come just two signings, one for free and one for a fortune.

Clive Wilson was the freeman, signed from QPR when his contract had expired. Making his debut today, he looked a quality player despite being played out of position at right-back. In contrast, Chris Armstrong looked completely out of sorts, lacking both the drive and initiative expected from a signing of his magnitude. Recalled Romanian international Ilie Dumitrescu was still seemingly unable to come to terms with the speed and the passion of the English game; his flaccid contribution serving only to silence that dwindling number of fans who shared his name and number on the back of their own replica shirts. Ronny Rosenthal's novelty value was fast waning, his ability to waste goalscoring opportunities matched only by his inability to remain upright when in full flight. Increasingly he was looking like Liverpool's cruel revenge for their ill-judged purchase of Paul Stewart.

The lack of competition for first team places was best highlighted by the appearance of Gerard McMahon. No more than a promising kid with few apparent skills to elevate him above the many who pass through the Spurs' youth system, McMahon had inherited Klinsmann's now-vacant number 18 shirt but sadly none of the enchantment brought to it by the former owner. Truly it was hard to think of many in the home side who would command a regular Premiership place in any side other than Tottenham's.

The home defeat by Liverpool (1-3 following a late consolation goal as the visitors got sloppy), was the third game of the new season, and left Tottenham with just one solitary point. That had come on the opening day from

Dream On

a laboured 1-1 draw at Manchester City. A home defeat
the following Wednesday against a revitalised Aston Villa
had intensified the build-up to the Liverpool game and
the need to avert early talk of crisis. Now with a second
consecutive home defeat, Gerry Francis again bemoaned
his injury woes:

'I felt to come off 2-0 down in the first half was a bit harsh;
having said that, I thought Liverpool were tremendous. I
think they would be my tip to win the title.'

It must have been so encouraging for the Spurs faithful
to hear their manager concede defeat in the title race after
just eight days. There was little more good news for his
own players:

'I think [Liverpool's performance] is the sort of yardstick
you've got to look to to try and achieve as a manager. Last
year we played them three times and didn't lose to them.
From the team that played last year, we've got five players
out for one reason or another and I think at times it shows.
I've been in this position before as a manager on a number
of occasions, and you have to dig down and get things sorted
out; hopefully get a couple of players back, and hopefully
sign a couple of players as well.

'The squad needs a lift. If Darren Anderton and Sol
Campbell are back that will give us a lift. I felt that Clive
Wilson today had an excellent debut playing out of position
on the right hand side. But I think we all realise we've all
got a hard job to do.'

So how close was he to making a signing?

'We're not really close to be perfectly honest. Some
people we may be interested in are not available because
of the time of year. A lot of the people we were interested
in have gone. A lot of the people we were interested in are
not for sale. I've only got a certain amount of money to

The Way We Were

spend, that's basically the Nicky Barmby money. I'd at least like to get two players, but the money isn't a great deal in terms of the prices that some players are going for.

'After next Wednesday's game [at West Ham] we've got a little break which could be a godsend for us, as that would hopefully get both Darren Anderton and Sol Campbell back. Those two players in particular will give us a big lift. I think if we do that, and what with two or three other bodies to come in – very important bodies – you're looking at half a team again and I think that will make us a lot stronger and give us all a lift.'

So, not only is the title race conceded, but the manager admits that half of his current team is not up to the job and in line for imminent replacement. Liverpool manager Roy Evans had little need for excuses, and had the kind of selection dilemmas that his counterpart could only dream of.

'We have three excellent strikers,' said Evans afterwards. 'We talked about competition for places and [with Stan Collymore injured] Robbie Fowler stepped in and scored a training pitch goal – a dart to the near post which we practised on Thursday. But he's not a replacement for Stan – it's competition for places which is good from our point of view.'

With that, Roy Evans joined his squad back on the coach for the journey back to Merseyside, his thoughts more concerned with players he may have to leave out rather than those he would need to draft in.

For Gerry Francis, the honeymoon was over. Whose patience would snap first? That of the supporters or that of his chairman? Given everything the club had gone through in the preceding five years, a poor opening three games hardly spelt crisis with a capital C. Alan Ball was having a

Dream On

far worse time of it in his new job at Maine Road; champions Blackburn had also lost two out of three, and the big spender down the road, Bruce Rioch, must have been wondering if he'd somehow bought the wrong Dennis Bergkamp. Even the most fatalistic Spurs fan had seen the team in far worse scrapes and knew it would eventually come good. What Gerry would have to address in the short term search for league points was the very un-Tottenham-like style his team had adopted, and to understand fully just how much that went against what the home crowd wanted and perhaps were prepared to tolerate.

'Push and Run' was a term coined by Arthur Rowe to describe the style of play adopted following his appointment as Spurs manager in 1949. A player would be expected to Push the ball to a colleague, then Run into space to accept a return. It was a simple philosophy, but one that demanded its exponents should have the skills, vision and fitness for it to succeed.

Rowe had a simple, straightforward way of coaching, encapsulated by succinct instructional phrases: 'Make it simple; make it accurate; make it quick', he would exalt. 'He who holds the ball is lost.' Every pass made demanded a subsequent movement to give the player in possession a further option for distribution. Moves were thus kept flowing, with short accurate passes ushering the ball and players upfield at a speed to bewilder the unwary. The Leicester City players once told Bill Nicholson – who played wing-half for Rowe – 'We hate playing against you because it's like trying to catch pigeons'.

Eddie Bailey, inside-forward at that time, felt that, '... We did things naturally, as a moving game. Consequently when you played with someone, you knew what he

The Way We Were

was going to do. The object of the exercise was to make a pass, get somewhere quickly and get the return.'

Of course to make it work the passing had to be accurate, and as a wonderful first-time passer Eddie Bailey's role was fundamental. But even if you didn't possess Bailey's ability – 'the best first-time passer of the ball at that particular time', according to Bill Nicholson – the style of play facilitated the assimilation of good habits. 'It became easy to push the ball and run off it,' said Bill, 'but also not to kick the ball too far in the distance because the shorter you pass the ball, the more accurate you can be ... hence push and run.'

Rowe had originally joined Tottenham in 1921 as a schoolboy, signing professional in 1929 and playing 210 games for the club before injury ended his playing days in 1939. A brief coaching post in Budapest was terminated by the commencement of World War II, whereupon Rowe joined the armed forces and eventually took charge of the Army's football team. Four post-war years spent with Southern League Chelmsford were hugely successful, and served to remind Tottenham of their former player's managerial potential.

When manager Joe Hulme was dismissed by Spurs in 1949, he left behind a team assembled over the previous three post-war years that had yet to fulfil its potential. Arthur Rowe was appointed as Hulme's successor and recognised the qualities he had inherited. Just one fresh face was brought in, that of future England manager Alf Ramsey, but the Push and Run tactics galvanised the previously moribund Tottenham team.

In his very first season, Spurs won the Division Two championship by nine clear points. In his second season, 1950–51, newly promoted Spurs stormed to the Division

Dream On

One championship for the first time in their 69-year history. The following season they were runners-up.

Rowe held a belief that football 'is a lovely passing game' and he inherited skilled, open-minded players who were receptive to his innovations. Goalkeeper Ted Ditchburn was already established as a fixture in the side, as were Nicholson and Bailey. Ron Burgess was an intelligent wing-half who captained Spurs for eight seasons. Adapting to the simplistic tactics of Push and Run greatly restricted the extravagant playing style of Burgess, whose long, defence-splitting runs were now replaced by short, one-touch passes. That this great player not only adapted to the new demands, but also accepted that such cramping of his style was necessary for the good of the team, indicated the degree of support new manager Rowe commanded.

According to Rowe, the system was the fulcrum of the success, as he explained in 1960 in the *Encyclopedia of Association Football*: 'The great thing we built on basically was accuracy. We had two or three great performers and we had a lot who were not. But they were all made to look great players because of the system we adopted and because they played in a winning side.'

It was a period of prowess unparalleled in the club's history, but one that appeared to end almost as soon as it had begun. Rowe kept faith with his championship-winning side, despite results that indicated changes were due, and in the face of an increasing ability by opponents to stifle the Push and Run tactics. Three subsequent seasons in charge saw his side finish tenth, sixteenth and sixteenth again, before ill health finally forced Rowe's retirement in 1955.

Rowe's successor was his assistant, Jimmy Anderson. The team that Anderson inherited in 1955 contained some good footballers and some good footballing habits. Anderson

The Way We Were

himself had been at the club for almost 50 years but was better known for his scouting abilities. True to form he was able to add quality players like Bobby Smith, Cliff Jones and Maurice Norman to the side. However, Anderson's forte was not team management and Spurs slumped to finish eighteenth after his first season in charge. With Bill Nicholson now operating as his assistant, fortunes revived and the team finished second and third in 1957 and 1958 respectively. When ill health forced Anderson to resign after just three years in charge, it was to 39-year-old Bill Nicholson that the club turned to maintain the tenuous link with their championship side of 1951.

As with his two predecessors, Bill Nicholson was a Spurs man through and through. He had already been at the club for over half his life, and, despite five full years lost to the war, had clocked up 345 appearances as a tenacious wing-half during a seventeen-year playing career. The success he had enjoyed as part of the Push and Run championship side obviously left a great impression on him. His teams were to adopt those tactics with a renewed verve, and further signings were specifically made to comply with the proposed style of play.

From the moment he took over in October 1958, every decision taken by the manager can be seen as a calculated move towards creating the side that was to sweep all before it within three years. Bobby Smith, Terry Dyson, Ron Henry, Cliff Jones, Peter Baker and Maurice Norman were all at the club and known to Nicholson. But pivotal players were still missing from the mental jigsaw being put together by the Spurs manager. His army days would have done much to confirm a belief that a team, any team, operating as an effective unit, needs a leader to inspire and to motivate. There was only so much the manager could do before a game; he needed an alter ego to continue his work on the playing field.

That man, Danny Blanchflower, had been induced to go to White Hart Lane from Villa Park in 1954, as much by the charismatic aura that had first brought the name of Tottenham Hotspur to his attention as a kid growing up in Belfast, as by the blandishments of Jimmy Anderson. Spurs had narrowly beaten Arsenal to his signature not only by outbidding their London rivals, but also by the way in which Anderson had emphasised to the player the footballing merits of such a move. Blanchflower enjoyed considerable success with the Northern Ireland team he captained, but his early days at Spurs were a low key period where managers came and went while the team coasted along living off past memories.

Blanchflower had achieved some notoriety at Tottenham for taking the initiative and reorganising the team mid-match when circumstances had dictated. In Jimmy Anderson's view this had been a capital offence and the player was dropped for supposedly undermining his manager's position. Under Bill Nicholson, however, such a trait was seen as a quality to be encouraged. Nicholson had been at White Hart Lane for 22 years and had no need to feel threatened by a player who had the confidence to take a captain's decisions when it mattered. For a decade, Blanchflower had played football in his own individualistic way, and at the highest level. He led Northern Ireland to a quarter-final place in the 1958 World Cup in Sweden, based on '. . . our new tactics: we equalize before the others have scored.' Nicholson rightly felt that his experience should be exploited to the full.

That first season under Nicholson, 1958–59, saw Spurs finish eighteenth in the league. But important steps had been taken to bring the success that the club, and now the players hungered for, ever closer. Despite being aged 33, Blanchflower was reinstated as club captain and Nicholson took the brave decision to construct a side around the attacking wing-half. Time was not on their side, and few of Tottenham's transitional seasons could be endured if the current squad was to achieve its potential.

Nicholson played the transfer market like a silent assassin. Unlike today when the media trumpet a move before talks have even commenced, the late 1950s still saw such negotiations conducted with stealth. Clandestine meetings, gentlemen's agreements and firm handshakes saw players bought and sold in the manner of prized livestock. Bill Nicholson had a poacher's eye for a potential Spurs player, and would frequently return from scouting missions with the signature of his quarry in the bag.

Dave Mackay was captain of Hearts and captain of Scotland, but when Bill went hunting north of the border, he came back with Mackay's name on a contract. Mackay first caught Nicholson's eye when, as assistant to Jimmy Anderson, he also looked after the England under-23 team for manager Walter Winterbottom. 'Dave [Mackay] played in the under-23s against England and I was rather taken by his play and particularly his attitude [which he later described as 'bubbling over all the time out there on the field'] . . . so naturally I made an enquiry about him and was very surprised when they [Hearts] said they would talk business. I went up there and signed him in a very quick time.' A brave decison and at £30,000 a record fee for a defender. Particularly an injured one, as at the time of the transfer Mackay hadn't recovered from a broken foot. 'I'm not fit,' he apologised to Danny Blanchflower, 'but wait until next season.' Notwithstanding the incapacity, Blanchflower '. . . could see right away that we would suit one another.' Another piece of the jigsaw fitted into place. Fired by the apparent abundance of riches to be had ('I was a firm believer in having Scotsmen in my team') Nicholson returned to his favourite hunting ground and stole away with Dundee's goalkeeper, Bill Brown.

And so a pattern emerged. A system. Players to fit that system. New players to perpetuate that system.

The year before the Double season was almost a dress rehearsal for the real thing. Most of the team was assembled, and all that remained was some fine tuning of tactics and possibly the signing of one or two players in key positions. Danny Blanchflower told what happened next.

'On the first Saturday of October, Mackay, Brown and myself went to Belfast for the Northern Ireland v Scotland match. Scotland won comfortably with some new faces in their team. John White was the one that impressed me most. On Monday morning, when I returned to White Hart Lane, Bill Nick was waiting for me.

'"What about John White?" he asked.

'"First class," I said, "good positional sense and smooth ball control."

'"I can get him for £20,000," he said.

'"Don't miss the first plane," I said.

'Bill had it all arranged. He just wanted confirmation. John White was signed before the day was out.'

In December 1959, the final piece of the jigsaw was slotted into place when Les Allen moved across London from Chelsea.

Danny Blanchflower again: 'At this time I began to think we could do the Double. It was a judgement of instinct and experience. I had seen Manchester United just miss it in the 1957 Cup Final when Ray Wood, their keeper, had been clobbered in the early stages of the match by Peter

The Way We Were

McParland. They had won the league by eight clear points. I remembered that well because we were second, with a frankly mediocre Spurs team.

'I told some of the players that I thought we could do it. "Oh yes," they said, as if they did not disbelieve it, or maybe they didn't know what I was talking about. Then I mentioned it to Bill Nick. He looked at me cautiously, as if it were another of my fancy ideas. Then he surprised me. "I was thinking about that myself," he said.

'We agreed that we all had to believe in it to do it. We must create the right atmosphere.'

But it was not to be that season. A cup exit to Blackburn and some sloppy league performances saw Spurs finish third that May. But lessons had been learned and the hunger for success had been intensified.

In 1960–61, Spurs won the Double. The Football League championship and the FA Cup both captured in the same season. The first time it had been achieved this century. A record number of wins, a record unbeaten start, a record number of away victories, a record for the fewest first team players used and over two million spectators paying to watch.

But the results and performances were only part of the story. That historic season and the events that led to it set a yardstick against which all future Spurs players and Spurs teams would be judged. It was as if the club had never existed before this time. The way this team played, the way the manager operated and the way the season unfolded all became encapsulated as The Spurs Way.

Football played simply, with the emphasis on attack. Flowing moves that swept the length of the field. 'Engage,' Bill would yell when a player lost the ball. 'Disengage,' he would counter when Spurs were back in possession. 'When

Dream On

you've lost the ball you engage your opponent but when you win the ball you disengage – you try to lose them. I told my players to just think of those two words when you're out there on the field.' Passing was the basis of his strategy, but Nicholson recognised fitness as a prerequisite for all the necessary running involved.

The Spurs Way was never a formula that could be precisely defined, committed to paper or coded or analysed. It was rather an amalgam that evolved through the vision of a few great men and the efforts of many more. Spurs fans will tell you that The Spurs Way encompasses all that is great about the game of football, and to a large extent that is correct. Entertaining, attack-minded football played by a team liberally sprinkled with stardust.

There is no right or wrong way of playing football. The precepts of the game permit endless permutations of tactics, formations, moves and opportunities, many of which will triumph. But few will bring glory. Because glory is success matched with beauty; success with flair; success that brings praise and is worthy of renown.

As Danny Blanchflower memorably expounded its relevance for Tottenham Hotspur: 'Football is not really about winning or goals or saves or supporters . . . it's about glory. It's about doing things in style, doing them with a flourish; it's about going out to beat the other lot, not waiting for them to die of boredom; it's about dreaming of the glory that the Double brought.'

Years later, in 1984, Irving Scholar held a reunion for the Double side to coincide with the release of a book – *Glory, Glory* – that he had helped persuade Bill Nicholson to write. The former stars came from far and wide to attend – Bill Brown from Canada and Peter Baker from South Africa. To Scholar, these were his real footballing heroes. It was, in his own words, a dream come true to share a room with such illustrious names. The normally self-assured Scholar recalls being racked with nerves at the thought of the speech he was to give. His long hours of preparation paid off, however, and his words were warmly received by the assembled throng who, until then, had cause to treat the club's new owner with cautious reserve.

'Every time this ground is opened,' he ventured, 'someone, somewhere thinks about you. You may think you're forgotten, but you are not.'

Mingling socially afterwards, none other that Cliff Jones approached Scholar and requested an autograph for his copy of *Glory, Glory*. 'I'm not telling you again,' Scholar snapped at the Welsh wizard, 'piss off and come back in two minutes . . . just like you used to make me do!' Having just found out that the young Irving had patiently accumulated at least six autographs from his playing idol despite receiving similar reprimands, Cliff Jones simply roared with laughter at this new twist to fate.

The Double side, together with the team which broke further records in the two succeeding years, achieved success with glory. This glory could easily have gone to Manchester United. Or to Wolves, or to any one of several teams who had come within a whisker of being the first club this century to win the Double. But it was Tottenham who made it happen first, and moreover did it with panache. And for that Tottenham will always be a singular club. And much credit must go to manager Bill Nicholson.

Bill Nick, as he was almost universally known, was to remain in charge of the club until 1974. His style of management became the accepted Spurs way of management, because so much was achieved with Bill Nick at the

Dream On

helm that it became hard to remember success at Spurs without him.

Dave Mackay, who remained a fixture in the Spurs side until 1968, remembers how, 'We didn't bother about other teams. We played as we wanted to play. Occasionally we lost matches, but there wasn't the fear of other teams. We wanted to entertain. After we'd played and won against a very good team, but hadn't played particularly well, Bill Nick acted as if we'd lost the match. He'd be so disappointed in the way we'd played.

'All the top teams would come to White Hart Lane to play football. They wouldn't expect to win, but they would play to win. Whereas the weaker teams would come and all they'd want was a 0-0 draw. But we would go to Liverpool or Manchester United and we would try to win, and we would expect to win.

'It was just a marvellous time to play football. We were the best team in England at that particular time [1960–63]. We'd go places and get beat, or we'd get beaten at home, but every game the players genuinely thought that we would win.

'Bill is a one hundred percent man. He likes everything one hundred percent, and this is what he looks for from his players. But he didn't mix with his players; he was apart from the Spurs players – you would very rarely have a chat with Bill Nicholson. He'd be there at training but when training was over he wouldn't sit around or anything like that. But everybody respected Bill Nicholson and worked hard for him because they all enjoyed it.'

Dave Mackay said that joining Tottenham was '. . . probably the best thing I've ever done in my life.' Probably because it wasn't work but a love affair. Danny Blanchflower told a story that encapsulates the team spirit of the day: 'The

The Way We Were

players were obsessed with football for football's sake, as Arthur Rowe had told me when he signed me for Spurs. Jones and White and Mackay and Harmer and Dyson were constantly competing with one another, throwing small coins up in the air, catching them on their foot, flicking them up onto their forehead and then nodding the coin back into their pocket. They would do the same at hotels with oranges, sometimes standing on restaurant tables even, and they continued to improvise and improve with these games.

'Jonesy would sometimes challenge me to do it. "Look son," I would tell him, "when you can do that with a coin and a ball at the same time then come and see the old pro." He loved that.'

Irving Scholar too remembers the team of that era as containing '. . . players who would still make a best-ever Spurs team from all sides since the War. I've always believed that a really successful team contains at last three world class players. And Spurs, at that time, had probably four in White, Mackay, Blanchflower and Jones. Four of the best players ever to play for Tottenham. Each one of those four could walk into any team, at any time.'

The seal of approval for Bill Nick's methods was that his success was not a one-off fluke. By applying his rules he extended the Double team's success for a further two years, before going on to create a second Spurs era of success that, while not matching the heights of his early 1960s teams, still propelled the club to further fame and glory. The Double season in 1960–61 was followed by another FA Cup win in 1962, and then an historic European Cup Winners' Cup triumph in 1963. Bill Nick and Spurs were re-writing the book on glory. Having seen his own championship side of 1950 grow older together, Nicholson was more aware than

Dream On

most of the need to continually throw some new ingredients into the pot to keep the potion fresh. Scoring goals was the least of the Double team's worries (over 115 league goals that season) but when the opportunity came along to sign a twenty-one-year-old goalscoring sensation from AC Milan, Nicholson had no hesitation in breaking the British transfer record to capture a homesick Jimmy Greaves in December 1961. Seventy-two goals in 79 appearances over the next season and a half tell their own story of this signing's importance to Spurs. It was a classic Nicholson signing – he had filled a gap that no one but he had seen.

Four barren years between 1963 and 1967 saw Bill Nick further raid the transfer market to bring in replacements for his aging Double side. He was not afraid to buy big if the need arose. As typified by the Greaves swoop, he acknowledged that there was no substitute for class and the importance of getting the right player to fill a position. They cost what they cost. Players were often bought mid-season, and bedded in for several months so that they would be attuned to the team's system by the start of the next full season. Transfer records were broken again and again as Tottenham's determination to get their man made them vulnerable to exploitation from selling clubs.

Pat Jennings replaced Bill Brown in goal; Alan Mullery came to cover for Blanchflower and Mackay; Cyril Knowles came in to replace Ron Henry at full-back; Mike England took over at centre-half from Maurice Norman and Alan Gilzean came to partner Jimmy Greaves up front. At the same time, there were players coming through the ranks who cost the club nothing but who were to prove just as valuable as the big-money signings: Phil Beal, Joe Kinnear and Steve Perryman amassed over 1,500 appearances between just the three of them.

The Way We Were

The 1967 FA Cup win was a premature success for a team that was still being built. Between then and 1971 when the trophies next began to arrive, two more key purchases were made – Martin Chivers and Martin Peters. Quality players for key positions. Record buys to complete a picture.

Despite three trophies in three years, by 1974 Nicholson was finding the going tough. Constant warring with modern players who failed to share his principles was wearing him down. The generation gap had grown too wide for Bill Nicholson to bridge. But while he knew he was no longer the man for the job, he knew a man who was. However, just as the Leeds directors could ignore the recommendation of departing icon Don Revie and appoint Brian Clough instead of Johnny Giles, so Tottenham made an ex-Arsenal captain, Terry Neill, the manager in preference to Bill Nick's choice of Danny Blanchflower. Heresy. At a stroke these decisions consigned both Tottenham and Leeds to seasons of transition. The Tottenham directors simply did not understand their role in the scheme of things. They did not understand that they were the privileged custodians of a legacy it was their duty to preserve for future generations. Quite simply, they did not understand The Spurs Way. Thus when Bill Nicholson left in September 1974, another link with the Double era had been severed. Now it was just the fans who remained.

Since Nicholson's departure, managers have come and gone, but none have approached his record of success. Given time, David Pleat might have proved a worthy successor. Only he of subsequent managers seemed to understand what was expected of a Spurs manager in terms of performances and standards. His short spell in charge was characterised by near misses (third in the league, FA Cup finalists and League Cup semi-finalists), and gave much entertainment

Dream On

along the way. After Pleat's premature departure, Spurs seemed to lose their way, with only the 1991 Cup success to show for their efforts and outlay.

Ossie Ardiles, a player who would have graced the Double side, had a far better grasp of The Tottenham Way when he succeeded Venables. His teams played expansively and he bought expensively. Like the great managers - Shankly, Busby, Paisley and Nicholson – Ardiles believed in a passing game. He also encouraged self-belief in his team: the Famous Five forward line went out each game expecting to score goals and not clouding their thoughts worrying about the opposition. However, those great managers had one quality sadly lacking in Ardiles – they made few mistakes in the transfer market. Given more time and different circumstances, Ardiles may have evolved into an outstanding Tottenham manager. But he was an idealist who fell victim to changed times. His emphasis on attacking football – at the expense of defence – was an unrealistic strategy in a 42-game Premier League. He had no eye for the defensive requirements of a team, and assistant Steve Perryman seemed sadly unable to cover for this deficiency.

When Ardiles was fired by Sugar in the autumn of '94, it was a merciful release for everyone. Both he and Perryman were finished at the club they had served so loyally; it was a rotten way to end their association with Spurs. Maybe, one day in the future, both may be able to renew ties rather as Bill Nicholson was welcomed back into the fold after a sabbatical. Certainly, you can see why Glenn Hoddle ran a mile at the suggestion of a return to White Hart Lane. His fear of tainting a memory held dear by the Spurs faithful was fully vindicated by the Ardiles/Perryman experience.

The Way We Were

Enter Gerry Francis; not a Tottenham man, but definitely a Sugar man.

'Gerry doesn't want to use a chequebook,' says QPR owner Richard Thompson, 'because the minute he does he puts himself open to blame for making mistakes. By having no chequebook he can always say "I have no money", which gives him a tremendous image within the game. He doesn't want a chequebook, which is why he'll tell Alan Sugar not to let on how much money they have to spend. Because otherwise people will know they've got a lot of money. That's not the reason at all; the reason is that he doesn't want any money to spend.

'He's a terrific coach, and tactically, he's extremely shrewd. There's no doubt about it. He's a tactician; a pure tactician and a very good tactician. I respect Gerry as an individual, but I can't work with him. Whatever club he may be at, he will always have the upper hand over the board because of what he needs as a person to satisfy and make him feel comfortable in the position he is taking on. He'll give it 100% on his terms. [He is reluctant to tie himself down to a long contract.]

'He is like that because of what he has seen in the industry. He is a realist about the industry; that is why he has become what he is – to make himself invincible as an individual. He has seen that four or five bad results can take you from hero to villain.'

Gerry had no real reputation to live up to at White Hart Lane. Most Spurs fans would have been vaguely aware of his existence at Loftus Road, and the older ones would recall his playing days as a dynamic and aggressive inside-forward and captain of Don Revie's England team. In truth, he'd had a heroic career, every bit as gutsy as Dave Mackay.

Dream On

Like Mackay, his trademark was his combativeness allied to a level of skill that belied his size and swayed the odds in 50:50 challenges. Two shocking injuries to knee and spine were overcome in a manner that speaks volumes about his determination.

Francis made his QPR debut in March '69, and spent four full seasons playing alongside Terry Venables, eventually succeeding him as club captain. Under Dave Sexton, QPR peaked during the 1975–76 season when they sat atop the First Division taking 27 points from 30 in their final fifteen games. However a win by Liverpool in their final game consigned Rangers to the runners-up spot. Alongside Gerry Francis in that team were the likes of Frank McLintock, John Hollins, Phil Parkes, David Webb, and Stan Bowles. There is no doubt that many of Gerry's ideas and strategies date back to that era and the influence a great coach and colleagues had on him.

Gerry's career seems to criss-cross that of Terry Venables with a spooky frequency. Venables paid £425,000 to bring Francis to Crystal Palace in 1979. Then just two years later, Venables crossed London to take over at QPR and promptly re-signed Francis for his second stint at Loftus Road. Further playing stints at Coventry, Exeter (player-manager), Cardiff, Swansea and Portsmouth took his total of league appearances beyond the 500 mark. He succeeded Bobby Gould as manager at Bristol Rovers in 1987, before being coaxed back to Loftus Road for a third time by new owner Richard Thompson in 1991.

For Francis, managerial experience has been gained the hard way. There has never been – until the Spurs job anyway – the option of the chequebook route to problem solving. His triumphs have come from making the best use of the resources at his disposal. As with Kevin Keegan, he has the

The Way We Were

ability to motivate his players; to inspire ordinary players to stretch their capabilities beyond their expectations. His inspirational playing career is the perfect 'caps on the table' answer to back up his arguments. He is no theorist: he has been there and done it.

Whilst at Bristol Rovers he dug deep into his own pocket to finance player purchases. This spawned an arrangement that he should in turn benefit when such players were sold on for substantial profit. When he joined QPR, a similar clause was incorporated into his Loftus Road contract. Rangers owner Richard Thompson readily acknowledges that his club are minnows in the Premier League, who cannot hope to survive without selling players. When Francis stipulated that he should receive an annual percentage of the squad's potential worth, Thompson concurred; any increase in the value of the club's assets (i.e. the players) could only be good for the continued health of the club. If the price to be paid was that the manager was on a commission of sorts, then that was a price worth paying. And so every year for the three years that the contract ran, Gerry Francis received a payment commensurate with the year-on-year incremental value of his squad. And a nice little earner that turned out to be.

'He did very well,' said Thompson. 'He earned a lot more than anyone on the playing staff. A lot more.'

His talent for galvanising the careers of players who were going nowhere transformed the likes of Les Ferdinand and Andy Sinton into England internationals who would go on to command multi-million-pound transfer fees. He turned cheap buys like Ian Holloway and Clive Wilson into valued Premiership players. But he was less successful when buying fresh talent. His hankering after Bristol Rovers players could be regarded as an unhealthy obsession. With the exception of Ian Holloway, the transfers of Gary Penrice and Devon White couldn't be termed terrific business. Only Trevor Sinclair has really justified his manager's outlay – a £600,000 buy from Blackpool who when sold will produce a profit that will dwarf the modest purchase price.

Gerry's adroitness in the transfer market will be sorely tested at Spurs. He has never had access to big funds as a manager, and has previously relied on bargain buys and youth players to bolster his teams. He is clearly more at ease with pliable players (and pliable backroom staff) – those he has made into better performers, for which they owe him. This is no bad thing as it has helped him cultivate a rapport with his players that brings the best out of them. This is not a reaction he would get from multi-million-pound signings who are supposed to be the finished article. Unless of course those he buys – like Chris Armstrong – are not yet the finished article.

It was commendable that Gerry never rushed out to spend the £7 million or so earmarked by Alan Sugar for pre-season signings. But his conservatism could prove equally expensive. The Tottenham man who went out and bought Tottenham-style players this summer was unfortunately the manager of Chelsea. In Gullit and Hughes, Spurs missed out on two players perfectly suited to their current needs – one a charismatic leader by example because of his presence and sheer talent, the other a proven line-leader/target man and a perfect foil for Teddy Sheringham.

In fact Tottenham had been offered Gullit first, but the Dutchman's preference for playing sweeper meant the move was a non-starter. 'What do I want with a sweeper?' Gerry Francis is alleged to have told Dennis Roach, the agent brokering the deal. It is a cruel turnaround considering how often in the past Chelsea have outbid Spurs for players (as was the case with Chris Waddle and Richard Gough) only for those players to snub the west Londoners in preference to the playing traditions at White Hart Lane.

Francis has also geared his team tactics around the all-for-one mentality; he creates not a team but a unit of which he is the leader. When the team defends, it defends as a unit with all ten outfield players contributing. When defence turns to attack, again the team attacks as a unit. This is a commendable strategy – albeit the long ball being an essential ingredient – and given the required levels of fitness and individual skill to ensure each player can play their part, it can be blindingly effective.

Although defenders may not baulk at the opportunity to go forward, many attack-minded players aren't keen to tackle back when the need arises. It was team orders like this that didn't help Spurs hold on to Jurgen Klinsmann and Gica Popescu. Which highlights a further worry about Francis – his man-management skills.

Both Klinsmann and especially Popescu found difficulty in adjusting their play to Gerry's system. It was no secret that Klinsmann preferred playing under Ardiles, who gave the German ace, together with the other four members of the 'famous five' forward line, only nominal defensive duties. When such a cavalier attitude to defence cost Ardiles his job, the team felt a collective culpability at their part in his downfall. This made it that much easier for Francis when he arrived. The players he inherited were receptive to his demands; they knew that organisation was the key to getting Spurs back on an even keel, and accepted the new manager's tactics and methods without histrionics. For Francis and Spurs, the only way was up and favourable early results appeared to vindicate his actions. Francis was able to appeal to their sense of guilt on the one hand and

Dream On

professional pride on the other, dishing out rollickings without come-back. He was fortunate that Klinsmann, unlike Popescu, was a rare jewel: a world-class player who was enough of a team-player to toe the line. And if Jurgen Klinsmann wasn't going to rock the boat, there would be no challenge to the manager's authority. Francis was home and dry.

But once the season was over, the two World Cup stars were off like a shot. The question must be asked as to whether a more flexible attitude to Klinsmann could have seen him stay for a second year. (Popescu was a different case as Francis probably felt the Romanian wasn't suitable for the rigours of the Premier League.)

The subsequent purchase of Chris Armstrong was also badly handled, causing a highly publicised outburst from Teddy Sheringham, who, it was implied, felt he should have been privy to Gerry's plans for any proposed attacking partner. When Teddy apparently found out about the signing of Armstrong through the media, it led to a very public appraisal of his perceived future at the club.

The same transfer deal also rang warning bells with Nicky Barmby. Despite much stuff and nonsense about family pressure to return to his northern roots, perhaps the real reason for his wanting away was that he saw his favourite position going to Chris Armstrong, thereby compromising his England prospects. As Middlesbrough manager Bryan Robson was later to confirm: 'Nicky feels he can further his England career more by playing through the middle or just behind the striker. At Tottenham, when Gerry bought Chris Armstrong after Klinsmann had gone, Nicky Barmby read it as, ". . . well he's definitely not thinking of playing me through the middle, it will be Teddy Sheringham and Chris Armstrong." That disappointed him.'

The Way We Were

Perhaps Robson was being a little disingenuous. After all, there was no reason why Francis could not have played all three together with Barmby just behind the front two. More to the point was the fact that Robson – who as part of the England coaching setup had worked with Barmby – could guarantee him the perfect position within his own team, while off the field a north-east base would facilitate a harmonious home life, it being no secret that Mrs Barmby was not particularly enamoured with life down south.

And so one of the Premiership's most promising talents left Tottenham for £5.25 million to join newly promoted Middlesbrough – many people's favourites for the drop. The money was secondary – what could it buy in this day and age? Particularly coming as it did immediately pre-season when the bulk of transfer wheeling and dealing was over. It was a humiliating blow to the club that any player should make such a choice, and must have been particularly hard for those charged with persuading promising youngsters to sign at White Hart Lane. A Nicky Barmby, no less than a Jurgen Klinsmann, comes along but once in a generation. To have and to lose two such players within one summer recess is a black mark against the Tottenham management, a bitter disappointment to the supporters and a major question mark against the club's supposed ambitions. The extent of Tottenham's loss and Middlesbrough's gain was hinted at by Alan Hansen when he positively drooled over Barmby '. . . a terrific player . . . what a signing . . . he's got a wonderful future and if I was Terry Venables I'd keep playing him'.

If Francis is to succeed as a manager, he must learn to cosset his stars. Key players like Klinsmann and Barmby should have been kept in the fold. If their egos needed massaging, their hands needed holding or their bums

Dream On

needed wiping, then at £250,000 a year Gerry should be first in line with the Andrex. Being a manager is as much about keeping stars as it is about buying them in the first place. So Klinsmann left, Barmby felt unwanted and Sheringham was unsettled.

So is Francis the right manager for Spurs? Given that the definition of a big club manager is one who defines the long term strategy for the club; one who buys and sells players, decides on the playing style and generally controls the playing side, then for Francis – the man who will not sign a contract and works only on a month-to-month basis – the case remains unproven.

Not, though, in the view of lawyer Douglas Alexiou, a Tottenham director since 1980. He emphasises that the appointment of Francis was a case of the club getting their priorities right and dismisses this season's problems as an unfortunate set of circumstances. 'Gerry had to come in in a difficult situation; he had to paper over the cracks before he could knock it all down and replaster. He's got half his team from last season, which wasn't the team he would have wanted necessarily, so he's got to start all over again. He's totally back where he started. Arguably he's worse off.'

Perhaps Francis is tailor-made for crisis management, his experience at QPR being directly relevant to the ongoing situation he has to face at Tottenham. Previously, as a manager at one of the Premier League's smallest clubs, his job was to make the best use of the players at his disposal, forcing him to fit his tactical approach around his limited resources. Man-management and organisation became paramount requirements. But a manager at a big club like Tottenham must possess additional qualities because big clubs are expected not merely to survive but to win trophies. The manager must have the knowledge, the experience and the skill to define a particular playing policy. He can then coach the players to carry out his plans, and if he finds they are not up to it, purchase their replacements.

What characterises the records of the great managers – Busby, Paisley, Revie, Nicholson – is that they were supreme players of the transfer market making fewer mistakes than their rivals. They knew when to buy and when to pay big money for that special player who could transform a good team into a great one.

Malcolm Allison and Dave Sexton were great coaches. As is Don Howe. But they could not make the transition into being great managers. Is it to be Gerry Francis's fate that he finds it beyond himself to step up from being an excellent coach and manager of a small club to that position at a big club? Unfair and premature according to Douglas Alexiou, who stresses, 'This is the first time he has really had the opportunity to be with a big club that historically has bought star players every year. Previously he has not been in a position where he has gone out and spent the three, four, five million pounds or whatever it might be these days, at QPR and Bristol Rovers. So you have to give credit to someone who, on a very limited budget, has managed to go and scout the lower leagues and find players and bring them through. And if he paid £600,000 for Trevor Sinclair, well, he's worth £3 million plus today. That's not a bad bit of business.' Precisely. But is this talent a prerequisite for the manager's job at Tottenham Hotspur?

At least Douglas Alexiou gives him unwavering support. (Being one of that rare species, a gentleman in football; this is not to be confused with the directors' traditional vote of confidence.) 'The man does know his football. He knows what makes a good player, and I think he's very well

Dream On

organised – a good coach. He knows the system he wants to play and the players know what is expected of them. And if you look at his record [at Tottenham] of wins, losses and draws with a team that has been through a true transitional period and with off-the-field problems at the same time, it's a very good record.'

Long after the Liverpool coach had departed, and long after most of his own players had left for home, Alan Sugar's RollsRoyce pulled out of the club car park and turned right into Tottenham High Road. The short journey to the North Circular Road took him past the Duke of Devonshire pub, where a dozen or so fans were drinking on the pavement, still lamenting that afternoon's defeat. On seeing Sugar's car with its distinctive number plate, the temptation to blame the chairman for all their frustrations proved irresistible.

'You f*****g c**t,' shouted one.

'Get your f*****g money out,' shouted another.

For Sugar, with family in tow, it was a bad end to a bad day. As he continued his journey around the North Circular Road, he once again found himself questioning whether this football business was really one he wanted to be in.

Chapter 4

Tomorrow Belongs to Me

You can imagine the cat-kicking, tea-cups-flying mood that Alan Sugar was in by the time he got home. The trouncing by Liverpool had left Spurs with just one point from three games. His £4.5 million signing Chris Armstrong was playing more like Neil Armstrong – leaving Sugar far from over the moon. The club record transfer may have been one small step for manager Gerry Francis, but it was one giant step for a chairman who may have a Roller but only a part-time chauffeur.

If any Amstrad recruit had performed so woefully, you sense Sugar would have had the poor unfortunate fired on the spot and escorted from the premises. But what was he to do with someone to whom he'd only just given a four-year contract worth £6,000 a week? The fans were on his back, taunting him with wads of cash and chanting for him to get out his chequebook. The press were already talking of a crisis. His own manager had already written off the club's title chances. Few potential signings wanted to come to White Hart Lane, and those that did were unaffordable after Arsenal had queered the pitch for every other club by agreeing to outrageous personal terms for Dennis Bergkamp.

So when the phone rang with a reporter looking for a reaction to the breaking story of Jurgen Klinsmann claiming he'd only left Tottenham because Sugar had lacked ambition, a red mist formed before Sugar's eyes. You can picture him pacing up and down the length of his lounge that Saturday night. Suit jacket thrown over an armchair, belt slackened, shoes kicked off, tie loosened, talking out loud in an empty room and gesturing wildly as he contemplated the unfairness of it all. Like a Care in the Community patient who holds a four-way conversation with himself in the middle of Oxford Street, the calming voice of reason was struggling to make itself heard, and the rage built to boiling point.

He'd taken over the club when it was believed to be two bob away from receivership. He'd put together a rescue package, sorted out the Midland, weeded out the slackers and deadwood, overseen the stadium development, made money available for players, straightened the books, seen off Venables, taken on and beaten the FA and signed the most promising young manager in English football. For what? So the fans could hurl abuse at him and his family? So that a German international who'd done a runner on him could now tell the world that he'd have been happy to stay at the club if only Alan Sugar had not been such a money-grabber with short arms and long pockets who charged the player trade price for the shirts he signed for charities?

It was ridiculous. Sugar knew he was being unfairly painted as the villain of the piece despite only ever having had the best interests of his club at heart. Who needed this hassle? Life was too short to put up with this nonsense, and at 48 he was looking to enjoy his hard-earned millions, not end up with grey hair and ulcers.

A disturbed night's sleep failed to lift his black mood, and when the press returned that Sunday in search of quotes, Sugar had made up his mind. If his enemies could use the press to slur him, then he wasn't beyond using the same medium to make his views known. He had friends in Fleet Street, and therefore there was every chance that a couple of discreet calls should be enough to secure a decent back-page splash in Monday's tabloids.

Alan Sugar may be lots of things in the eyes of Spurs supporters, but he certainly isn't poor. But 'poor Alan Sugar' is a sentiment that comes to mind when you take a closer look at what the man has done for Spurs and the scant praise received in return.

Unlike many of today's new breed of football chairmen, Alan Sugar never took the short-cut to riches via the property boom. The 1980s was a period when single property deals could net millions in profits for those individuals who found themselves in the right place at the right time. A fifteen acre industrial wasteland could be bought for very little in a recession, but a fifteen acre industrial wasteland with outline planning permission could be sold for a considerable sum in a housing boom. You just had to know the cycles. Of course there were casualties, and it's probably true that for every high profile Irving Scholar or Matthew Harding, there's a guy sleeping on a park bench with a helluva story to tell. But nevertheless, a whole bunch of suits to whom an MBA is just an oily British motorcycle found they had a bank balance ending in seven noughts and convinced themselves that they had a Midas touch they could henceforth apply to any business, but particularly to football.

Dream On

Sugar, on the other hand, had come up the hard way. From humble Hackney origins, he left school at sixteen and within five years had sown the seeds of an empire in consumer electronics. His vision in realising the vast untapped potential for cheap home computers was matched by his drive and determination to make the whole thing happen via manufacturing partners in Japan, Hong Kong and Taiwan. Alan M Sugar Trading (Amstrad for short) rose from market stall obscurity to one of the UK's most recognised electronic brands, bringing its founder a personal fortune in excess of £100 million. As he told *Business Age* magazine, 'We [Amstrad] did a lot for this country. We brought computing to the masses. We brought word processors to the masses. We brought satellite dishes to the masses. No one else did. We did it. I did it.'

To use an Alan Sugar term stolen from TV's Del Boy, he is no plonker.

To cite Del Boy is a harsh analogy but not strictly wide of the mark. Sugar is a native Cockney; a blunt, hugely confident, thrusting entrepreneur with drive and a forceful personality that makes it difficult for people to look him in the eye and say 'No'. Del Boy, courtesy of BBC scriptwriters, may not have progressed from street markets and a council tower block, but if he were ever to 'crack the big one' and move up into the Bentley, private yacht, villa in Marbella and Essex mansion strata, would he really appear that much removed from the Alan Sugar we picture addressing THFC board meetings, ramming home his point with a prodding forefinger and no uncertain language? Thundering at his legal team before sending them to do battle with the octogenarian bureaucrats at the FA? Enjoying the lavish perks of directorship in the boardroom at wherever Spurs are playing? Or simply swanning into

Tomorrow Belongs to Me

Monaco harbour to sign Jurgen Klinsmann in a flourish of champagne, dosh up front?

Sugar tells the story of how, during that dramatic race for Klinsmann's signature, Jurgen came on to the phone and asked where Sugar was making the call from.

'If you look out of the window,' Sugar replied, 'you will probably see a blue boat bobbing about in the harbour. That's me!'

History doesn't record the later conversation when the deal was done, but it is difficult to imagine the signing ceremony going through without Sugar rubbing his hands and murmuring 'Lovely jubbly'.

None of which is meant in any way to denigrate a man who, let's face it, stepped in when no one else would lift a finger. The man actually put his hand in his pocket and coughed up £7.5 million to secure the club's immediate safety, even paying Terry Venables' share on takeover day. Just by his association, the banks backed off and accepted that here, at last, was somebody at the helm of THFC with financial clout who knew what he was doing.

And sure enough, the overdraft came down, the borrowing stopped, the books were ironed out and, not surprisingly given his history, anyone who didn't toe the Sugar line was ironed out too. Which included Terry Venables when Sugar felt that his 'partner' was now the remaining obstruction to his Tottenham blueprint for the future.

But a funny thing happened to Alan Sugar along the way; something that was to have a profound effect on the club's future: he became a Spurs fan.

The more we see Alan Sugar in action, and the more we learn about what kind of person it takes to run a major Premiership club these days, the question is no longer 'Why Sugar?' but 'What took him so long?'

Dream On

Alan Sugar never pretended to be the kind of loyal, lifelong fan that traditionally buys into the club of his boyhood dreams when such a calling comes. Although Sugar has said that in his youth he was regularly taken to White Hart Lane by his father, and although he also admits to having a brother who is the archetypal Spurs nut, the truth was simply that you couldn't be a successful market trader if you didn't work Saturdays. And so the young Alan Sugar worked Saturdays, became the country's most successful market trader, and left the frippery of being a football fan to those in his family who had the time.

When the invitation came from Terry Venables in 1991, to help him in his long-running saga to take over the club, you can imagine the dilemma that faced the now middle-aged Alan Sugar. Certainly, it would not be a cost-effective investment; several million pounds invested in the Abbey National would doubtless provide a greater return. And he knew he'd get his money back with the Abbey National. Nor did Sugar really need the distraction of involvement with Tottenham: Amstrad was suffering badly at the hands of the recession and now was not the time to neglect his cash cow. Despite a running battle with City analysts, shares in Amstrad were still sufficiently buoyed that he could cash in his personal holding and walk away to a retirement of spectacular luxury. In a nutshell, it was an opportunity he didn't need.

But there was one thing that all Sugar's trappings and success had not brought him. Status. Being a successful industrialist in the UK is only marginally more glamorous than having leprosy. The fact that you may have created thousands of jobs, or boosted exports, or improved living standards counts for little with the British public. The City bestows notoriety on quirky caricatures; a fat crook or a

Tomorrow Belongs to Me

sharp fraudster, a long-haired know-it-all or an autocratic peer of the realm. To really make the news you have to fail spectacularly and lose everything; or be caught with your hand in the till; only then will we know who you are.

For a man like Alan Sugar whose only further education was at the proverbial school of hard knocks, his background, his accent, his dress and his manner would have fallen foul of the class apartheid that firmly places a man not by his achievements but by his social credentials.

Despite being a self-made multi-millionaire, a man who would continually feature in the *Sunday Times* list of Britain's richest men, Sugar, like most successful company chairmen in this country, was an unknown face outside of his boardroom. To buy into Tottenham must have appeared a heaven-sent opportunity to announce at last his existence to the wider world. Though in the view of successful businessman turned Crystal Palace chairman Ron Noades, the dangers of vanity are endemic. 'I don't think people like Alan Sugar go into this business for an ego trip,' he said, 'but then they open their mouth and find themselves on the back page. Then it becomes an ego trip because you get elevated to a status your normal business wouldn't provide you with.'

Football has such a hold on the nation's psyche that its protagonists appear daily on TV, radio and in the press. There is a football-dependent industry that demands that there cannot be a day when there is no football news. Something must happen, or be made to happen, to fill the allocated time and space. Since football's quantum leap from sport to show business over the last decade, anyone remotely involved in the game at its top level has sprung to semi-celebrity status. Although kids may still idolise the players, their chances of actually emulating those stars and

Dream On

making a playing career in football are minuscule. But not to worry! You could one day become a player's agent and get your own column in the *Sunday People*. Travel the world wheeling and dealing as you tout your clients on a monster global market. Or maybe you'd like to become a football author. Nick Hornby's epic of unrequited love for Arsenal, *Fever Pitch*, crossed all barriers and propelled its author into literary stardom. How about being a soccer writer for a daily paper? You get to meet the stars, get your picture published next to your articles and maybe even host your own programme on Sky Sports, where you invite all your mates along so they too can be asked for their autograph when next they walk down the street. Too ambitious? Then start your own football fanzine and before you know it you'll be on Radio 5 Live putting questions to government ministers.

It must have seemed to Alan Sugar that everyone involved in football was better known than he was. He would also have been aware of the degree of national fame afforded to his would-be contemporaries in Glasgow (David Murray), or Italy (Silvio Berlusconi or Gianni Agnelli), or any number of American cities where entrepreneurs became more famous than the sports teams they had bought.

So Sugar must think to himself, 'Yeah, I fancy some of that.' For the price of sticking his hand down the back of his sofa to see what loose change he can turn up, he can take a controlling interest in a company worth three times his investment. (In fact, Sugar had only two months previously sold 42.75 million shares in Amstrad plc, raising £33 million for himself.)

He knew the business was in a mess, but a cursory look indicated the massive potential lying dormant. He will of course have nothing but contempt for the 'bungling

Tomorrow Belongs to Me

cowboys' of previous regimes who had brought the club to its knees, but what better way to prove his business acumen than by dramatically turning the club around? Whatever he does will hit the headlines, and a modicum of success will earn him the lasting gratitude of half of north London. The fact that he would be rescuing the club held sacred by so many of his family must also have been a further incentive.

He knew nothing of football, but then he could leave that to Terry Venables, a man for whom everyone had nothing but praise. He'd just pop by one day a month to see how things were going.

And so the invitation was accepted and an alliance was forged. As predicted, Sugar's profile was raised to a degree no Amstrad stewardship would ever bring. It was a shame that much of this was due to the lengthy Venables/High Court drama, but nevertheless if the object of the exercise had been to promote Alan M Sugar, then it had succeeded spectacularly. If it had been to turn Tottenham Hotspur FC into one of the country's dominant clubs, well that hadn't really happened.

What Sugar was now discovering was that a tight, orderly, well-run club isn't necessarily a successful, trophy bagging, all-conquering winning machine. Premiership fodder like Norwich, Ipswich, Coventry or QPR were renowned for those same virtues he now brought to Spurs, but the price for their financial sanity was mediocrity. Modest grounds; modest gates; modest players. If they find or groom a star he will eventually have to be sold to ensure that the books balance. And gradually, Sugar realised that he wanted more for his money than just complimentary letters from his bank manager and having to watch his team surrender three points each week to clubs who were prepared to gamble today and pay the day after tomorrow.

Dream On

Alan Sugar is a winner, and investing millions into a losing football team was having an increasingly limited appeal. But if he wanted 'his' club to be able to compete on level terms with the other big boys, he would have to compromise his stance.

Urban myths have long been rife about Sugar's lack of 'in-house' knowledge about the game of football. Whether Sugar ever actually said 'What is this Double everyone keeps on about?' is debatable. What is more believable is that he may once have openly expressed his admiration for the Victorian values behind clubs like Wimbledon FC.

This unfashionable south London club have a sound but simple financial plan based on the assumption that they will achieve no more than a comfortable mid-table league position each year, and go out of the cup competitions at an early round. This modest premise dictates all their spending, particularly the money available for new players, and the wages paid to existing ones. As a result, the club have yet to pay more than £1m for a player, and have the smallest wage bill in the division.

If the club fails to reach its budgeted targets, then it sells a player to make up the shortfall. Everyone at the club understands and accepts the rules. Which player goes is largely decided by the availability of ready-made replacements. For this purpose, manager Joe Kinnear has a complex and exhaustive file that surely encompasses just about every player currently turning out for pro, semi-pro, amateur and Sunday league teams in England. Files on these players are kept and updated by a nationwide army of scouts who report back to Kinnear on availability, current form and estimated transfer values.

Throughout the season, Joe and club owner Sam Hammam criss-cross the country to watch players who may one day

Tomorrow Belongs to Me

get the call. Often taking in two games a day, Sam takes a delight in these clandestine scouting missions for 'his' club. The pair think nothing of driving 200 miles north to take in an evening game where reports indicate a player who may have Wimbledon potential. This hands-on policy, where most managers would delegate such tedious chores down the line, reaps dividends. There are bargains to be had out there and Joe Kinnear knows better than most where to find them. Wimbledon doesn't buy stars, it makes them. And by selling on average one player per season, Wimbledon can survive despite the lowest home gates in the Premiership and despite winning only one major trophy in its history.

Full-back Warren Barton cost Wimbledon just £30,000 from Maidstone United, but was sold on to Newcastle for £4 million in June 1995. A year earlier, John Scales, a £70,000 signing from Bristol Rovers, netted £3.5 million for Kinnear when he moved on to Liverpool. Terry Phelan was scooped up by Wimbledon after just 45 games for Swansea, and sold on to Manchester City for £2.5 million. Keith Curle was similarly snapped up after 40 games for Reading, before he too was sold on for £2.5 million to City. You can't fault book-keeping like that and to a trader like Alan Sugar who made a fortune from the motto 'Buy low, sell high', you can see the attraction.

The fans at Wimbledon in turn expect nothing but 100% effort and are extremely grateful for whatever modest success owner Sam Hammam and manager Joe Kinnear can coax. Just getting to the Premier League and staying there against all the odds must be one of the greatest achievements in English club football.

So it may well have been that Sugar, and truthfully many other Premiership club chairmen, envied the simple home-spun economics of Wimbledon FC. The trouble is, Spurs

Dream On

fans would not tolerate such a low level of achievement, and what was surprising Sugar was that he felt the same way.

In July 1993, Alan Sugar wrote the following when addressing complaints from Spurs fans about his apparent lack of ambition:

'I am not, and nor have I ever professed to be, a football expert. I love watching the game, I love supporting Spurs, and I want to make Spurs successful, but I do not have the knowledge or experience to even begin to suggest how the team should play or what players should be bought and what players should be sold.

'Contrary to rumour, I do not want Tottenham to be another Wimbledon. I want them to be the best club in the land, the best in Europe. My dream, like that of any other Spurs supporter, is for Tottenham to win the Premier League, the FA Cup, the League Cup and the European Cup and as many trophies as possible. I want them to play good and entertaining football in the great tradition of Spurs, so that Spurs fans not only enjoy success, but enjoy watching that success.'

The bug had bitten deep. Off came the gloves.

The trouble is, there is little in football so dangerous as a rich fan in the boardroom with dictatorial power. Such 'super fans' are increasingly cropping up in the boardroom of clubs for whom financial pressures have forced a relaxation of previously stringent vetting routines. These rich fans buy their way to a place on the board, yet rarely have they supported the club with the passion and commitment of those on the terraces and generations of season ticket holders. Once in place, they convince themselves that their financial sacrifices on behalf of the club, which they view as having paid their dues, give them the right to speak and act on behalf of all other 'fellow' fans. Anything they do is said to be in the best interests of the club, as if they alone are able to decide what those best interests are.

And out of the window goes objectivity. Like any business, football clubs need to be subject to certain checks and balances that ensure decisions are taken for the correct commercial reasons. When a fan runs the board and wields the chequebook, these checks and balances cannot be relied upon to transpire automatically.

Luckily in the case of Spurs and Alan Sugar, the problems he inherited forced him to remain squeaky clean in all his subsequent dealings, in full knowledge that the FA were ready and waiting to clobber the club given the slightest suspicion of any culinary skills in the bookkeeping department.

However, as the Klinsmann episode illustrated, simple naïvety can be just as damaging for a club when a fan plays the transfer market. Klinsmann's departure was a blow to both Sugar's club and his pride. The Spurs chairman was finding it hard to accept that he had been outsmarted through his unwillingness to interpret the contractual small print. Sugar was adamant that the German had reneged on his promise. Obviously it depends on which way you look at it.

'You can forgive me for being naïve,' he said, 'but Gerry Francis is not, and both of us would have put money on him [Klinsmann] seeing out the second year of his contract.'

The back pages of the tabloids all contained the same story on Monday 28 August, best summed up by the *Sun*'s headline, 'Spurs For Sale'. In a rant that covered three pages, Sugar lashed into Klinsmann via an 'exclusive' given to one of the paper's football writers, Ben Bacon. Over in the *Daily Mirror*, much the same stuff appeared under the

Dream On

banner 'Alan Sugar opens his heart to Harry Harris'. Sugar had let rip at everything that had been bugging him that weekend. The papers lapped it up, with headings like, Two faced Klinsmann talks a lot of bullshit and, referring to the yobs that had abused him after the Liverpool game, 'I could not go to sleep. I could not get their hate-filled faces out of my mind.' Or how about, 'I've worked my nuts off for this football club, I don't need the hassle of all this total rubbish' and even, 'Let them get someone else in, an entrepreneur, a wine bar owner with £50 million. If anyone thinks they have got the money, and they could do a better job than me, then come forward. Give me back the money I'm owed, purchase my shares and I'll be off for the benefit and good of the club.'

All good stuff for selling newspapers, but not exactly commensurate with the kind of public image other football chairmen were trying to cultivate. Sugar appears to grant himself special exemption from criticism, despite the frequency with which he lays into others.

In the City this behaviour is just about tolerated in the absence of a truly effective watchdog. Sugar will ridicule Amstrad shareholders who fail to agree with his low estimation of his company (when he is trying to buy it back from them for, in their eyes, a pittance). Those shareholders who question his tactics use the AGM as an opportunity to 'mouth off' and are credited, according to *Business Age*, with the inability 'to find their arse with radar'. Retailers are referred to as 'the arseholes of the world'.

The man flies by the seat of his pants and lives by his instinct. In the past this has secured spectacular successes. Buying up Sir Clive Sinclair's computer business gave Amstrad a telling edge over his rivals, while an unexpected

Tomorrow Belongs to Me

conversation with Rupert Murdoch ultimately led to several million satellite dish sales. Sometimes the instinct lets him down, as it did in 1988 when Amstrad launched the 'revolutionary' PC2000 computer series which flopped to the tune of several hundred million pounds and took Amstrad to within a whisker of going bump. Some would also say that his instinct failed him when he bought into Tottenham Hotspur. As Sugar himself admitted to *Business Age*, 'The quickness of moving into something and smelling something was one of my attributes. Well, the instinct was wrong. I felt that the guy in question [Venables] was not just an expert on football but perhaps a very wise and astute business person. That was where I was wrong. Had I realised that then, I would never have gone into the Tottenham transaction. I never had any intention of spending time there. It was going to be an investment and I would give my input from a commercial and marketing point of view. There had to be experts in there to run it. It took nearly two years before the shit hit the fan but let's say there were certain eyebrows raised after six months.'

During his involvement with Spurs, there had indeed been many occasions when Alan Sugar's shit had hit the fan. But by the autumn of 1995 several Premiership chairmen were voicing concern at the frequency with which they were getting splattered.

Just three days before the new season had started, another 'exclusive' to the *Sun*'s Ben Bacon had Sugar branding Arsenal as 'gutless' for the way they handled the George Graham sacking. Sugar's opinion that the Arsenal board should have acted more swiftly once Graham's financial indiscretions had come to light was in fact shared and voiced by many in the game. However, for the chairman of Tottenham Hotspur FC to say as much in banner

Dream On

headlines across the county's best selling paper was something else.

'Arsenal are a gutless lot,' ran the quote. 'They've got no balls. If he [Graham] is guilty of what he's said to have done, his employer should have sacked him immediately. If he were my manager, I would have acted at once – it's taking money from the club.'

Continuing in the same vein, Sugar moved on to Arsenal's new signing, Dennis Bergkamp. 'Arsenal have taken an almighty risk. There's no way he is going to have the same impact as Klinsmann. If Bergkamp thinks he is going to set the world alight, he can forget it. There is no way it is going to happen. Arsenal got him because they needed a bit of cosmetic marketing.'

True or not, it wasn't the right thing to say. Compounding his error, he went on: 'I don't think Spurs could ever sign a superstar like a Klinsmann or a Bergkamp again. These guys are floaters. They'll go anywhere, play for anyone who pays them the most. Arsenal can't just wave off almost £8 million though. How could they get their money back? They have spent a load of money which is unrecoverable if something goes wrong. At least with Klinsmann he came, conquered and went – and we got our money back.'

The fact that Spurs had reported Bayern Munich to FIFA precisely because they hadn't received a fair price seems to have been forgotten here. Finally, just in case there was anyone left at Highbury not yet insulted, and giving a possible indication that Sugar was still smarting from having to pay over the odds for Chris Armstrong, there was this to say: 'If Bergkamp doesn't start popping them in . . . he will be under immediate pressure. As the season progresses and the fog, ice and cold arrive, his approach could change – especially when someone gives him a good kicking, an elbow in the ribs or a whack in the earhole. I'm shocked how much Arsenal have spent. I even think it's somewhat irresponsible. It will be interesting to see whether their new manager Bruce Rioch has the qualities and capabilities of George Graham. That must be a concern for the club.'

And one final parting shot at the suggestion that Arsenal were talking about further foreign signings: 'They are good talkers that lot, aren't they?'

The Arsenal board would still have been flicking off the smelly stuff the day after this outburst appeared, when a Premier League meeting had been scheduled to ratify – of all things – the Chairman's Charter. This was an agreed set of principles concerning the behaviour of club chairmen in aspects such as respecting individual rights, the hiring of managers and suchlike. The timing was just perfect for Arsenal's David Dein, who lost no time in pointing out to Sugar the potential consequences of such outbursts. To Dein's credit, his argument was diplomatically phrased along the lines that such comments could 'stir up rival sets of fans'. Of course this was utter tosh as both sets of supporters already had more than enough perceived reasons to dislike one another. Could he really envisage the North Bank launching into a spontaneous chant of 'If you all think that the Tottenham chairman's remarks are inflammatory and not consistent with his own club's policy clap your hands . . .'? Or perhaps he was more concerned that Finsbury Park would echo to the sound of gloves being slapped around faces as rival fans challenged one another to pistols at dawn to settle this slight once and for all.

Privately, David Dein probably felt the remarks were born out of envy, which was closer to the truth and akin to what most genuine Spurs supporters were feeling as

Dream On

Arsenal grabbed the headlines and the glory while Spurs went bargain basement shopping.

Sugar tried to defend his outburst by maintaining his published remarks had been taken out of context – not easy in a 1,500-word interview. To Arsenal's credit, they failed to rise to the bait and maintained a dignified silence over the matter.

Two weeks later, at the Arsenal AGM, the degree of anger felt by Arsenal fans was seen when the first question directed at the board concerned their club's lack of official response to Sugar's insults. Chairman Peter Hill-Wood replied that he had received a letter of apology from Alan Sugar (perhaps Arsenal's refusal to mix it made him feel like a cad?) and that the matter was now closed. 'We will forgive and forget,' he stated, adding after a pause and to wild cheering, 'Well at least we'll forgive . . .'

What Arsenal were too polite to say in public was that they were increasingly flabbergasted by much of what was occuring at the other end of the Seven Sisters Road. Not only had the Gunners beaten Spurs at their own game of 'The Price Isn't Right', but the new-look Highbury with its near-40,000 capacity and all-star playing squad under the disciplinarian management of Bruce Rioch stood in stark contrast to their near neighbour's 'let's see what tomorrow brings' attitude.

Gerry Francis had confirmed his continued employment by the club, not by signing a four-year contract, but merely by extending his handshake agreement and adding the reassuring comment that he'd 'give it another year'. You really got the impression that Francis was at a loose end for the next twelve months and the Spurs job would fill in nicely until something decent came along. Unfair probably, but what other conclusions can you draw? Of course Sugar wasn't going to push the contract issue in light of the compensation he'd just had to negotiate with former manager Ossie Ardiles. A month-to-month agreement could work in favour of both parties, but did nothing for those looking for signs of long term strategy in a world of short term madness. How could Francis hope to attract new players to the club when his own commitment was so loose? How could the club hope to convince fresh young talent that their footballing future should lie at White Hart Lane when the obvious first question from any parent would be 'If the future is so bright then how come you won't commit yourself to it?'

It is well documented that the young Nicky Barmby was only swayed to sign for Spurs because of the favourable impression conveyed by then-manager Terry Venables. Even existing players must have been eyeing the remaining years on their contract, knowing that a career can flourish or die on the whims of an incoming manager. Just look at those signings made by Ardiles (Scott, Kerslake, Dozzell, Dumitrescu) who were now just highly paid reserves under Francis. Just as promising winger, Andy Turner, had failed to get a look-in under the Ardiles regime, so Erik Thorstvedt now sat out every game under Francis as second choice 'keeper.

The North Stand redevelopment has been postponed, leaving the Paxton Road end of the ground looking like a giant bus shelter. Capacity is pegged at 33,000, and retrenchment is the order of the day under the cost-cutting regime of Claude Littner. The inability to spend in the light of glaring team squad deficiencies is seen as a virtue rather than a vice. When the new player kitty was further swollen by the £5.25 million Middlesbrough paid for Nicky Barmby you couldn't help but feel that Sugar was more pleased with the short term ramifications of such healthy cash flow, rather than the long term consequences of losing one of England's brightest young talents.

Sugar's unnerving preoccupation with money was again highlighted during a highly embarrassing televised rant on BBC's *Sportsnight* at the end of August.

'I don't think Tottenham have ever had a manager [like Francis] who was told sometime in June that they have £7.5 million to spend and the money is still there. I mean, any other bloke we may have had in the past *[Hi Tel! Hi Ossie!]* would have spent the money in a week and we would have had a load of donkeys running around the field – just gone and bought anything, just for the sake of it. But Gerry doesn't do that. He's one of those guys – I know it might sound commonsense to most people – who wants to look at a player. Check them out, he wants to see what they had for breakfast. He wants to know what their family life is like – you know, what kind of character they are. There are all these agents about, sending you a tape of a player, Carlos Kickaball or something. You watch him score three goals and within two days you have him wearing a shirt and signed. I think you've got to take your hat off to him [Francis] for not being intimidated, for not buying a load of dross.'

Both chairman and manager were showing signs of inexperience in the needs of a big club operating in today's cash-rich Premier League. A manager given complete control over the playing side by a chairman who is desperate for someone to trust in. The manager brooks no interference in his methods and in return receives absolute power, no real guidance from the board, no guarantees about longevity, just a book full of signed cheques. This might have been fine in the days of yore when football was less of a business.

Tomorrow Belongs to Me

But with the amounts involved today, more thought must go into the process of buying and selling players.

This sets the club on a dangerous course drawing parallels with the George Graham era at Highbury. Perhaps the Arsenal board have more reason than most to be concerned at the situation they see developing at Tottenham.

It's funny to think of a boardroom autocrat like Alan Sugar, getting upset because he isn't liked. Mrs Sugar would no doubt vouch that he's a kitten at home, never happier than when he's having his tummy rubbed or getting the back of his neck tickled; drying the dishes in one of those aprons that make the wearer look like he's wearing stockings and suspenders.

But the public face, the face the rest of us see, is the one so memorably portrayed by Hunter Davies in an interview he tried to conduct for the *Independent* in 1992.

'He strode in, glared at me, looked at some messages on a screen, picked up some papers, then strode out again. Stockier than in his photographs, beard just as aggressive, demeanour just as miserable.

'"I can't believe my ******* eyes," he was shouting at some legal adviser in a room farther down the corridor, loud enough to be heard all over Essex. "What the **** is going on? I'm not taking this ****. If that document does not ******* turn up, your job is on the ******* line, you ****."

'Eventually he came back, picked up more papers, tore out a fax that was coming through, glared at me again. The phone rang and he shouted at someone down the line for being an idiot, then hung up and glared at me again, indicating get on with it, cat stolen your tongue? I've got work to do.'

Hunter Davies asked him of his faults: '"I do too much. I don't delegate. I don't trust people enough. I shout and scream and get very annoyed, especially when people wind me up." He glared at me again. Are you happy? "No, I'm a miserable sod."

'I have noticed that in all your photographs.

'"It's deliberate. A PR man once told me never to smile for newspaper photographs. When your firm makes a loss, it will print your photo on the financial pages with you smiling."'

The man appears to be a tyrant and a bully, but he wants to be loved. He wants his efforts for the club recognised. From his early associations with the club, he was famously needled when Terry Venables basked in the glory of Tottenham's success while Sugar was relegated to the periphery of events. The crowd chanted for Venables the manager, but not Sugar the chairman and financial saviour. That's just the way it goes in football, but that particular penny has yet to drop with Sugar.

When he is criticised, he is immediately on the attack, giving out better than he gets. Unfortunately, he has grown used to getting his own way. It can't be often that Sugar has a stand-up ding-dong slanging match with someone who is is prepared to stand their ground and argue their point. You just don't do that with your chairman, do you? So, as Hunter Davies discovered, perhaps he has got used to winning arguments by intimidating bar room tactics where he just bellows and jabs his finger and repeats his point over and again until his opponent concedes defeat.

But that approach doesn't work when you are dealing with other Premiership chairmen of equal standing. You can't be a bully in a playground that's already full of bullies. And it particularly doesn't work on television, best illustrated by the awful *Sportsnight* rant against Jurgen Klinsmann on 30 August. Responding again to Klinsmann's 'no-ambition'

Tomorrow Belongs to Me

accusation, Sugar went through his bellicose repertoire, slaughtering Jurgen for being two faced and slaughtering the Spurs fans who had abused him that Saturday.

'I don't need to put up with this aggravation. Because people say to me that's normally what football's all about. I don't need that. I don't need to drive out of the football ground with my family sitting next to me in the car frightened and intimidated – not for something I haven't done. I've only done good.'

Kate Battersby, writing in the following week's *Daily Telegraph*, highlighted a further flaw that had surfaced during the programme.

'To this viewer, the very worst part of the interview was when Sugar gave us his idea of how Tottenham fans should behave towards him. He magnanimously conceded they have every right to ask "Mr Sugar, we were wondering what's happening with the buying and selling of players?" What is all the Mr Sugar bit? Why should fans address him as if they are the below stairs staff? They are not in his employ. On the contrary, he is answerable to them, although that is another concept he has not quite got his head round yet.'

In the *Observer*, Alan Hubbard was also underwhelmed by his performance: 'Hurling away Jurgen Klinsmann's No.18 shirt in disgust and saying he wouldn't wash his car with it, was a tasteless little episode which dragged football back down towards the gutter at a time when it is desperately trying to scrape the smelly stuff off its boots.

'Much as he may wish to be loved, Sugar will never find romance in football, no more than you would expect in any arranged marriage. You sometimes wonder if Sugar gives a fig about football. His chequebook may be in the game, but is his heart? And his absurd notion that he resurrected

Dream On

Klinsmann's career exposed a naïvety that is alarming even for a football club chairman.'

It was a shame that a few crazy interviews had turned many closet allies against Alan Sugar. For in truth his battles with the FA had given him much credibility within the game. When Tottenham were severely punished after the investigation into financial irregularities, Sugar alone stood up and said the punishment was unfair and that he would fight it. If Bill Shankly had once pronounced football to be more important than life or death, then the FA's fine of £1.5 million backed Shanks's judgement by demanding a price far in excess of that compensation usually awarded for loss of life. Of course it was unfair that the FA could appoint Terry Venables as England coach and then penalise Tottenham for offences committed during his time. Many in senior positions shared Sugar's view, but none were prepared to back publicly his crusade.

The bungled case against Spurs stemmed from the FA acting in their capacity as overlords of the professional game, but prosecuting on behalf of the Football League under whose jurisdiction the offences had been committed (pre-Premier League days remember?). Where the arbitration panel found in Tottenham's favour was that Tottenham were now in the Premier League, and thus no longer in (or answerable to) the Football League. Therefore the FA/Football League had no right to deduct Premier League points. It was like a shop-lifter stealing from Marks & Spencer. If the shoplifter had got caught while still in the store, then the Marks & Spencer security staff could search and detain the suspect. However, if the suspect made it home before the crime was discovered, those same Marks & Spencer security staff could not march into the accused's home with the

Tomorrow Belongs to Me

same rights to search and interrogate they enjoy in their store.

By the similar token the arbitrators ruled that a ban from the FA Cup was not permissible for impropriety committed in the Football League. Marks & Spencer could ban the thief from their own stores, but not from going into Tesco as well.

The only area where the FA was upheld was over the matter of the whopping fine. The misdeeds were a breach of football regulations rather than the more serious laws of the land. The Tottenham crime was one of 'non-disclosure'. Although the previous highest fine was £105,000 inflicted on Chelsea some years back, it was argued that – notwithstanding the fact the offences were committed under a previous regime – it was some time after Alan Sugar first knew of the malpractice before it was reported. The fine stood.

To all intents and purposes it was a great victory, all down to one man who turned from zero to hero overnight. Unfortunately, success went straight to Sugar's head. Where previously he had often turned for advice to fellow Spurs directors Tony Berry and Douglas Alexiou – and even former chairman Irving Scholar – Sugar now felt he knew it all and no longer needed the benefit of their accumulated wisdom. The spate of foot-in-mouth outbursts had shown this was not the case, and caused acute embarrassment to everyone who holds the club dear to their heart.

Spur of The Moment fanzine reminded Sugar that as chairman he is a figurehead and must shoulder the blame when things go wrong, whether or not it is his fault. It asked Sugar to stop acting like a spoilt child who has had his pocket money taken away.

Dream On

Manager Gerry Francis must have been privately embarrassed by his chairman's public outbursts, and was probably the only one at the club who told him as much. With adverse press comment from respected sporting writers, Sugar cannot have failed to realise he had boobed. Sure enough, he disappeared off the face of the earth for a while and let the team do his talking for him. Like David Dein, Ken Bates, Irving Scholar, Richard Thompson and Martin Edwards, Alan Sugar must realise that as the man at the head of the table, he will come in for stick when things get a bit rough. All the aforementioned have had to put up with far worse than Sugar has yet suffered and did so willingly because of their umbilical love for their club or their acceptance that vitriolic criticism comes with the territory. He has got to realise that you can't suddenly become a football fan in middle age and expect history to be kind to you.

In fact, if Alan Sugar wants a lesson in the cruelty of history and football, he could look no further than his predecessor, Irving Scholar.

Irving Scholar was chairman at Tottenham for seven years between 1984 and 1991, having spent the years immediately following the 1982 takeover – effected in conjunction with Paul Bobroff – loosening his business ties in Monaco while Douglas Alexiou performed the duties of chairman. He took over during a financial crisis precipitated by the building of the West Stand. He was hounded out a decade later following a financial crisis precipitated by the rebuilding of the East Stand. Perhaps Alan Sugar should make a mental note never to commission a new stand . . .

During his term at White Hart Lane, Scholar introduced and implemented a succession of innovative projects that transformed the club and opened the eyes of many within

Tomorrow Belongs to Me

the game to commercial possibilities previously unconsidered. All of the initiatives were spawned by a burning desire to make Tottenham a great club. Like Alan Sugar, Irving Scholar recognised the importance of a sound financial base from which to operate. However, he never let this consideration divert attention from his primary objective, which was to bring the glory, glory days back to White Hart Lane.

As a fan himself, Irving Scholar knew as much as anyone the importance of this me-too tie between supporter and club. It could be argued that his actions once he took charge were merely an extension of this search for the feel-good factor, that he was just a big fan with a big chequebook. But that would be to confuse Scholar's short term tactics (star acquisitions like Venables, Waddle, Gascoigne and Lineker) with his long term strategy.

In fact, Scholar's whole period at the club can be characterised by a continual juggling act of trying to bring the biggest and best players to White Hart Lane, coupled with the ever present drive to generate extra income to pay for such a policy.

Throughout his period at the club, Scholar never received a penny, refusing to take any salary for what he saw as his 'pursuit of excellence' for Tottenham. He enjoyed a convivial relationship with the playing staff, without succumbing to the degree of informality that some younger chairmen in the game enjoy with their star assets. Alan Sugar's spectacular falling out with Jurgen Klinsmann would never have happened if Scholar had been chairman. He remains on good terms with those stars like Hoddle, Waddle and Richard Gough who chose to leave Tottenham against his wishes. He had a very strong perception of the proper way to behave in these matters. There were many occasions when comparable situations were tackled and resolved discreetly without recourse to the kind of public mud-slinging characterised by the club's current custodians.

He recalled that towards the end of his managership, Bill Nicholson found it increasingly difficult to deal with the players on personal matters. It was no surprise that Scholar was a long-time admirer of the Liverpool way of doing things, where chief executive Peter Robinson relieved successive boot-room managers of the anxiety of keeping their players financially content. Scholar felt he had a role to play in this area (perhaps it was no coincidence that when Graeme Souness assumed many of Peter Robinson's functions, Liverpool lost their way).

Scholar's pro-active role in the players' contractual arrangements inevitably brought him into conflict with some of his managers. Most notably, Keith Burkinshaw and Terry Venables. The former felt he should control the commercial operation – he once blew a fuse because no one had informed him that the club had applied for a Kosher licence in order to be able to cater for Jewish functions – while the latter simply felt he could do a better job of running the club and should be in charge of the whole shooting match. For his part, Irving Scholar simply loved the players and was determined to do the best he could for them. And it was a love given freely. Scholar liked to think that one of the traits that marked out a big club was the ability to retain a family feeling. To this end, he and Douglas Alexiou always made a point of going to see injured players laid up in hospital. He felt families have an obligation to look after their own. When it appeared that Danny Thomas would never recover from his horrendous knee injury, Scholar, rather than immediately claiming insurance, gave the player a new contract for a year with a 16% salary increase.

Tomorrow Belongs to Me

In 1985, towards the end of his time at the club and in an attempt to ensure a final pay day, a hesitant Ossie Ardiles came to see his chairman. He asked for a one-year contract at £75,000. Faced with an indifferent response, Ardiles immediately backed down to £70,000 but Scholar still refused to discuss the matter. The talk drifted on in a desultory way for a few minutes before Scholar, seemingly exasperated with this pointless conversation, abruptly told Ardiles to 'piss off'. Taken aback, Ardiles rose to leave, tentatively saying as his parting shot, 'You think about it . . . yes?' 'No I won't,' came the reply. 'You can have £80,000 and a two-year contract. Now f∗∗k off!'

The club behaved magnaminously to the players. After all, Scholar always said he never wanted paupers in the dressing room. When Graham Roberts joined the club he was living in rented accommodation and even Gazza had been earning less than a fortune at Newcastle. He applied the same principle to those who came up through the ranks. For example he encouraged the agent Eric Hall to renegotiate the contract of David Howells.

Acting on professional advice and totally in line with fiscal requirements, loans were given to many players without any firm intention of repayment. Scholar believed that as the loans were sanctioned by the plc, there was no need to disclose them to the Football League as part of the players' salary package. To Scholar, the failure to declare the loans was a technical breach of football regulations explained away by the desire to be generous to the players. As vice-chairman Tony Berry observed, 'Irving would never have done anything deliberately that would have got the club into trouble.' Besides, everyone else was probably at it.

His total immersion in the running of the club inevitably

brought him into conflict with his employees. He could not actually pick the team, but made his views clear to successive managers about whom he favoured and which targets were ripe for the next chequebook flourish. Just as his fancy flitted between prospective signings, so did his interest wane in successive managers. Keith Burkinshaw walked out in protest at what he saw as boardroom meddling. Peter Shreeves survived just two years of indifferent results. David Pleat's personal problems could not withstand the irresistible lure of Terry Venables on the horizon. Despite these comings and goings, Tottenham was undeniably a big club under Scholar's regime. Only two trophies were won, the UEFA Cup in 1984 and the FA Cup in 1991. But in between there were near misses, European adventures and star signings.

If Alan Sugar's first ten years in charge are as fruitful as the Irving Scholar years, then he will have done well. What Alan Sugar must avoid, though, are those pitfalls which brought about Scholar's downfall.

The playing side is probably not an area where Alan Sugar would feel qualified to meddle nor one where Gerry Francis would welcome his interference. Although it must be said that the firing of Ardiles was in part due, in Sugar's view, to the unsatisfactory way in which he dealt with playing affairs. No, where Scholar really came unstuck was that he lost the support of the fans.

The average fan was largely oblivious to the catalogue of benefits for which Irving Scholar can claim credit. Good chairmen take the long term view, which means that some of their decisions or actions may never be appreciated. The chairman may have a three-year financial plan. The fan just wants to know who the team are playing next Saturday and how the team got on last Saturday. This is not a criticism, merely a recognition that the fans' perspective tends to be the immediate short term and needs to be addressed in some way if unnecessary grief is to be avoided.

Although Irving Scholar was very proud of his work at Tottenham, he didn't create a platform for chronicling his achievements. Though ready to admonish publicly the football authorities – on one occasion he fulminated against the iniquities of Mrs Thatcher's ID card scheme to the House of Lords – he was strangely reticent to engage in personal PR to explain the club's policies. This meant that when things started to go awry he had accumulated no credit with the fans.

Quite the reverse. The lack of communication between the club and its fans stimulated the formation of an intelligent resistance movement spearheaded by the Tottenham Independent Supporters Association (TISA), determined to have its say on the way the club had, in their view, got their priorities all wrong.

The late-'80s financial bust hit Tottenham hard. Poor business decisions and poor professional advice were punished severely, dealing the club a near fatal blow and Scholar was the obvious fall guy.

By the time the crisis was resolved in the summer of 1991, Scholar was gone, having been bought out, despite a last minute attempt by Robert Maxwell to intervene, by the Terry Venables/Alan Sugar dream ticket. Ironically, by then most of the problems had gone too, and the question must be asked whether the crisis was really as severe as some were keen to paint it. The successful FA Cup campaign that year, with the promise of Europe to follow, did much to alleviate things. Paul Gascoigne was promised to Lazio for a sum that would wipe out most remaining debts. The East Stand was completed and generating a healthy income from its remaining standing area, its extra seats and its 36 corporate hospitality boxes. Interest rates had fallen so the banks were looking to make friends again. The loss-making acquisitions were being ditched one by one, and the impending Sky TV deal was about to bring huge financial benefits to the new Premier League clubs. But for Irving Scholar it had all come too late.

The press had carried out such an effective demolition job on his character, they barely had time to ponder the ethics of their openly encouraging an employee to take over from his boss. In any other business such tactics would see the employee summarily fired – which is indeed what Alan Sugar did for business efficiency reasons later on.

Today, debts of £8 million are no big deal and it seems quaint to recall the furore over such a sum. Fresh revenue sources have given Premiership clubs a long term stability and untold wealth they could only have dreamed about back in the crisis days of 1990/91. Indeed, Liverpool have raised over £10 million in the last five years via rights issues, and yet still borrowed £7 million from their bank to finance an ambitious transfer policy. Similarly at Everton, a rights issue in 1994 raised £9 million and resolved their debts at a stroke. Compare this with the Tottenham rights issue of 1993 when only £6 million needed to be raised. Such figures beg the question as to whether the crisis that cost Scholar his club could have been orchestrated and exaggerated in the hope of pushing Tottenham into bankruptcy, with the intention of then buying it back cheaply from the receiver with little or no obligations to existing shareholders.

Today, Irving Scholar is not even afforded the modest privileges extended to former players. He is probably the only ex-chairman who has to buy his own season tickets and feels that he would not be made welcome if he used

Tomorrow Belongs to Me

them. However, a legacy of his years in charge is the warm reception he does receive from other Premiership clubs, notably Arsenal, Liverpool and Manchester United.

There have of course been attractive offers to return to football with other clubs, but it's not easy, as any committed fan will verify. Home is still in Monaco, and work is occasionally London's West End. It is strange for someone once so involved with the club now to be so peripheral. Scholar, as a lifelong Spurs fan first and foremost, admits to concern about the power vested in Alan Sugar, and the questionable desire Sugar may hold for the club to recapture glories its chairman cannot know. Scholar tells the story of how shocked he was when his erstwhile partner and chairman of the plc, Paul Bobroff, surveyed the sweep of White Hart Lane and commented on how good it feels to know one owns all this. It is such passive echoes that Scholar now sees in the current regime. For all his power-brokering, Scholar never regarded Tottenham as his own personal fiefdom – although his desire to have a finger in every pie may have given that impression. Probably the hardest thing for him to take was not losing control, but being made to feel unwelcome and receiving the antagonism of the crowd who were manipulated by both Venables and supporter groups.

There are still certain ties with the club – Alan Sugar is suing Scholar (and former finance director Derek Peter) over the undisclosed player loans which cost the club such a hefty fine in 1994. Perhaps this action is probably no more than Sugar covering himself against a possible counter attack from Venables, but it does serve to highlight how far Scholar is from any reconciliation with the club. Tony Berry regrets the estrangement because, 'He [Scholar] is Tottenham through and through. His knowledge is immense. He gave advice freely [to Sugar] and then gets smacked in the teeth.'

The pictures have come down in his office, and contrary to what Terry Venables may have said in his book, they were not of Scholar and his players, but just memorable moments and important people in his life. He loved to reminisce – his penchant for historical trivia questions was endured by friends and foes alike – so much the better if he could do it with former Spurs players. They were always welcomed at the club. Phil Beal once surprised him when, after enduring another tedious display by a Venables team, the ex-player asked enigmatically, 'They're not your heroes, are they? We were your heroes.' It is probably true that while he rubbed the teenage stardust out of his eyes, he always appreciated that, like the players, his passion had become a way of life. Unlike them, he chose not to be paid for the privilege.

Maybe Irving Scholar was just an innovator who simply moved too fast and too far for the times. Maybe if he had trusted his instincts all the way down the line instead of hiding them behind the corporate view on controversial issues like the Shelf, he would have won through.

For unlike most of the Premier League directors, he is a true fan.

Chapter 5

Mind The Gap

If August had been a bad month for Spurs, then September was much, much better. Five games, five wins and Chris Armstrong at last finding his goal touch.

To huge relief and not a little surprise, the first win of the season finally arrived in game number five, against Leeds at White Hart Lane. It was not a totally convincing performance by Spurs, and maybe Leeds had their minds on an impending UEFA Cup clash with Monaco. But at least it postponed further talk of crisis which would surely have followed a third successive home defeat.

Unlike most managers who use the post-match press conference to bemoan dodgy refereeing decisions, bad luck or the injustice of injuries, Leeds manager Howard Wilkinson makes a point of living up to his image as a straight talking Tyke. The disappointment was clear to see as he faced the assembled press, compelled, however painful, to tell the truth as he saw it, seemingly getting cathartic release in the process.

'I've been saying all week that Tottenham had too many

experienced players, too many good players, and too good a manager for them to accept what had happened to them recently on the pitch, without doing something about it. So their vigorous, fighting, scrapping, scratching, wholehearted approach – with some good football thrown in – was no surprise to me and wouldn't be a surprise to the players.

'The corner [from which Howells had scored the opener] was a disaster for two reasons. For one, we knew that was a corner [routine] they worked. They took the same corner at West Ham, but then Howells volleyed it instead of heading it. So we knew that might happen – one of three corners they do [someone had been doing their homework]. So somebody has forgotten something. And secondly, once it did happen, not getting to him to close him down, even if you don't stop the header . . . so that's dozy as they say in Sheffield. You can't do that. Particularly when you know where the sniper is, and you know what gun he's using. There we are. Pop!' He slumped into silence, and stared at the untouched beer that had been placed before him at the conference table. No journo was prepared to interrupt his train of thought.

Gerry Francis for once was a little more upbeat. A different tempo maybe, but there were still snatches of the same old song as he bemoaned injuries, lack of cover, and the fact he couldn't even spend the money he'd been given.

'Well, I'm still hovering on the crest of a crisis, boys,' he began. 'Very pleased with the result. Very pleased with the performance. Good game. Lots of commitment from both sides, marred a little by the fact that David Howells has broken a rib. I thought against West Ham [the previous match a 1-1 draw] we showed a lot more commitment – the sort of commitment I was used to last year from November onwards. We've taken that commitment into today's game and come out of it with three points. Which is a start.

'Darren Anderton [starting a match for the first time this season] obviously makes a major difference. He gives us another dimension. He ran out of steam towards the end, which was understandable really.'

Gerry's mood was only soured when a reporter, noting that Ilie Dumitrescu had vanished from both the team and subs bench after a lacklustre display against Liverpool, enquired after 'the Dumitrescu situation'.

'Situation?' snapped Gerry. 'There's no situation. He's not in the side. Simple as that. Ilie has worked very hard at the pattern of play we do, and he's doing extra little bits of work with me and the players. You have to remember that Ilie left as soon as I came here, to go to Seville [on loan]. Therefore he hasn't done the sort of pattern of play work that the rest of the boys have done. And in the few games that we've played, although he's worked very hard, he has left us a little bit open on certain situations. Since Ilie has been out [of the team] I think we've looked a lot stronger, and a lot tighter. It's not Ilie's fault, it's just that the other boys have worked at it a lot more. We've won and drawn so far without him. It comes easier to the other boys because they've had seven months of doing it, whereas Ilie hasn't had anything at all. I'm pleased how hard he has worked. I'm pleased with his application. But at this moment in time, the team is better suited with people who know the system.'

At Sheffield Wednesday a week later, those people who knew the system brought Spurs their first away win, Sol Campbell making his first appearance of the season, covering in midfield for David Howells.

Win number three, a midweek Coca-Cola stroll over

Dream On

third division Chester, was notable only for two goals from Chris Armstrong – his first for the club. The 4-0 scoreline effectively killed the tie, and provided further ammunition for those who felt the two-legged format of this opening round to be no more than a financial sop to lower division fodder. Still, it was Tottenham's first clean sheet of the season which probably said more about Chester's attack than it did Tottenham's defence.

For Gerry Francis and Clive Wilson, the next game would have that added frisson that comes from returning to your old club. Both ex-manager and ex-player would be assured a warm reception at Loftus Road, but would their presence serve to inspire the players they'd left behind? Certainly that seemed the case after a torrid first half in which Trevor Sinclair ran the Spurs defence ragged, while Clive Wilson had his worst game so far for Spurs. A 0-1 deficit at half-time became 0-2 within a minute of the restart. Terry Venables had come to scout his England prospects, but Teddy Sheringham and Ian Walker were doing little to further their cause in front of their former coach and those watching live on Sky Sports. Until . . . well until Spurs moved up a gear and won comfortably 3-2. That they had the gear to use was never in doubt, it was just typical Spurs that they seemed to need the challenge of a two-goal deficit to propel them into raising their game. Two goals from Teddy Sheringham, making it five in three matches, secured Tottenham's fourth consecutive win.

Win number five came against Wimbledon the following Saturday, with two more goals from Sheringham. Win number six came midweek in the return against Chester, with a further two goals from Teddy Sheringham, who was rapidly developing a fruitful partnership with Chris Armstrong. Win number seven came against Nottingham

Mind The Gap

Forest . . . at least that was the plan, but nobody had told Forest, who won the game when a long distance punt from Steve Stone sailed over the head of Ian Walker. It is a long standing custom at Tottenham that they always let Forest win at White Hart Lane. Forest tend to reciprocate by losing the return fixture at the City ground. Both sets of fans appear to understand this protocol, which was why there was only muted disappointment amongst Tottenham's biggest crowd of the season so far. However, Gerry was obviously unaware of the background to the game.

'For the first 25 minutes there was probably only one team in it, and we needed to get a couple of the breaks that came our way.'

With that, Gerry launched into his favourite topic, excuses.

'I think it has been very disappointing for us, as a team, that we've never once this season been able to pick our strongest team. Chris Armstrong missing the game today [with a dead-leg] was a blow, and we know Darren is still out. Having said that, we've had a very good run, and I thought we started very, very well and it must have been 30-odd minutes before Forest had any sort of attack against us. But they defend very well, get a lot of numbers back behind the ball and they limit your opportunities.

'I felt it looked to be, without doubt, a 0-0 game, up until Steve Stone's tremendous goal.'

Don't laugh.

'Although I would obviously be disappointed that we would lose our run, I thought if any goal deserved to win it, it was an exceptional goal like that. However, having spoken to the player just now, he has ruined my weekend completely because it was meant to be a cross. From our point of view, we accept that Forest are a good side, they

Dream On

have shown why they are unbeaten; tough opposition. It's only the second time we haven't scored a goal, and we've got to bounce back and get on a run again. We are still unbeaten away from home and we want to keep that going.'

Almost unheralded, Ruel Fox had made his Spurs debut against Forest. Signed from Newcastle for £4 million, it was a strange buy, given that the priority should have been to try to rectify the chronic early season defensive problems. With Dean Austin playing like a man dispossessed, a Premiership-grade right-back would have been high up most fans' shopping list. But Gerry was clearly more worried by the lack of quality support for Armstrong and Sheringham. With the bulk of his pocket money now spent, the presumption was that the team would see the season out with the current defence. Not that anyone in the press room was ever going to push Francis on the matter.

The post-match press conferences at White Hart Lane follow a format that is as well-choreographed as any West End farce. Premiership protocol insists that both managers present themselves to the assembled media after each game for a question and answer session. The game ends; the managers make their way to the press lounge; the press ask the questions and the managers provide the answers. Done. However, what actually takes place is somewhat different.

For a start, it usually takes Gerry a full hour to get from the dressing room to the press lounge. At first it was assumed that the inordinate delay in walking 40 yards was simply down to him bollocking the team after another home defeat. However, as results improved, it became apparent this was just wishful thinking.

Fortunately, for the hacks anxiously pacing the press suite, checking watches as deadlines come and go, the visiting manager can usually be relied upon to make an appearance within about 25 minutes of the game ending. With the team bus idling outside and no responsibility to corporate sponsors or guests, the press conference is his only chore before the journey home.

For Gerry Francis as home manager, there appear to be other priorities. Reporters now expect the time lapse and make use of it by compiling their provisional match reports. Shorthand squiggles on an A4 pad are translated into tomorrow's back pages, laboriously dictated over mobile phones to transcribers who need every word over two syllables spelt out in full. Those at the cutting edge of technology use lap-tops to bash out their reports in noisy two-fingered frenzies. The room then empties with a dash to the car park to collar players for their pearls of wisdom as they in turn dash for their cars.

If the game has been covered by Sky's cameras, then Gerry can be seen immediately, but only on the press room television sets as he is interviewed from the dressing room. A hush falls as the press boys take this opportunity to furiously scribble down his quotes, a good 40 minutes before he will appear in person and repeat everything they have already heard. If the press are particularly unlucky, there will also be a BBC *Match of the Day* interview for Gerry, as well as phone-in soundbites for London's commercial radio stations.

At long last, with the ground long emptied, the High Road still, the visitors departed and even the press room bar closed and shuttered, word finally filters down that 'Gerry's on his way'.

Like a headmaster arriving at school assembly, Gerry makes his entrance. Seats are taken and a hush descends. Now out of tracksuit and into smart jacket and tie, he is flanked by the imposing figure of Spurs press officer, John

Dream On

Fennelly. While Gerry takes his seat, Fennelly remains standing behind his charge like a presidential bodyguard, and surveys the hacks as if any one of them is likely to unleash a weapon.

Except that the press find it hard to unleash even a decent question. There is an embarrassing silence when the only sound comes from the noisy air conditioning fan, before Gerry, realising nobody is going to ask him anything, will then launch into his interpretation of the game beginning with the customary 'Well gents . . .'

Gerry's monologue is couched in the usual manager-speak where the boys always done well and there are already lots of promising signs. To his credit, he does speak clearly and distinctly, without the umms and errs that make you wonder how some managers ever got through their job interview. Before too long, Gerry will remind the assembly about his injury woes, listing at length those players missing and how difficult it is to cover for their absence from such a restricted squad. He will also be at pains to mention by name those players departed in the summer, so that history men like Barmby, Klinsmann and Popescu feature as frequently as if they were still on the club's books.

Throughout his speech, Gerry will stare down at his tabletop, as if reading a script. Only occasionally will he glance up, taking a sip of the orange juice placed there for him, but still avoiding eye contact with his audience. (The QPR fanzine *A Kick Up The Rs* memorably described this technique as 'Gerry giving another interview to his shoe'.)

When his ramble comes to a halt, Gerry will again sip his drink, while the press in turn stare down at their notepads, willing someone to pluck up the courage to ask a question. When someone does, it is usually a real humdinger along the lines of . . .

Mind The Gap

'Three good points today, eh Gerry?' or 'Another goal for Teddy, eh Gerry?' or the favourite, 'You must be pleased with the lads today, eh Gerry?'

It is simply amazing to witness how time and again, nobody is prepared to actually ask the kind of question we have all been discussing prior to the manager's arrival: like why Gerry persists with full-backs who are obviously not Premiership material? Or why he is so cautious in his choice of substitutes? Or how he can defend his direct play tactics?

So anyway, off Gerry will go again, giving the underarm 'questions' the full answers they don't deserve, before again coming to a meandering halt. Another painful and embarrassing silence ensues, before Gerry effects merciful release by saying 'OK boys?' and gets to his feet to leave.

'Thanks Gerry,' they all chorus, as they too rise to their feet as if in the presence of royalty.

To the novice, this is the end of the press conference. But in fact, it is only just about to start. As Gerry exits through the rear doors of the press room, he is followed by a stampede of Wapping's finest who have sat patiently through the preceding charade with lips firmly buttoned. What happens now is that an 'impromptu' conference is held behind the bike sheds, where all those name reporters who have been biting their lips can now unleash the real questions in search of those elusive, 'exclusive' answers. This second conference is supposedly 'for the Mondays', i.e. those daily papers who need an angle to fill their pages after the weekend papers have carried the match reports. The quotes given here are the ones you will read in the *Sun* and the *Mirror*.

It is a shame that the newspaper circulation war prevents the searching questions being asked in front of rival ears.

Dream On

It is also a shame that the potential risk of upsetting the Spurs manager, and presumably incurring his ire, produces such a pat-a-cake repartee of mundane questions and answers.

However, even innocuous questions can backfire. One example, from that post-Forest game press conference, perhaps serves to illustrate why so many choose to suffer in silence and how even gentle deliveries can sometimes backfire.

In an effort to break the strained silence, one novice hack fed the following line to Gerry: 'When Darren comes back, will you have him in the centre or out on the wing?'

Pretty innocent question you would have thought, given the recent purchase of Ruel Fox to play in the right-wing position where Darren Anderton first came to prominence. Gerry disagreed, and his caustic answer had many in the press room making mental notes never, ever, to stick their own neck above the parapet.

'Well I think if anyone has done any homework, or has actually seen us play or has actually spoken to me or Darren, I think it is plainly obvious that Darren is going to play in the middle of the park, where he wants to play and where I think is his best position.'

Gulp. The temperature in the press room dropped by several degrees. Gerry continued, 'I think he has been playing there for me since last year, at every opportunity. So obviously, that, for me, is his place. And even more so, it is the place that he really wants to play. So I don't envisage any change on that.' The poor hack noted down the reply, and then was swallowed up by the hole that had conveniently opened up in the ground.

Such are the concessions to Sky TV and the national team,

that Spurs played just one Saturday fixture during the whole
of October. Following the Forest defeat, the team faced a
trip to Everton. Not the glamour game it may once have
been, but a chance to avenge the 1-4 FA Cup semi-final
mauling of last April.

The long journey up the M6 precluded Sunday lunch
for the travelling fans, but those hoping for hearty fare at
journey's end were to be sorely disgruntled. Once upon a
time Liverpool was the third wealthiest city in the British
Empire. Today, a drive through the city centre on a Sunday
afternoon should be enough to send shivers down the spine
of any Euro '96 organiser.

The concept of Sunday trading doesn't seem to have
reached this outpost of pre-deregulation Britain. The 24-
hours-a-day trading revolution has long since spread out-
ward from London's Soho and West End to encompass
even the most somnolent suburbs. There are few parts of
the capital where, at any time of day or night, you can
be more than ten minutes' drive from a pizza, a kebab, a
cappuccino, a burger, a pint of milk or a salt-beef bagel.
Here in Liverpool at two in the afternoon, the only sign
of life came from the shadowy figures flitting in and out
of the boarded up bookmaker's or lurching from pubs and
disappearing down narrow back alleys. The journey to the
stadium, following city centre signposting, takes the visitor
through a *Mad Max* landscape that has drivers instinctively
reaching to check their doors are locked. Row after row
of red-brick terraced housing gives way to vast areas of
grassed-over dereliction; what the Luftwaffe started in the
Forties, the slum clearance programme completed in the
Sixties. It is surreal to see so many streets without a single
parked car; to see kids playing football in the street in the
sure knowledge that no motor vehicle will come along to

Dream On

disrupt their game; to see washing fluttering on lines strung zig-zag across back alleys.

Underpasses, flyovers and deserted university sprawl finally give way to the usual redeveloped town centre where all the chain stores are hidden inside a concrete hanger. Those streets that haven't been demolished for roundabouts and car parks now contain shops whose anonymous wares are hidden behind graffitied shutters. The one-way traffic system swallows up the unwary driver, routing the poor soul past deserted bus depots and streaked concrete office blocks before spewing him out again, back the way he came.

English football grounds may have become safer havens in recent years – two thorough body searches either side of the visitors' entrance would detect any weapons carrier – but they have failed miserably to meet the demands of a public spoilt by the High Street fast food revolution.

It may once have been that pie and Bovril was the nearest most fans ever got to 'eating out'. But not now. A nation of casual grazers expects more than the basic rations most stadia offer. It is indicative of the thinking of those who still run our clubs that they think it quite acceptable to pay, as Everton recently did, £5.5 million for one player, Andrei Kanchelskis, and then expect the 4,000 paying punters who travelled 200 miles from London, to feast on powdered tea, powdered coffee, Wagon Wheels, Mars bars, crisps or 'meat' pies. Is this what they serve in the Directors' Lounge? Is this what they think the fans eat at home? Is there a catering manager who gets paid to compile these menus? What on earth makes club officials think that supporters, who will have spent a considerable sum of money travelling to the ground and buying a match ticket, will then be satisfied with a bag of crisps and powdered tea? It is a sad truth that the filling station

Mind The Gap

down the road will be a better source of nourishment than any catering concession found in a modern Premiership ground. A freshly made sandwich for its customers is still beyond the capabilities of a club that has a £5 million wage bill for its employees. While this remains the case, fans will continue to spend their money in pubs and corner shops, arriving at the ground as near to kick-off as is possible. And that's not just a potential recipe for disaster, but a proven one. And all because the away fan is regarded as an unavoidable nuisance rather than a source of revenue. What other business could treat a section of its customers so indifferently and still survive?

The newest stand at Goodison sits at the Park End of the ground, and must run with ex-manager Mike Walker (father of Spurs 'keeper Ian) as the greatest disappointment in recent Everton history. For years the traditional visitors' end, it now comprises a single tier cantilever econo-stand, of a style, design and scale totally out of keeping with the rest of the ground and thus totally in keeping with football's current Topsy-like construction boom. Once upon a time, Goodison Park was one of the biggest, grandest and most luxurious grounds in the country, its double-tier stands a monument to football's most famous architect, Archibald Leitch. Today, looking at the ramshackle collection of ill-matched structures that ring the pitch like bowed-head mourners around a graveside, it is hard to imagine when that time may have been. The irony is that having been one of the first to undertake the conversion to all-seater status, Everton are paying the penalty of being pioneers; their largely pre-Taylor development comparing unfavourably with their peers who had the benefit of Football Trust financial aid and could draw on the experience of bodies like the Football Stadia Advisory Design Council (FSADC).

Dream On

Home fans pay £15 to sit behind a goal and survey a landscape that encompasses the good, the bad and the ugly of football architecture. To their left is the monstrous main stand, three tiers at vertigo-inducing angles in a 1971 classic from the *well-it-looked-good-on-paper* school of design. Sight-blocking roof supports and tacked-on executive boxes hint at a serious lack of pre-planning. Allowing the eye to skip over the corner site which bizarrely houses the church of St. Luke the Evangelist, the opposing goal houses the unpronounceable Gwladys Street End, a bastardised 1938 Archibald Leitch design with plastic seats bolted in where they were never intended. The theme continues around the fourth side, where classic Leitch features like the blue and white ironwork – duplicated at Roker Park, White Hart Lane and Ibrox – are now clumsily boxed over with plywood to carry advertising hoardings.

It doesn't take too many minutes of pondering this sorry mish-mash of conflicting styles, before the question comes to mind: where did all the money go? It is only comparatively recently that transfers and wages have spiralled to absorb the gate generated revenue. When you check the Everton programme and count the eight First Division championships, the seven runners-up consolations and the twelve FA Cup final appearances, all evenly spaced over 105 years of history, you are reminded of why Everton are regarded as founder members of the 'Big Club' syndrome. In 1948, 78,299 watched a Merseyside derby at Goodison, as many as watched Everton win the FA Cup at Wembley last year. Even in that post-war period, all four sides of the ground had double-decker stands that had cost a total of £121,000 to build over a 31-year period. So where did all the money go?

The steep admission charges now being levied at every

Mind The Gap

top flight club reflect the huge outlay incurred in the move to all-seater stadia, plus the spiralling cost of assembling and keeping a squad of highly paid stars. For the first time, clubs can actually explain, if not entirely justify, their pricing policy by pleading that the kitty is empty. But they've had 100 years to prepare for this moment and yet it still took them all by surprise.

Everton's current capacity of 40,000 is less than it enjoyed in 1894. True the stadium is now all-seater, but three of the four sides need upgrading, particularly the Bullens Road Stand where the bulk of the travelling Spurs fans found themselves plonked in late October.

Everton's participation in the Cup Winners Cup the previous Thursday meant that their match with Spurs had been put back a day to Sunday. A dull 0-0 draw with Feyenoord of Rotterdam didn't bode too well for Everton's continuing involvement, but a healthy enough 33,629 had turned up this afternoon, including a sizeable contingent from north London.

Out on the pitch, with 30 minutes to kick-off, players were beginning to emerge for their pre-match warm-up. In dribs and drabs, players ran out to a smattering of applause that reflected each individual's popularity. Those confident of their standing, like Andrei Kanchelskis, ran from the tunnel with a vigorous sprint, acknowledging the welcome with a disarming wave and grin. Those less sure of their appeal ambled on in twos and threes to aggregate their applause, before embarking on the ritual of small-talk and stretching exercises with which players while away the minutes.

The Spurs fans, as do most away fans, gave a generous reception to all their own team, although a discernably louder one to firm favourite Teddy Sheringham. With

Dream On

Darren Anderton still crocked, Teddy was undisputed number one with the fans. SHERINGHAM 10 was still the most popular combination seen on the back of fans' replica shirts, although new additions like NAYIM 50 (YARDS) showed that terrace wit was not completely dead.

Both teams contained a fair smattering of internationals, and there was no shortage of young fans seeking to augment their autograph collection. Most players have perfected the blinkered stare that allows them to enter and exit the players' tunnel without actually catching the eye of those zealots holding out pen and pad for a precious signature. Once out on the pitch, they are on safe territory providing they don't stray too close to the perimeter and risk eye contact.

One player however was bucking the trend. As a wayward shot flew high into the stand at the Park End, a track-suited figure jogged to the touchline to retrieve the ball. One enterprising young fan saw his big chance and intercepted the player with a programme to be autographed. The player stopped and signed with a flourish, but then found that by the time he had finished that one brief signature, there were three more kids with books waiting for him. As he signed these three books, the penny dropped with every other kid, and within seconds the player was ten-deep in autograph hunters.

After a couple of minutes of frantic scribbling, the throng had barely reduced, and the player looked over his shoulder at his team-mates who had by now started to make their way back down the tunnel as kick-off approached. Eventually, after a good five or six minutes, all the autograph hunters had been satisfied, and Erik Thorstvedt ambled sheepishly back onto the pitch to complete his catching exercises.

Mind The Gap

The number 13 on the reserve 'keeper's back was an ironic reminder of how Erik's final years at the club had not gone the way he would have hoped. Niggling injuries had cost him his automatic place in the starting line-up, back at the beginning of the 1994–95 season.

'It's a weird thing – I don't get injuries where I break my leg or suchlike, I just get things sneaking up on me. I think . . . phew what next?'

Ossie Ardiles was forced to throw in young reserve 'keeper Ian Walker, a chance seized and never released. As the end neared for Ossie in October 1994, he reinstated Thorstvedt for a vital Coca-Cola cup tie at Notts County, Walker having failed to keep a clean sheet in any match until then. The game ended in a 0-3 defeat, and although Thorstvedt kept his place for the following game against West Ham, Ossie was then fired and caretaker manager Steve Perryman restored Ian Walker to the side. Once Gerry Francis arrived a week later, Erik's first team career at Tottenham was finished.

With a contract due to expire in the summer of 1996, Erik knows that his 33rd birthday will bring with it a free transfer and the opportunity for one big payday from a final move. Of course he would prefer to finish his days at Tottenham on a high note, but acknowledges there is little chance other than Walker suffering serious injury. Erik is philosophical about his fate, readily praising the young 'keeper who had recently broken into Terry Venables' England squad: 'I said it when he [Walker] was 17 – he was going to play for England. And Walks is just a really good goalie. He's not Peter Schmeichel dominant – perhaps a bit more like John Lukic, laid back. But he does well all the time, and you can't argue with that.'

Such praise contrasts with the 'welcome' Thorstvedt

received when signing for Spurs back in 1988. A catastrophic FA Cup defeat at Bradford had signalled the end for Bobby Mimms. Erik came straight into the side, and despite a few hiccups – notably the televised howler in his debut against Forest – soon provided a reassuring presence behind a distinctly shaky defence. Not long after, there appeared a somewhat scurrilous newspaper piece in which Mimms slated Thorstvedt. 'Mimms just said I was big headed . . . arrogant . . . I didn't mix. I had not one friend at the club. He said he'd tried to make me feel welcome at the club from day one, but that I didn't want to know. It was just a terrible piece. I can understand him being bitter, but that article was just lies. Still, everyone at the club thought it was hilarious; the players were just laughing their heads off in the dressing room.

'When I came to the club, he [Mimms] never spoke to me. Never. In training you say things like "well done", but he never said that one single time. Not once.'

Does Thorstvedt get on with Walker? Does he encourage him? 'Yeah, definitely. All the time. We don't mix socially, but we are good friends. He has supported me when I was playing, and I do the same when he's playing. We get on okay. But that Mimms thing was just so out of order, it was terrible. And it really hurt me because my local press in Norway picked it up before I'd even read it myself! I've just got absolutely no respect for him, but he's the only one.'

Thorstvedt quickly became a firm favourite with the Spurs fans. He adopted the habit of throwing his gloves into the crowd after each game; a gesture particularly appreciated at away games where a desultory wave was the most the travelling fans had come to expect in acknowledgement. He was dubbed 'Erik the Viking' (after a film of that name), and even had his own terrace anthem: 'I love

Mind The Gap

Erik the Viking; Erik the Viking loves me'. When things were going well, the fans would chant 'Erik, Erik, what's the score?' and he'd hold up the required fingers to show the tally. 'Erik, Erik, gis a wave' also got a response and the crowd loved him all the more. Trivial incidents really, but serving to illustrate how little it takes for a player to win the hearts of the fans, and how few players bother to make the effort. Of course there have been bloopers where Erik has cost the club points, but his accumulated credit always saw him through.

Truthfully, there were many who still saw him as the club's number one 'keeper. Sure, Walker was a good shot-stopper, with incredible reflexes. But his reluctance to come off his line to deal with crosses was a serious flaw in his game. Walker would appear rooted to his line whenever a high cross flashed across his area. In the absence of a really dominating central defender, such crosses were frequently met by an in-rushing forward forcing a miraculous point-blank save from Walker. All praise to the 'keeper, but the lingering question was always whether in the first place the cross could have been intercepted with a modicum of anticipation and technique. Both club and 'keeper recognise the deficiency and under the guidance of Spurs' goalkeeping coach Pat Jennings, Walker feels the special sessions are paying dividends.

It would also be nice to see Walker rollocking his defence some more. In the absence of a commissar in the Mackay/Perryman/Roberts mould who would remonstrate with their colleagues, mistakes now go unchastised if not unpunished. If a defender gets it wrong these days, captain Gary Mabbutt prefers a quiet encouraging word in the ear. Many Spurs fans would rather see the kind of fireworks Graham Roberts could ignite, when his rabid reaction to a

Dream On

team-mate's gaffe left no one in any doubt that the incident would not be repeated.

Walker, like Pat Jennings, is not of that ilk, and is probably not about to change. He appears to accept his defence's shortcomings, and his role in picking up the pieces. Erik Thorstvedt, as with his mentor Ray Clemence before him, was a shouter and a hollerer (although it went against the grain for someone brought up in the stillness of Scandinavian dressing rooms). They both would prowl the extremes of the area like a caged animal, bawling out defenders and shouting instructions where necessary.

At age 24, Walker is not a kid nor a novice. He is first choice goalkeeper for Tottenham and a member of the England setup. No longer can he be excused for reasons of age or maturity. He married during the summer, and is presumably on a very substantial salary. However, there is still about Walker the air of a youngster who can hardly believe the position in which he finds himself. He looks very uneasy during media interviews, and though he has managed to avoid the drink/driving/drugs scandals that his contemporaries see as a rite of passage, *News of the World* readers were entertained by his wife's tales of his sexual prowess. His garish playing kit, foppish hairstyle and frequent appearances in youth style magazines are all in marked contrast to his unassuming on-field persona. Has it all come too soon and too easy for Walker? Certainly his father's footballing connections would have opened a few doors, but there is no doubt that Walker junior has an inherent talent for his metier. At Spurs he will have benefited from expert coaching from masters such as Ray Clemence, and currently, Pat Jennings. So why haven't fans taken to him in a big way?

Well for a start, the Spurs crowd has been somewhat

Mind The Gap

spoiled over the years with a succession of international class keepers. Pat Jennings and Ray Clemence accumulated 921 Spurs appearances between them, while Erik Thorstvedt has 96 Norwegian caps to date. But they can also remember how stop-gaps like Tony Parks, Mark Kendall, Barry Daines, Milija Aleksik and Bobby Mimms all displayed flashes of brilliance, but were unable to achieve the consistency to retain a regular first team place. Is Walker really going to be the next Pat Jennings?

Whatever the answer, it will come too late for Erik Thorstvedt. He stoically acknowledges his position in the pecking order, and is content, if not happy, to see out the final year of his contract. The one consolation that has kept Erik going throughout his difficult year has been his undisputed position as first choice goalkeeper and captain of his country.

Erik admits that it is the qualifying games for Euro '96 that have kept his mind focused when his regular match practice has been limited to Avon Insurance Combination fixtures. Spurs reserve team coach Chris Hughton speaks highly of Thorstvedt's professional application to a role that he could have considered beneath him.

'I've got nothing but admiration for Erik,' Hughton conceded. 'He is a model pro. There is no side to him. Quite the opposite – he has a generous spirit. Obviously he's not Gerry's number one choice, but he still works hard at his game because he's ambitious to get 100 caps.'

'You are,' admits Erik, 'a bit in two minds when you play for the reserves. Obviously you want to do your best and everything, but in the other sense you don't really want to be there. We won the league last season on the last game of the season. Charlton were three points ahead of us, but we played them in the last game and won 2-0 to take the

Dream On

Football Combination title on goal difference. There was a victory photo afterwards and you are thinking "Am I really going to go for it or am I going to hide behind someone else . . . ?" But when you play you have to do your best.'

Next to his 1991 FA Cup winner's medal, the 1995 Combination title may have seemed small beer. But Erik was nevertheless determined to celebrate the victory over Charlton that night. No one at the club had had the foresight to lay on any kind of celebration. However, much to everyone's amazement, Erik pulled from his kitbag a magnum of champagne with which the team could toast their success. 'Holsten was finishing its sponsorship,' recalls Erik, 'and they were giving everyone, all the first team players, magnums of champagne. So I just brought mine in.

'Luckily I have been having this Norway thing as well to keep me going. We are ranked [by FIFA] at number four in the world [England aren't even in the top twenty], and I'm the captain of the team. I'm like a world superstar who plays at St. Albans [home venue for Spurs reserves] every week! Because of that I have to be really disciplined and motivated to keep going. I always have the next qualifying game in mind. That's what is always in the back of my mind. That's what I'm training for – when I'm pushing myself that's the carrot that is dangling in front of my eyes.

'I knew Walks would start the season even if I had done brilliantly pre-season – which I didn't. I knew I was facing an uphill struggle. Obviously I'm here to play in the first team and that's what I want to do. But even if I had been perfect pre-season, I think Walks would have started anyway.

'I will always say, I'm here to play for the first team. I will never admit anything else. If I'm not playing, you can choose two paths really: you can try and give yourself a rest by saying "from next summer I will probably be somewhere else"; or I can just work hard and get my [injured] back 100% okay. For an outfield player you can take things more in your own hands – you can tackle harder and run harder. As a goalie you can only react to what other people do, therefore it is sometimes very frustrating – particularly if you've made a mistake and want to make up for it, because you don't always get the chance to do so.'

If Erik was seeking to impress Francis pre-season, clangers in Sweden and at Ibrox would not have gone in his favour, although his colleagues would have been impressed with his ability to arrange free drinks wherever they went in Norway.

'Pre-season is a bit of a hit-and-miss affair; it has always been like that for me, particularly when it comes to crosses and things like that. You've got to get into the judgement of distances. The situation I find myself in, I can't afford to be anything other than fantastically incredible. I'm not happy with what happened but I'm not killing myself over it either.'

There was another incident on tour that brought back memories for Erik, when he and Gary Mabbutt, his room-mate, arrived at the Stockholm room to face the realisation that they were sharing a small double bed.

'No way,' protested Erik. 'It's the floor for you Mabbs.' A case of once bitten, twice shy for Erik who had faced a similar dilemma during his spell with Moenchengladbach. On his first night away with his new team-mates, he sampled the delights of the old-style family hotel which the German club used before home games.

'It was my first game, and there was just this one big double bed for me and my room-mate, Andreas Winkholt. Strange, but there you go. Anyway, I was soon fast asleep, and I must have thought I was back at home. So I wrapped an arm and a leg over the person next to me . . . Andreas woke with a bolt and put up one hell of a struggle! We both toppled onto the floor and eventually he flicked the lights on. I didn't know the language, so it was difficult for me to explain away what I had done. Still, I was lucky as Andreas could have shopped me to the other lads . . . at least I don't think he did! Although the players did laugh whenever they saw me, but I don't know the reason for that.'

The Spurs game at Everton that Sunday finished 1-1, with Chris Armstrong at last scoring his first Premiership goal. The game was typical of most that Spurs had played away from home this season. True they remained undefeated on their travels, but they lacked that killer instinct to finish off inferior opposition. Draws against Manchester City, West Ham and now Everton (all 1-1) represented six lost points from games Spurs had at times dominated and from which they had carved enough chances to win comfortably. At this stage in the season, those six points represented the difference between mid-table anonymity, and a top three position.

At the head of the Premiership, Newcastle were setting a cracking pace. Although the Spurs fan who expected their team to challenge seriously for title honours had yet to be born, there was always the nagging feeling that it would be jolly decent of the club if there was maybe a little league interest beyond Christmas for once. However, traditionally Spurs were a cup side, and so the next two games for Spurs would serve as indicators for what the rest of the season may hold: an away Coca-Cola Cup tie at Coventry was to be followed by a home league match against Newcastle on the Sunday.

Mind The Gap

Although just three days after the Goodison game, another huge turnout of Spurs fans swelled the gate at Highfield Road and must have given both Francis and Sugar further indication of the hunger for success at Tottenham. With Coventry having a rough old time in the league, Spurs must have fancied their chances of a win on the night. Which, of course, is when Spurs are at their most vulnerable. Twelve months earlier, at the same stage in the same competition, even Ossie's woeful team fancied its chances against lowly Notts County, who were subsequently relegated to Division Two. The 3-0 defeat then sealed Ossie's fate, and should have served as a warning for those players about to take on Coventry. But no. After cruising to a 2-0 half-time lead, and just as at least one fan was thinking 'I reckon Spurs could go all the way in this competition', Coventry had woken up and pulled off a remarkable 3-2 win.

It was the kind of performance that had the fans – and surely manager Gerry Francis – wondering if any progress at all had been made since Ossie's departure. Ruel Fox had been cup-tied, but Chris Armstrong had shown all the lazy traits that had highlighted his latter days at Palace. Sheringham had simply drifted out of the game, and Ian Walker once more displayed his lack of mastery in his own six-yard box. Afterwards, Gerry talked about the brilliance of that first-half performance, contrasting it with the subsequent collapse. In truth, Spurs had never been more than competent; anything approaching brilliance would have seen far more than just two goals go in against a wretched Coventry side. Tottenham's inability to capitalise on their superiority had finally cost them dearly. One cup down, only one more to go.

Four days later, a far better performance saw Spurs take a 1-1 draw from the Newcastle game. Kevin Keegan's side

Dream On

was bristling with talent and really had the look of all-stars about them. Against Spurs, they moved the ball about with confidence and no little skill, with Keith Gillespie in particular giving a terrific display of wingplay in the first half. Somewhat against the run of play, Sheringham put Spurs ahead, but as was increasingly becoming the case, it was a lead they could not hold on to. There was little doubt that Newcastle would claw their way back into the game, and just two minutes into the second half their equaliser came, from David Ginola. It was to be the end of the scoring, but not of the action.

Afterwards, in a packed press lounge, both Kevin Keegan and Gerry Francis enthused about the quality of the game, and its entertainment value. No one thought to question the confusion of entertainment with quality. Sure, the match had been enjoyable in the typical English blood and thunder way. But it had also been error strewn, tactically naïve, badly paced and physically exhausting. At least Newcastle had attempted a passing game, albeit one that got progressively ragged as players sagged from the sheer effort of covering so much ground. Spurs, true to the Francis diktat of organisation before flair, became increasingly content to hoof the ball upfield in the hope that Chris Armstrong could use his pace to create an opportunity.

As an end to itself, this game may indeed have provided some high jinks, and certainly an opportunity for everyone involved at Sky Sports to hype it up and air those old clichés about 'best league in the world'. It 'would sustain the British game as a spectacle, worthy of world audiences if others could repeat it' trumpeted Rob Hughes in *The Times* the next day. What nobody was saying however was that such fare was poor preparation for the demands of Continental competition, where skill and tactical nous were needed along with athleticism.

After the second round of the three European club competitions, only Nottingham Forest of the English clubs remained. This contrasted with six Spanish clubs, five French, four German and four Italian sides. And some of these countries had only lost representatives because they had had to play against one another. Perhaps an equally telling statistic was that no English sides had managed a goal in the five return legs played.

Despite the grandiose ambitions of the Premier League, clubs were still prioritising those attributes needed for league success (or survival) at home, at the expense of those more expansive skills that would serve them well on the European stage. All the talk is about the winning of trophies, rather than qualifying for Europe. To this end, English club sides play more 'important' competitions and more games than any other European country. But it's not just the number of games our sides play, but the way we play them too; three games in eight days is not unusual. The schedule is dictated by television and the maxim of play more matches – earn more money. The traditional Saturday and Wednesday fixture slots are no longer sacrosanct, putting the emphasis on recuperation from the last encounter rather than preparation for the next.

It can only be hoped that the unexpectedly early elimination of Manchester United, Liverpool, Leeds, Everton and Blackburn will inspire critical self-analysis. Just as the best of the European teams have added English strength to their skill, so the English clubs must attempt to emulate the methods which have enabled their Continental counterparts to breed more skilful and stronger players. They must look at diet, at training methods (the major clubs in Europe train twice a day on at least two days a week), at lifestyle (R&R actually means rest and recuperation to the Europeans, but apparently Rock & Roll to the British), and especially to preparation – fewer games and a more sensible schedule means being able to treat each game as a special event.

In England, the influx of foreign players has undoubtedly brought an extra dimension to the Premier League. Foreign coaches must now be encouraged to do likewise because, according to Britain's favourite German, it is 'good for any country to attract outsiders. They bring their own special ideas into the game. Then it is up to the individual player to take out of it what he wants.' The emphasis by the FA is wrongly placed on *what* to coach rather than *how* to coach. This fails to allow for a wider range of tactical approaches than the FA's predilection for either direct play or direct play. It is to be hoped that the appointment of a technical director will set new standards applicable all the way down to schools level.

Thinking of the longer term, there can be little doubt that those who have been demanding a reorganisation of kids' football will find increasing support for their views. A renewed emphasis on skill, an enjoyment of the game for its own sake and, perhaps most importantly, earlier and greater control by professional clubs, are all areas where European sides have already taken the initiative. A move in this direction has already been made by encouraging the professional clubs to widen their catchment area by becoming centres of excellence for the young. However, schoolboy fixtures still come first thereby restricting club involvement. So at an under-15 international level the English schoolboys will face their counterparts who have already spent a number of years being groomed by the leading professional clubs in their country.

Mind The Gap

This is not to say we should ditch those aspects of the English game that are real plus points. Passion, organisation and the will to win are all qualities our clubs should maintain; indeed Arsenal managed to win the Cup Winners Cup in 1993 and reach the final the following year by doing exactly this. And when big clubs do succeed it is despite habitual self-indulgence. The prevailing view of the English professional by their Continental counterparts, according to Erik Thorstvedt, is that '. . . they drink too much. They just eat rubbish. They don't train properly. But what they do have is this will to win . . . this incredible determination.'

As the Duke of Wellington once remarked of his army: 'I don't know what effect these men will have on the enemy, but, by God, they frighten me.'

Would that it was still so.

Chapter 6

Love Thy Neighbour

To fans of Spurs and Arsenal, the match on 18 November was not simply *a* derby, but *the* derby. Such is the vastness of London, and the insularity of its inhabitants, that a trip around the South Circular, through uncharted territory like Dulwich, Catford and Thornton Heath can invoke compass, rations and passport preparations.

When a drive across the traffic-snarled capital can take as long as a dash up the motorway to Coventry, it is hard to accept that the term 'local derby' is meant to encompass even those trips to far-off Wimbledon, Chelsea or West Ham.

Only in the *A-Z* is London one city. The distance that separates N17 from SW6 or E6 may not seem great when running your finger across a map, but is enough for your clothes, your haircut or even the drink you order at the bar to betray your origins. At least in Coventry the locals talk funny and you know where you stand.

Ask a Spurs fan about a proposed visit to Villa Park or Highfield Road, and you'll get chapter and verse on what

Dream On

route to take, what pubs to visit, where to park up, and where to get a good take-away or a blinding post-match Balti. Ask the same question prior to a fixture at Stamford Bridge or Upton Park and you'll get blank looks and shrugs. Decorate the lounge and listen to the game on Capital Gold is the best advice on offer.

The borders between Arsenal territory and Spurs country blur as they overlap. At what point does the Seven Sisters Road change its allegiance? Both clubs share much the same north London catchment area, within which there are loyalist strongholds and rebel enclaves. Wherever you live in north London (or Essex or Herts), your neighbour is just as likely to be an Arsenal supporter as a Spurs fan. There is usually one character at work who goes to West Ham, or another who is a Chelsea nut. But they are merely tolerated and their opinions disregarded as inconsequential. Statistics will inform you that one in four men has homosexual tendencies, and one man in ten is a regular user of prostitutes. But who do you know who supports Crystal Palace?

As a fan of Spurs or Arsenal, you live, work, eat and drink with the enemy. For every *bona fide* supporter who actually goes to matches, there will be a dozen more whose attendance has lapsed but who still follow the club's fortunes and classify themselves as fans. Once upon a time, it was casual fans such as these who would turn up for particularly attractive fixtures, or on public holidays – and certainly on derby day – to provide those extraordinary attendances that litter the record books. Those few games a year were enough to satisfy their craving for live football yet maintain their credibility as an 'active' fan. Today, such fans have been marginalised by the money-up-front membership schemes facilitated by smaller, all-seater stadia. To turn up on match day seeking admission, with no more than cash in hand, is a fruitless exercise when even fixtures against lowly opposition bring out the 'house full' signs.

But in the workplace, or down the pub, these disenfranchised fans can be as partisan as any season-ticket holder. It is often the case that the loudest gloaters or the sternest critics turn out to be those who have gleaned their knowledge vicariously from edited highlights and the tabloids.

With no telltale racial or religious divide, the enemy will infiltrate all walks of your daily life. Every other cabbie, barman, shop assistant, neighbour, or tradesman who comes to your house will support the other lot and have a mini-kit hanging in his rear window just to annoy you. A cup final appearance will have red or white flags sprouting from the most unlikely places. White or red ribbons will decorate every other car aerial. Daubed sheets will suddenly be draped from the windows of a neighbour you thought you'd known intimately for twenty years.

Hence the rivalry. Not the contrived rivalry where you are adopted by another team to be their chosen rivals for geographical expediency. But the genuine 'enemy in the camp' rivalry that compels you to ridicule or be ridiculed. The French have a phrase for it – *les frères ennemies:* brothers in conflict.

'Monday was not Monday at school,' recalls Arsenal vice-chairman David Dein, 'if you couldn't rib the non-Arsenal fans about their results. Particularly if Arsenal won and Spurs lost. That set the week up. Maths, geography and history paled into insignificance.'

Although on the other side, Daniel Stern agrees with David Dein. Perhaps it is their common background of north-west London grammar schools and youth clubs, albeit

Dream On

a generation apart. Like his father and younger brother, Daniel is a Spurs season-ticket holder and shareholder. Allegiances in this part of town are decided at birth. Bizarrely not in the case of one of Tottenham's most famous fans, Morris Keston, who explains, 'When I first went to Tottenham during the war they shared a ground [White Hart Lane] with Arsenal. If I'd gone the week Arsenal played I'd have been an Arsenal fan but I had to go the week Tottenham played so I became a Spurs fan.' But then there were no football traditions to be passed down to young Morris, unlike the inheritance in the Dein and Stern families.

'I remember being at school in the early 1980s,' recalls Daniel Stern. 'We [Spurs] were actually doing quite well. But then in Sixth Form college Arsenal started taking over, and I got all the abuse. And that's when I started thinking that football is everything, and that your team has got to win on a Saturday. And if they don't, your life is miserable at school until the next week when the team has a chance to put things right.

'As you get older, you realise it's only a game. But you don't lose your affiliation to your team. I think people who may change their affiliation to follow a team that has just started winning – they can't understand the game. Because I love Spurs more than I love football. Unless a match has any real interest concerning Spurs – like Arsenal who I would always want to lose, every time without question – then there's no link for me. I am first and foremost a Spurs fan, and then a football fan. I don't feel the same passion when I watch England. For me, if England win, then great. But I would never go and watch them.

'I think you build up your affiliation when you are known as a football fan as a child. When you are at school, and you

Love Thy Neighbour

are known as "the guy who goes to Spurs", when Spurs lose, you're the one who gets the grief. But when Spurs win, you're the one who comes in wearing your Spurs shirt and lets everyone know how happy you are.

'But now, I'm more realistic. There are only three trophies to be won each season, and so the other 89 teams aren't going to win anything. And after having been so many years with Spurs winning so little, you become resigned to the fact that you don't win something every year. After our success in the early eighties – going to Wembley seven times in my first two seasons with a season ticket – when we stopped going to Wembley, it was "Why? Why aren't we going to Wembley? Why aren't we in the cup final this year?"'

Morris Keston has cultivated many friendships with both players and officials at the club, and tells a story that nicely illustrates the lengths some people will go in the Arsenal-Tottenham game of one-upmanship.

Through his long-standing friendship with Terry Venables, Keston had got to know George Graham when he was an Arsenal player. Keston would often run into Graham, particularly when Arsenal were due to meet Spurs. It appeared that whenever Graham saw Keston before a derby game, Arsenal went on to win. The two began to believe that maybe their meetings were not simply coincidental, but harbingers of fate. Thus when the two teams were scheduled to meet, George Graham would make a point of seeking out Keston – his lucky omen. Keston in turn would take evasive action, thinking that Spurs' chances of success depended on his avoiding the Arsenal man before the game. On the eve of one derby match, Keston thought his team were safe as he had successfully avoided Graham over the preceding days. However, late on Friday evening, the doorbell rang at Keston's flat. It was George Graham.

Dream On

Ignoring the protests of Keston's wife, Graham began to systematically search the flat, eventually coming to a locked door, the toilet. Graham stood upon a chair and knocked on the glass above the door. Keston looked up in amazement to see the grinning face, thus sealing his team's fate.

'I've seen you,' shouted Graham. 'Now we will win tomorrow.' Which of course Arsenal did.

Most fans will be able to tell similar tales, albeit with less celebrated protagonists. It is no use taking a holier-than-thou attitude by refusing to cast the first stone. Defeat in the derby game means social hell for those losing fans, with salvation only coming from a victory in the return fixture.

A historian will tell you that the rivalry dates back to 1913, when south London Arsenal moved their base across the river from Woolwich to Highbury, encroaching on Tottenham's north London territory. Six years later, in 1919, that insult was compounded when the league programme was resumed after the suspension forced by the First World War. Tottenham had finished bottom of the First Division and were scheduled for relegation. However, as the division was about to expand from twenty to 22 clubs, their place in the top flight looked safe, as it was decided that no clubs would go down and the top two in the second division would simply be promoted to make up the requisite numbers. What actually transpired however was that strings were pulled and favours called in, resulting in Arsenal, who had finished only sixth in Division Two, being promoted to replace the relegated Spurs in the top flight. With Alan Sugar still but a twinkle in his father's eye, the decision remained uncontested.

Although Spurs bounced back with a vengeance, winning the Division Two championship the following season, and

Love Thy Neighbour

the FA Cup the year after that, the next 30 years saw Arsenal make all the headlines while Spurs were relegated twice more. Arsenal became arguably the world's most famous club side, as they won the First Division championship in 1931, 1933, 1934, 1935, 1938, 1948, 1953 and the FA Cup in 1930, 1936 and 1950.

Tottenham's Double at the start of the Sixties established them as north London's top dogs for the rest of the decade. It was an exceptional team that transcended parochial boundaries, and it also gave birth to the media's ambivalent love affair with Spurs, going into ecstacies about the attacking style of play. Thus, even when Arsenal were galvanised under Bertie Mee to emulate Tottenham's success with a Double of their own in 1971, the acclaim they received was muted and grudging by comparison. Poor unloved Arsenal had to win the 1971 FA Cup after being drawn away in every round, and coming from behind in both the semi-final and the final. They played 64 matches that season – clinching the championship with a win at White Hart Lane in the final game – and yet were still able to beat Liverpool – a team that had conceded only one Cup goal and 24 league goals all campaign – in extra time. That their success was achieved by grinding out results through hard work, team spirit and the cautious tactics of Don Howe (suited to a team of competent pros laced with the odd wild-card flair player) should not detract from their triumph. The Gunners' achievements, though, were not assessed on face value but instead compared unfavourably to the cavalier style in which Spurs had swept the board a decade earlier. No team could have stood that comparison.

Arsenal fans then and now resent the lack of respect for what was after all a pretty astounding achievement. All the more so since it came after almost seventeen barren years.

Dream On

Instead of 'brilliant Arsenal', the tag 'boring Arsenal' was coined to accompany 'lucky Arsenal', bestowed out of envy because of the club's phenomenal pre-war success. If the modern Arsenal was born in that Double season, then 'boring Arsenal' is the birthmark it must always carry.

Amy Lawrence has been an Arsenal fan since the age of six. Twenty years older, she has been fortunate enough to make a career out of her passion. After cutting her teeth on the Arsenal fanzine, *The Gooner*, she is now an established football writer and assistant editor on the football magazine *FourFourTwo*.

'When you support a club like Arsenal,' says Amy, 'it's more than just a relationship. It's like you take on the family. You take on the club, you take on the players. You develop relationships with players past and present. You take on the history, you take on the personality of your club which you have to defend. And you have to represent it to people and it becomes a part of you. When I meet someone and they ask who I support, and I say Arsenal, they get an impression of me because of that. And secondly, being an Arsenal fan, you tend to find you actually have to defend yourself for it. So there's an extra element of pride, of defiance – you have chosen to link yourself with this quite pictorial beast. People have opinions about it – almost everyone who knows about football will make a judgement about you because of your links with Arsenal. If you said you were a Coventry fan or a West Ham fan, people would just say "Oh really?" There are only a handful of clubs about which people have such really fixed ideas. Arsenal is one, perhaps Millwall is another . . . Manchester United, and Glasgow Rangers in Scotland.'

Success at one club will always be qualified or enhanced by the degree of failure at the other. Thus did the years of

Love Thy Neighbour

1987 and 1988 set the pattern for the years to follow. When George Graham was appointed manager at Highbury, and his mate Terry Venables took over at White Hart Lane, it was to signal a period of almost total domination of Arsenal over Spurs and was perhaps the catalyst for much of the ill-feeling that permeates today.

Spurs and Arsenal were drawn together in the two-legged League Cup semi-final. Under David Pleat, Spurs had perfected a pattern of play that appeared to satisfy their dual objective of success with style. An all-star five-man midfield, with Clive Allen as lone striker, saw Spurs win 1-0 at Highbury in the first leg. Three weeks later, in the return at White Hart Lane, Clive Allen again scored to put Spurs 2-0 ahead on aggregate. As any Spurs fan will testify, this is a dangerous position for their club to find themselves, particularly when playing against the old enemy. Sure enough, Arsenal were able to score twice and send the tie into a third deciding game for the right to meet Liverpool in the final.

The omens were bad when Spurs won the toss for the right to host the match, and the omens deteriorated further when Clive Allen again put Spurs in front. The half-time PA announcing how Cup Final tickets would be allocated for Spurs fans was also an ill-judged move. Just as the only way to beat Arsenal is to leave your scoring so late that they have no time for a reply, so the best way to beat Spurs is to allow them an early goal and all the time in the world to fall prey to complacency.

So it was that two late, late goals broke Spurs' hearts and took Arsenal to Wembley. The champagne that Irving Scholar had put on ice in anticipation of a home victory was generously redirected to the away dressing room; a magnanimous gesture given that the Spurs chairman felt

Dream On

the pain of defeat every bit as much as those fans who fought up and down the High Road late into the night.

David Dein was touched by the gift. 'Irving, you're a good loser,' he said to his friend in admiration. 'I've had a lot of practice,' was the reply.

'They were probably the most nerve-wracking, exciting, tense matches between the two clubs that I can remember,' confesses the Arsenal vice-chairman. 'I'd like to think they were enjoyable, but in truth I cannot remember truthfully enjoying any Arsenal-Spurs game. There is too much tension, too much at stake. In a way it's almost painful. It is masochism. It is pain and pleasure combined.'

To Spurs fans, the fact that Arsenal went on to beat Liverpool in the final was of minor irritation. It was those two home defeats (three if you count that season's league match), and particularly the manner of the defeats, that really hurt.

The opportunity for revenge was presented and taken when the two sides met at Wembley in a 1991 FA Cup semi-final. A 3-1 Spurs win prevented a possible Arsenal double. Such was the superiority enjoyed over Spurs until then, that the Arsenal supporters filed out of the stadium in shocked silence. It was to be the highlight of Terry Venables' reign at the club, eclipsing even the cup final win over Forest five weeks later. To this day, many Spurs fans will cite that win over Arsenal as the highlight of their Spurs-supporting life.

When the fixture was reprised in 1993, it was Arsenal's turn to upset the form book, beating Spurs 1-0 with a Tony Adams header. The game had a curiously unsatisfactory air to its outcome; the result neither lifting Arsenal fans to the heights enjoyed by their rivals in 1991, nor quite serving to erase their misery of that earlier defeat.

Love Thy Neighbour

Amy Lawrence vividly recalls that game: 'I remember particularly arriving outside Wembley. Perhaps because we'd seen it all before in 1991, we weren't so nervous or excited and people weren't so bitter. But second time around everyone knew what it was all about. Arsenal were obviously going there looking for revenge, while Spurs were cock-a-hoop thinking "we've done this before and we can do it again". But the atmosphere outside Wembley for the hour or so leading up to the game was despicable. It was so unpleasant it actually tarnished the game for me. I couldn't even enjoy the game because I was so tensed up by what I'd seen outside the ground. It was absolutely horrible the way people were insulting one another just walking down Wembley Way; the aggression in people's eyes, people pointing at one another and inciting trouble with all that false bravado.

'I was with my family – something I don't generally do. I remember a gang of Tottenham fans trying to piss against the car and being really aggressive. I've seen it before and can deal with it, but my family were horrified. I ended up feeling guilty about it and trying to defend football – the "beautiful game". But it seemed anything but beautiful.

'I believe it's not the most glamorous of derbies. People will talk about Manchester derbies, or those in Glasgow or Liverpool [where much is made of the fans' ability to mix and mingle without segregation], and only then the north London derby. Perhaps that's because there are so many different types of London derby that it is diluted a bit. But I've been to quite a lot of derbies, those in Manchester and Liverpool and so on, and in my mind, none is as bitter or as full of hatred at Arsenal-Spurs. Particularly in the last three or four years when it has got worse. People seem to feel things in these

Dream On

games that they don't normally feel in their life. Things bubble up.

'In a sense, you can compare it to the Cantona thing. For 99% of the time he's a volatile character but he'd have his great times and he'd have his bad times, but he dealt with situations. He'd be a bit on the edge, but he'd be all right. And then he flipped. It got too much. And I think Arsenal-Spurs games, to their respective fans, are the same. The fans go to other games, and win or lose, there is always this edginess about football, but they cope. But there is an underlying – almost animal thing – inside, and it erupts at Arsenal-Tottenham games. You snap, and you become the lowest common denominator. I am least proud of myself and my excesses as a supporter at an Arsenal-Tottenham game. It is almost like an instinct.

'But I must stress that I am only talking about the 90 minutes of an Arsenal-Spurs game. Outside of that, I've got pals who are Tottenham fans who are very, very close friends. This worst aspect of ourselves only really emerges during the game.'

Like Spurs in 1991, Arsenal went on from the derby semi-final to win the Cup, but easily eclipsed their rivals by lifting the European Cup Winners Cup the following year. Spurs entered a period of scandal, disgrace and management upheaval.

Under managers George Graham and Ossie Ardiles, the characteristics of the two clubs became almost polarised. With six trophies in eight years, Arsenal began to out-distance Spurs to an embarrassing extent. Indeed it could be argued that if Graham had not left in disgrace, and instead taken Arsenal to a third championship and a sub-sequent Champions League place, there would have been

Love Thy Neighbour

a Manchester United/City syndrome where one club is practically beyond the reach of the other . . . for ever.

Arsenal season-ticket holder Harry Lansdown is tall, slim and fair-headed, and enjoys an unusual thrill for any football supporter: he bears an uncanny resemblance to his team's most expensive ever signing. In August, a middle-aged Chinese man in a take-away, situated in a rather insalubrious road called Tollington Way N7, almost collapsed in a fit of excitement when Harry strolled in. He believed the Dutch international superstar Dennis Bergkamp was asking him to fry up some prawn crackers. Harry owned up to his true identity, but did not have the heart to speculate out loud as to whether the real Bergkamp would ever consider hanging out at such an establishment. Still, he was granted a free meal when Dennis finally broke his goal-scoring duck, and he was recently given a t-shirt by his friends with the unique lines: *There's a guy works down the Chinese who swears I'm Dennis Bergkamp.*

In another life he helped produce the acclaimed BBC2 historical football series *Kicking & Screaming*. Harry is convinced that Tottenham's problems have no quick fix.

'I don't know what is wrong at that club, but something is deeply wrong. There seems to be some inner mental strength lacking. I don't think any Arsenal fan, for all the frustrations we sometimes have, would want to swap with Spurs – you know, pretty football and no success. To us it was summed up in the semi-final against Everton. That was the year everyone said Tottenham's name was on the cup after they'd played really well at Anfield in the sixth round. Then they go up to Elland Road and it was like men against boys. They were hustled out of it because Everton wanted it more. You would *never* see an Arsenal team in a semi-final go down like that. You may see an Arsenal team outclassed, but not outfought. And to lose 4-1 ... when have you ever heard of a team losing 4-1 in an FA Cup semi-final whey they're both from the same division? That was the most disgraceful performance I have seen in a long while, and that is why I wouldn't want to support Tottenham. You never know on the big games if they are going to bottle it.

'Arsenal are the only London side who win anything. You know when Spurs last won the championship? The Beatles hadn't even been *formed!* Bill Haley was Number One in the charts. We're the only London side who can take on the north; the north thinks London football is a joke, the only team they fear is Arsenal.'

John Harris rivals Morris Keston in his allegiance to Tottenham. Coming from a family where both father and grandfather were Spurs fans, John's memories stretch back to the mid-Fifties. He agrees with Harry on Arsenal's special status but feels that they have blown it in spectacular fashion.

'Arsenal have always, in every way, been a better club. Until Mr Graham came along and completely ruined everything they ever stood for, and reduced them to rubbish. Here was a club that had values. But they weren't in such a rush to get rid of Graham. If there had been a way of keeping George Graham as manager, they would have done so in spite of what had gone on. If you were working for a firm, and you took a thousand pounds out of the petty cash book, the police would be called in and you wouldn't have been allowed back to clear your desk.'

For 1995/96, Arsenal with a new manager, Bruce Rioch, were once again muscling in on traditional Tottenham territory. This time it wasn't geographical encroachment but rather the wholehearted adoption of the 'success through style' ethic that Spurs had pioneered 35 years previously. With purse strings not so much loosened as slashed, Arsenal spent more on one player – and a Tottenham-type player at that – than they had ever spent before. The pre-season purchase of Dennis Bergkamp, an exciting but erratic attacker, was a classic Tottenham ploy. They had spent heavily against anticipated success. It was Arsenal drawing a thick line under everything that had gone before. The 'boring' tag, the spendthrift policies, the sterile football, the siege mentality and, most of all, the recent George Graham 'bungs' scandal were all consigned to the history books as the Arsenal board finally gave their fans what they had been clamouring for all along. They turned them into Tottenham.

The real Tottenham, meanwhile, were quietly turning into Arsenal.

According to Amy Lawrence, 'Convention dictates that the image of Arsenal is staid, dour, organised, while Tottenham is flair, excitement, slightly reckless, beautiful, poetic. I find that interesting because being who I am as a person, those perceived Tottenham attributes are the kind of things I go for in life. And yet I chose Arsenal.

'Arsenal have always got more heart, more determination than Spurs. Another convention, maybe true, maybe not . . . but the theory is that Spurs are a bit more flippant; either they'll be great or they will get stuffed. Arsenal . . . they'll keep going, they'll never give up. They've got more spirit than Spurs. According to convention anyway.'

Whilst understanding what makes the two clubs so different, Amy Lawrence was also shrewd enough to realise that it was only precedent, that could be radically altered if the manager was strong and clear-sighted enough.

Dream On

Manager Gerry Francis had no Spurs pedigree to cloud his decision-making process; his brief was solely to bring stability to White Hart Lane. His chosen route was that used to great effect by successive Arsenal managers; organisation became paramount. The team attacked as a unit and defended as a unit, with nine men behind the ball if (and frequently when) necessary. With no creative playmakers as characterised by the likes of Hoddle, Waddle and Gascoigne, the ball was frequently hit over – rather than through – the midfield. To the White Hart Lane fans, such tactics were anathema and contravened the very spirit of the game. But when they brought results, well maybe a little fence-sitting was in order before the placards came out.

Equally, Alan Sugar had no qualms about the route Francis might choose to take. Success through whichever course chosen would be welcome. However, Sugar's acquired business acumen forbade him from sanctioning the kind of spending he viewed as profligate, and thus while Arsenal bought proven quality in Bergkamp and David Platt, Spurs refused to pay the going rate for top quality. Chris Armstrong and Ruel Fox represented gambles – could they do more for the new club than they had done for their old one? At a combined price in excess of £8 million they illustrated well the inflated price of buying a Premiership lottery ticket.

Spurs fan Daniel Stern only partly agrees: 'Now that I accept only three teams can win anything in a season, I'd like to see Spurs play good entertaining football, like last season. We had a good cup run and finished seventh in the league; it was a very enjoyable season. We didn't win anything but all the games were sold out and I would say it was a good exciting season.

'The trouble at Spurs now is that they are not a big club.

Love Thy Neighbour

They don't spend the money the other clubs do. That isn't necessarily bad as I feel that paying £5 million for a player is absolutely insane, and we have now twice paid over £4 million for what I consider to be very average players. I think the whole thing has gone totally crazy, but it will calm down.'

For both sets of fans, this was one game where the performance was of secondary importance to the result. Nothing less than a win would suffice. Any long-term strategies and lofty, idealistic principles could safely be laid to one side for an afternoon of blood and thunder mayhem. Frank McGee in the *Observer* succinctly set the scene: 'Arsenal versus Tottenham is like no other derby match in any of the great soccer centres of Britain. It is not based on the sectarian barbarism of Glasgow; it lacks the bitter jealousy of Manchester City's bids to catch up again with United; there is none of the internecine strife which splits families on Merseyside. It is more like neighbours who detest one another so much, for reasons long forgotten, that getting one up on the other lot makes a fan's day.'

'I don't like the local derby,' confesses Harry Lansdown. 'I think there is too much hatred and I don't like it. It's artificial. I think that we are all north London boys at the end of the day. What I mean by that – and it may sound a bit snobbish – is that compared to the rest of the country we're basically more cosmopolitan. There's less racism. It's not as tribal as it is in the north. We get criticised by northern clubs for a lack of passion, but football is not our whole life – we have other things in our lives. We are not Sunderland fans.

'What that means is we should be able to go to the game, really want to win, enjoy lots of piss-taking, lots of jokes about Nayim or not winning the league. But that

Dream On

should be where it stops. I don't like the atmosphere in the ground at those games. Too much hatred. Spurs have become obsessed by Arsenal. They threw a whisky bottle at Ian Wright in the last game. I read their fanzine and to be honest there is more about Arsenal than Tottenham. And I look at people who write that stuff and think, "Get a life".

'I think the players ought to make more of an effort. I think Ian Wright and Gary Mabbutt, or whoever, should make comments in the programme. They should come out on the pitch and say, "Look we don't want all this hatred – it's getting out of hand". Because sooner or later there is going to be this *massive* fight at Arsenal-Tottenham. At the last game at Highbury, it was 1-1. But if Ian Wright had scored in the last minutes it would have all gone off. The Clock End – Spurs – would have all come on the pitch and there would have been a pitched battle. If something isn't done about it soon, that's going to happen. It's unnatural. It's like that nasty Liverpool-Man. United thing. All this talk in the Spurs fanzines of calling the Arsenal "The scum" . . . fanzines were born out of Heysel and they should remember that.'

Actual expectations for the match differed between the two camps. Perhaps due to the consistent success enjoyed in recent years, the Arsenal fans had come to place less importance on beating their north London rivals. Their team were still title contenders, starting the season at odds of 6-1 to land the championship. Spurs were just another team to be overcome in that quest, a distant 33-1 for the title (and with the year failing to end in a '1' could not even be expected to lift a cup). Spurs were perceived as having already been outmanoeuvred both on and off the pitch. It would be irritating to lose to them, but a minor hiccup in the scheme of things. Life would go on.

Love Thy Neighbour

Harry Lansdown is scathing in his dismissal of Spurs, but probably representative of what many are thinking.

'Historically, there are only three teams who ever win anything, who consistently win trophies: Liverpool, Manchester United and Arsenal. Covering the last fifteen years or so, through the Eighties and into the Nineties, everyone else is left standing with maybe one trophy.

'I always felt there was a special role for Spurs; they were glam. They were great at attacking but they couldn't really defend. But you really didn't care, and you could feel special about them.

'I think West Ham had that as well in a similar way, with their "academy". But West Ham have lost it completely – they are just an ordinary struggling club now. But I think Spurs too have lost their "specialness". They barely come up in conversation any more. I feel Newcastle have taken their place as that glam, attacking club who maybe won't be that consistent. In the same way, Forest have maybe taken West Ham's place as that special footballing club that does well in Europe and everyone quite likes them. But Spurs have become merely competent – and that's their worst nightmare.

'If Spurs beat us, that will be the highlight of their season. But if Arsenal win, that won't be the highlight of ours. Because God knows what could happen to us this season. We've already beaten Manchester United – which Spurs certainly won't do. So to us it's a big game, but to them, it's a huge game. Winning for them would be like their championship, because it's so rare that they beat us. And for the first time in a couple of years, we are going there still in the title race.'

Warming to the topic, Harry takes a further swipe at the new Tottenham policies.

Dream On

'Tottenham are messing about in the transfer market, buying reject players. Once again, everything is on the FA Cup. It always is for them. They never seem to get in Europe any more; the last time they came up against Feyenoord and couldn't score in either game . . .

'I used to think that they were as big a club as us, but I think we've gone ahead of them now. If Arsenal win the league in the next two or three years, and get into the Champions League, then we've just left them behind. That's what I'd really like. Then we could start liking them. That would be terrific.'

For Spurs fans, the inferiority complex inherited from the barren Venables years placed an irrational importance on beating the team now, according to age and upbringing, referred to as 'The scum', 'Gooners' or 'the Arsenal'. Indeed for many, the rivalry of late has degenerated into an almost paranoid hatred, giving recent fixtures a gladiatorial atmosphere. Certainly for Spurs fans, a preoccupation with how Arsenal have fared can overshadow even their own team's achievements. 'How did that lot get on?' is the almost frantic whisper heard as the crowds stream away from White Hart Lane. A convincing Spurs home win can have the gloss taken off in seconds at the news of an Arsenal away success.

Many Spurs fans probably share Morris Keston's enigmatic feelings: 'I don't hate Arsenal fans but I hate the Arsenal. Nobody told me [as a Tottenham fan] that I had to. It just develops. Over the years I've had many good friends among the Arsenal players and managers but you just don't want them to win.'

It is hard to find an Arsenal fan who enjoys the annual visit to White Hart Lane. While Spurs fans will eagerly await the Highbury fixture, their counterparts actively dislike both

Love Thy Neighbour

Tottenham's ground and its seedy environs, drawing unfavourable comparisons with the new-look Arsenal Stadium and the comparative affluence of Highbury and Islington.

Amy Lawrence is unabashed about her dislike of White Hart Lane. 'I go to Spurs once a year, to watch Arsenal. As a journalist, I certainly ought to go to Spurs a lot more; I ought to watch visiting teams at Spurs. The other day I toyed with the idea of going to see Newcastle at Spurs, and I just thought in the end . . . "Aw, I just don't want to go to White Hart Lane! I can't face going there twice in one month". When one goes to White Hart Lane, you want to get out of there as quickly as possible. Amy recognises the dilemma her role as a journalist brings. Frequent visits to Tottenham are increasingly an occupational necessity but emotional tribal convictions have a far deeper hold that are difficult to shake off.

want to get out, to get back home.

'I even live in Highbury now. Was it a deliberate choice? You can view it whichever way you will – I love living there. It was definitely one of the places I was trying to get somewhere to live. With all due respect, if I was a Tottenham fan I wouldn't particularly want to live in Tottenham because I don't like the area, but I do like Highbury.'

Since the development of the Clock End, and more recently the North Bank, Arsenal Stadium is indeed a ground with a feel-good factor in which the home supporters can take much pride. The twinned East and West stands are hopelessly outdated, but still serve their purpose better than Tottenham's much more recently rebuilt East Stand. The Clock End suffers, as do most pre-Taylor stands, from being designed as standing terracing and then having to endure enforced seating. But against all odds, it is the new North Bank stand that has most won

Dream On

the hearts of true Gooners. It fulfils its function on every level – capacity, facilities, aesthetics – and all controversy over the demolition of the terracing and the debenture bond financing of the new structure has receded into the background.

From Arsenal's point of view, the Stadium's only drawback is the capacity of barely 39,000. Every home game is a sell-out and there is no doubt that the potential audience is far greater than that which it can currently satisfy. The same problem is also faced at White Hart Lane. A capacity of just 33,000 is simply not enough in an age when the purchase of one star player can account for an entire season's gate revenue.

For the derby game, Arsenal were allocated just 4,000 seats, occupying the south-west corner of the new Park Lane stand. It would give the visitors an early chance to compare facilities. Thankfully, they would be in no position to judge the new stand on looks alone, for it comes a very poor second to the stylish North Bank.

To assuage the disappointment of the ticketless, Arsenal would be showing the game live at Highbury on their giant video screens. A further 8,000 fans would therefore be rooting for the Gunners, further proof, if ever it was needed, of the potential audience for the game. The fact that each of those proxy Arsenal fans had to pay £10 for the pleasure of watching the transmission pointed up yet another area where fans can, and surely will continue to, be exploited. Is it naïve to wish that in these circumstances, a club would charge no more than necessary to cover their costs? Probably.

Harry Lansdown was one of those fans without a ticket, although he had been offered a pair at £100 for the Arsenal section. He had politely declined the offer, preferring to

Love Thy Neighbour

save the money in anticipation of a celebratory post-match meal.

'Although,' adds Harry, 'I have to say, there is no better feeling than coming out of Tottenham, and driving back down the Seven Sisters Road, away from all the rough parts, to arrive back at the much nicer Islington. All the Arsenal cars have their flags and scarves and banners out and are hooting away. You are arriving back in "your" part of London. The worst thing about losing to Spurs is that where I live, Finsbury Park – Stroud Green Road – you never see Tottenham cars. But if we lose the derby on Saturday, then believe it or not, on Sunday they'll all come down from Enfield and Edmonton in their Vauxhall Novas, driving about in their blue and white, hooting. So if we lose I'll stay at my girlfriend's to avoid all that.'

For Bruce Rioch, it would be his first north London derby, although he was no stranger to Birmingham, Liverpool and even England-Scotland clashes. For Ian Wright, however, yet another suspension would mean his missing the game; a major blow to Rioch's preparation.

'I think so far Rioch has done everything right,' was the view put forward by Harry Lansdown. 'He's only bought two players, which is good, and he has only bought really good players. I think Rioch has the sense to know that David Platt is going to get goals – he just is. And he took a chance on Bergkamp. Rioch probably thought that Bergkamp is such a star that even if it didn't work out, he could sell him on. And besides, he knew enough to know that Bergkamp would find the space he wouldn't find in Italy. After not scoring for six games, he's now got seven in nine games. Plus his all round effect on the club has been huge. Psychologically it has been huge. You feel good going to Spurs with him in the side.

Dream On

'Everyone knows about the Ajax setup, and knows that's where Bergkamp is from. So you have a real pride in that as well. And he's a big match player, scoring in the big games when you need him. He scored against Manchester United. He scored at Elland Road. He always scores for Holland against England when it's needed. So I'm hoping that he'll score against Spurs. Because he knows it's a big game. And if he's wound up, that's good, because his one fault is that he's sometimes a little laid back because he is so good. All I can say is that he's better than I thought he'd be. Different, but better.'

But worth the £7.5 million that Arsenal spent on him?

'Yes, because it wasn't my money. Suppose he had only cost £5.5 million? I wouldn't be enjoying the fruits of that £2 million saved. I don't care what he earns or what they paid for him, as long as he plays well. What I don't want is for the club to buy Jimmy Carters for half a million.

'You know the Spurs fans are going to be looking jealously at Bergkamp every time he gets the ball. It's really up to Bergkamp – the whole game revolves around him as far as I'm concerned. If he has a good game, then he can run the game. What are Mabbutt and Sol Campbell going to do? They are not going to be able to cope with him. If he has a good game, then everything will flow from him. If he doesn't, then it will probably be a draw. Either way, I can't see Spurs beating us.

'Sheringham will be knackered after the England v Switzerland game on Wednesday. It's just a shame that Ian Wright is suspended and misses the match.

'You know, Ian Wright did a funny thing which I don't think he'll do at White Hart Lane because it would cause a fight, and it nearly caused a fight at Palace. We went to see Palace play Arsenal last season ['94/'95], and Wright was again suspended. It was quite boring – but we were playing quite well and were 2-0 up when suddenly the Arsenal section went barmy, absolutely barmy. Everyone started singing, "Ian Wright, Wright, Wright."

'We were all looking around wondering what was going on, when suddenly he stood up – he was right in the middle of the Arsenal fans – and waved. The only player I've ever known do that. Surrounded by family and minders he was. The Palace fans went beserk! They all started going "Judas! Judas!" It could have caused a riot, but it was a great gesture. It would be brilliant if he did that at Tottenham, but I don't think he'd have the nerve to. But then you never know . . .'

The fervour on the terraces was unlikely to be matched by the players, despite the clichéd rhetoric trotted out on such occasions. Gerry Francis and his squad had prepared for the match with their usual behind-closed-doors policy that excludes press and public from their training sessions. Arsenal on the other hand offered a lesson in accessibility, holding open house for the media in recognition of their role in the proceedings.

Manager Bruce Rioch was looking forward to meeting up with two of his old boys – both Sheringham and Armstrong had played under Rioch at Millwall. In fact Rioch had sold Sheringham to Forest for £2 million in July 1991, replacing him with £75,000 budget-buy Chris Armstrong a month later.

Arsenal captain Tony Adams was a veteran of numerous derby games, and knew the party line the fans wanted to hear: 'Tottenham-Arsenal games are the big fixtures in the calendar. Everyone I know looks at the fixture list at the beginning of the season to see when you are playing Tottenham. It's a big game. It's like when you are going to play Man. United or Blackburn.'

Dream On

For the team, playing Tottenham may indeed be like playing Man. Utd or Blackburn, but that observation hinted at a failure to realise exactly what the derby meant to the fans. Defeat at the hands of Man. Utd or Blackburn, former and current Premiership champions, could be excused or forgotten in the space of the journey home. Not so defeat at the hands of Spurs.

'They are high profile games,' confirms David Dein. 'We have to mount enormous security at Highbury. There is always damage done to the ground by Spurs fans [the toilets in the newly seated Clock End were trashed by Spurs fans on the day the stand was opened two seasons ago]. That is the game where we are all on Red Alert. It is the most high profile game of the season. Our policing, our stewarding has to be top notch.

'In a way, speaking as an administrator, a draw is the best result. Because then you know both sets of fans go home with honours shared. As an administrator, I know that if either side wins, there will be retribution from the other side. Always. By and large it's under control in the stadiums. But who knows what goes on at Kings Cross station or Highbury Fields? There are problems.'

Of course as professionals, it would be quite right that each game ought to be treated as important as the next, every game is a cup final, the only important game is the next one blah blah blah. But the fans would still like to believe that in each of their heroes there is a heart that beats faster on derby day. Given that of the 22 players in the starting line-up, only four – Sol Campbell, Teddy Sheringham, Tony Adams and Paul Merson – are native Londoners, that may be a little optimistic. Still, Adams tried to sound convincing: 'Some of my best pals are Tottenham supporters,' he ventured. 'We've not done bad over the past

Love Thy Neighbour

few years at White Hart Lane. It will be tight again this time. There is an abundance of talent on show. Hopefully it will be entertaining with an Arsenal victory, although sometimes the skill factor suffers in derbies because of the blood and guts. It's always a special feeling going to White Hart Lane.'

This was more encouraging.

'I remember the League Cup semi-final success in 1987. Because that came early in my career, it left a strong memory that always comes back whenever I play at White Hart Lane. It's like playing at Anfield. After we won the championship there [in 1989], it's always a special feeling.'

Perhaps it is best left to Arsenal's other Londoner to definitively sum up what is so special about derby day. Is the Spurs game really any different?

'Yeah, I believe so. It is a big game. It is one game ... well you can't afford to lose any game, but you know ... this is the fans' game as well. But, yeah I look at it as the biggest game. You know, it is big. Big.'

But do you approach it any differently to other games?

'No, it's just the same you know. It's the boss's first one, so, you know, we just approach it as the same but all the players know, you know, how important, but as I say, every game is important, but, this one does just stick out as something special.'

Do you, like Tony Adams, have a lot of Tottenham-supporting friends?

'No, not really. No, it's not because, I, you know, I don't come from that side of London, so no, I haven't got any. They are mainly Arsenal and Chelsea fans.'

So is it important to them?

'Yeah, course, yeah, it is, very. You know. You see the

Dream On

passion tomorrow with the fans, and it is important with the fans. It spoils their weekend you know.'

Speaking the day before the match, were there any special pre-match rituals for this game?

'For me? Well now I'll go to Waitrose and get the dinner. I'll go home, cook the dinner and just relax for the rest of the evening and just get ready for the game and eat the right foods.'

The right foods?

'Loads of pasta and Jelly Babies. We've been told to eat 'em. We had a dietician in not long ago who said Jelly Babies are good for you. I don't even like them but if someone tells me they're good for you, then they're good for you.

'I'll go to bed about 11 o'clock. I'll get up about 9 o'clock tomorrow morning. Glen Helder will pick me up and we'll go for a pre-match meal [at a golf club in Barnet; the regular venue for London games]. I'll have something like spaghetti on toast. Some breakfast like cereal with banana on top. And then just relax and watch telly, then we get the police escort to the game.'

And afterwards?

'If we win, I'll be in the Players' Lounge. I don't usually go in a lot of players' lounges anyway. So even if we win – even when we win – not if, when, I won't go in. But yeah, it's big.'

So there you have it: it's a big game.

A big game with racial overtones according to many. Not the usual problem with idiots abusing the black players. Thankfully, that particular brand of hooliganism has been virtually eradicated. Although not entirely, as Arsenal, and Ian Wright in particular, found out when the latter was mercilessly abused by visiting fans during a recent

Jurgen Klinsmann, he came, he saw, he conquered *(Above)*

Chris Armstrong, £4.5 million potential and not all of it wasted *(Below)*

Head and shoulders above Arsenal – Gary Mabbutt a fan's
man, a player's man (*Above*)

Alan Sugar, master of all he surveys (*Below*)

John Fenelly
(Tottenham Press Officer)
and Gerry Francis.
Just what
the manager ordered,
another press call
(Above)

Tottenham directors Tony
Berry (left) and
Douglas Alexiou
emerging from the
Law Courts with
something to smile about
(Left)

Ian Walker –
Tottenham's future
in his hands
(Above)

Erik Thortsvedt
in happier days
(Left)

Bergkamp
shows how its done,
despite the attention of
Howells and Dozzell
(Above)

Ilie Dumitrescu
– right man wrong time
(Left)

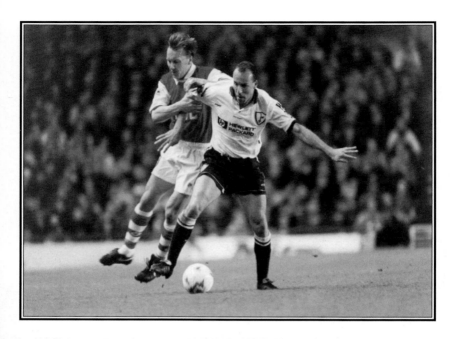

Ronny Rosenthal – playing to the system *(Left)*

Sol Campbell – Tottenham's Mr Versatility
doing the business against Arsenal
(Bottom left)

A sight for sore eyes,
Darren Anderton in first team action
(Below)

'Stop Sheringham and you stop England'

Love Thy Neighbour

Coca-Cola Cup second leg fixture at Highbury.

'He scored a hat-trick here against Hartlepool,' remembers David Dein. 'They had a handful of spectators come down, probably less than 1,000 fans. But they were chanting "Get the nigger off the pitch." Shameful. He said, "What do I do about it?" I said we bring it to their chairman's attention. We say this is unacceptable behaviour. Say something to your fans. Sort them out.'

Amy Lawrence agrees it is despicable and points out that it doesn't just occur off the pitch. 'But then I also wish that people wouldn't abuse Ian Wright both on and off the pitch. I've seen instances where Wrighty might retaliate on the pitch for something someone has said to him. The crowd are asking themselves what he's playing at, risking a booking. But I know what he's doing. I know what that other player has been saying to him. If I was him, I would be the same, I can identify with that.'

So obviously can Tottenham's Clive Wilson, though he feels Ian Wright may be an unfortunate exception as, 'Most teams have a black player so it is difficult to say you black bastard and not mean your own team-mate. I can't say a player deliberately tries to wind you up.' There may be more tolerance today – 'I recall playing at Derby [at the start of his career], going to take a corner and being showered with bananas' – but Clive Wilson thinks there is still some way to go. 'Because we are footballers and we are black we seem to be more acceptable in certain circles. This is totally wrong. We've got to be acceptable because we are black, not because we are footballers.'

For Spurs, the problem is the misconception that most of their supporters are Jewish, and thus the club has become an easy target for every bonehead with a crew-cut who thinks that swastikas make good facial tattoos, that Hitler was one of the lads and that every problem from the Ozone Layer to the price of lager is down to a worldwide Jewish conspiracy.

Football grounds have long been a healthy recruitment source for right-wing organisations. Some clubs, like Leeds, Chelsea and West Ham, are traditionally notable aggressors, with active factions within their support who promote neo-Nazi activities. In truth, there are probably only a handful of individuals at each club, but they are able to exert a disproportionate amount of influence because the views they promote appear to offer plausible solutions to those not prepared to make their own minds up. It is a sad fact that there will be in any sizeable football crowd, perhaps several thousand supporters who see nothing wrong in chanting anti-Semitic abuse at Spurs fans; in hissing like escaping gas or, more commonly, to use the generic term of *Yiddo* to denigrate all Spurs fans.

Club officials and players are probably less aware of the extent to which this is prevalent than the supporters who travel away and encounter such treatment almost habitually. Even at places like Old Trafford, the headquarters of a plc as well as a football club, it is a deeply disturbing sight to witness the notorious K-stand, with hundreds of grown men, many with families, *Seig-Heiling* and hissing at visiting Spurs fans.

But it is the visit to Stamford Bridge that is the low point of most Spurs fans' season, knowing they will have to listen to endless choruses of 'The Jews are on their Way to Belsen' sung lustily to the tune of 'Ossie's on his way to Wembley'. Ironically, even at Arsenal where the fan base is surely no different to that at Spurs, the term *Yid* or *Yiddo* has been widely adopted as a convenient term of abuse for Tottenham supporters.

Love Thy Neighbour

'For me,' says Amy Lawrence, 'as an Arsenal supporter, that's the most difficult thing to come to terms with. In fact that's almost the only thing I actually feel embarrassed about in my association with Arsenal. Although I would say that in the majority of cases, the simple association in the heads of people singing "Yiddo" is that Tottenham equals Yiddos – they're not saying anything particularly against Jewish people.'

David Dein agrees. 'The shouts of "Yiddo" is a learned behaviour pattern. I'm not sure they know what they're saying. It's ignorance. The enmity stretches far back – it's local rivalry. I sit on the anti-racism committee. We do arrest people for racist behaviour. We want people to have a good time, to have fun, but within the confines of the law. Arsenal should be seen as a family and a fair club. We don't want antisocial behaviour. And anti-Semitism is antisocial. The big problem is that the police can't arrest 500 people at a time.'

Officially, clubs will always condemn any such behaviour from their fans, but there isn't a great deal they can do without more active support from the bulk of decent supporters who are equally appalled at such boorish behaviour. With club stewards increasingly replacing police officers inside grounds, a fan now has to commit a pretty offensive act before he stands the risk of reprimand, let alone ejection. Closed circuit TV may serve to pinpoint troublemakers, but when most stewards are virtually unpaid volunteers offering their time in exchange for a free match ticket, which of them is going to risk their neck by seeking to confront violent thugs? A dayglo vest carries little of the authority that a policeman's uniform commands, and assaulting a steward carries few of the penalties incurred by attacking a police officer.

Dream On

In addition, the advent of all-seater stadia has placed fans in the same seat for every game. The choice to move away or dissociate oneself from troublemakers has been removed. Equally, the option of publicly reporting louts to a steward carries hidden menace when that same gang of louts will be back in those same seats for subsequent games. Sometimes it really is easiest to just keep quiet and exchange raised eyebrows.

The players of course could set more of an example. After all, in Italy, France and Germany they had a special anti-racist day when players stood up and were counted. Even the sponsors sacrificed their shirt logos for a more important message. However, in England, it was left to Nike to produce a commercial featuring Eric Cantona and Les Ferdinand to do the PFA's work for them. The campaign *Kick Racism Out of Football* which was supported by all the football authorities, though worthy, was too little, too late. What was needed was a lot more than small ads in club programmes.

It's a sad fact that many English players are generally clueless about this sub-text to the game, as they are about most aspects of a supporter's life. When asked about his awareness of the racial overtones to the derby game, one Arsenal player confessed his ignorance:

'Er . . . no, not really. Sometimes I get a lot of stick from fans, then some are as good as gold.'

But they call Spurs fans Yiddos . . .

'Yeah . . .'

You don't think that is genuine racial hatred?

'Oh I don't get involved in that. I don't get involved in the racial side. I don't know what a lot of it means.'

But what do you think when they say things about Ian Wright, who is a friend and a colleague?

Love Thy Neighbour

'Yeah ... I just think it is part of the game. It is unfortunate, but as I say, sometimes I get stick off away supporters, you've just got to do it as water off a duck's back. When they are having a go at you, that means you are playing well. If they are not having a go, you are not doing too much damage towards the other team. That's the way it is a lot of the time. Certain players do get picked out a lot, which isn't right, but, you know, how are we going to stop it?'

By standing up and saying it's not right?

'Yeah, it's not right, and then what? And then you've got to start throwing people out the ground ...'

Spurs fan John Harris has stronger views on the subject, believing that the anti-Semitism is co-ordinated by extremist groups.

'The National Front have engineered that Tottenham become the target club, so that the polarities – the east and the west, West Ham and Chelsea – have got a target. It gives them a reason to operate.

'I can remember going back to the days of Richardson [former chairman of Tottenham]. They [the NF] started selling their magazine outside Tottenham. So I went to see Richardson and asked him what he was going to do about it. I told him that if the selling was allowed to continue, his club would begin to lose its support.

'He said he wasn't going to do anything. 'So I said right. I went round and got the mayor of Tottenham – and all the councillors as well – and announced we would go and stand behind the goal and make notes about what was going on.

'So Richardson, when he realised the mayor was involved said okay, he'd put something in the programme, which he did.

'Thankfully, it never really got bad at Tottenham because

they were the target. The NF got their support from West Ham and Chelsea and we gave them something to hate.'

It doesn't help the situation that Spurs fans have themselves adopted the term 'Yiddo' as a tribal badge of convenience. After so many years of hearing the word used as a term of abuse, it is now interpreted as a sign of recognition by Spurs fans. Blue and white Israeli flags with the Star of David are often on view at White Hart Lane. On one level, this could be construed as a positive force. It means that to be a Yid (i.e. Yiddish or Jewish) is not viewed by Spurs fans as something to be denied or ashamed of. They are in effect saying 'Yes that's right, we are the Jewish club. What of it?'

The trouble is, many Jewish Spurs fans are not so keen on this development. They find terms such as Yid or Yiddo to be singularly offensive in whatever context they may be used, and would prefer that their co-fans didn't encourage its usage. The club itself is unlikely to get involved in the argument; like most clubs they are the last to know what their fans are feeling.

A club once allowed a racist banner to remain draped over their Main Stand for the duration of a league game, seemingly unaware of what was going on or unable to comprehend its effects on many visiting and home fans alike.

Alan Sugar has even gone on record as saying the Yiddo chants do not offend him, even though Mrs Sugar demurred after one of her earliest visits to White Hart Lane.

The chants don't offend Tottenham's Jewish player Ronny Rosenthal, who puts it down to 'going with the flow'. But then Ronny's equanimity enables him to ignore the anti-Semitism which is often specifically directed at him. 'By ignoring it, you let those who are doing it know they are being paid no attention.'

Love Thy Neighbour

As it transpired, the salient chant at the game was not one of 'Yiddo', but the taunting of Arsenal fans with endless chorusing of 'Nayim from the half-way line.' Since that May evening in Paris, when the former Spurs favourite had beaten Seaman with an outrageous lob to secure the Cup Winners Cup for Real Zaragoza, Spurs fans have taken every opportunity to remind the world of what had, in truth, been an improbable sucker punch for Arsenal and its fans.

Now, some six months after the event, even if the joke was beginning to pale a little, it appeared that Spurs fans had at least found a more palatable successor to their previous antiquated anthem, 'Three-one; we beat the scum three-one'. (The fact that Nayim's goal had not been included in the 'Tottenham goal of the season' contest was a sore point among many who cast their votes earlier in the season.)

With ten minutes of the match gone, it was slowly dawning on the Spurs fans that their team was being pulverised by Arsenal's skilful play. Spurs were left chasing shadows as Arsenal fans roared 'Ole' to ten-, twelve- and in one case, seventeen-pass movements that moved the ball from flank to flank. It wasn't that Spurs were playing badly, just that Arsenal were so much better. Sheringham and Armstrong were reduced to the role of spectators, starved of service by team-mates fully occupied in rebuffing wave after wave of Arsenal attacks. A goal had to come, and in the absence of Ian Wright, it took Bergkamp just fourteen minutes before his effortless far post volley left Walker flat-footed. It was the Dutchman's eighth goal in nine games. 'Bergkamp from the six-yard line' was now the refrain echoing around White Hart Lane, as the Arsenal fans seized the moment for a volley of their own.

Dream On

This was Arsenal at their Tottenham-best. If the real Tottenham were looking for comfort, it was that they didn't fold as once they might, but retained their shape in the face of an onslaught few Premiership defences could have withstood.

A second Arsenal goal could have proved decisive, but it never came during that masterly opening spell, and as if taking encouragement from this reprieve, Spurs began to find their confidence. An equaliser came after 29 minutes, and it came with a movement that encapsulated everything Gerry Francis had been trying to do at Tottenham. From defending an Arsenal corner, the ball was cleared to Teddy Sheringham on the edge of his own penalty area. With the whole Tottenham team defending as a unit, there was no point in simply lashing the ball upfield, and so it was passed back to Dozzell, while Teddy started making ground. Dozzell spread the ball to Armstrong, who in turn unleashed Ruel Fox on the right wing to run at the furiously back-pedalling Arsenal defence. His early whipped cross found all but Tony Adams out of position and Sheringham, having covered the length of the pitch, headed past the flapping Seaman. That goal was Teddy's fourteenth of the season and 78th in all for Spurs. It was a triumph for all the qualities that Francis holds dear.

Half-time gave Gerry Francis a chance to rearrange his forces. He had not foreseen the trouble that Bergkamp had caused by dropping deep and giving Merson the space for running at the defence through a strung-out midfield. Centre-back Colin Calderwood recalled that, '. . . they passed it better than us and looked very good, but although they had a lot of possession, we didn't feel they were getting through'. Gerry took a less complacent line. Accepting that he couldn't always anticipate the way the opposition would play, he relishes the break as it gives him the opportunity to provide a counterpoint. As Gary Mabbutt put it, 'We were giving them too much space and we were losing our cohesion.'

Sol Campbell was instructed to mark Merson tightly and the team were urged to stick to the principles of what had now become a very well-honed pattern of play.

Defensively as Colin Calderwood later explained, this meant '. . . everyone working off each other,' to restrict the opposition's attacking options. 'He [Francis] wants you to put your body position in a certain way so that it is very hard to play the ball into their central striker so they have a starting point [for attack]. He doesn't want teams to have time on the ball. It's especially important around the box to close them down, and that means getting right in their face. It certainly helps defenders when a cross comes in under pressure because you can adjust your position. If someone is not under pressure you wonder what to do and that's when the doubts creep in. Physically it's hard to defend this way but the results have kept everyone at it.'

The latter stages of the first half demonstrated that the Spurs attack was beginning to find its range. Colin Calderwood again: 'The defender is encouraged to hit long balls over the [opposing] full-back. Gerry wants the ball put into certain areas and expects the forwards, especially Chris Armstrong, to make a run for it. It is important to test teams out via the space behind them. But if they become aware [of the tactic] the emphasis is switched to the space in front of them. He wants the ball crossed into the box at certain times. He doesn't want two or three passes played. So, if your route is blocked, you must try to get into the box from the other side.' And this is the only time individual skills are prioritised. According to Colin Calderwood, this '. . . allows

Dream On

Darren Anderton, Teddy and Ruel to try different things to get into the box because that's what makes them exceptional players'.

The second half became a triumph for Tottenham's organisation over Arsenal's skill. What a turn-up. As Ian Ridley was to later comment in the *Independent on Sunday:* 'It is not unusual for a north London team to be well organised and direct, to show resilience in adversity. It is unusual for that team to be Tottenham Hotspur.'

There was an air of inevitability about the next goal, a classy shuffle by Armstrong before firing low and hard past Seaman on 55 minutes. The Arsenal threat had seemingly been stifled, and as Fox continued to whip in a stream of wickedly tantalising crosses, Spurs looked far more likely to extend their lead than Arsenal ever did to equalise. Despite a nervy final few minutes when the height of Adams supplemented the Arsenal attack, Spurs remained in control to a degree unimaginable during that opening half hour.

The 2-1 defeat was Arsenal's third in four away fixtures, and a blemish on their record of previously only conceding six goals.

'I'd say it must be a long time since Arsenal have been opened up so many times as they were today,' said Gerry Francis afterwards. 'I'm very pleased with the performance as well as the result. The second half performance for me was outstanding. At the start of the game, for fifteen minutes, I felt we gave them far too much time, far too much room. The boy Merson, dropping deep, was causing us a few problems.

'I was able to change things a little during the game, but it was a little noisy. I really needed to get to half-time to change things as I wanted to. We were able to put one or

Love Thy Neighbour

two things right, and to be perfectly honest, I thought the second half was as good a performance as I've had since I've been here – considering the opposition, and the number of chances we created throughout the game. Ruel Fox played probably his best game yet for us. He was outstanding and the chief tormentor and supplier throughout the game. 'That's one defeat in ten now, and we are three points behind the team in third place. I can't fault the team.'

Gerry then moved onto autopilot.

'We've had our problems. We lost Clive Wilson just before the kick-off. We've had Darren out, we lost the three players in the summer. We've only had nine defeats in the league in all the time I have been here which shows good consistency. We are the only team in the league still unbeaten away from home. In five of the six games we've had to come back from being behind . . .'

Arsenal manager Bruce Rioch was finding it hard to reconcile his side's opening blitz with its later capitulation.

'In a local derby where you expect no quarter given in terms of space and time, we found ourselves making a lot of space and making a lot of time for ourselves. We felt that in that spell we needed to convert some of the play we had, and fortunately we got the goal that the play warranted. But at half-time we weren't completely happy with the spell after the goal. We appeared to take our foot off the pedal, not move the ball as well, as swiftly, as accurately.

'I thought it was a very open game for a derby. It's the first one I've been involved in between Tottenham and Arsenal but I've played in derbies where there has been no room at all to play the game, so it was far more open as a game than I anticipated.'

Reminded that both Tottenham scorers once played under him at Millwall, Rioch paid them generous tribute.

Dream On

'Teddy Sheringham is a goal-scorer. If you set him high enough targets, and encourage him to achieve the targets, then he could reach 30 goals a season, in almost any season. As I said when I sold him from Millwall to Forest, he can score with his feet, left or right foot. He can score with his head; near post, middle of the goal, back post. He can score with power, score with touch. He can bring people into the game. He's a good player.

'Chris is more direct; his two great strengths are his pace and his jumping ability. If he can ally goals to those qualities, he's always going to be a threat. It's a good combination. But Sheringham is the key.'

Daniel Stern admitted to feeling 'incredibly surprised' at the way the game turned out. 'I thought we were going to lose 4-0 at least. And for the first twenty minutes that looked likely. Then we did something tactical – we played the long ball! And it worked. Cut out the midfield. And they had Bergkamp but we didn't have Klinsmann any more. It wasn't all long ball by any means. But there is a worrying amount of that going on though.

'The best thing about winning was that if the score had stayed at 1-0, it would have been "Bergkamp from the six-yard line" for ever more. And that would have entered the mythology. So we beat them on songs again which is both good and unusual for Tottenham. We would never have been able to sing "Nayim from the half-way line" again obviously. But I think Tottenham played incredibly well in the end. I think it was the best one since the Gazza semi-final . . . We didn't want to leave the ground.'

Many Arsenal fans were streaming for the exit before the final whistle. It was just another bad day at White Hart Lane for them. Thankfully, there had been no serious

Love Thy Neighbour

crowd trouble in the ground, although reports filtered through of the usual skirmishes in the High Road. One steward apparently riled the Arsenal fans, but when his actions were reported to a supervisor, they were exonerated with the claim that 'There are a lot of offensive people around here'.

It could have been worse. Arsenal's goal and the subsequent celebrations by fans revealed a considerable number of them had bought seats that placed them outside the allocated visitors' section. This often happens for games where demand from visitors far outstrips supply. Maybe some of these fans unwittingly bought tickets from the army of touts who still ply their trade outside the ground, or simply took advantage of the various credit-card booking facilities that ask only your card details, not your allegiance.

Either way, there were several very unpleasant scenes as Arsenal fans celebrating the opening goal were confronted by some very angry Spurs supporters. The stewards were mostly able to defuse the situation, albeit at the expense of the intruders who were led away for their own safety. It's true that clearly visible signs indicate which areas of the ground are for 'home supporters only' and warn of the threat of ejection for those ignoring such segregation. But it's a great shame that sitting with opposing supporters should not only be banned, but could potentially be harmful. Quick action in removing those fans unquestionably avoided some serious violence, but it is nevertheless a sad sight to see a father and son ejected from the stands amid a baying mob of hateful faces, all for the heinous crime of cheering their team's goal.

The situation was particularly bad in Legends, the reserved section in the Lower East Stand. For a substantial financial consideration, Legends members and their guests

Dream On

can enjoy the usual pre-match meal and hospitality packages. Hosted by former Spurs stars – hence the name (which perhaps fails to live up to expectations when you find Denis Bond or Paul Miller is your host for the day) – the game is watched not from the usual enclosed executive box, but out in the open via a pseudo directors' box with padded seats and the kind of ample legroom not afforded to mere season-ticket holders.

Unfortunately, being situated in the heart of the home support (slap bang in the middle of the former Shelf actually), this presents problems when invited guests turn out to support the opposition. Previous home games had highlighted this confrontation waiting to happen, but the Arsenal game brought it to a head. When a good dozen or so guests leapt to their feet to celebrate Bergkamp's goal there was a very real possibility of violence. As angry Spurs louts turned to remonstrate, and it became apparent there were no police or stewards to intervene, the situation got very ugly. The louts were able to approach the Legends section and hurl some nasty verbal abuse, complete with obscene gestures, at what were some very well dressed – and by now very frightened – guests and their embarrassed hosts.

All the much hyped anger and hatred of this fixture was encapsulated in two or three minutes that did both Spurs and many of its fans no credit whatsoever. Eventually the arrival of stewards, helped by the passive response of the Arsenal-supporting guests, allowed the anger to dissipate and the moment passed. The subsequent Spurs goals saw the same louts turn to the intruders and taunt them. The stewards seemed content to duck a confrontation so long as actual physical violence was avoided. Luckily there were no more Arsenal goals to further inflame matters, but many decent Spurs fans were left to recall

Love Thy Neighbour

how much safer Highbury had been when they have been the 'intruders'.

Gerry was doing his best with the playing staff and making great strides. But the fans and the admin staff still had much to learn about the inherent responsibilities of being a Big Club. In this respect they could do a lot worse than try to live up to the example set by the directors of both clubs. The die-hards though would probably rather not hear Tottenham director Douglas Alexiou's assertion that 'Although there is rivalry at board level, as long as I've been involved [15 years] we've been great friends'. Perhaps it couldn't be otherwise given that Alexiou and Arsenal director Danny Fiszman were at school together and David Dein's eldest son, Darren, enjoyed work experience at Alexiou's law firm as part of his studies. Moreover, it was as a result of a dinner party on Alan Sugar's yacht in the South of France just before the season began that Master Dein and Miss Sugar first met and subsequently became 'an item' in the *Sun*. The social relationship between the respective parents has been maintained notwithstanding the public slagging off Alan Sugar gave to Arsenal over the 'spendthrift' transfer policy.

Although it is not Arsenal's style to retaliate in kind, there was annoyance and embarrassment on both sides. As David Dein put it, 'Being a director brings with it privileges, duties and responsibilities and a certain code of conduct.'

To Tottenham vice-chairman Tony Berry, 'Being a director is very important. It's something I enjoy. It's not an ego trip – ego is something you strive for so that you represent yourself well in other people's eyes. The real excitement for me is being able to drive in the front gates, park your car and go upstairs. It's nothing to do with what other people feel. No matter how well I did at Blue Arrow, no matter how successful I was, the biggest thing for my father, had he lived to see it, would have been for him to see me as a director of Tottenham. He wouldn't have believed it. He used to stand at the Paxton Road end and first took me when I was six. I used to go regularly when I was nine. [Berry subsequently played for Tottenham as a junior, finishing up in senior amateur football.] Like Scholar, if for some reason the directorship ended tomorrow, I would still go.'

With the cost of his corporate box and season tickets, the price and commitment of being a director doesn't come cheap, about £50,000 a year. 'It's a tradition,' he says simply of his desire to entertain clients and friends. 'You just have to have them.'

For derby day, Douglas Alexiou had invited his Arsenal friends, so he '. . . watched my guests exercise restraint without managing to hide the glee on their faces [when Bergkamp scored]. And then when we scored and scored again, I exercised restraint myself.'

Afterwards in the boardroom it was handshakes, congratulations and commiserations. 'I remember once,' said Douglas Alexiou, 'Robert Bellinger coming up to me and saying "well done, you deserve it, you thrashed us." Well you know that directors of football clubs who have been directors for a while know how to behave themselves. You have to be magnanimous. You just say well done, or well played, whether you have won or lost. Smile and say good game. It is one of those unwritten rules. You say well played, as the players do.'

A nice cosy scene, a world away from the hostile environment of the ground and boisterous music at TGI Fridays in Enfield where after leaving 'a happy dressing room', Gary Mabbutt stopped off on his way home to have a meal with

Love Thy Neighbour

his fiancée and father. Although Spurs fans were in the majority, Arsenal shirts were clearly in evidence and the atmosphere, though rowdy, was never threatening.

Chapter 7

Sky's The Limit

Throughout November and December, Gerry's revolution continued. His team yomped through the Premier League, born upon the back of good old 4–4–2, turning average players into good players, and an average team into one that, while not always winning or being particularly entertaining to watch, was certainly hard to beat.

When Bolton's Scott Green thumped the ball past Ian Walker just two days before Christmas, it was the first goal Spurs had conceded in 602 minutes of play, stretching back to Bergkamp's 14th minute volley on 18 November. A new club record had been established, all the more remarkable for the fact that Gerry was operating with virtually the same pool of defenders that had secured the sacking of Ardiles. In a transformation worthy of a *Dirty Dozen* script, the Spurs defence was now operating as a cohesive unit. Although injuries continued to play havoc with team selection, players could be drafted into the side, or played out of position, yet still shine because everyone knew the rules of the system and their role within it. The reserves under Chris Hughton,

Dream On

and the youth team under Des Bulpin were also playing to Gerry's system and performing even better in their own leagues, creating a reservoir of players who could be drafted into first team reckoning without the usual clash of cultures.

With Arsenal despatched in the derby game, next up was a 500-mile round trip to Middlesbrough for a tricky Tuesday night fixture. Boro's all-new Cellnet Riverside Stadium is located on a remote out-of-town site, far from the kind of facilities – food and drink amenities, car parking and public transport links – it would be reasonable to assume as essential for survival in any other field of entertainment. Only in football could 29,000 people be expected to patronise an establishment where so few concessions had been made to creature comforts.

Nevertheless, Spurs quickly sold out their allocation of tickets and consequently were able to offer their non-travelling fans the opportunity to watch the game live on the big screen back at White Hart Lane. The installation of the giant Sony Jumbotron high above the new South Stand is unusual in that it has provided an authentic new facility for the committed, while generating a new source of revenue for the club. With Premiership clubs retaining 100% of home gate receipts, it is no surprise that more of them are turning to the option of buying the hardware so that away games can be transmitted. Given that all top-flight games are already covered by TV cameras, it is a logical step to ask permission from the host club to make a signal available, pay whatever rights fee is necessary, and engage a commentator to describe to the punters what they are watching.

Tottenham, however, appeared reluctant to embrace the concept fully. Minimal promotion kept the 'crowd' at White Hart Lane down to a gathering of around 3,000 that

Sky's The Limit

Tuesday night, all cosily squashed into the lower tier of the North Stand. Given the right promotion, it would not be unreasonable to expect crowds of at least twice this number to watch away matches on the big screen. At £7.50 per adult and £5 for juniors, admission prices for the Middlesbrough game were pitched at a level just the right side of the grumble threshold. Presumably a lesson had been learned from a previous experiment when Whites social club, adjoining the ground, had charged a whopping £15 for the dubious privilege of watching away games on an oversize TV screen in their lounge.

Although the quality of the Jumbotron picture was surprisingly good, it was still a strain for many to peer the length of the pitch to see their heroes in action. Technical problems meant that most of the match was received with no soundtrack and the absence of crowd noise made it an eerie experience. However, Tottenham's positive start to the game encouraged most fans to overcome their inhibitions about cheering on a team 250 miles away, and the event created its own atmosphere. Commentator Gary Bloom had been drafted in to add the touch of hype deemed necessary on these occasions, but despite his best attempts to convince that he was actually at the Riverside Stadium, by the time Chris Armstrong scored the only goal of the game after 71 minutes, it had become apparent that Mr Bloom was secreted somewhere at White Hart Lane watching the same live feed as the fans. He won few friends with his infuriating insistence on assuring the crowd how Spurs were about to secure a famous win, despite a good fifteen minutes remaining in which, as any Spurs fan will tell you, things could and usually did go wrong.

But Gary Bloom was as good as his word, and if not a famous win, it was certainly commendable. Middlesbrough

Dream On

away on a cold Tuesday night would have had most previous Spurs teams (and managers) settling for a narrow defeat. But Gerry and his tactics have given Spurs some substance and three welcome points took Spurs up into the top three of the Premiership, as well as preserving their unbeaten away record.

And the form continued. Away to Chelsea finished 0–0. Home to Everton finished 0–0. Home to QPR was 1–0. Away to Wimbledon also saw a 1–0 win. Glory, glory stuff it was not. More, who dares sins. And so to the home game with Bolton, on 23 December.

Bolton Wanderers were bottom having lost every single away fixture so far. Spurs had lost just one game in fifteen and a win would take them to second place. Nosebleed territory. The league table indicated that this would be a formality, but cynical Spurs fans (i.e. those 99% who remember life before Gerry Francis) were still reluctant to believe that a lifetime of false dawns and promises could so easily be consigned to the dustbin. And the cynics were proved correct.

Cruising towards a comfortable, though not convincing, 2–0 win, Tottenham's title charge took a tumble as they eased their foot off the gas and conceded two in two minutes. On the face of it, a mistake by full-back Justin Edinburgh allowed Bolton in for their first goal (thus ending the 602-minute clean sheet sequence). But Gerry, never happier than when having a moan, blamed a bizarre incident prior to that goal for his team's collapse: the Jumbotron. Used during each match to show live pictures of the play, it can be something of a distraction to the fans. Indeed Kevin Keegan had demanded a halt to the action replays during Newcastle's game back in October, though on that occasion BSkyB were covering the match so the replays were more intrusive than usual.

Sky's The Limit

During a lull in the action, an astute camera operator had scanned the West Stand only to find that Mohammed Ali Amar (aka Nayim) was the club's guest for this particular game. The image of Nayim sitting in the stand was flashed up on the giant screen, and the crowd went bananas. *Nayim from the half-way line* echoed around the ground in a frenzy of hero-worship that surpassed any reception he had received during his time at White Hart Lane. The players were oblivious to what was going on, aware only that their actions on the pitch were not responsible for the reactions off it. To compound matters, PA announcer Gary Stevens, a former player and someone who really should have known better, came on air to ask that everyone 'Show your appreciation of our guest today, Nayim'.

This may have cleared up the mystery, but it only served to launch a further series of chants and celebrations and the sudden party atmosphere seemed to distract the Spurs players. It was then that Bolton struck twice. It seems a mite harsh to suggest that the concentration of the home team could be so flimsy, or that battling Bolton's first away point was so fortuitous. Still, despite missing out on second spot, the Spurs fans took the 2–2 draw in their stride, perhaps even mildly reassured that, after all, there still remained some traces of the unpredictable and irrational Spurs of old.

It was certainly the ghost of Christmas past that haunted Spurs on Boxing Day. Another two points slipped by at Southampton as yet another 0–0 draw did little to justify Tottenham's lofty league position, or win new friends. It was true that Spurs were not losing – one defeat in seventeen was now the record. But they weren't always winning either, and the goals had certainly dried up. With only Sheringham and Armstrong seemingly able to find the net, their combined barren spell left the club bereft of alternatives up front. Fox had managed only two goals in nine appearances and Ronny Rosenthal just two in twenty. With a trip to Blackburn next for the last game of 1995, a win was essential to salvage something from what had so far been a typically dire Christmas return of two points from two games. Could they manage to finish 1995 undefeated on their travels?

Of course not. The 2–1 result flattered Rovers, but was enough to end the Premiership's only unbeaten away record and represented only the fourth away league defeat Spurs had suffered since Gerry had taken charge over a year ago. Now, with only Manchester United to visit White Hart Lane on New Year's Day, there remained the distinct possibility that Spurs would end the holiday period with a paltry two points out of a possible twelve.

The Manchester United game is always a big attraction at White Hart Lane, and had been one of the initial matches targeted by Sky back in August for live transmission. For Spurs, it would be their fourth game in ten days over the holiday period, a factor on which Gerry held strong views.

'I cannot see why we can't have a Christmas break. I have been in this game for 27 years and have yet to spend one Christmas with my family. We must learn from the Europeans who have been doing this for years and who relish the chance to rest, recharge their batteries and get their injured players back to fitness.

'Here, we play two of our most exciting games, Blackburn and Manchester United, back-to-back in the space of a few days. Unbelievable. It means that we are playing four games in ten days, virtually a game every other day.'

Gerry had felt strongly enough about the issue to write to the Premier League proposing a ten-day break from 23 December to 2 January, and he apparently wasn't alone in such thinking. 'I got a great response: 80% from the letter I

sent out to the other managers. It has to go to the Managers'
Association to be voted on, and then put to the Premier
League who have to decide.'

With Sky ruling the roost, however, such an argument
was unlikely to cut much ice.

The traditionally long Christmas holiday in England provides television with a captive audience of couch potatoes.
Harsh weather, poor public transport and severely depleted
funds deliver unto programme schedulers the great British
public on a plate. Movie premieres and variety shows draw
best-of-year viewing figures. If major sporting events could
also be rescheduled for this time, then they too could be
expected to pull in TV audiences far in excess of what the
same fixture might draw on a warm August evening. And
with the audiences comes the lucrative advertising.

Thus it was that Sky Sports had scheduled six live
transmissions of Premiership games over the ten-day
Christmas/New Year break. Crucially, they had secured
matches to be transmitted at times when historically
there had been no football; following the traditional full
league programme on Boxing Day, Sky had scheduled
a double-header on 27 December with two Premiership
games shown at 6pm and 8pm.

For armchair fans this was no bad deal. The losers were
those clubs that had drawn the short straws and who were
to be the dancing monkeys that entertained the rest of the
nation; those fans and players called upon to sacrifice their
quality time on the altar of TV ratings. But this was nothing
new; it is increasingly the price being paid by the Premier
League for selling out to BSkyB.

Before 1988, English football received less than £5 million
per season from TV's cosy gentlemen's agreement, and even
in 1988 Greg Dyke had paid just £44m for ITV's exclusive

Dream On

four-year deal. Sky's Premiership contract of almost £200 million in 1992 was therefore a huge windfall but, by the same token, a huge gamble. Sky's finances at that time had been in a bad way; the station was haemorrhaging cash with too few viewers, little subscription income and massive debts incurred during its launch and subsequent tussle with rival satellite station BSB. Sky had won that particular battle, but there was a very real danger that the war would be lost.

British viewers had been slow to embrace the concept of satellite TV, with fewer than 10% of homes possessing a dish in 1991. The process of conversion was not helped when, following Sky's eventual devouring of BSB (or 'merger' as Sky laughingly referred to the transaction), thousands of former BSB subscribers found their newly bought receiving equipment was no longer compatible with Sky's signal. Swift action by Rupert Murdoch and, in particular, his appointed head of the new BSkyB, Sam Chisholm, saved the company. They slashed operating costs, staffing levels and, many would say, production values. At a stroke they saved millions in running costs, but they still needed a product that would capture the nation's imagination and trigger a stampede for satellite dishes. Only then could their transmissions stop going out 'free' and unscrambled, and the lucrative subscriptions be introduced.

In 1992, the new-born Premier League was delivered from the womb of the Football League. Sky beat off competition from ITV and delivered its £200 million slap to the arse. The cry that went up confirmed a healthy baby. If the Football League had been the mother, then subsequent lab tests showed that Sky was the father. And Sky had done to the Football League what all fathers must do to make babies.

It was then that the debate should have taken place over

the so-called 'listed events'; those sporting occasions deemed important enough to be protected from pay-TV by an Act of Parliament. Sure, Sky would like the FA Cup final – if not the Boat Race. But who cares when the Premier League is really the only competition that matters? For among the dross that a 60-match season of live games is bound to contain, there will be enough jewels to justify even Sky's hype.

Criticism from fans that top class football was being relegated to a minority channel was ignored by the clubs themselves, despite initial reservations that their sponsorship income might be decimated by the drop in television audiences. Besides, the clubs had been promised payments and exposure far in excess of anything they had previously received. Sky's commitment, not just to live transmissions but to preview, review and discussion programmes, in conjunction with their determination to raise production values, quickly enhanced the new League's status. This in turn forced a reaction by the other media who were fearful of being left by the wayside. Commercial radio and the tabloids in particular responded in a manner which brought a quantum leap in the perceived importance of football. Under Sky, the game blossomed from being merely a 90-minute action spectacle, into an art form worthy of discussion and analysis. Sport as drama. Sport as soap opera. If it was always the most important sport in the country, it was now the second, third and fourth most important sport as well.

Although Sky supremo Sam 'We must get rid of the possibility of 0–0' Chisholm couldn't introduce any quick-fix to ensure games were more entertaining, he did, in his own sensitive Antipodean way, take steps to introduce added 'value' in the form of a two-hour build-up to matches, the pubescent Sky Strikers, half-time pop groups, firework pyrotechnics, the parachute displays and the inflatable sumo

Dream On

wrestlers. However he quickly learned verisimilitude, and saw that the real way forward was more cameras, better analysis, SloMo action and dressing room/players' tunnel interviews. The gimmicks were quietly ditched and the overall presentation now has both substance and style. The only major criticism that can be levelled is that of unashamed hype; Alan 'This is an awful game' Green from Radio 5 Live would never be acceptable to Sky's mandarins because BSkyB do not have bad Premiership games.

A hectic schedule that tallies over 100 live games per season (three times as many as terrestrial TV covered pre-Sky) has prioritised the effort behind production. Sky's team have an unerring ability – it would be insulting to call it luck or simply a knack – to capture every incident of note in every game. They really do bring you, in slow motion and from a variety of angles, every shot, tussle, foul, near-miss, save and goal. Every spit, sneer, dig, gesture and oath is captured and replayed to wow the viewer. Under Sky, for the first time, the armchair fan can truly consider himself better off than the fan at the ground.

Although wages at BSkyB are not reckoned to be on a par with those paid by Independent Television, the satellite channel has no problem in attracting and keeping the best producers, editors and camera operators in the industry. There is a buzz about working for Sky Sports, because if you want to be in live sport, Sky is simply the only place to be. While Sky may be at Old Trafford for a Manchester United v Newcastle title showdown, the fact that their colleagues at ITV are probably earning more by covering Millwall v Portsmouth at a three-quarters empty Den, is not envy-invoking.

ITV strive to give the impression that they are still major players in the live football stakes, but of course they are no

Sky's The Limit

such thing. For the company that once held exclusive rights to top class league football, they have fallen a long way and it shows in their commitment. Despite having some potentially attractive contracts (the Champions League and the Coca-Cola Cup), and punditry big guns such as Terry Venables and Jack Charlton, a programme featuring a major cup tie may only go on air ten minutes before kick-off, and be off the air within minutes of the final whistle, leaving no time to do justice to the event.

Far too many incidents are missed by ITV's cameras, which are as guilty of ball watching as any second rate defender. When Newcastle played Arsenal in a vital Coca-Cola Cup game, David Ginola was sent off after a violent tussle with Lee Dixon, causing a touchline altercation between the rival coaching personnel. It was an incident that hogged the back pages of every newspaper the following day. Not one ITV camera could shed any light on who had been the aggressor. You just know that with Sky, the incident would have been captured from all angles and replayed instantly to clear up any controversy. The BBC probably would not have missed it either, for they too have consistently demonstrated why the viewing public hold their output in such high regard. But like ITV, their time has been and gone, despite their tradition.

With every passing day, the ability of the two terrestrial networks to compete is weakened as more homes subscribe to cable and satellite. By the end of 1996, more than one in five homes will be connected and a critical mass in excess of 5 million attained.

When Sky's £304 million (including BBC and estimated overseas rights sales) beat ITV's £262 million to secure the Premier League contract purely on the basis of money, it is debatable whether the chairmen realised that subscription

Dream On

was around the corner. As the only means by which Sky could hope to challenge the revenue generated by the larger terrestrial audiences it was inevitable. High advertising and broadcast sponsorship income were simply incompatible with the low audience penetration of satellite and cable in 1992. For the first time in the history of commercial television, audience size ceased to matter. With the prime football competition only available on their channel, must-see demand by the fans resulted in a concomitant must-pay response by Sky.

For Sky, the success of the Premier League has surpassed even their wildest dreams. By moving Sky Sports to a subscription basis, albeit for an initial £5.99 per month, the Premier League contract quickly became a licence to print money and was the catalyst that moved the previously ailing TV company from debt to profit in the space of a year. As Vic Wakeling, at the time Sky's football boss, now their Sports Controller, proudly confirmed just one year into the Premiership contract, 'Sky Sports subscriptions are just going through the roof. It has been the quickest ever take-up for a subscriber channel. Quicker than the movie channels, quicker than anything America has ever seen.' Profits in the six months to the end of December 1995 were £106.3 million – more than £4 million per week. Subscriptions accounted for more than three-quarters of that sum.

With the success of Sky Sports, BSkyB has been able to pursue an expansionist policy. Its massive investment in digital broadcasting, to begin in 1997, will coincide with the next Premier League contract, which could be transmitted by pay-per-view (PPV). The PPV technology has existed in the USA for some years; it is the first choice for major boxing contests so it was no surprise when the Tyson-Bruno fight in March 1996 became the first sports event to make

Sky's The Limit

viewers pay specifically for the privilege of watching it. Notwithstanding that those punters had already paid a subscription to the broadcasting channel, Sky Sports, this was a double whammy which encountered fierce opposition. Nevertheless it was a successful one in terms of revenue, if not profit, the media hype being funded by a massive advertising and promotion campaign. More than 600,000 paid between £9.95 and £14.95, strengthening the station's belief that what worked for boxing could work for football – at least for similar heavyweight clashes with perhaps a championship at stake. Indeed, if it wishes, it could do so under the current contract, as the Premier League threw in pay-per-view rights.

However, the British TV-viewing public have been spoilt by a diet of 'free' TV sport, to the extent that they now expect free and instant access to all major sporting events as a divine right. Of course sport on TV has only ever been 'free' in that there was no specific or ongoing charge demanded. Little correlation was made between payment of the BBC licence fee and the year-round provision of world class sport. Even less correlation was drawn between ITV's sporting agenda and the acceptance by viewers of advertisements before, during and after every match, bout, heat, race, frame or innings, supplemented in the last few years by broadcast sponsorship.

Sky have tried to soften the blow to their satellite subscribers by 'adding value' to their premium channels. Sky Sports 2 and Sky Sports Gold joined the portfolio and specialist interest channels like MTV, Bravo and Discovery were bundled into a 'multi-channel package' that helps disguise the real cost of receiving Premiership football.

Sky have also taken steps to distance themselves from the tag of being a 'satellite channel'. Despite the fact that to

Dream On

most of the viewing public, Sky is now the generic term for all satellite TV, Sky are aware that home dish sales will never increase at the rate they once did. It is to cable that they now look for more subscribers – by 1999 Sky will be available in more cable homes than dish homes – while greater efforts are made to encourage pubs and clubs to join up.

The government's decision in 1995 to allow all-day Sunday opening in English pubs will not have gone unappreciated by Sky. From the point of view of the brewers in general and Carling in particular, the pub take-up has been a godsend. For the fans as well: 'Most football supporters have actually been proved wrong about Sky,' enthuses TV football producer and Arsenal fan Harry Lansdown. 'I certainly have. It has lifted the whole quality of the coverage. I would not want things to go back to the way they used to be. But then again, neither I nor most of my friends have a subscription. Pub football is brilliant for away matches you'd never get to, or for big games of general interest. It's something no one particularly anticipated.'

Sky's Sunday games traditionally kick off at 4pm, and thus for three years were denied to the lunchtime drinking crowd who would be forced by law to vacate the premises at 3pm. Sky incidentally are adamant that their 4pm choice for Sunday kick-off was a shrewd one, as Vic Wakeling explained: 'I had noticed that ITV's biggest viewing audience of the year, back in February 1992, was for the Spurs v Forest League Cup semi-final that got delayed by a bomb scare. The game kicked off about an hour late, at 4pm, yet pulled in a huge audience. I think by opting for this later kick-off we get a lot of viewers we would otherwise miss.' Probably true, but viewing figures for Sky's live games are still but a fraction of those previously enjoyed by ITV. The average Sky audience for a Premiership football match is around

Sky's The Limit

940,000 viewers. Only a few games have ever topped the two million mark. This compares poorly with the six million ITV were averaging in 1991 and can still pull in for 'the big match'. A week after 1.3 million tuned in to see Spurs v Manchester United, ITV attracted nearly nine million to the Arsenal-Newcastle League Cup tie.

Not that Sky themselves would be unduly bothered as Kevin Morton, Media Director at the advertising agency J Walter Thomson, explains: 'Audience size really isn't that important. If subscribers are up-to-date with their subscriptions but choose not to watch an event, so what? It's like leaving your food in an expensive restaurant. Audience figures are only important in that they give an idea as to the popularity of what you are transmitting, and therefore whether you will have poor subscription renewals. The reason why broadcasters are willing to bid sports rights up to stratospheric levels is simple. First, sport has been proven to be the strongest force in building subscriptions, more so than films. And second, it draws in the elusive young, upmarket male viewer.'

By the end of 1995, with a full season still to run of the original Premiership contract, steps were already being taken by Sky to ensure its smooth renewal. In truth, it is hard to see the contract going elsewhere. The only question is how much will Sky be paying for the privilege? With bidding expected to reach the £800 million level – talk of £1 billion was not being discounted – the BBC and ITV are out of their league – literally. The terrestrial 'giants' cannot compete with Sky and its seemingly limitless funds. This was acknowledged in a flurry of deals that saw Sky kick the BBC out of its bed, and allow ITV to climb in.

At the end of 1995, Sky signed a deal to tie up exclusive rights to the rest of the Football League as well. From

Dream On

August 1996, Sky Sports will broadcast up to 60 live Football League games per season, including, for the first time, Divisions Two and Three. Sky will also gain access to the League Cup showing live games from as early as the First Round with the final exclusive to Sky Sports, although ITV share the live semi-finals and retain a highlights package. From the 1997/98 season ITV will also have exclusive rights to the FA Cup final plus highlights of the Football League for their own *Match of the Day*-type round-up programme. And where does all this leave the BBC? Until 1997 it remains Sky's junior partner with recorded action from the Premier League, the FA Cup and England internationals. But then what?

So far as a regular diet of league football is concerned, Auntie is yesterday's woman, only surviving a bleak future as a part-time football channel on a bi-annual blow-out of World Cup and European Championship tournaments, courtesy of the European Broadcasting Union (EBU) and its relationship with FIFA and UEFA. But here as well, it is a question of how long the authorities are prepared to suffer the decreasing audiences of the terrestrials in the face of increasing cash offers from satellite and cable.

For this latest package, Sky signed a £25-million-per-year, five-year deal. Petty cash for Sky, but for the Endsleigh minnows a vast improvement on their previous deal. It may not make those clubs rich, but it will certainly help raise their profile and enable them to strike better commercial deals.

Sky has confirmed its position as both the paymaster and ringmaster of football. It is now the biggest producer of sports programming in Britain, with a budget of £100 million (£10 million more than BBC and more than twice that of ITV). On the face of it, Sky are facing an apparent abundance of material, and will be struggling to find the airtime to show all these live

Sky's The Limit

games and associated programmes. In fact, the opposite will be true. For just around the corner is the digital revolution, an advancement in technology that will give broadcasters such as Sky almost limitless channels with which to bombard the nation's living rooms.

Current satellites are limited in the number of transponders they carry. It is these transponders that beam the TV signals down to earth. One transponder can only carry one TV channel at a time – rather like a telephone line only handling one call at a time. Some satellites may only carry sixteen transponders which makes rental time on each transponder pretty expensive when the satellite may have cost several hundred million pounds to launch into orbit, and may only have a projected life of ten years before its batteries expire. Digital technology in the new generation of satellites means that now each transponder can carry a huge number of channels simultaneously. Capacity is therefore up, while costs per channel correspondingly nose-dive.

To broadcasters like Sky, this is a godsend. They will be aiming to persuade their customers to trade up to digital decoders and to this end have already rented time on two ASTRA satellites devoted to digital television. With the cost of actually beaming the signals into homes now reduced, the station could have, if it so wished, hundreds of different Sky Sports channels, each dedicated to a particular niche. Every sport could have its own channel (complete with subscriptions and/or pay-per-view plus advertising of course). Every event that Sky covers could be shown live and uninterrupted. Single sport channels will become no more strange than magazines dedicated to one sport.

Then, if Sky so wish, every camera at major football games could have its signals transmitted down a channel of its own. The viewer at home could flip between different channels and see the same match from different camera positions. Behind the goal? Main stand? Touchline dugout? No problem with digital technology. Sky could even decide to regionalise its coverage, promoting local derbies that may be of limited national appeal. There could be separate sports channels for England, Scotland, Ireland and Wales.

Unlimited sport, endlessly.

This is not some flight of fancy. It is about to happen. Agreements have been signed in Italy and France which make pay-per-view a reality. For the 1996/97 season, Telepiù in Italy and Canal Plus in France will offer league matches on a pay-per-view basis. Canal Plus – owners of the leading club Paris St Germain – will launch, in partnership with the French league, a new channel. This will enable viewers, after payment of a monthly membership fee of £12 and the one-off purchase of a special £70 receiver, to choose any game from an *à la carte* menu of nine first division games for the price of £6. What Canal Plus do today, Sky can do tomorrow. In fact their current contract, which doesn't expire until the end of the 1997 season, allows them the opportunity to learn from the Italian and French experience.

But this time the Premier League chairmen may be ready for them. Suppose just half of the 2.5 million adults who watched Newcastle-Manchester United were prepared to pay a fiver to see it live on PPV. A reasonable expectation given that the cheapest seat at St James' Park was nearly three times that amount (if you could get one). Then that one match would have produced £6 million. Extrapolate that across the fixture card and the contract suddenly becomes worth billions. Perhaps more than even Sky could afford on its own.

How can BBC or ITV ever hope to compete? With

only two channels, and neither dedicated to sport, they cannot. Unless either broadcaster intends to launch its own dedicated sports channels (which would probably have to be satellite-based anyway because of limited terrestrial frequency availability), then they must resign themselves to being minority providers of sporting television. ITV has limited advertising revenue, and the BBC limited licence revenue. They both have a brief to provide entertainment across the spectrum – light entertainment, drama, news and original programming – and already come in for much criticism for the volume of sport they carry. Indeed, a key factor in Sky securing rights to golf's Ryder Cup was the amount of airtime Sky could promise over the BBC.

The responsibility now lies with each sport's controlling body to decide whether acceptance of Sky's inevitable cheque can offset the decreased exposure inherent in a move to the satellite channel. Ominously, David Elstein, BSkyB's Head of Programmes, has warned, 'We'll carry on making sure our subscribers have the best possible service. The important question is that the sports have a right as well as the viewers. For a long time sport was underpaid, and the viewers got a very low-cost ride. The balance of power has changed and the sports are entitled to get what is available in the market.'

Elstein sees political interference as running against the principle of allowing market forces to decide who should be allowed to watch what. The 'principle' that any event should be available free as a 'right' to the armchair fans appals him.

'Sport owes nothing to the armchair fan,' states Elstein. 'Absolutely nothing. The armchair fan doesn't put a penny into sport. If the BBC and ITV want to put money into sport competitively with Sky, then let them do so. One thousand

Dream On

million a year is spent on network television; three times what Sky spends and ten times what Sky spends on sport. If you want the public to have more access to free coverage of major sporting events, then campaign for a higher licence fee; campaign for the BBC to change its spending patterns. But don't tell sports they have to subsidise the viewing public at home. They don't.'

For now, Sky are the premium event channel for sport and movies. They have moved from being a downmarket, second rate ITV clone, to being an emerging champion of popular culture. Their football, boxing, golf and World Cup cricket all draw those elusive ABC types and free spending younger viewers that advertisers seek. They supply, through their range of specialist channels, premium quality entertainment.

But where does that leave football? For although those who represent Sky on our TV screens are undoubtedly committed to the best interests of the game, can those who actually run Sky be trusted with its welfare?

The original TV contract with Sky was the best deal on the table at the time, but scarcely the best deal available. The price was too low, and too much was simply given away out of naïvety. The Premier League had been so keen to sign with Sky, it had omitted to retain control over its own product. It had been unaware that Sky intended to repeat the live game in its entirety only hours after the original transmission. This was something the BBC and ITV had never done, and so the thought had never occurred that this could be part of Sky's agenda. Nor had the clubs quite anticipated the hours that Sky intended to devote to dissecting every part of the Premier League action it had secured. Not that this proved to be a disadvantage, quite the contrary, but at least they should have paid more for

Sky's The Limit

it. As a result of that one deal, Sky are probably earning over £100 million a year from their football contract. The Premier League receives around £40 million, which when split twenty ways doesn't amount to a tremendous deal even for the top earner, Newcastle United (£3.1 million in 1995/96).

Before the Premier League rushes to sign a new contract for whatever sum Sky offer, they really should do some serious research into how much their product is actually worth, because they still have little idea of its true value. Of course they will be offered a better deal than was on the table five years ago, but how much better? And how much more is fair? Double? Treble?

A major consideration for the Premier League must surely be whether they should be running their own TV channel, so that the benefits currently creamed off by Sky could be passed directly to member clubs. If soft-porn outfits like the Fantasy Channel can do it, why not the Premier League? It just needs the willpower and the expertise within the Premier League to make it happen. After all, these days it's not the medium: it's the message.

The potential benefits of such a scheme would outweigh the start-up and operating costs, which, come digital TV, would be a fraction of those incurred by Sky today. It would also act as a useful insurance policy for that rainy day when Sky may find a new champion for its subscription drive. There are valuable lessons to be learned from the way that both snooker and darts were heavily promoted by television, before being unceremoniously dumped when ratings subsequently slumped. Those sports suffered traumatic post-TV depressions, with acrimonious splits within their ruling bodies and a dramatic loss of earnings for all involved.

Dream On

Come the digital revolution, the move will inevitably come from Sky to cover every Premiership game live, and making those transmissions available on a pay-per-view basis. But if technology makes this possible, wouldn't the Premier League itself be the best organisation to ensure that such a dramatic step was handled in a manner sympathetic to its member clubs?

With dramatic developments appearing to come on stream almost daily, control of rights is a prerequisite for ensuring that future wealth stays within the game. There will certainly be no more five-year contracts next time around. The current Sky package could be 'unbundled'. Pay-per-view could be retained until its implications are thought through, and that won't be until technology is available in the home and a stipulation made that a club can access recorded action 24 hours after the event, which would enable it to tie up with local cable or regional television. Similarly, other 'historic' footage should be retained for these outlets and for video. Recorded highlights can be sold again for probably three times the current *Match of the Day/Sportsnight* going rate of £4.5 million to either ITV or BBC. And the price for the big prize, Live and Exclusive, will go through the roof, because BSkyB can't afford to lose. They know they are in a no-win situation. Win or lose, their share price will take a hammering. If they win the annual payment may well reach £150 million. If they lose it will be a menu with no main course.

One way out of the Catch-22 situation for them would be to offer the Premier League a percentage of every subscription – up by more than three-quarters of a million in the last year – in a partnership deal. As David Elstein has said, 'What the game is worth is changing as technology changes'. And this time around it is essential that a master-servant relationship (or at the very least senior-junior partnership) is established, with football calling the shots.

They must not forget about overseas rights fees either. Despite the worldwide popularity of Premiership football and the expertise of CSI (who sell the matches on behalf of the Premier League), there is little likelihood that the much quoted £304 million will be achieved because of the unrealistically high estimated return back in 1992.

The irony is that the Premier League may not be able to do this or any other deal for that matter if the Office of Fair Trading (OFT) comes to the conclusion that it is operating a cartel, or that the present contract unduly favours BSkyB. In which case the way would be open for the big clubs to do their own deals direct, which might then bring the BBC or ITV back into the game, or even allow for the creation of a new network. The start-up costs of Tottenham TV may be prohibitive on satellite but it could certainly book time on cable so that, for example, supporters could switch on to away games. After all, that's only an extension of the White Hart Lane Jumbotron.

Sky are dismissive about competing bids and remain firm favourites to seize control of the Premiership TV contract again. However, the spectre of serious competitive bids from a Mirror Newspapers/Carlton Television alliance and a consortium of Pearson and MAI, may precipitate them into attempting a pre-emptive strike. But Sky already hold one trump card in that their present contract allows them to match any rival offer. With their recent acquisitions of the Football League, the Coca-Cola Cup, the FA Cup and England internationals, next season will see Sky broadcast over 150 live games. But will they be able to resist the urge to abuse their power to influence the game? And if they go in that direction, who will stand in their way? They have the money and the power to fund and enforce any changes they wish in the structure of divisions below the Premier League. And even in the Premier League they may draw the line about televising Coventry or Wimbledon, except when they draw 'glamour' clubs.

English rugby league has been turned from a winter game into a summer game after an £87 million injection from Sky's owners, News Corporation. Who can say that Sky will not become the driving force behind a Premier League Division Two, giving them a combined 44 clubs to pad out their sports channels? Maybe they would decide that the August to May season is in need of revision. With so many teams out of title contention before the half-way stage (and thus producing a glut of 'meaningless' fixtures), Sky could well decide that two short seasons are better than one long one, with results from each mini-season aggregated as a preamble to play-offs. It already happens in Switzerland and Denmark, and is symptomatic of the same thought process that has led to the incessant tinkering with the European Cup format, that virtually removes all possibility of 'big' clubs being eliminated from the competition before they have had a chance to generate some serious television revenue.

At present, Sky appear to dictate the agenda for the Premier League, a fact acknowledged everywhere but Lancaster Gate. Without Sky's money and Sky's exposure, most Premiership clubs would never have accumulated the commercial wealth they have today. The wages spiral, the transfer merry-go-round and the refurbishment of stadia have all been funded to a great extent by the commercial revolution – a cash windfall unimaginable just five years ago – largely brought about by Sky's ceaseless promotion of Premiership football. If clubs had been too eager to climb into bed with the fledgling satellite broadcaster back in 1992, they will

Sky's The Limit

soon be presented with perhaps a last chance to slip out and shape their own future. Failing that, it may well become apparent, to use Sky's own promotional slogan, that there can be, 'No Turning Back'.

The reasons why Sky has done so well from its association with the Premier League were all too apparent in the Spurs v Manchester United game transmitted on New Year's Day. Despite the hype in the channel's prolonged build-up, the match more than exceeded expectations, finishing 4–1 to Tottenham, and severely denting United's title aspirations.

Both sides were depleted by injuries and forced to reshuffle their line-ups. For Spurs, Mabbutt missed his first game of the season, and there were recalls for Ilie Dumitrescu and Darren Caskey (his first game since Gerry's arrival fourteen months ago) to replace Fox and Dozzell. In Mabbutt's absence, Sheringham was made captain for the first time under Gerry Francis.

For United, the defence was almost unrecognisable, with regulars Irwin, Pallister and Bruce all absent. To add to United's woes, an injury to 'keeper Peter Schmeichel in the pre-match warm-up meant manager Alex Ferguson had to move quickly to reshuffle his pack. The team-sheets had already been handed in to the referee, and United had no substitute goalkeeper on the bench. The referee was told that substitute Paul Scholes, who had recently been ill, was feeling poorly again. Could they take him off the bench and replace him with someone else? Reserve 'keeper Kevin Pilkington perhaps? Understandably, both referee and Gerry Francis had no objections. Thus United were able to begin the match with a reserve 'keeper on the bench. When Schmeichel's injury proved too much and he failed to come out for the second half, on came Pilkington.

Dream On

By then, however, Spurs were 2–1 to the good. Two further goals after the break were enough to give Spurs their best win of the season and consolidate their league position at joint third with Liverpool. For those home fans at White Hart Lane, the performance and the result was a welcome, if belated, Christmas present.

For Sky and its audience watching at home, the afternoon was another boost for Premiership football. The channel manages to bombard the viewer with a barrage of facts and analysis without distracting from the spectacle being watched. Until, that is, the commentators are forced to interrupt the action to promote forthcoming attractions. The Schmeichel injury was picked up on as early as the fourth minute, and monitored throughout the first half, so that it was no surprise when he was substituted.

Through it all, commentator Martin Tyler was able to interject snippets of facts and gossip that, once again, sought to reinforce the impression that viewers at home were seeing much more of a complete picture than those actually at the ground; even the traditionally sedate White Hart Lane was made to seem a cauldron of noise thanks to Sky's clever use of crowd amplification. And when Sheringham's opening goal drew strong appeals for offside, once again Sky's camera angles were spot on to show exactly why the strike was rightly allowed.

The negative aspect of so many stars missing from the two line-ups was countered with the fact that there were still thirteen internationals on the field. Mabbutt's absence was explained as being a precautionary move by the Tottenham manager, who did not want to risk aggravating his captain's injury, because Tottenham's other central defender, Colin Calderwood, was already banned from the next important

Sky's The Limit

game – Hereford in the cup. No one in the ground would know this until later.

Some factors were beyond Sky's control, notably the too-high camera rostrum at White Hart Lane that makes much of the action seem too distant. The bird's-eye view of the pitch precludes the atmospheric action shots that incorporate a crowd backdrop. To compensate, the channel made good use of their other cameras at ground level. With Sky's images (but not sound of course) appearing simultaneously on the giant Jumbotron screen, it was noticeable that players would steal a discreet glance up at action replays after being involved in a near miss or a particularly controversial incident.

With Spurs romping to a 4–1 lead by the 64th minute, the significance of the score was emphasised when TV viewers were reminded by Tyler that in the ten previous meetings between the two sides, United had won seven and drawn three. This deftly led into a reminder for those at home to phone in their vote for the man of the match award, the 0891 number costing 'only 20p a call', which in turn was followed by reminders to tune in to further live games for the following two evenings.

With the match finally over, the summarising facts and figures were screened which, rather than serving to baffle the viewer, in fact helped bring home United's supposed domination (55% of overall play) but lack of fire-power in front of goal (22 attempts on goal, eleven on target, one goal scored). With a dedicated sports channel, Sky could then take the time to leisurely consider points and discuss highlights from the match, with no need to wrap up all the issues in two minutes flat like ITV and BBC traditionally have to do, before making way for the news.

The employment of visual pyrotechnics to illustrate, for

Dream On

example, the length and direction of a defence-splitting pass are instructive, though does Andy Gray have to pretend to be a video jockey as well as a football analyst on *Monday Night Football*? Further, as Andrew Baker commented in the *Independent on Sunday*, 'The set still resembles a late-70's cocktail bar and every time Gray reaches up to the rack next to him you expect him to bring down a Pina Colada or Banana Daquiri instead of a video'.

A buoyant Gerry Francis was interviewed via a link-up to the Spurs' boot room, and was able to get in a few sideswipes at those pundits who had previously written off his side, and particularly those who had questioned his purchase of Chris Armstrong, scorer of two goals.

So, a good evening all round, for Spurs, for Sky, and for Newcastle, who saw their lead at the top of the table remain at four points. For Manchester United, it had indeed been a miserable festive season, with away defeats at Leeds, Liverpool and now Tottenham almost erasing their championship hopes. Alex Ferguson had been beset with injuries to key players, forcing him to change his line-up more often than title-chasers would prefer. But if United were still fine tuning their system on the pitch, there was no question that off the pitch, their system was the envy of every other Premiership club. And for that they could thank Tottenham, and in particular, Terry Venables' worst ever transfer deal.

Chapter 8

Top Gear

In an era where clubs are forced to acknowledge that gate receipts alone cannot sustain them, even through a successful season, the importance of commercial and merchandising revenue cannot be overstated. Of all Premiership clubs, perhaps only Manchester United have fully grasped the opportunity, and are now reaping the rewards for three years of hard work and commonsense principles. And when it comes to merchandising, the Manchester United story is the Edward Freedman story.

Edward Freedman, merchandising director at Tottenham for a short while under the Venables/Sugar regime, was initially hired by the man whom he cheerfully refers to as his mentor, Irving Scholar. Appointed in 1987 when turnover was less than £500,000 per annum, that figure had been quadrupled to the largest operation in the league before Freedman was allowed to go to Manchester United in 1992.

From the moment Irving Scholar took over the club in December 1982, he had set about creating an environment

Dream On

where the club could generate sufficient funds to finance its celebrated raids on the transfer market. Within a year, Tottenham had become the first football club to go public, wiping out their debts at a stroke. That same year saw another first, a multimedia advertising campaign through radio, TV and press. Depicted as a disaster by Terry Venables in his autobiography, the campaign was, in fact, a considerable success, selling season tickets and boosting gates for potentially unglamorous fixtures with teams like Coventry. It was only halted when a spell of poor on-field performances clashed with the positive propositions the ads portrayed.

Former ticket office manager Chris Belt and Mike Rollo, who has been the commercial manager since 1984, were constantly exhorted to come up with ideas. Together with their chairman, their initiatives, many unashamedly borrowed from more enlightened customer-friendly businesses, led the way in changing the relationship between a football club and its public.

Appalled at the low number of season tickets on offer, Scholar allocated new areas of the ground to them and slashed a waiting list that would otherwise have taken years to satisfy. Fans were also offered the chance to buy two-year season tickets at reduced rates, and home games were graded to align pricing with the attractiveness of the opposition – a practice now widely imitated.

A merchandising drive was undertaken, capitalising on the untapped demand for club-related products and services. The Tottenham logo was redesigned and copyrighted, to thwart pirates who were cashing in on the club's image. Successive deals were struck with kit suppliers, culminating in a ground breaking deal with Umbro in 1991, when Spurs became the first club to receive £1 million a year – more than Manchester United – and the kit was launched at the FA Cup final. It was a deal that did much to cement both the sportswear revolution and re-position Umbro as a major leisurewear supplier.

Dismayed by the spectacle of fans queuing for tickets at the decrepit ticket office, the move to telephone sales and the acceptance of credit cards was innovative for football when already commonplace throughout the leisure industry. The premium rate Spurs-Line service was inaugurated, again a first for a football club. Fans dialled to hear club news and gossip updated on a daily basis. This proved a massive financial success, not least because Irving Scholar was said to phone it all day, every day whenever he was away from the club. Moneyspinners such as Spurs videos and books were launched, and Spurs became one of the first clubs to utilise mail-order and produce their own catalogue. In fact, so successful were these ventures, that Scholar was tempted to take over the production and distribution of licensed ventures for other clubs. And this is where the trouble began.

The purchase of sports and leisurewear clothing companies Hummel, Martex and Stumps, and the ticketing operation Synchro Systems saw the club getting involved in areas peripheral to their core business. The debts incurred during the acquisition, running and subsequent loss-making sale of these companies were a major cause of the club's financial crisis in the late 1980s.

'People get confused,' says Freedman, 'when discussing Tottenham's merchandising, and bring up subsidiary companies like Hummel and Martex. These had nothing to do with the merchandising of Tottenham Hotspur, which was profitable, successful and a very good business.

'I discovered that the football side was seen as the all

important side of everything that ruled the club. Directors were always looking for the Saturday, for the match. Very few directors actually knew, or were involved in, the merchandising side of things. This wasn't the interesting part of the game.'

When those directors did get involved, their lack of expertise cost their clubs dearly. Freedman recalls, 'I saw that clubs, for short term gain, would sell their long term future. People who knew their business, in say scarves or mugs, would go along to a club and offer them small amounts of money – maybe £500 or £1,000 – for a licence. Clubs took that money thinking it was a sum they never had previously. They were happy to leave the merchandising to these so-called "experts" from outside. But to my mind, the clubs were getting the thin end of the wedge, taking the five or ten percent while the outsiders were taking the other 90 percent.

'There were also a lot of people attracted to football merchandising who were cowboys. They weren't always telling the club what they were doing or how they were doing it, or exactly how much they were making from their licences. It had to be monitored and policed.'

So why wasn't Freedman able to stay and ensure long term growth?

'For a number of reasons. After the [Sugar/Venables] takeover, I was called into a very hostile meeting with the Tottenham board. I was seen as Irving's man and, particularly, Irving's "friend". I had questions thrown at me by Eddie Ashby [then helping Terry Venables run the club on a day-to-day basis]. But I had all my facts and figures to hand, and passed them around the table, inviting anyone to pick holes in them.

'Sugar then read the balance sheet pretty quickly, and

commented that things weren't really that bad after all. The meeting changed its tone, and I was given a chance to continue.'

It was the non-payment of a bonus, due for the previous year's performance, that was to drive a wedge between Freedman and the new board.

'It became clear that Tottenham were never going to pay me my bonus. They even tried to bring in a friend of Eddie Ashby's to work in merchandising. I told them – as managing director of merchandising – that wasn't on and that I was going to go home and remain there until the bonus was paid. Things got a bit heavy and they said more or less, "Don't come back", so I made my decision to leave, whether I got my bonus or not. I just didn't want to carry on.'

Having been at White Hart Lane for five years since 1987, and a supporter since a boy, Freedman felt deeply concerned by much of what he experienced personally and what he observed around the club.

'I phoned Colin Sandy [then Tottenham's financial director] and told him that I felt it would be in the club's best interest if I sat down with him, and Alan Sugar, and had a chat. I told them I could feel what was happening at Tottenham [the day-to-day problems in running the club], and felt that what I had to say would be in both their interests.

'I never got a reply.

'I gave it a week, then rang one final time, repeating my previous offer to have an off-the-record chat, at a time and location of their choosing. I got a phone call back half-an-hour later from Colin Sandy. He said he'd spoken to Alan Sugar, who felt it was a good idea, and could I meet him at 3pm Thursday at Terry's club Scribes?'

Freedman still cannot help laughing when telling this

story. The penny still hadn't dropped with Sugar. Freedman told them, 'Colin, you and Alan are obviously living in a different world, and so forget it. Leave it.'

He continues, 'The pair were at that time still totally committed to the idea that Venables knew what he was doing, as well as having a lot of confidence in Eddie Ashby. I suppose when you go into business with someone like Venables, you've got to give the man a good chance.

'But it wasn't going to cost him anything to see me for half-an-hour. And whatever he learned – whether he then discarded that information or not – I was inside the operation.

'I was very bitter when I left Tottenham, and felt convinced that one day things would all blow up. In fact, on the Thursday night after Venables had left, Sugar phoned me and said: "You know he's gone?" Which of course I did. He actually said he'd like to talk to me about it now. I agreed, but I must have been half asleep. When I came to my senses, I asked myself, *why should I?* I phoned him and pointed out that I did in fact work for another club now, and that before any meeting could take place I would need Sugar to fax through the questions that he wanted answering. I also said I'd like to tell my chairman of any proposed meeting.

'I never, ever, heard from him again.'

If Edward Freedman thought he'd left his problems behind at White Hart Lane, he was soon to find that things could be just as chaotic at Old Trafford.

'In my first week, I dug out all the licensing agreements the club had made with anybody. Every single one, and I put an end to them. Everything I could, I took totally in-house. We sourced the product, bought it for a price and sold it for a price. Total control over our products, and of course the margins were better.

Top Gear

'I had no office, just a Portakabin alongside the shop, and an assistant I took on. My first task was to look at the retail area. There were approximately twelve people working in the whole merchandising division. Our mail-order operation had one telephone with one person answering the phone and one person despatching the goods.

'My first priority was not only to get as many people into the shop as I could, but also to serve them. The amount of money we were taking was being limited by the number of tills we had in the shop. People were waiting to pay, so we eliminated that wait. We had eleven tills, and so I proposed we should double that to 22. "How?" they asked. Easy, by putting a new till in next to an existing one. We doubled turnover on a matchday by that one simple scheme.

'On a more strategic note, we were aware we had to have much larger premises. I also looked at the mail-order situation, which was a nonsense with just one phone. So we brought in more bodies and more telephones and more people to do the packing. We improved the catalogue and began using the programme to advertise our merchandise.

'Next, I got to thinking how, on a matchday, Manchester United attracts people from all over the country. So how can we get to those people who don't come to the ground every week? Maybe we can make our product available in other areas away from the ground. There were frowns as people thought we'd be taking custom away from ourselves, but as I told them, we couldn't cope with the level of business then anyway. People were coming to us from all over, but couldn't get into the shop.

'So I looked at starting a wholesale business, where we would supply retailers with our products. That again was something I'd started at Tottenham.

'The next issue I pondered was how we reached the

Dream On

consumers. I decided that we might be able to sustain a Manchester United magazine. I went to the chairman with this proposed project and said, "Look, this is the first time I've come to you with a project, but I've got a feeling on this one. I could lose money on the first year. But I think it will do a lot more for us than if we look upon it purely as a balance sheet exercise".

'I argued that through the magazine we'd be reaching people who don't come to the ground. I said I felt we had a very "sexy" team with players like Ryan Giggs. I said look at *Shoot* and *Match*. They carry 20 pages each issue on Manchester United players, and we get nothing from that.

'And so we started the magazine, and I think that magazine was one of the biggest contributors to the appeal of Manchester United.' In fact, with sales of over 100,000 it is Britain's biggest selling football monthly.

'We did a survey and found out that 83% of the people who buy the magazine only come to one match a year. So the magazine was a wonderful tool for merchandising. A couple of times a year we will put in a merchandising catalogue which is enormously successful for us. Then we brought out bi-monthly videos, which we'd never done before.'

Freedman's spectacular success at Old Trafford made other clubs sit up and take notice. The trouble is, few clubs are prepared to make the commitment or the investment that Manchester United have.

'Of course, other clubs look at what we do, and think if they do the same then that's the answer. That is not the answer. You can't just revoke all your licences. You can't just start up a wholesale business. They think, "You have a magazine; we'll have a magazine". But let me tell you, I have been reading the current Manchester United magazine and I've had a good hour and a half's read. Interesting football reading. Pick up any other club's magazine and that's not the case.

'Newsagents all over the country are now full of football magazines where once there was just *Shoot*, *Match* and *90 Minutes*. But no one seems to see what the difference is, what the quality difference is. We've got to look at everything through the supporter's eyes. We give them a magazine that they want to buy because it tells them about Manchester United. About Manchester United players. About the football. And the photography is as good as any other magazine in the country. To have a feature on the club's vice-president or to advertise a mobile phone company down the High Road is not what that magazine is about.

'Too many decisions are made with no thought given to the supporters. I still have a battle at Manchester United; we put the logo on certain products I wouldn't want to put it on. You don't want to brand everything that comes along.

'I said earlier how, if you are not getting what you ought to be out of a licensing agreement, then you should do it yourself. However, I think if you then look at what you've done, and it appears you have turned a very small licensing operation into a mega-business, then there is possibly a case for licensing out. If you are talking about mega-money, and if you can get guarantees over the next five years or whatever. But you must build up the perceived brand value first. Don't devalue the brand. Keep the brand strong.'

When people think of football merchandising, they immediately think of replica kits, the most salient manifestation of club merchandising. Manufacturers like Adidas, Reebok, Umbro, Pony and Nike vie for contracts with top clubs, knowing that the rewards can be enormous. Adidas has sold 500,000 of the current Newcastle shirt, fuelling a

Dream On

tenfold growth in turnover to £40 million in less than five years, and meaning that almost one percent of the country's population owns one.

Contrary to popular belief, Spurs were in fact the first club to utilise three kits in one season back in 1986. However, it is Manchester United, more than any other team, who cop the flak for changing their strip so often, with so many of their change strips appearing to be blatant fashion opportunism.

'Whether I personally think we ought to have three kits in a season, I'm not sure. But I have no control over that. It's already in the contract with Umbro which was signed years ago. Manufacturers have given out a certain amount of money on a contract, and they want to get their money back. But if supporters are making complaints about kit changes, those complaints have got to be taken on board. In any business you must listen to the people buying the goods.' Not a view common or popular in the football industry.

With United's current Umbro deal set to expire in 1998, the club are making sure they do their homework before entering into any new deal.

'We have been working for three months solid to determine "the value of kits", because no one knows what the true value is. People tell me that it is fantastic that Liverpool have got £23.5 million over five years for their kit deal. But I'm not sure. Is it fantastic? Why is it fantastic? Is it because we, Manchester United, only got £15 million?

'So we've gone through kit supply and kit production in detail. And asked questions like: what is a kit worth? What does it cost? What can it be sold at? We have all the documents from our kit suppliers, we know exactly how many shirts we have sold, how many shorts, how many socks, how many jackets. We've got costings and selling prices and we've got supporter analysis on what they want.

Top Gear

So now we feel we know how much a manufacturer could or should earn from a kit deal.

'Now we've got a good idea of what our value is, we can argue from a position of strength. Too often the benchmark had been simply to compare the proposed deal with what had gone previously.'

Subsequently in the face of stiff competition, Umbro renegotiated their contract and, in February 1996, signed a new agreement until 2002, guaranteeing Manchester United minimum earnings of £58 million.

The fans themselves seem to be taking a more philosophical approach to merchandising. After all, they reason, nobody forces us to buy the stuff. And if it is tat, they won't.

'It's true,' concurs Freedman, 'I think one of the nicest things since I've been here is that I don't have to fight people every day by justifying what we are doing. The fans do it for us.

'Take the megastore, which is a 5,000 square foot shop. I *really* found it embarrassing that I'd look out of the window of my office above the shop and see people standing in the pouring rain, queuing to get into the shop. We opened the megastore because there was a demand for it. I also think the fans understand that the money we take through merchandising goes back into the club; to buy players; to improve the stadium. The fans haven't got a problem with that.

'It would be wonderful to have a stadium where you don't have to charge money and you could give away kits. But it's an economic world and we try not to rip off the fans. We've got a very discerning fan base. Fans know you can buy a sweater for £30 and if we try and charge them £40 or £50 they won't tolerate it. They are not stupid. What we try to

Dream On

do is get the same value, the same product and enhance it with a Manchester United logo. And if we can do that, and compete with the normal retail prices, then I'm happy and they're happy.'

Despite the strides in Freedman's four years at Old Trafford, there is still much to do before Manchester United can feel they have achieved their full potential. Eyes are being cast overseas.

'We've done very well in the UK, but what about abroad? You go all over the world and you see NFL products everywhere. Ask the people there what they know about American Football, the answer is "not much". But have they heard of Manchester United? "Oh yes, we've heard of Manchester United!"

'So, if there was a Manchester United product for sale, would they buy it? "Of course", they say. So now we've got another big area to look at. That's our next big step. Export.'

Given the runaway success of Manchester United's merchandising push, with turnover exceeding Old Trafford gate receipts and almost matching the entire turnover of Tottenham Hotspur Football Club, why are other clubs lagging so far behind?

'Well for a start, Manchester United is a massive club. The only possible comparison in recent years would be Liverpool.'

Possibly, but five years ago, Glasgow Rangers were bigger than Manchester United. And Arsenal had just won the league. And even Spurs were arguably up there with them. So there were five contenders, but now Manchester United are in a commercial league of their own. What happened to the others?

'Well, there is a factor called investment. Without invest-ment, you can't get a return.'

Top Gear

Freedman could have added that they were sadly deficient in the basic tenets of common sense.

'Imagine each of those clubs getting a phone call tomorrow morning from their manager, who was raving about a player who may, or may not, turn out to be sensational. But it would cost the club a million pounds to buy that player and find out. The club's attitude would be to say, "Well, for only a million, so what? Go and buy him!" But you phone any Premier League chairman and propose a commercial investment of £100,000 listing both the up-sides and the possible down-sides, how many of those chairmen in the Premier League would give the project the go-ahead?'

Freedman knows from experience the answer is none. Well, perhaps one.

'Let me tell you a story. We get all of the clubs [apart from Tottenham] wanting to visit us, to see how we are doing things. What they do about it I don't know, but they are always welcome. We had this one phone call from a major club. From a chairman respected for his commercial expertise, who said that he'd seen the operation at Manchester United, thought it was absolutely fantastic, and could his architects please come up and look at the warehouse?

'I asked why Manchester United's warehouse? Why not Marks & Spencer's? Or Tesco's? Surely they have a better operation than we have? After all, we inherited four walls and some racking, that's all the warehouse is. But he was adamant.

'So the chairman sent up two chaps, one a consultant, the other an architect, and I said the same thing to them. Why have you come to see our warehouse?

'They admitted they were paying lip service to their client. Their client had seen our operation and believed the secret was the warehouse. He'd seen our warehouse and he believed everything happened because we had "a warehouse". The consultant said he knew that wasn't true, and that he realised it was the people who were running the operation. So, I showed them around, and then we went back to my office for a coffee. I asked them, "What next?"

'They said, "Are you prepared to come and do the same for our client?"

'I laughed. I told them their client wouldn't pay me the money for a start [Freedman had dealt with that particular club previously and they'd wanted him on the cheap then]. And what were they going to tell their client anyway? That they'd "seen a warehouse"?

'That's absolutely true. He [the chairman] didn't have the perception to conceive what was behind this £23 million operation. What the structure is. What has gone into it. He just saw "a warehouse".'

Manchester United's 'secret' is no such thing. It is just a down-to-earth philosophy applied as it would be to any other service business – give the customers value so they will come back for more. But football's chairmen by and large cannot seem to grasp that basic premise. And so, although there are notable pockets of excellence where clubs are at last waking up to marketing, for many the hunt is still on for the quick and cheap fix.

'I had a phone call from another chairman,' continues Freedman, 'who came up here to see our operation. Before he'd even left the warehouse he was asking me to go back and work for him! This with my chairman only four paces behind us.

'I declined, of course, and four days later this chairman phoned me and said that he'd now got someone to do the job, and could that person please come up and visit our premises?

Top Gear

'So this chap came and sat in my office for an hour, and it soon transpired that this chap had no experience in the field we were discussing. Some time after, when someone asked me what I'd thought of my visitor, I had to admit that I'd found him a comedian.

'"Oh, did you know he was?" they asked. I said "I'm sorry . . . ?"'

'"That's his part-time job! He actually is a comedian around clubs in the evening!" That chap who'd come to see me was the chairman's best friend, and he thought he'd get him to run his merchandising operation!'

As the saying goes, you couldn't make this up.

If Manchester United can climb, in three years, from £2 million to £23.5 million turnover in merchandising, that surely hints at the possible wealth for the Premier League as a whole. There are probably tribesmen in undiscovered Amazon rain forests who have yet to see a white man, but who are wearing Chicago Bears caps and LA Raiders puffa jackets. The English Premier League has the potential to emulate basketball's NBA, the wrestling WWF or American Football's NFL. With soccer being the world's favourite sport, and England the founding father, there are none of the constraints that have been faced by America's manufactured sports in their wish to expand their fan base overseas. Courtesy of television, Premier League clubs are well supported in the Far East. The Manchester United magazine sells nearly 20,000 copies in Thailand and a local Malaysian edition is about to be launched. By contrast, Premier League merchandising is conspicuous by its absence.

The NFL brand has an image that has been carefully manufactured and sold to the world as skilfully as any Marlboro, Coca-Cola, Harley-Davidson or Levi's product. Buying branded NFL merchandise buys you into the lifestyle, and the premium prices seem merely to enhance the value-for-money cachet. And the Premier League? Well you can buy Premier League crisps, although not for much longer as the manufacturer, KP, is reported to be pulling out.

'We've been very fortunate in football,' admits Freedman. 'There has been a lot of money thrown at football. Some of it has been caught. Some if it has slipped through the fingers. Some if it is still slipping through the fingers. But it isn't because anyone has got clever out there.'

Rather than protecting its integrity, only accepting sponsors in a secondary role and thereby turning over a more valuable product to television, the Premier League has gone for the easy option. It, alone of the major European leagues, has unforgivably allowed title sponsorship – a beer company for pity's sake – and continues to sell its licences on the basis of a new source of income rather than as a result of a planned policy. For instance, Freedman is appalled at how cheaply the League sold the rights to use its name in a sticker deal.

'What they try to do is side deals. Little deals with people that come along, like the clubs were doing five years ago. Look how little they sold the [Premier League] sticker collection for. And they think that's the best deal they've done! But if you look at the structure of sticker deals, and how much money there is in sticker deals, you'll soon realise that the one deal they did for the whole Premier League, Manchester United could do for themselves. And make more money.'

And what will they do when the next TV deal is negotiated?

For Tottenham at least, it's not all bad news; perhaps just a case of must try harder. Or simply must aim higher.

Top Gear

On the field, despite his conscientiousness, there is still a doubt as to whether manager Gerry Francis will succeed at the highest level. And the same accusation can be made of the man running the off-field activities, Claude Littner.

Put bluntly, Claude Littner is seen as Alan Sugar's hatchet man, although he no doubt would prefer the title of trouble-shooter. In hot-spots around the world, Claude has been called in to act as Amstrad's Mr Fix-it; his master's voice with a brief to get the corporate train back on the rails, leaving a leaner and fitter outfit as his legacy. When the departure of Terry Venables left a vacant chief executive position at White Hart Lane, he was an obvious candidate, particularly as Tottenham's train hadn't so much gone off the rails as ripped up the track and used it to fire the boiler.

For Alan Sugar, Claude is the perfect man to leave in charge of the day-to-day running of the club. Well perhaps at least until Sugar junior, son Daniel, finishes his apprenticeship and assumes Littner's mantle. Still only in his mid-forties, there are plenty more Air Miles for Claude to clock up once his tenure in N17 is over. In the meantime, he is doing a great job, as he himself will tell you. And if you don't agree, then more fool you.

'I'd love to explain why we are doing so well but I can't,' is Claude's riposte to a enquiry about the club's business strategy, confirming that Tottenham's gain was a great loss for the diplomatic corps.

Claude's problem is that, unlike co-directors Messrs Alexiou and Berry for instance, he is not a long-time fan (hence his reported suggestion that the club ought to utilise local referees after once again having to pay travelling expenses for a match official), and therefore cannot appreci-ate where the fans, his customers, are coming from. Instead, his sole aim seems to be to improve the existing situation. He

Dream On

therefore plays by the book, using his experience and MBA qualification to attempt to solve the maverick problems that are endemic in the football business. Up to a point, this works. But there's the rub: an improvement in the mess he inherited is viewed in isolation as a success. No one would doubt that the club is thriving now, with the receipts to prove it. But perhaps Claude's lack of product knowledge prevents him from taking the club that extra step, where success is judged not merely on what has gone before, but on what could possibly be.

His two major deals with Pony (kit suppliers) and Hewlett-Packard (shirt sponsors) are viewed by Claude himself as major achievements, simply because they show a substantial advance on the previous agreements with Umbro and Holsten. But the sums involved, particularly for the shirt deal, are no great shakes compared to the deals signed by clubs, who also appreciate precedent, but place the emphasis on what can be realised in today's expansionist climate. It begs the question of how the current regime would have coped in a pre-Premiership era and highlights how Tottenham have not optimised their true commercial potential, especially given finance director John Sedgwick's explanation in the *Financial Times* that, 'We're not so dependent on gate receipts now or even on the performance of the football team'.

This was probably best illustrated during the one year that Jurgen Klinsmann spent at the club. The full-blown Klinsmania that swept England that season should have been a godsend to Tottenham's bottom line. But the accounts show that merchandising turnover only rose by £66,000 over the previous season though profits rose to more than £600,000. This was a missed opportunity that Claude attributes to Klinsmann's 'unwillingness to co-

Top Gear

operate' with the club. The other side of that argument is represented by Klinsmann's lawyer, Andy Gross, who was dismayed to have travelled to London from Switzerland specifically to find some common ground with Claude Littner. No co-operation could be agreed for player/club initiatives. The club even refused to stock the official Klinsmann magazine which would certainly have sold many more than the 15,000 copies it did if it had been readily available in the club shops. In contrast, a much tougher cookie than Klinsmann, Eric Cantona, has struck a mutually beneficial deal with his club on a number of merchandising items.

Where once Tottenham, in the persons of Irving Scholar and Edward Freedman, were pioneers, the club now slavishly follows others. When it became known that Manchester United had secured a blockbuster £6 million deal with the video company VCI, Claude was reduced to phoning VCI with the plaintive cry of 'What about us?'

'You disappoint me if you don't think we do an exceptional job,' bridled Littner, at the implication that there is someone out there doing a better one. If he is to change, then it will only come via a directive from Alan Sugar, whom Claude refers to as 'a very clever man, a wise man. I say that as someone working for him.' From Sugar's point of view, Claude has done everything asked of him; reducing costs and boosting turnover. The squeals from staff at White Hart Lane – especially at the reported introduction of a telephone call logging system – will merely convince the chairman that Claude's draconian cost-cutting measures are hitting home.

What isn't in dispute is the personal control that Claude Littner exercises, as a result of which Tottenham cannot be accused of an Arsenal director's confession that, 'We err on the side of generosity'. Quite the contrary: to avoid writing out cheques for small amounts, when there was a shortfall in ticket applications, for example, staff were encouraged to send back the balance in the form of vouchers which could be redeemed against club merchandise. Further, Sunday ticket sales are discouraged because of the reluctance to pay overtime rates. As someone who knows both Littner and Sugar wisecracked, 'The reason Alan likes him so much is that he is the only bloke he knows who is meaner than himself'.

Post-Venables, there was undoubtedly scope for some fat trimming, though not from the chief executive's salary; Claude earns well into six figures making him among the highest paid directors in the Premiership, notwithstanding his tranche of share options which, when exercised, may take him into the millionaire category.

'It's chalk and cheese compared to the old regime. It's a tight, sharp company now, with tough working principles. There are systems in place; there is harmony because people understand what is required of them. People understand the company's objectives. There are no people working to different agendas. If you write that it [Tottenham's business strategy] is just a cost-cutting exercise, that will be a very shallow piece of reporting,' says the man who is alleged to have cancelled milk deliveries to the club because it was cheaper to buy from the supermarket, and who charged club captain Gary Mabbutt for the use of the corner flags at his testimonial game. But perhaps one can go too far; as someone who worked with him explained: in football 'You were expected to act in a way that modern business found unacceptable. There *was* too much laxity [at Tottenham]. He had to sort that out and in doing so often used a sledgehammer to crack a nut.'

Littner continues, 'Ignoring the football side – though we

are doing very well at the moment – it's a very successful operation. You don't get over five million cost-cutting.' True, but it is only half the story. The 'five million' to which Claude refers is the clubs's profit, but only after taking into account some severely reduced year-on-year costs. The previous accounting period had seen some hefty legal bills and a whopping £1.5 million fine paid to the FA. Since then, increased ground capacity and some of the highest seat and season ticket prices in the Premiership has boosted income. If the criterion was satisfying the major shareholder and producing profits for the plc, then it was a job well done. However, for some this was not enough. In the view of one shareholder, 'If we could have protected the soul and tradition at the same time, it would have been a major achievement. Unfortunately we are some way short of the second part.' Maybe it is time to dust down Keith Burkinshaw's famous quote: 'There used to be a football club over there . . .'

If true, this is a disappointing state of affairs given that Claude had his cards marked for him when Alan Sugar asked both Tony Berry and Douglas Alexiou to interview him prior to appointment. 'Let me tell you,' Alexiou told Littner, 'a football club has a soul. Whatever we do we must not lose our soul.'

Comparing today with yesterday, Alexiou does find some plus points. 'Irving Scholar had a wonderful house style. "We will see what comes round the corner, then we will decide what to do", was, in its own way, wonderful. He had tremendous flair. This is a much more thoughtful, thorough organisation. Sometimes a bit of discipline isn't a bad thing, as long as it is balanced.' Alan Sugar agrees: 'It's not the kind of social club for the lads to meet up in the wooden shed any more . . . Fact is, it's an institution that has to be run properly and have tight financial controls. So you can't say to hell with everything, let's just enjoy the football.'

But that doesn't mean you have to sell tickets in the directors' box. Throughout the Premier League, most members of the football fraternity – visiting managers and coaches – will be welcomed in the home directors' box and lounge. At Tottenham, with priority given to paid-for seats by thirteen vice-presidents, there is no guarantee that a manager won't end up in the East Stand. Especially if you are Ted Buxton, ex-Tottenham employee and current England scout.

The Annual General Meeting was a chance for the board to announce some healthy profit figures for the 1994–95 season, as well as to reassure supporters that a steady hand was now steering the good ship AMS Tottenham. The meeting, held at the Boxholders' Lounge in the West Stand, is a popular event for those fans who have bought shares in their club, and who like to think such a purchase gives them a say in the running of it. For many, it is their only opportunity to share a room with the Spurs hierarchy, and have the opportunity to fire off questions with the right to expect a reply. Strictly speaking, the discussion should be on the club's fiscal performance, but in truth the financial aspects are glossed over and it is only at the Q&A session that the meeting tends to come alive.

The broad facts are set out in the Annual Report, but few of those present would have been that interested in wading through 30 pages of accountant-speak. Those that could be bothered would have seen that the club were announcing a profit for the year of £5.3 million, up six-fold from the previous year's £885,000. Turnover was also up by about £3 million, to £25,083,000 and, not surprisingly, most of the club's running costs had been reduced, notably

Claude's admin expenses which were down by a whopping £1.5 million per year. That's a lot of milk.

Also detailed in the report was the £50,000 paid indirectly to Sugar for his services at the club, together with a further sum of £22,185 by way of interest on loans since repaid. After tax, there was still enough left in the kitty for the board to pay a dividend of 3p to every shareholder. Not exactly a windfall for those with just one framed share hanging on their lounge wall, but a tidy sum for the likes of A M Sugar of Chigwell who had accumulated 8,150,535 of them. With the club capitalised at around £50 million the chairman's majority shareholding was now worth more than twice his original stake.

At a previous AGM, Alan Sugar had come in for criticism from a shareholder who proclaimed his familiarity with the workings of the City. This man had told Sugar he 'must be dreaming' if he thought he'd create a market for Tottenham shares; that sports and leisure industry shares like those of Tottenham were of no interest whatsoever to City financial institutions. Sugar, who has made little secret of the fact he saw his involvement in Tottenham as an investment on which he hoped to show a profit, said that although he respected the chap's experience, he intended to prove him wrong.

And he has. The only way the club's shares would increase in value was if they were actively being traded. From under 100p per share at the time of the Venables resignation, Tottenham shares have risen in value to over 300p each, triple the original offer price. Indeed, two institutions are listed in the Annual Report as having a significant holding of Tottenham shares. This is a major achievement for the club and an indicator of the stability and long term confidence from within the City. More than this, though, it reflects the

Dream On

fact that football, at least in the Premiership, is a high growth leisure industry. Fund managers seemingly can't get enough of football club shares.

With the accounts swiftly dealt with, the chairman was able to move on to the part of the meeting that perhaps he dislikes most, unlike his predecessor who so enjoyed the cut and thrust of football issues that he often intercepted the questions directed at his team's manager, questions from the floor. Alan Sugar never seems particularly at ease when called upon to perform in public. Sure, he is hardly lacking in confidence, but his seeming inability to tone down his naturally abrasive style is a recipe for a PR disaster. Not that he shies away from the task. Far from it. At this year's AGM, it was only Alan Sugar and Gerry Francis who got to speak, despite the rest of the board being in attendance. Given that the directors owe their appointment to their business expertise, it was strange they were not allowed the opportunity for public speaking. It can only be hoped that things are different at board meetings.

From a footballing point of view, the chairman's address in the annual report struck a defensive note which echoed previous outbursts against escalating transfer costs.

'The start of this season,' it began, 'has seen a dramatic increase in the cost of player transfers in the British transfer market to such an extent that commercially it is impossible to compete if the fortunes of the club and the Company are to remain intact in the long term. Irresponsible spending of money that we do not have will simply result in the all too familiar financial crisis that the club and its supporters have seen over the years. I am confident that with strict financial control, a good youth policy and a responsible and experienced coaching department, we can build a championship winning team within the next few years with a depth of squad to give us consistency.'

Perhaps few had read this statement, or maybe its implications had yet to sink in. Certainly, when the floor was opening for 'any questions' there was no rush to query the club's stance. Initial questions covered routine matters that allowed Alan Sugar to rattle off routine answers. Yes, the South Stand development was complete. The club was just commencing the process of applying for planning permission for the proposed North Stand, and no, there was as yet no date for the commencement of work. Sugar's explanation was that he [the club?] didn't want to put in more seats until he knew he could sell out the ones he already had. Given that virtually every game at White Hart Lane was now playing to capacity attendances (average gates at over 30,000 were up by more than 10%), it will be difficult to justify this argument at the next AGM if work has not begun by then.

Alan Sugar also confirmed that he was still the personal guarantor for the club's bank loans. He made light of this issue, perhaps an indication that the sums involved were not likely to cause him too much personal grief should he ever be required to bale out the club once more. Originally thought to have been taken out to underwrite construction costs for the South Stand, now that the project was complete, it was unclear to what purpose the money was earmarked. New players perhaps? Or to finance the new North Stand? Whatever, there didn't appear the need for such extensive borrowing. But then Alan Sugar would never be seduced into becoming a benefactor. Despite, or because of, the return on his capital, Tottenham would remain first and foremost a business risk, and one he was happy to share with his bankers. Indeed a few months later in April '96, Alan Sugar reduced his shareholding by 10% as part of an £11 million rights issue to fund further stadium redevelopment including the rebuilding of the North Stand, raising capacity to 36,000 in the process.

The meeting moved along, and the first note of dissent arose when a season-ticket holder complained that his ticket no longer gave him free admission to watch reserve team fixtures. Sugar acknowledged this would remain so as long as the club played reserve 'home' fixtures at the ground of St Albans FC. When the new training ground in Chigwell was ready, it was expected that reserve fixtures would switch there and once again season-ticket holders could enjoy their former privilege.

These responses were rattled off by Sugar in a perfunctory manner, as he was fed with notes and whispered advice by Claude Littner. Quite why Claude himself was not called upon to answer specific questions is a mystery. He is, after all, in charge of the day-to-day running of the club, but his role for this afternoon seemed to be as personal prompter to Sugar.

For the chairman, a meeting that had started so well took a downward turn when another question from the floor took him to task. A fiesty woman, who announced herself as a teacher at a drama school (and who accordingly declined the use of the microphone offered to her), listed a string of grievances broadly covering the cost of a day out at White Hart Lane and the perceived poor quality of the Pony replica shirts.

Sugar bristled, as protocol forced him to suffer in silence as the list of complaints came thick and fast. Rarely looking up from the copious notes he was scrawling, he allowed the criticism to run its course without interruption. The fading collars on the Pony shirts was a known problem and one over which the club had already received many complaints. Full refunds, he assured, were available to those who so wished. As to the price of food and drink within the stadium, there was little he could do about this matter which was determined by outside caterers. This, of course, was surprising, as the club would surely retain some degree of control over such matters. But one suspected that Mr Sugar, and the rest of his board for that matter, may have had little idea or concern for the prices charged within the ground for tea, coffee or the ubiquitous burgers. It would have been instructive to ask the assembled board perhaps to name those food and drink items they thought were available at the catering concessions, and perhaps hazard a guess at the prices they thought were being charged.

Still, Sugar did his best to cover the points one by one, but was not allowed to complete his answers. When the shareholder then interrupted him for a second time, it was all too much for his trigger temper to bear. Throwing down his pen in disgust, he delivered a withering broadside that attempted to put the poor woman firmly in her place.

'Madam,' he laboured with undisguised sarcasm. 'If the only point of you being here is to advance your acting career, I don't think there is any point in continuing this discussion.'

At that moment, the whole tone of the meeting changed. Regardless of the perceived provocation, Sugar had snapped at a woman who was both a supporter and a shareholder. There were audible intakes of breath, and several 'tut-tuts' as the jibe went down very badly indeed. Nevertheless Sugar ploughed on, wrapping up the discussion with another dose of gratuitous irony. 'I'm glad you had no bad points to make about Tottenham.'

Those present at a previous year's AGM may recall a similar incident when a Canadian lady took the chairman

Dream On

to task. The woman had been trying to pre-book match tickets from Canada, pending a visit to England. Her gripe concerned the club's inability to deal effectively with her telephone enquiries. Sugar handled the question in a not unsympathetic manner, stating that he too had fallen foul of the club's switchboard system, and promised that a new, more efficient system was on its way. However, after the meeting, during the low-key autograph-signing sessions that takes place, the same lady sought out Sugar. Sensing her approach, Sugar looked up and without even waiting to discover what her intentions were, said: 'Madam, I hope you are not here to cause trouble, for that would not be the tone of today's meeting'. At this she turned on her heels and marched off, presumably to sell her shares and take a vow never to return to a club run by such a man.

Maybe Alan Sugar will eventually master the niceties of social protocol. Maybe he would argue that you don't amass a personal fortune by being pleasant to people. But fortunately the afternoon had a saviour.

As the topic moved away from club affairs and on to playing matters, it was Gerry's turn to field questions. Which he did, it must be said, with much aplomb. In stark contrast to the brittle, almost self-conscious persona that Gerry seems to adopt for post-match press conferences, the Gerry on display this afternoon was a warm, witty and engaging individual who diffused any remnants of tension by simply charming the supporters with his honesty, and obvious enthusiasm for Tottenham. Like most people in the audience, Tony Berry was pleasantly surprised by the manager's performance.

'I thought it encouraging that he found it so easy. He always seems so diffident, so tentative. He doesn't speak easily. He showed a lighter side that sometimes doesn't come through on television or other interviews. I thought he saw the meeting had got into a difficult phase, something Alan was sorry about afterwards. We both had another meeting to go to so we rushed out together, but in the car park Alan admitted he wished he hadn't risen to the bait. But fortunately Gerry diffused the situation. In many ways he has a similar quality to Sugar; you hear the same story wherever you are. There is no ducking and diving; frankly, what he told the board was what he told the shareholders. From that point of view they are both of a similar nature. If they've got something to say, then they'll say it. At least you know where you stand.'

Gerry took the trouble to stand up when answering questions, a small mark of respect to the audience that was not lost on them, and he was happy to give expansive answers to even those questions that perhaps never warranted them.

Commensurate with the team's buoyant current form, few questions were openly hostile to Gerry. Tactics, transfers and player selection came up for discussion – the position of Erik Thorstvedt, the acquisition of Ruel Fox and the health of Darren Anderton. But Gerry gave a good account of himself. Nor did he shy away from tricky issues. He also joked that he wasn't as naïve as some may think and was well aware of which players he needed to get rid of. 'Judge me on my results,' he asked. 'If I've got it wrong, then this will be my first and last AGM.'

He even managed to elicit a smile from the drama teacher by cheekily suggesting that her support of the club could be taken a stage further by 'having more children,' thereby facilitating the youth development policy.

The non-selection of Ilie Dumitrescu was patiently explained, using statistics (only six wins in the eighteen appearances made by the player since his arrival) to justify the tag of a 'defensive liability'. The player, said Gerry, would be sold the moment a suitable buyer could be found, as would defenders Scott and Cundy. He did remind supporters, however, that all those named were currently on long-term and extremely lucrative contracts which would make it hard for other clubs to match such favourable terms.

An interesting point raised was who would eventually succeed Gary Mabbutt as club captain. Gerry responded that, if necessary, he would buy a captain, giving an indication that he believes the role important enough not to be simply awarded to any player on a seniority basis, thereby insinuating that there was no one currently at the club who fits the bill. Which is a shame, but probably a reflection of what most supporters already presumed.

Indicating Bill Nicholson, who was sitting at an adjoining table, and perhaps with reference to the 'I'll give it one more year' comment, Francis paid homage to the former manager's achievements. 'I'm here to emulate what this man has done before me,' he said. Then, in a none-too subtle reference to his chairman, Gerry said he would commit his future to Tottenham, 'as long the club remained in a position to win things'. Gerry had already made it clear the current squad was not strong enough to mount a championship challenge. This fairly and squarely placed an obligation on Alan Sugar to make cash available, as well as giving the manager a get-out clause if those funds never materialised. Clever man.

As the meeting wound down and supporters drifted away, there was an unmistakable optimism about the club and its future. True, there had been a comparable mood only a couple of years earlier, when Terry Venables and Alan Sugar had combined for a wise-cracking double-act worthy of Morecambe and Wise. Only after the subsequent acrimonious split did Venables reveal the act had been staged for public consumption, after the pair had agreed that the AGM was not the place to reveal the knives that were already out.

But Gerry's sparkling rapport with the fans had erased any distaste caused by his chairman's earlier outburst. The touching deferral to Bill Nicholson was a nice gesture appreciated by all. Particularly, as the club itself seemed unwilling, or simply unable to recognise the importance of tradition and the expectation it fuelled. Bill Nicholson was approaching his 60th anniversary with the club, but one you somehow felt was more a source of embarrassment than of honour to be celebrated.

Probably Messrs Alexiou and Berry are privately embarrassed by the hard-nosed business practices which leave no room for sentiment. They may even concur that the tradition of the club is being undermined. As someone on the inside succinctly said, 'Although we f**ked up the business end, we have always done things with style.'

Well that scenario has been well and truly turned on its head. And who is to say it is for the better? It may still be football the Sugar way, but not as Bill Nick knew it. Poorer in spirit, if not in the pocket.

Chapter 9

Walking Alone

If you can't enjoy the day out when your team plays at Anfield, then you really shouldn't be in football.

For those fans travelling north to support Spurs, the match on 3 February would provide a rare opportunity for a bit of glory-basking. Admittedly it would only be in the afterglow of last season's epic FA Cup sixth round win, but for Spurs this season, despite losing only two away matches, Gerry's safety-first tactics had removed glory from the agenda and there had been few notable scalps. With all the really interesting away games still to come, maybe Anfield would be where things moved up a gear. For the Spurs players, out-fought and out-thought by Liverpool just one week into the new season, there was professional pride to be salvaged. That and the pressing need for three points to consolidate a top five position if realistic hopes of a UEFA Cup place were to be sustained. But for the Spurs directors, the day would set them on course for an embarrassing confrontation with their former chief executive, Terry Venables. It would also illustrate a continuing disregard for footballing

Dream On

protocol and provide further ammunition for those who lament the passing of the old Spurs ways, off the field as well as on.

Of the 3,000 fans travelling north that day, the older ones would remember a time, not that long ago, when going to Liverpool was a rite of passage. If you could say you'd followed your team to Anfield, you were treated with an added respect not accorded to those who merely went to home games, or who only travelled to those 'safe' towns like Ipswich, Coventry or Luton.

The reasons were twofold. For a start, no matter how well Spurs would be playing at the time, they could never manage a win at Anfield. Sometimes they were simply thrashed (7–0 in 1978 seems like only yesterday for those who were there); sometimes they were even given a two-goal lead before being overhauled. The fixture became one of football's best known statistics: Spurs hadn't won at Anfield since 1912, the year the Titanic sank. It got to be an obsession with successive Spurs teams and managers, to be the side that broke the jinx. For the fans too, some of whom will have lived and died without ever seeing a victory, above all others a trip to Liverpool became unmissable, just in case. After a 73-year wait, the win finally came courtesy of a Garth Crooks goal in March 1985. Since then, two further wins and some battling draws have revoked the hoodoo, but a good result at Liverpool will always lift the spirits, especially during an otherwise nondescript season.

The other reason has much to do with the violent nature of football supporting that permeated the game in the Seventies. Certain grounds, like Old Trafford and Elland Road, were renowned for the ferocity of their welcome and a day trip to these fortresses of parochialism was fraught with actual danger. It is alarming to recall just how lax the authorities were with regard to the potential and actual violence that took place in their city centres of a Saturday afternoon.

Liverpool was probably no worse than Manchester or Leeds for a wide-eyed southern innocent. It was just that the menace there was harder to reconcile with the media image that portrayed all Scousers as lovable mop-tops, armed with no more than a razor wit and a penchant for quotable quips. For visiting Londoners, the rules for survival were swiftly learnt. Foremost was no colours; hats and scarves (replica shirts came much later) gave away your allegiance; you could expect a bloodied nose and the offending items to be 'confiscated' by indignant home fans, who saw the exercise as no more than a justifiable tourist tax. Indeed, dress down was rule number two. Through successive eras, your Crombie overcoat, your sheepskin coat, your leather jacket or your trainers would all be liable to be snaffled should you be indiscreet enough to ignore the strict northern dress code. No talking dictated that if you went into a pub, you pointed at the drink you wanted. You particularly didn't ask for 'a light and bitter' which was the sure-fire giveaway of London roots. And you never, ever, knew the time. If a kid sidled up and asked you 'fer the time mister' you shrugged and upped your walking pace, because this was a notorious ruse to gauge your accent for the benefit of his older mates who would be loitering with intent out of sight.

But things changed.

The Heysel disaster in 1985 was a disgraceful episode for English football, but especially for Liverpool FC. The behaviour of their fans in Brussels that night shamed the club's reputation which had been painstakingly built up through the Shankly and Paisley eras. Four years later they were on the receiving end, when they suffered English

Dream On ˙

football's worst disaster as 96 of their fans had the life crushed from them at Hillsborough. As those awful pictures made headline news there could have been few English fans who could not empathise, their worst fears realised as years of flagrant neglect made it a tragedy waiting to happen.

Spurs fans would remember when they too played an FA Cup semi-final at Hillsborough in 1981. The crush at the Leppings Lane end of the ground was acute as thousands of Spurs fans arrived late from the pubs and motorway congestion. Many spilled over onto the pitch and were escorted around the perimeter to the sparsely populated Kop end allocated to Wolves. It went unremarked because it was the sort of thing that happened all too frequently at big games. If you can remember terraces, then you will remember the crush at big games. Crash barriers would twist and snap. Those agile enough would climb out of the danger area and kids would be passed overhead to a safe perimeter spot. It wasn't commonplace, but it happened. Which is why so many must have felt for the Liverpool fans that day. It could have been you. It could have been me. But it wasn't; it was them.

Reaction to Hillsborough brought about the voluntary ceasefire that had eluded endless initiatives from the authorities. Violence became unfashionable and impractical. To continue to behave badly at a football match was at last acknowledged as being uncool, moreover a mark of disrespect to those who had died. As if they hadn't mattered. The move to all-seater stadia, accompanied by stricter segregation, closed-circuit television and the ubiquitous ticket-only restrictions for visiting fans changed the character of the audience. Travelling to away matches ceased to be a spontaneous journey undertaken if a Saturday dawned clear and bright. Despite swingeing price

Walking Alone

rises, tickets were in short supply. Priority was given to holders of season tickets or club members who would be required to rise early and queue late. To be a true supporter required more than just The Right Stuff: you needed the right voucher too. The tacit acceptance that a seat ticket should cost more than a standing ticket ostracised many for whom football attendance was already becoming unaffordable. In their place returned a more mature away fan, who was prepared to pay the premium in return for creature comforts previously denied. In short, you got a better class of away fan. Sure, the boneheads could still seek out match tickets, but their boorish behaviour was in stark contrast to those around them. Violence both inside and around the ground was the exception, as travelling fans became more intent on buying a copy of the home team's fanzine than razing the local shopping precinct.

However, fans at many clubs rebelled, as they quite rightly saw themselves being sacrificed for the benefit of the born-again fan of the new football boom. At clubs like Spurs, Arsenal, Manchester United and Newcastle the directors could afford to take a cavalier attitude to fan loyalty. Stadia capacity had been drastically reduced and by and large, there was enough new money and enough new fans to demonstrate the law of supply and demand.

On Merseyside, where the recession had bitten longer and harder than most places, Liverpool FC were faced with the tricky task of simultaneously redeveloping a stadium and rebuilding a team. Initially they got their priorities wrong and the Anfield trophy room was deprived of its usual display of silverware. But today, the new look Anfield is a credit to the club, with impressive new stands on two sides making the ground one of the very few in the Premiership to hold 40,000. The transformation – executive boxes in

Dream On

the new Centenary Stand and tie-ins with sponsors like McDonald's acknowledge the harsh facts of commercial life – has been achieved without alienating their core support, despite the Kop redevelopment, and without resorting to a ticket pricing structure that brings out the placards of protest.

Although the club can guarantee a sell-out for most home games, they are unfailingly generous in their ticket allocation to visitors. Both inside and outside the ground, the atmosphere is charged, but without the air of menace that once prevailed. Visiting fans are welcomed and visiting colours are openly worn in the surrounding streets and pubs. Since the recession encompassed the South East, travelling Londoners have been less willing to flaunt their excesses. There was a period, during the late '80s, when the half-time flourish of mobile phones was an awesome sight as visitors made to call home in full sight of native Scousers or Mancunians, who were presumed still to live in the age of Bakelite and Marconi. In Liverpool today, where even the kids who 'mind' your car keep in touch by phone, the capacity for Londoners to maintain their edge has been eroded. Even the mock chorus of Liverpool's *You'll Never Walk Alone* anthem to the words of 'You'll Never Get A Job' ('Sign on. Sign On. With a pen in your hand . . .') is half-hearted.

The club's frequent brushes with tragedy and death have often seen the eyes of the world focused on Anfield. The fans have responded in a manner that has drawn admiration; where once they were feared, they are now respected. Supporters at Anfield know good football when they see it, and aren't afraid to show their appreciation, even if the team or player in question isn't wearing red. The generous reception afforded to Jurgen Klinsmann after he had dumped Liverpool out of the FA Cup contrasted with the mean-spirited booing that Neil Ruddock drew from the Spurs support in the same match, simply because he was an ex-Spurs player who had moved clubs for an improved package.

For Colin Calderwood, Ruddock's replacement in the Spurs defence, however the Anfield match turned out could surely be no worse than the corresponding August fixture at White Hart Lane. That day, the whole team had been steamrollered by a Liverpool side on top of their game. As a central defender, Calderwood had suffered more than most. He winces when he recalls the post mortem.

'At team meetings before a match, Gerry will allocate tasks, going through a list and saying things like: "Colin, you've got so-and-so at corners". And we must all acknowledge our names with a "Yes" so we all know that responsibility has been accepted. That way he knows you have heard and that you have acknowledged him.

'On a Monday after a game, we always sit through the match video; not the whole game, but the highlights that were on *Match of the Day* or Sky TV. And if a goal has gone in, and it was your fault, you know it. I think the whole team knows whose fault the goal was before we come in. Gerry doesn't persecute you for making a mistake, but he won't let it go unnoticed or without telling you.

'In the Liverpool game at home, they absolutely hammered us. They played us off the park. The best team we've played so far this season. And the video playback on the Monday was the Colin Calderwood show! "Colin Calderwood! What are you doing there?"

'Afterwards he will come to you and say: "You did this wrong, you were nowhere near him." You know what you should be doing, and most of the time people accept it. It is said in a way to help you put it right. With Gerry, you don't feel as if he is hammering you into the ground and you are never going to get up. He also knows that you will probably have to play for him again in the next match, and you want to do it for him. And you don't want to be highlighted in the video next time. You try to minimise the times you get mentioned in the meeting because you haven't been in the right position. Otherwise you just want to squirm.'

Calderwood hasn't had an easy time at Tottenham. For fans brought up on superstar signings, it was very much a case of 'Colin who?' when Ossie Ardiles paid £1.25 million for him in the summer of 1993. When that first season turned into a high profile battle against relegation, the apprenticeship at Mansfield and Swindon must have seemed a world away.

'Ossie had said to me: "You'll never realise how different things can be at Tottenham until you come here." And he was absolutely right.'

Colin was a regular fixture in the Swindon side that rose from the old Fourth Division right up to their dramatic Wembley play-off victory over Leicester that brought them into the Premiership. He had the good fortune to play for Lou Macari, Ossie Ardiles and Glenn Hoddle at Swindon, and all of them added something to his game.

'Lou's regime was all about getting yourself very fit, and becoming a team that moved all over the pitch, capable of running very hard for 90 minutes. And his training was geared around that.

'When Ossie came to Swindon, the change benefited everybody. We all seemed to revel in it. We were encouraged, no told, to get the ball off the goalkeeper and try to pass it. Not do anything fancy, just pass it to a red shirt.

'And things just went remarkably well for us. We were

never really going to be champions, but we were always in with a chance of the play-offs. And to be honest, I don't think any team wanted to get us in the play-offs, because, on our day, we were very good and capable of beating anybody.

'When Glenn Hoddle took over, he was an extension of Ossie. But defensively he would do a lot more work, particularly on how we would defend in certain situations. A little like Gerry Francis, but not so regimented. We were not told "This is where you stand!"

'But even under Hoddle, we were never great defensively. We were always liable to concede goals, but we were also very capable of scoring goals. Obviously with Glenn playing between two centre-halves, our job was relatively easy. We just used to pass it to him. We benefited from playing alongside Hoddle because if we gave him the ball and he did something good, it looked as if you had been a part of it. A small bit in the jigsaw perhaps . . .'

Colin had never worked to a bold career plan that would chart his rise to the top. But like most professionals, as he became accomplished at one level, he wondered how he would fare at the next.

'I'd been on holiday that summer when I saw in the papers that Ossie had got the Spurs job – and started dreaming!'

Calderwood's contract at Swindon ran out the summer they won promotion to the Premiership. The club had made two or three good offers to retain him, but manager Hoddle was off to Chelsea, and the lure of Tottenham proved too great for a player looking for a final career move at 28.

'I was surprised when Ossie did eventually contact me, and said that he'd like to bring me to White Hart Lane. It was when Neil Ruddock was linked with a move to Liverpool. The talks dragged on for five or six weeks, and the longer

Dream On

it went on the more I was convinced the move would never happen.'

But the move did go through, and Calderwood replaced crowd-favourite Ruddock. Despite a bright start, an inability to win at home plunged the team into a dour battle against relegation, eventually won by the slenderest of margins. The following season was little better, and Calderwood was dropped after six games as Ossie desperately searched for the winning formula that would help him keep his job. Did the players feel responsible for Ossie's eventual sacking?

'We were talking about that recently, whether the players should feel responsible for a manager getting the sack. The feeling was that the manager picks the team and dictates the tactics. So unless he's got no money and isn't allowed to bring in his own people, then it is basically his team. How he goes about things dictates how the team is going to do. So I think, although everyone feels sorry for a manager who gets sacked – and we did feel sorry for Ossie – quite a few of the players felt it was definitely coming.

'Steve Perryman was very good at coming up to you and talking you through defending in certain situations. But collectively, we probably never did it. Players like to be told what their responsibilities are. One or two of them deny it, but I think deep down they do. Some of the players would rather the manager say specifically, "You do this". And if it goes wrong, they can say, "Ah, but *you* told me to do it".

'Obviously, you can't take that literally all the time. But I think, especially in defence, people like to know what their partner is doing. Or what the rest of the back four is doing. But we didn't work at it. Under Ossie, we probably didn't do enough work to sort out the problems. Everyone said the problems were at the back, but I don't think it's as easy a job as everyone seems to think to sort out a defence, to get a team to defend. Because I don't think the defence was particularly bad.

'I should have kept all the newspaper clippings when they talked about "the worst Tottenham defence ever". I warned my family, I told them there were going to be things in the paper which they wouldn't want to stick in their scrapbook, but it is part and parcel of being at a big club.'

Calderwood was recalled for the first match under new manager Gerry Francis, and has remained, for the most part, a fixture in the side ever since.

'Looking at it now, it has been a blessing for me. That's very cruel, Ossie was a lovely fellah, but for me it's a fact. Although Ossie has made quite a bit of money recently by getting paid up by Tottenham and getting those jobs in Mexico and now Japan, I'm sure he'd love to trade all that for being successful at Tottenham.'

The last ten games under Ardiles saw Spurs concede 25 goals. Discounting that first thrown-in-at-the-deep-end debut against Aston Villa, the first ten under Gerry saw Spurs concede just four, with essentially the same personnel in the defence.

'Gerry has ideas on how a team should defend, and how everyone has a job to do. He has drummed it into us; he has made us work very hard. Sometimes it can get a wee bit tedious at training doing the same things. But his manner, and the way he gets you to work at something in training, demands that you do it properly. And it certainly benefits the team on match days. And because you get results on the pitch, you think, "He's right". Sometimes people can talk the biggest load of old rubbish, but because of the way they come across, you think: "Oh that's right, we definitely go along with that".

'Gerry is very good at putting ideas across, and what he

Dream On

is putting across is getting results. So everyone wants to do what he says and realise the importance of what we do in training.

'I think he is very good to work with, and the turnaround in my career backs that up. I've certainly benefited from the general improvement in the team, but also I've definitely improved personally by my involvement with Scotland. Getting into the Scotland side was not something I'd ever been close to. But being at Tottenham, I think your name is pushed to the forefront more than if I'd still been at Swindon. The publicity of being at Spurs – whether good or bad – had certainly helped me get into the squad.

'With Spurs, because the team has done better, I am playing with a lot more confidence. I feel I belong at Tottenham and that I have been a reasonable success here now, and so, personally, I feel I have found my feet in the Premier League.'

Colin is a hugely likeable man, with an easy, unassuming manner and an equable temperament. He seems to fit the bill as the kind of conscientious professional that would be an asset to every successful team. His career has been marked by low-key moves where he was happy to allow his playing record – and not an agent – to dictate terms. Both the moves, from Mansfield and from Swindon, took place when he was out of contract; the fees in each case being decided by tribunal. Although he is a family man with family responsibilities, it would be a surprise if Colin was one of the big money earners at White Hart Lane, but an even bigger surprise if that caused him to feel resentful or to rock the boat. There can't be many at White Hart Lane who would give *Gardeners' World* as their favourite TV programme, nor reply, 'I'd love a really nice lawn', when asked for remaining ambitions.

London has won him over – 'I used to hate coming into London to play a game. Detested it, but once you are here, everywhere else seems a wee bit quiet' – and there is every indication that Colin Calderwood could end his days playing at the highest level for Gerry. 'To be perfectly honest, if I knew I was going to stay here, I'd get around to laying that lawn.'

For the Spurs players, the countdown to the Liverpool match had started on Tuesday with the weekly running session at Chase Lodge, the council-owned grounds in Mill Hill on the edge of north London. (The new season will see the club move to its own purpose built training facility in Chigwell, Essex.) Physically it is hard to play the Gerry Francis way and Tuesday is perhaps the hardest day of the week when the emphasis is put on speed and stamina work to ensure the necessary fitness levels are maintained throughout the season. With drills that replicate the sort of running that could be expected in an actual game – penalty box to half-way line, box to box in sets of two or more – David Howells probably speaks for everyone when he says, 'The lads don't enjoy it and, to be honest, I don't think Gerry enjoys making us go through it'. But it goes a long way to explaining the comparative success of the Francis way of doing things. As Howells succinctly puts it, 'I think we are fitter now'. And of course they need to be, to fulfil the running that is expected from every outfield player.

After Tuesday's exertions, if there is no midweek game, Wednesday is usually a day off. On Thursday after training, at around 2pm, Gerry reluctantly gives his pre-match press conference. Although he obviously regards it as a chore, he does his duty diligently. It is the one day in the week the media can be sure of his attention, but fail to attend in person, and you can forget about trying to do the interview by phone. On the other hand, a couple of minutes of one-to-one chat after the conference have often stretched into an enjoyable and instructive hour or so, especially for the name writers who have made the tortuous journey from town.

Tomorrow, though, is literally another day.

By Friday, Dennis the gateman was under strict orders to keep out both press and public as the first team completed their preparations at the training ground. Gerry Francis and assistant manager Roger Cross attach great importance to this final workout. In fact, if a fixture is put back to Sunday, the training session is also put back to the Saturday. Youth team games scheduled for that day have been known to be switched so privacy can be maintained (and the best pitch used). The open house sessions that flourished under Ossie Ardiles are a thing of the past under Gerry.

A new addition to the squad for the trip to Anfield was £1.5 million Andy Sinton. The midfielder had been linked with Spurs for some time, but the move had been delayed by an injury to the player and the unwillingness of Tottenham to meet Sheffield Wednesday's valuation of him. As with all of Gerry's signings so far, there was a distinct lack of glamour, which left the fans indifferent. After making a name for himself under Steve Perryman at Brentford, Sinton was brought to QPR by then manager Trevor Francis. Once Francis had moved on to manage Sheffield Wednesday, he eventually persuaded Sinton to follow him north. When Trevor Francis was sacked, to be replaced by David Pleat, Sinton had a tough time both with injuries and with finding a way into a more free flowing system than he was used to. To the rescue came former manager, Gerry Francis. It had been Gerry who had sold Sinton to Sheffield Wednesday back in 1993, one of those inevitable transfers essential to

Walking Alone

keep QPR solvent, but not before he had helped the player attain international recognition. Thus Sinton would know what was expected from him in any side managed by Gerry Francis.

It was a typical Gerry Francis purchase. A known quantity; a player who owed Gerry and who could do a specific job in a specific position. At 29, it was not a building block for the future, but then compared with 34-year-old Clive Wilson, Sinton was a spring chicken.

For that last practice session before the trip to Anfield, the tactical plan was put through its final rehearsal to ensure no repeat of the August débâcle. As Teddy Sheringham recalled later, it was a more flexible approach than usual: 'We did a little bit of work on closing them down from the off. We pushed the full-backs right in on Steve McManaman, whichever side he was. That stopped them getting out. Then we had the centre-halves the other side of Robbie Fowler so he couldn't get in the channel from either side. We pressed on to their back three to stop them playing from the back.'

The mood was good and team spirit appeared buoyant. Anything spectacular met with applause from the players, while Chris Armstrong's attempts to do anything with his left foot other than stand upright met with unrestrained ridicule. During the nine-a-side match that concluded the session, Roger Cross was occasionally compelled to step in and halt the action to complain about the attitude of some players. Cross knows he has the full backing of Francis when taking training, Gerry often preferring to watch from the sidelines as a passive observer

'Roger Cross is a very good number two,' concurs Colin Calderwood. 'Obviously he's very comfortable with what Gerry says, but he is also very comfortable with his position. Once Gerry has had his say at half-time, Roger will come in

Dream On

and have his say. It's a hard job being a number two, because you might think you could do the job better yourself. Maybe Roger does, but you have to be loyal to your manager. Gerry gives him a lot of responsibility. Roger will take all the training, but Gerry will then pick out the forwards, or the defence, and take them away to work on something specific. Gerry doesn't come out and tell us what we are going to do in training, that all comes from Roger. And he is excellent at it. People respect him because he stands up and speaks to people.'

With training over, the players and the management drove their cars to South Mimms on the M25, where they boarded the coach for Liverpool. The journey to the Haydock Thistle hotel was uneventful, and the squad arrived in time for dinner. Although not allowed to leave the premises (and in truth, it would be a struggle to find anything within twenty miles to justify going AWOL for), bedtime was left to the discretion of the players.

Come matchday morning, there's another training session, this time loosening exercises followed by a gentle game, to blow away any cobwebs accumulated on the trip north. For most players this was a routine not encountered pre-Gerry, but one they took to as a welcome break from hotel confinement. On this occasion, it was a local school pitch that was host to players valued at £50 million. Back at the hotel, special lunch menus had been prepared by a dietician. Still, old habits die hard, and the recommended chicken, pasta and omelettes were declined by several who stuck with the tried and tested steaks. The post-meal tea and toast united the squad once again. And they wonder why English players can't settle abroad.

Twelve miles away down the East Lancs Road, the Tottenham directors were showing signs of flagging. Their long day had begun with a drive to Stanstead where an 18-seater hired from Atlantic Airways was waiting to fly them to Speke Airport. On arrival they piled into a coach which took them direct to the ground. Fatigued and hungry, the Tottenham directors could only dream about the kind of lunch their players had enjoyed. With the clock ticking its way towards half-past two, stomachs were definitely rumbling in the Anfield directors' lounge, as it became obvious that the meal they were expecting was not going to materialise. One can imagine the whispered asides that passed between directors and wives as it began to dawn that crisps and peanuts may well be thought to constitute a balanced meal in this part of the world.

To immense relief, platters eventually arrived, but the tired chicken drumsticks and ham sandwiches did little to lift spirits nor sate appetites. Claude Littner was left to pillage the cheese board and perhaps ponder on life the other side of the cost-cutter's axe.

For two men in the room, however, the sight of such obvious discomfort amongst the Spurs directors was a source of wry amusement. Terry Venables and longtime pal Morris Keston had flown that morning from Heathrow to Manchester on a scheduled British Airways shuttle. The breakfast then had been substantially better than the office party buffet now being served. The FA limousine that had whisked the pair down the M62 to Liverpool had hardly allowed time for adequate digestion, before lunch was taken courtesy of the sponsors' lounge. The role of England Coach may be a thankless task, but you'll never go hungry in the search for the perfect striker.

Venables would be a welcome face at most clubs, but in truth couldn't always expect an invitation to that inner sanctum of hospitality, the directors' lounge, especially if Tottenham were the opposition. Today, however, the presence of his companion Morris Keston would ensure all doors swung firmly open.

Business has been good to Morris, and Morris in turn has been good to Tottenham. He has been following the club over land and sea for more years than he cares to remember. It is almost 30 years since the infamous bust-up when Tottenham players absconded from their official FA Cup winners reception at the Savoy to party on down at Morris's shindig at the Hilton. The Spurs directors were none too amused and for a long time after he was shunned by the club he loved. Directors come and directors go, but Morris just hangs on in there. Today, in his sixties with a shock of white hair and a physique that has seen slimmer days, Morris is still the superfan. Indeed, to many people at many clubs, Morris Keston is 'Mr Spurs'; a kind of roving ambassador. Before home games, if the directors bothered to look up from their lunch, they might spy Morris outside the entrance to the main West Stand, greeting the visiting football dignitaries who are invariably good friends. Recently Jimmy Greaves halted a rehearsal for ITV's *Sport in Question*, telling the audience he had seen an old pal, whereupon he left the podium and went straight over to Morris, who was in the audience, and embraced him in full view of everyone present.

Once upon a time, Morris had ambitions: 'To have a ticket to the tea room in every ground in the First Division'. He was offered directorships by several clubs. Ernie Clay, owner of Fulham when they were in the top flight, offered him one saying he could be chairman in a couple of years. 'I'll accept on one condition,' said Morris. 'What's that?' asked Ernie. 'That I can go and watch Tottenham every week.'

Well Morris never made it onto the board, but must now

Walking Alone

realise he is better off out than in. The directors' box is no place for a fan when you can't cheer a goal, jeer Ian Wright or even get up and walk out when the tension gets too much. Morris may not be able to boast too many of the current team as dinner guests, but, like Irving Scholar, one suspects that his real heroes have long since hung up their white shirts.

His long-time pass to the Oak Room in the West Stand, where a visiting manager or VIP used to get a cup of tea and sandwich on the house, has been withdrawn as entry is now restricted to those prepared to pay handsomely for the privilege, or be lucky enough to be a guest of the directors. Hence a warmer welcome for Morris at Anfield than at White Hart Lane, and no need for the tactics adopted earlier by the official Spurs party. What a sight they had made, storming into Anfield like a swoop squad of VAT inspectors. Alan Sugar with son Daniel, daughter, wife and Spurs-mad brother. Claude Littner, finance director John Sedgwick, Mr and Mrs Douglas Alexiou, Mr and Mrs Igal Yawetz.

'They can't all be directors . . .' bemoaned the jobsworth responsible for vetting entry to the directors' room. 'Course they are!' countered Sugar as he swept the party past the bemused official, collecting as he did Claude's son and cousin who had initially been rebuffed.

With the Sugar/Littner camp in one corner, and the Venables/Keston camp in the other, it was left to Douglas Alexiou and wife Shirley (daughter of former Spurs chairman Sidney Wale), together with Igal Yawetz and wife to mingle with their Liverpool counterparts. Never one for small talk when there was work to be done, chief executive Peter Robinson soon retired to his office along the corridor, leaving David Moores and some old-time directors and wives to hold the fort.

Dream On

Once in his element in such situations, Terry Venables now remained detached, no longer feeling the need to move among the throng, wisecracking or exchanging pleasantries. Scouting missions such as today's presented him with a welcome opportunity to switch off for 90 minutes and enjoy a game over which he had no influence or responsibility, and for which he could not be subsequently blamed, libelled or sued.

From now until June, his attention would be focused on the European Championships. His England team were, as host country, expected to emulate their 1990 World Cup semi-final place. But regardless of the eventual outcome, he had already made clear his intention to vacate the position when the tournament was over and his two-and-a-half-year contract had expired. For then Venables faces a High Court libel action brought by the man standing not ten yards away, Tottenham chairman Alan Sugar. There was also the possibility of further cases, this time instigated by Venables himself, against the *Daily Mirror*, the BBC *Panorama* programme, and the much talked about wrongful dismissal action against Sugar and Tottenham.

Since his unceremonious exit from Tottenham, Terry's career has roller-coastered to a degree that has made many wonder how he has retained his sanity. What he has undeniably retained, however, is a strong sense of injustice at his treatment, and a determination to see those he thought of as 'bully boys' exposed. It is a fair cause, but one that if played to a finish will surely end in tears.

Some time earlier, Morris Keston had posed a question to Venables, seeking qualification on what it would take to make his friend stay on as England coach. 'If your team won the Euro '96 championships; if the FA doubled your salary; if the FA's international committee publicly apologised for

Walking Alone

their previous lack of faith in your abilities, would you then stay on in the position and guide England to the 1998 World Cup finals?'

'Under no circumstances,' replied Venables firmly, with an admirable conviction that was perhaps stronger than his logical reasoning. For he would surely pay heavily if he took on those who were better able to suffer the quirks of the legal system.

The primary grievance stems from the settlement offered by Alan Sugar when Venables was ousted from his position as chief executive at White Hart Lane in 1993. Sugar offered to buy back Venables' shares in a deal that was alleged to be worth around £4.5 million. Venables felt this offer was insufficient. After all, he reasoned, he had overseen a steady upturn in the club's finances and felt that his pay-off should more accurately reflect this. Although at one time close to an accord (Sugar sought Morris Keston out to thank him for his endeavours in trying to get Venables to settle), things took a turn for the worse, and after an acrimonious and very public dispute, Venables ended up having to sell his shares on the open market for around £3 million. He had already started to pay for his principles. That strong sense of discrimination (and possibly the need to replenish his bank balance, receiving a reported advance of over £200,000) spurred him into an autobiography in which he took the opportunity to put his side of football's most public dispute. This merely served to exacerbate the situation as Alan Sugar and co-director Tony Berry promptly took great exception to some of the comments and issued writs for libel.

Before he was appointed England coach, the FA were made fully aware of the extent to which Venables could become implicated in lengthy and potentially damaging court action. But still they concurred that he was the

Dream On

right man for the job, and efforts were made to heal the rift between Sugar and Venables, one that saw the England coach barred from White Hart Lane ('Why should I welcome a man at my club who is suing the arse off me?' stormed Sugar), and thus hampered in his scouting mission. Only personal intervention by Sir Bert Millichip saw Sugar lift the ban, and indeed postpone the pair's proposed High Court showdown until after the European Championships. Venables' staunchest ally, the agent Eric Hall, who had suffered the same fate, was not so lucky, as Sugar extended his life ban. When asked how anyone could extend a life ban, Sugar replied that he believed in reincarnation and he was taking no chances of Eric Hall coming back as a Tottenham fan.

There was no doubting the commitment of the FA to stand by their man. Graham Kelly, the FA's chief executive, went so far as to state that he felt that a campaign was being waged against Terry Venables. 'What I'm concerned about,' commented Kelly back in the autumn, 'is not so much Terry Venables' off-field activities; all I'm concerned about really is what he does so far as the England team is concerned and there is no doubt about it that he has improved the England team in the 22 months he has been in charge. He has brought young players through in the team. He is raising standards. This is permeating down to the youth international teams.'

However, by December 1995, some within the FA were apparently getting cold feet. In particular, Liverpool's Noel White and Oldham's Ian Stott, both prominent members of the FA's international committee, made public the concern they felt about the premature need to renew the England coach's contract before the European Championships and at a time when his legal problems showed no signs of evaporating. On the contrary, the impending DTI inquiry

and the arrest of Venables' business associate Eddie Ashby
perhaps brought home to them in spades the seriousness of
the allegations.

In truth, such caution was not unwise, but was nevertheless a severe blow to the pride of a man like Venables. His
decision to walk was a brave one, but one subsequently
muddled as it became unclear whether the motive was the
FA's failure to back him, or the welter of litigation that lay
ahead. As far as Alan Sugar was concerned, 'I don't think
it has got anything to do with me. No one told him to
resign. No one told him to take the job either. That's a
decision he made himself. When he took the job he had
as many legal cases with me as he's got now. Nothing has
changed really.'

Sympathy for the position Venables found himself in was
widespread, tempered however by an acknowledgement that
his own stubbornness may have contributed to his situation.
'Take the money. Walk away. Fight another day,' was the
advice offered by Morris Keston upon his friend's dismissal
from Tottenham. That advice was ignored, as it seems was
much offered by other good friends who were alarmed at
what they saw as serious lapses of judgement in Venables'
business and social life. In particular, the running of his
Kensington club, Scribes West, attracting as it does many of
the game's personalities, including players and their agents,
is seen at odds with the necessity for Venables to retain his
objectivity.

'When,' according to Richard Williams in the *Guardian*,
'some of those players make regular appearances in his
England squad, it is hard to avoid the unworthy suspicion
that a certain amount of favouritism is going on.' Perhaps it
was his determination to dispel this notion that brought him
to Anfield to run the rule over further England hopefuls, in

Dream On

particular Liverpool's forward pairing of Robbie Fowler and Stan Collymore, who were peripheral to his plans, but who would soon need to be brought on line if they were to feature at all in the European Championship.

In the pubs around Anfield, Spurs fans mixed freely with home fans, and trade was brisk at bar prices that appeared to be pegged at pre-war levels. Another guaranteed 40,000 sell-out saw touts move amongst the pub crowds, asking to buy or sell any spares. Outside the ground itself, the actual presence of ticket touts was far less noticeable than outside the main entrance at White Hart Lane. Perhaps the police on Merseyside interpret the laws more strictly than their Metropolitan counterparts. Certainly there was no shortage of takers for what seats were being offered. A season's best 40,628 packed the stadium to its rafters, and as Spurs kicked off attacking the Kop end, expectations were high from both sets of fans.

But it was the Liverpool fans who were most disappointed at half-time. Their team had been unable to break down Tottenham's well marshalled defence, and looked increasingly at risk from their visitors' counter attacks. Both Collymore and Fowler, so dangerous in Liverpool's midweek victory at Villa Park, were subdued and peripheral to the action, while Mabbutt was proving once again what a loss he would be if Spurs failed to renew his contract. His smothering of the Liverpool attack was exemplary and reduced the home team's options to erratic raids down each wing which, much to the delight of Gerry Francis, were being promptly and efficiently dealt with. Goalless at half-time was more than satisfactory for the visitors; what was now needed was one of Gerry's half-time tactical briefings that would turn one point into three.

Walking Alone

Up in the boardroom, half-time saw the predictable scrum for tea and biscuits, as the merits of what had passed were discussed with the nearest neighbour. For the visiting fans, half-time saw the welcome opportunity to empty bladders bloated to bursting point with local ales. The solitary urinal in the visitors' enclosure was soon awash as it struggled, as did the catering concessions, to cope with 3,000 customers with just fifteen minutes in which to satisfy all and sundry. The urinal at least fulfilled its function, but the paucity of catering facilities once again reminded away fans how low down on the list of priorities they were.

Within fifteen minutes of the restart, the home crowd were openly howling their displeasure, as it became apparent their side and its 3–5–2 formation had garnered no fresh insight into how to break down Gerry's good old 4–4–2. Of the four strikers on display, only Chris Armstrong looked capable of breaking the deadlock, although Teddy Sheringham again impressed his England manager with his intelligent promptings and link play. An injury to Sol Campbell threatened to disrupt Tottenham's composure, but substitute Stuart Nethercott was able to hold the fort despite the introduction of Ian Rush after 83 minutes.

With barely seconds remaining, both sides could have snatched the points; man of the match Chris Armstrong forcing a fine save from James, while McAteer shaved the post as play switched ends. The final whistle saw Liverpool fans dismayed at their team's inability to close the gap on Newcastle, and possibly already calculating that the two points dropped had seen their side slip from second to third place in the Premiership. For the Spurs fans too, 0–0 represented a disappointing return from a game they could, and perhaps should, have won with a more cavalier attitude which Gerry seemed unprepared to adopt. Still, it speaks volumes for Tottenham's progress that 'only' a point was felt to represent a poor return from what is traditionally Tottenham's most troublesome match of the season.

'I watched them a lot on video and teams have tended to let them have the ball,' said Francis afterwards by way of explanation. 'I was determined not to let that happen.' Indeed, Francis was to praise his side for what he claimed was a 'magnificent team performance'. One that had seen Liverpool 'outplayed and outworked on their own pitch'. Writing in the *Sunday Times*, Joe Lovejoy was restrained by comparison: 'Although Spurs were particularly well-served by Mabbutt whose excellence in central defence was heroic, and Calderwood who was not far behind, this was essentially a team effort in which every individual played up to, or at least very near, his best.'

Andy Sinton on his debut had been quietly efficient; contributing little but doing enough to hint that he might prove less erratic than Ronny Rosenthal, who replaced him for the final few seconds of the game. For Colin Calderwood, the afternoon had gone some way towards exorcising the ghosts of the previous encounter with Liverpool.

The scramble by fans to exit the stadium and join the dash for the motorway was in sharp contrast to the boardroom, where the pace was more leisurely. At last some substantial fare had materialised, and chefs were serving those still seeking nourishment. After accepting the white wine offered by Noel White, Terry Venables and Morris Keston retired unobtrusively to a corner. Seeing their isolation, they were approached by Alex Fynn, who somewhat mischievously proceeded to take Venables to task.

'People are encouraging me to sue you,' ventured Alex.

Walking Alone

'They are telling me that apparently some of my material can be found in your autobiography.'

'That's funny,' replied Venables. 'Because I was thinking of suing you.'

'What on earth for?'

'Because of the criticism you made on the Richard Littlejohn show. Both you and he were out of order.'

Venables listed at length the points he contested. In exasperation at the verbal battering he was receiving, Alex repeated his assertion that Venables himself had been out of order regarding his autobiography. Unfazed, Venables dismissed the accusation out of hand.

'That's typical,' said Alex, 'of an attitude that is prevalent in football. You see things in black and white. There are no shades in between. In your view I have a case to answer. That's all that counts. You never think you might be culpable in some way. You say, "If you are not for me, you must be against me". But I am neither for you, nor against you. I will never forget the consideration you showed to me when you didn't know me from Adam.' This was in reference to the time Venables made himself and his team available for interview. 'But that doesn't mean I am unable to criticise your business activities. No harm was intended. Maybe a little knowledge is a dangerous thing.'

Venables was unmoved. 'The damage has been done,' he shrugged and gestured to Noel White. 'It's the same with him. What's the point of apologising in private after criticising me in public?'

'But surely as a public figure you are fair game for criticism?' countered Alex. 'And you know mistakes were made. The reason you feel so hard done by is that you surround yourself with people who only tell you what you want to hear. Criticism comes as an unpleasant surprise.'

Dream On

With a thumb in the direction of Morris Keston, Alex ploughed on. 'Why didn't you listen to this man? A true friend who tells you what you need to know rather than what you want to hear. You certainly would be better off if you'd taken the money and lived to fight another day. You could have walked away with money in your pocket and still be in the top job now.'

'So it's fair that I helped to turn the company around but don't get to benefit from that?'

'Of course it's not fair. But that's business. As an employee or junior partner you are at the mercy of the man who owns the company. He made you a reasonable offer, but you wanted more and had to settle for less. You feel that you are owed; that's what all this is about.'

Sensing that his tone had become hectoring, Alex tempered his comments. 'Why don't you settle? Who needs it? You are resigning a job you want to keep, and for what? The chance of losing more money? Neither of you will win.'

'Maybe it won't come to that,' said Venables, enigmatically suggesting that the dispute may not end up in court. But nevertheless he was adamant that his cause was just. 'It's about what is right. In life you can't let the bully boys win. What sort of place will the world be for my grandchildren if people can just do what they want?'

'I admire your stoicism,' countered Alex. 'I don't know how you can keep going with all this hanging over you. You should give up the court case not the job. You were lucky to get the job in the first place and you should try to keep it.'

'Lucky?'

'You were the right man, appointed for the wrong reasons, at the wrong time.'

Venables was genuinely puzzled. 'The wrong reasons?'

'Yes. You should have been appointed in 1990 but you

weren't because you were not the FA's type of man. Four years on you were appointed, but you were still not their type of man. And anyway, for the last couple of years you have wanted to own a club, not manage one. The reason you were chosen was a political one. Why do you think Bert Millichip changed his mind [he was reported to have said Venables would only enter Lancaster Gate over his dead body]? UEFA were under pressure because none of the four home unions qualified for USA 94 and with the Asian and African lobbies pressing for an increased World Cup allocation, FIFA were threatening to grant it at Europe's expense. Sitting on the UEFA executive committee, Bert Millichip was told in no uncertain terms that he had to get his house in order. Europe needed a strong England. For the first time in their history, it served the FA to go with the choice of the people and the professional game.'

The conversation was interrupted as the Spurs directors prepared to leave. Alan Sugar is rarely at ease away from his own patch and he soon announced it was time to go. And when Alan Sugar goes, everyone goes. After some frantic scurrying about to collect coats, the entourage departed as suddenly as it had arrived. The rush for the door took the party past both Venables and Keston, who were blanked with consummate ease by both Alan Sugar and Claude Littner. Igal Yawetz and Douglas Alexiou both paused to offer farewell handshakes and best wishes, returned by Venables with a wry smile for one and a degree of warmth for the other. The atmosphere noticeably eased, and Tottenham secretary Peter Barnes – travelling back on the slower yet surely more convivial players' coach – took the opportunity to saunter over for some friendly banter. When he too had left, Venables turned to Keston

Dream On

and remarked that, 'He had to wait until the others had left before coming over'.

'What do you expect Terry?' came the rebuke. 'He has a mortgage to pay.'

Chapter 10

Wholesale/Retail/Import/Export . . . ish

'Who's that?' asked Irving Scholar of the youngster making his debut for Southampton against Tottenham in 1986. 'Some local kid,' replied David Pleat, not realising that his chairman was already enamoured with the boy.

In 1991, Matt Le Tissier decided the time was right for a career move, and he signed for Spurs. Contracts were lodged with a solicitor in London's West End and the transfer fee would be set by a tribunal as Le Tissier was out of contract. The deal represented a coup for Irving Scholar who was somewhat beleaguered over Tottenham's grave financial predicament. Come the run-up to the new season, the Spurs chairman would be able to announce that his club had captured one of English football's brightest prospects.

As often is the case at Tottenham, things didn't work out quite as planned. By the summer, neither Scholar nor Le Tissier was at White Hart Lane. The chairman had bowed to public pressure and sold his shares to Alan Sugar. The player had bowed to fiancée pressure from the soon-to-be

Dream On

Mrs Le Tissier who had made it perfectly clear – 'We're going nowhere' – that a move to London was out of the question for the childhood sweethearts. With the Le Tissier transfer low down on the list of Scholar's priorities as his position at Tottenham hung by a thread, he respected the player's predicament, annulled the agreement and was thus denied his swan song.

In 1996, that archived contract was in danger of being dusted down as Gerry Francis made several unsuccessful approaches to lure Le Tissier to White Hart Lane. As Southampton flirted with relegation, they knew that a tumble out of the Premiership would surely see their most prized asset exercise a contractual clause and seek a move that would keep him in the top flight. Encouragingly, Le Tissier had told Francis that Tottenham was 'my kind of club' and that if he was going to move then Tottenham would be top of his candidate list. Perversely, he apparently told Chelsea vice-chairman Matthew Harding that he'd love to play under his boyhood idol Glenn Hoddle. In fact Le Tissier, to echo his wife's earlier sentiments, was going nowhere until his own club's fate was decided.

Under Hoddle, it was easy to picture how Le Tissier's capricious skills would be indulged. But under Francis? It was hard to imagine the Spurs manager accommodating Le Tissier by compromising principles that had already seen off a world class 'slacker' like Gica Popescu, who was now drawing rave reviews for Barcelona. Just where would the player fit in? Would he complement Anderton in midfield? Or was Le Tissier to be an expensive insurance policy against Anderton failing to recover from his long term injury? Or was there a sinister long-term plan to sell Anderton once a ready-made replacement had been bedded in? But what was perhaps most startling about Gerry's interest were the

Wholesale/Retail/Import/Export . . . ish

similarities between the player he wanted to sign, Le Tissier, and one he was desperate to unload, Ilie Dumitrescu.

Dumitrescu was clearly out of favour with Gerry Francis, who felt that the player was unable, or simply unwilling, to adjust to his tactical requirements. It was a decision Gerry had apparently arrived at early on; within four games of taking over in 1994, Dumitrescu's season at White Hart Lane had ended. He was packed off to a shop window in sunny Seville where no doubt the hope was to attract the attention and pesetas of Barcelona or Real Madrid. Poor Ilie had always been very much an Ossie Ardiles player, and must have feared the worst when Gerry arrived. But surely he couldn't have envisaged that the descent from World Cup hero to Premier League flop would be so rapid. For Tottenham, there was little credit to salvage from the episode, but the agents didn't do too badly.

'I was talking to Ossie Ardiles,' recalls Dennis Roach of the summer of '94, 'about certain players he was looking for, and I suggested Dumitrescu, whose agent I had a contact with. Ossie got very excited about the player. After a few weeks' consideration about what he would like for his side, Ossie decided he would like to buy Dumitrescu. So I was authorised by Tottenham Hotspur to go and sign him.'

Dumitrescu's club, Steaua Bucharest, were resigned to selling their star, providing they received $US 2.5 million (£1.6 million). Dennis Roach was convinced he could secure this fee for the club, which was why lesser bids from Padova and Cologne were rejected. Spurs were interested in Dumitrescu, and a deal was struck for much more than the asking price, £2.5 million. In addition, an agreement was made that would see Spurs play Steaua in friendly matches, with the proceeds being split between the two clubs. Steaua's commercial representative, Constantin

Dream On

Matei, admitted that, 'We were not comfortable with the system [the transfer of players to the West] and we therefore felt we had to trust Dennis Roach, who is very experienced in these matters. We were happy with the business he did for us.'

What then happened however was that Steaua deducted their £1.6 million and passed the balance of the fee received – around £900,000 – on to Roach. This amount was then divided between the player, the player's agent, Roach's representative and Roach himself. Dumitrescu probably got around half the amount while the agents split the rest. The only reason all this came to light was that one of the parties was a little indiscreet.

It was the sum of money that was divided among the agents that caused some consternation to Alan Sugar when he realised that a great chunk of his club's money had not gone where he thought it had. 'In fairness, those commission arrangements were made with the Steaua club. My invoice went to the Steaua club and therefore Mr Sugar probably didn't know the breakdown of commissions, only the total amount of money involved,' adds Roach by way of qualification. Further investigative work by the *Mail on Sunday*'s Simon Greenberg uncovered more details of the deal. According to Greenberg, 'Sugar's experience was limited in dealing with Eastern European clubs and so he had nominated Roach to act on his club's behalf'. Roach in turn had invoiced Tottenham for a 'finder's fee' which Sugar now refused to pay, telling the agent in no uncertain terms that he'd already had his money. What probably narked him was the subsequent discovery that, according to the terms of the arrangements, Roach was entitled to be paid by both the selling and the buying club. Similarly, the agreement to play Steaua also went out of the window. Sugar pleaded ignorance to any payments that may have found their way through to Dumitrescu and the agents, pointing quite rightly to the fact that Tottenham had followed the correct procedure, although his threat that there would be 'hell to pay' if 'something has happened to a proportion of the money', was probably a result of his inexperience in dealing with overseas transfers. Like the Klinsmann transfer, the player appeared to get the better of the deal.

'Dumitrescu,' said Roach, 'had an agreement with his club, as did most of the Romanian team who went to the '94 World Cup, that, in the event they did well and got sold, then the player would get a percentage of the transfer. That was in Dumitrescu's contract. From my point of view, that is perfect; that looks after the player. I don't have to worry about that.' Steaua Bucharest were more than happy with their share from the deal. They were not at all bothered to see the player and the agents divvy up the balance; in fact the club took the attitude that Dennis Roach's involvement had greatly helped secure such a good price for their player.

The matter blew over, and Dumitrescu was left with a financial windfall and a good contract at Tottenham, but a move that wasn't turning out as he had hoped. Dennis Roach apportions a large share of the blame to the Spurs manager.

'Gerry Francis is not the best with foreign players. He doesn't seem to have the ability to talk to them. He is a very good coach, but perhaps he doesn't understand foreign players. Therefore, Dumitrescu was a big star from the World Cup, in a strange land, he's got his wife and kids there, stuck in a house that no one comes near. The only person who ever visited was the wife of Peter Barnes, the club secretary. He should have had an interpreter immediately, someone with him at the house.

Dream On

He was trying to find his own way to the training ground and turning up hours late because he'd got lost. It wasn't handled very well. Dumitrescu then got the needle, and his agent got involved in a slanging match at Mr Sugar's house. There were some unfortunate things said, and it was a fall-out. Once the fall-out came, then Mr Sugar – in Mr Sugar's way – started to look at things he wasn't interested in before.'

The player was left in an unenviable situation; a proven international midfielder and goalscorer, in a foreign country, with a manager who doubted his abilities and a chairman who felt he'd done a bum deal. When Seville said thanks but no thanks, Dumitrescu returned to Tottenham in the summer of '95. With Klinsmann gone, Popescu about to go and Barmby packing his bags, the 'famous five' were about to become slightly less than a dynamic duo.

'There are no problems, only opportunities' is a phrase beloved of dynamic businessmen, but one which could have been coined with football agents in mind. For Dennis Roach, other people's problems certainly provide opportunities for him to add to an impressive track record in cross-border transfers. His pioneering import/export brokering saw Trevor Francis and Des Walker move from Forest to Sampdoria, Clive Allen go from Tottenham to Bordeaux, Trevor Steven from Rangers to Marseille (and back again), Mark Hughes from Manchester United to Barcelona (and back again via Bayern Munich), Mark Hateley from Portsmouth to Milan to Monaco to Rangers and Glenn Hoddle from Tottenham to Monaco. More recently he was instrumental in taking Mark Hughes from Manchester United (where a one-year contract was all that was on offer) to Chelsea where a three-year deal was secured. Also Chelsea-bound via Dennis Roach, who

Wholesale/Retail/Import/Export . . . ish

has obviously cultivated that friend/client relationship with Glenn Hoddle, was Dan Petrescu from Sheffield Wednesday and Ruud Gullit from Sampdoria. He was even asked by his friend Michel Platini to try to get Eric Cantona a fresh start in England.

Roach is fully licensed by football's authorities, but doubts the credibility of a system that has seen him having to lodge a 200,000SFr bond with FIFA, while apparently unlicensed operators wheel and deal with impunity. As the Sheringham 'bungs' inquiry limps into its third year of Premier League investigation, it was only after the further Rune Hauge/George Graham fiasco that the FIFA players' licence became essential to stay on the right side of the authorities. This is important to Roach, as is the aim of using the licensing system to clean up a business where opportunists notoriously proliferate.

'We have an organisation called IAFA (the International Association of Football Agents) comprising all the top European agents. If it is supported by FIFA and the FA, it just gives some credibility to it. There are rules and regulations, and hopefully it will build and become respected.'

But there is still a long way to go in England, with authorities apparently turning a blind eye to unlicensed operators. 'In all the time that this licensing business has been going on, all these transfers are still being done by unlicensed agents. And the FA knows about them. And I know what's going on, but I can't report X club. They know about the club that brought in a South American with the help of an agent, who, after an investigation, was declared "an interpreter". Everyone knows the bloke's been an agent for years! And he is unlicensed. And unless they do something about that kind of thing the whole licence thing will collapse.

Dream On

'In Scotland, the first time a club was found to have used an agent, bang! Everyone's up in front of the authorities. It was all over the press and everybody is terrified. In England . . .'

In England, to finish Roach's sentence for him, the system is a mess. To work internationally an agent in theory needs a FIFA licence. To work in England, in practice, he needs a phone.

Depending upon who is telling the story, agents can be made out to be the game's greatest benefactors or its greatest scourge. Essential specialists or unqualified cowboys? Clubs have access to professional advice, so why should players be denied those rights? Players need the expert contractual and financial assistance that agents can give, but who is to say a particular agent is an expert in such fields? Unscrupulous agents can manipulate a player and make a great deal of money for themselves. And yet good agents have made their clients wealthy. Clubs complain about players' agents infiltrating the system, but those same clubs behaved like slave traders until they were forced, by the courts in the early 1960s, to do otherwise, and of course they use agents when it suits them.

It's no wonder that the FA have dithered for so long about imposing meaningful regulations. Particularly when you see the limitations of the licensing system introduced by FIFA, where an unlicensed agent can do anything except negotiate face-to-face with a club. FIFA rules say only licensed agents can act in transfers. But in England a solicitor can act without a licence following the FA's acceptance of a Law Society proposal that, because solicitors are qualified in contract law, they do not need to have a licence.

'People often wonder,' explains Mel Goldberg, a solicitor who specialises in sports law, 'if club A wants to buy a player from club B, why doesn't the manager just phone the other club direct and negotiate without the use of an agent. Well, the answer to that is to compare the situation to that of estate agents when buying a house. If you happen to know that your next door neighbour's house is for sale then of course you don't need an agent. But the truth of the matter is that, when you are looking for a house in a certain area, you want an agent in that area to supply you with a list of houses which may suit your needs. And that agent is entitled to charge a fee for supplying that information.

'Now if a club manager knows that a certain player is available, he doesn't need an agent. But not every manager knows what players are available. And there may be circumstances where an agent or an intermediary knows of a player who may be available because he is unhappy or that player's club, perhaps, wishes to cash in on the player's sale. It is in these kind of circumstances that an agent does play a useful role.'

But. There is always a but.

'But I would argue, why not use the services of a professional solicitor who has spent years studying and many more years in practice, as opposed to an agent who is not a professional person. Why do people use an unqualified agent who may be a second-hand car dealer? There are some good agents, but I take a view – confirmed to me by the chairman of a club recently – that a lot of agents who have lodged their licensing bond with FIFA have only been able to provide the funds for that bond by being involved in shady deals in the past. If you look at the list of licensed agents who operate with the authority of FIFA, some of them have dodgy backgrounds.'

The flaw in this theory is surely that solicitors or accountants are great people to bring in when the deal is about to be done, but are they the best for bringing that deal to the

Dream On

table in the first place? Solicitors or accountants will only charge a set fee for their services, usually based upon an hourly rate. They will not levy a percentage of the deal. There can be little doubt that clubs and players would prefer this method of payment. Indeed, players like Paul Gascoigne, Chris Waddle and Alan Shearer all had major transfers handled by a solicitor, Mel Stein. But there is no substitute for specialist knowledge, and in many cases the lure of a 20% cut on a £2 million deal is a great incentive for agents to get out there and make things happen. Solicitors may know the ins and outs of contract law, but agents are the great deal makers. If a club needs a left-sided midfielder, then an agent like Dennis Roach, because of his footballing expertise, is more likely to come up with the right answer. So much so that clubs who feel he may have turned them over have to go back to him because of his ability to walk into the boardroom of every major European club.

No actor or entertainer could hope to sustain a career without an agent representing their interests. In the USA it is the agent who rules the roost in sport and show-business, making the contacts, doing deals, talking figures and generally moving and shaking. Is there a fear that football agents in England could soon reach that status?

If you ask some people, one agent already fits that bill. Eric Hall is the man who, with Screaming Lord Sutch, introduced the word monster as an adjective, and can qualify the most outrageous line with the suffix '-ish'. He isn't football's most successful agent, and he certainly isn't licensed, but he is its most notorious. He's omnipresent in the media with his weekly column in the *People* and his own show on the cable station Live TV, and Giles Smith in the *Daily Telegraph* was ironically moved to comment: 'Some new broadcasting legislation seems to have come into effect, whereby all documentary programmes on the subject of football are obliged to include interviews with Eric, or make reference to him, not less than once every ten minutes. It's a welcome ruling and long overdue.'

In fact the FA are so keen to see such a maverick toe the line, that he was encouraged to proceed with a licence application. In a weak moment Eric agreed and accordingly was summoned to Lancaster Gate for vetting. Although not openly hostile, the examination took the form of appearing before a tribunal. After an apology – following the initial fact-finding questions – that they were just going through the formality of clearing a sensitive area, the chairman came to the point. 'Eric, forgive us for asking but do you have a criminal record?'

'Yes,' he replied, 'I do'.

Taken aback by the answer, a tentative follow-up was ventured. 'What is it?'

'*Careless Hands* by Des O'Connor.'

Amid some tut-tutting and suppressed laughter, the chairman tried to restore order. 'Eric, we are being serious.'

'So am I,' replied Eric, 'haven't you heard it?'

Perhaps it is this incorrigible behaviour that endears Eric to Graham Kelly, the chief executive of the FA, who despite appearances to the contrary, has a nice line in off-the-wall humour. He often greets Eric with a friendly 'How are you, monster?' at which Eric proffers one of his huge Havana cigars, accompanied by a stage-whispered, 'There's your bung, Graham'.

Under pressure from FIFA to sign everybody up, the FA told Eric it may, in future, be easier for him to go legit, as they were considering making the licence available for no cost. 'In that case,' countered Eric, 'I'll have two'.

Originally a record plugger, Eric made the move to

football after a chance meeting with Steve Perryman, at the time Tottenham's captain. Links with Tottenham have remained, although not always close ties. In 1991 he handled the players' cup final pool, although not without protests from some – notably Paul Gascoigne and Gary Lineker – who felt Eric was not the best man to look after their interests. Throughout the Venables era, Eric Hall maintained a high profile at White Hart Lane, representing the likes of David Howells, Steve Sedgley, Justin Edinburgh and Vinny Samways. However, when Terry Venables was ousted, Eric Hall was banned along with his friend from attending home games. Eric takes great delight in reading out loud the letter on THFC headed notepaper: '15 June 1993: Dear Mr Hall, I am instructed to inform you that you will no longer be permitted access to Tottenham Hotspur Football Club, and you are also asked not to telephone the club. If you need to communicate with the club with regard to matters relating to players, please do so in writing. Signed Peter Barnes.'

During that turbulent summer of 1993, Spurs defender Neil Ruddock was more vociferous than most about the perceived injustice many of the players felt over the Venables sacking. His outspoken views in the media took the player into direct conflict with his chairman and, after that, there could only ever be one outcome. Ruddock's agent, Eric Hall, helped engineer the player's departure from White Hart Lane, and his story of that move gives an insight into the machinations of transfer brokering.

'If Terry Venables had stayed,' begins Eric, 'then Neil would have stayed. But he didn't like Alan Sugar. Terry Venables was negotiating a new deal for Ruddock prior to his sacking. The deal Ruddock was on at the time wasn't tremendous. But Terry Venables knew the old show-business trick – you don't wait until your stars come knocking at

Wholesale/Retail/Import/Export . . . ish

your door for an improved deal; if they're doing well, you call them in and renegotiate a new deal.'

But before Venables could offer Ruddock anything, the bust-up with Sugar came to a head and Venables was fired. Eric Hall again takes up the narrative: 'Neil and his father-in-law, Paul Bennett, had a meeting scheduled at Alan Sugar's house. I met them prior to that meeting, at the Swallow Hotel in Waltham Abbey, when I told them what to say and what to do. They went off and I waited a couple of hours for them to come back. When they returned, they confirmed they had done what I'd asked them to, but Sugar was having none of it. They were told that Ossie would see them tomorrow at the training ground to convey any improved offer.'

But Ossie's offer wasn't what Ruddock had been hoping for. The player felt let down, and put in a transfer request. Almost immediately, Sugar circulated a memo within the club intimating that Ruddock could go if he so wished. With hindsight, Sugar must regret the haste with which he allowed Ruddock to leave. Tottenham had no obvious replacement and could envisage spending big money to get someone who might prove unable to fill Ruddock's boots. Eric Hall is in no doubt that Sugar's financial offer to the player could have been improved upon.

'Sugar never really tried to make it attractive for the player to stay. I believe if Ruddock had got a monster deal, he would have stayed. He loved it at Tottenham and didn't want to uproot his family to move north.'

As a last resort, Tottenham could have simply refused Ruddock's request and made him see out the remaining three years of his contract. The swiftness with which the post-Venables trauma blew over once Ossie arrived and got a few wins under his belt suggests that stance would have been best for the long-term interests of the club. Eric Hall agrees: 'Sugar could have dug his heels in and told Ruddock the new offer was the best the club were going to make. He could have told the player, "Look it's more than you are getting now. Take it or leave it; but if you leave it you're still here."'

But Sugar apparently made a snap decision that the troublesome player could go, and that was that. 'Typical Sugar,' quips Hall, 'act in haste, repent at leisure'.

It was just a question of the club getting the most they could from the transaction. 'To be fair to Sugar,' concedes Eric Hall, 'he didn't play games. He set a price, £2.5 million, and that was it. First in, first served type of thing. I got a phone call from Neil, telling me the club were going to let him go, and they were going to tell all the interested parties that day. The first to react were Ray Harford and Kenny Dalglish at Blackburn.'

Uncanny.

'I know Ray and Kenny very well. I said "Listen Ken, it's not official yet, but within an hour or so you'll be getting a call . . . two point five . . ." They didn't waste time and got their offer in straight away. They had their fax in within minutes. Two point five million.

'I phoned Graeme Souness at Liverpool, but it turned out he was here in London that day on business. So I got him on his mobile and told him the news. "Meet me at my hotel," he said.

'By the time I've got washed and changed and ready for this meeting with Graeme, everybody knows the news. Just as I was walking into Graeme's hotel my mobile goes and it was Terry MacDermott from Newcastle. He said, "Eric have you heard the news?" I said yes. He said, "We want to talk to him. We've faxed Spurs and they've accepted our offer. Can you come up tonight?" I said yes, fine. He said to me, "The only thing is, Blackburn have been in before us." He had a little go at me . . . ish, saying he didn't know how Blackburn had got to hear so bloody quickly when they'd only had the phone call themselves two minutes ago, and yet Blackburn had made their offer twenty minutes ago.

'So anyway, I unofficially met Graeme Souness, who then rang up Peter Robinson and David Moores [chief executive and chairman respectively] telling them he was with me at that moment, and had they heard from Tottenham yet? And if not, why not? And to get on to Tottenham right away because bids had already been accepted from Blackburn and Newcastle and so to get Liverpool's bid in right away. He told his directors to forget about typing a fax up, just get on to Tottenham and claim you'd "heard the rumour" about Ruddock being sold. So, about 40 minutes later after we'd finished our smoked salmon sandwiches and coffee, the phone goes and it's Peter Robinson confirming that Tottenham had now accepted Liverpool's bid.'

Unbeknown to Eric at this stage, Chelsea had also had a bid accepted. So Tottenham had now accepted four bids for Ruddock, all meeting the £2.5 million asking price. All within a couple of hours of the news breaking.

'So now the player can speak to whoever he likes,' says Eric, taking up the story again. Unofficial protocol stipulates that interested clubs must be seen in the order that the bids arrive, beginning with Blackburn.

'Kenny Dalglish was out playing golf somewhere in Spain [it was June to be fair], and so Ray Harford flew down to London that night. We met at a hotel, where he made an offer which wasn't really acceptable. I said what we were looking for, which they weren't too happy with. I know people think the club are moneybags, and that all players are on monster, monster wages, but it's not true. One or two are yes, but the majority aren't.

'That was a Friday evening. On the Sunday we flew to Liverpool. Graeme Souness met us in his car and took us back to his wonderful house. When we arrive, David Moores and Peter Robinson are also there, along with Graeme's wife Karen. And they really laid it on for us. There was gefilte fish – fried and boiled – there was smoked salmon bagels, apple strudel and smoked salmon sandwiches, there was chopped liver sandwiches. It was like a Jewish wedding. I said I hope you haven't done all this for me, and Karen said, "Are you joking Eric? We have done it for you, but only made it more". Every Sunday they have that same schtick.

'So all day long we are noshing, and as we sat around the table, I listed the things we were looking for. And everything I wanted, they've said yes to! A very good basic. A very good signing-on fee. A very good loyalty bonus. The usual three things which everybody has . . . ish. I thought, "I've blown it here". I mean, I went over the top, but they'd said yes to everything. By then, the Sunday, the transfer news had been all over the papers, and I suppose the Liverpool directors were thinking that if they didn't get the player, then Blackburn would. So they said yes to everything, except one thing. They wouldn't give Neil a club car. They said that nobody at Liverpool got a club car, but that they would definitely line up a sponsored car. It wasn't a big stumbling block, but I did my usual schtick, asking if they expected him to go car-less or what. They said, "Eric, we've agreed to everything, it's a monster deal as you would say". I said I know it's a monster deal, but he's got to have a car.

'The Liverpool directors said we don't do cars, but don't worry, he'll get a car, we guarantee. I said in that case, if it's guaranteed, put it in the contract. Say he will be supplied with a car. The Liverpool people were straight, monster straight people. They said they couldn't put it in the contract in case the club fell out with the sponsors the next day.

'So I went outside and walked around the garden for a few minutes, talking things over with Neil. I told him that for the money he was getting he could buy two Porsches. But we went back into the room and talked some more and finally did a deal whereby Neil could buy his own car. So we compromised.

'So the deal was done and dusted. We'd missed our plane by then, so Graeme Souness arranged for someone to drive us back to London that night. Neil stayed overnight with his friend Alan Shearer because Liverpool wanted him to have a medical the next day. I get in at midnight-ish, and there are messages on my answering machine. Phone Ken Bates urgently. Phone Glenn Hoddle urgently. Phone this one and that one urgently. Phone Howard Wilkinson. So I called them all back next morning, and explained how we'd agreed terms with Liverpool. I went back to Liverpool, who by now had sorted things out with Tottenham, and the deal was done that Monday.' Eric could now wear his bright red jacket and tell everyone who'd care to listen, what a wonderful club Liverpool was.

So Alan Sugar got his money, but arguably lost it again in trying to plug the gap left by Ruddock. Ironically, although he originally prospered at Liverpool, to the extent of earning international recognition, injuries, personal problems and his manager's glut of central defenders meant that less than a couple of years later Liverpool were listening to offers for the player. To give Tottenham their due, they came back for Ruddock according to Eric. Unrealistically though; the Sugar-Francis budgetary considerations meant they only offered £2.7 million and so the return trip never transpired. At least not yet.

Not all transfer deals are knitted together by agents. David Dein rates Arsenal's purchases of Ian Wright as, 'probably our best buy in the whole history of the club'. It was a deal that came about almost by chance, and was, for Dein, a model transfer transaction.

'George Graham identified Ian Wright and/or Mark Bright as being potential strikers. At that time, I was speaking regularly with club chairmen, including Ron Noades from Crystal Palace. It was natural to speak about players.

'I was on the phone to Ron, and asked him to tell me about Ian Wright and Mark Bright. Would he sell either of them? He said he was a "reluctant seller", and that it would take a lot of money to prise one or the other away. I asked him what he called a lot of money, so he said, "Like £2 million for Mark Bright", and that he wouldn't take "less than £2.5 million for Ian Wright". I asked him if that meant he would sell Ian Wright for £2.5 million. He said, "I suppose, if it was offered, I'd have to take it."

'So I said to him, "Ron, I'm offering £2.5 million for Ian Wright". The phone went dead. He said "Are you serious?" I said, "Yes, I'm offering you £2.5 million. You said you'd sell him for that, you are a man of your word, I'm offering you two and a half million."

'And to his credit, he stuck by his word. He said, "You've got yourself a deal". And Ian Wright was at Highbury that afternoon having a medical. George Graham was having – of all things – a golf day with the press. I rang through to him on the course, and said, "I've got good news for you: we've just signed Ian Wright". And so George announced it to the press when he finished his golf.

'Ian Wright was almost unique. When he came in, and

Ken Friar was doing the paperwork, he said, "Where do I sign?" We said, but what about your terms? He said, "Where do I sign?" He was not interested at all in salary or bonuses. Just, "Where do I sign?" And that speaks volumes to me.

'And once again, he had an extension to his contract recently. He wasn't interested in the money he was going to get, he said he just wanted to sign for Arsenal Football Club. He's one in a million. A gem. You want to have eleven players in the team like Ian Wright.' David Dein would have been distraught at Wright's transfer request towards the end of this season, but would have appreciated the reason, which had nothing to do with money but everything to do with his role in the team.

Gerry Francis would no doubt settle for eleven players like Clive Wilson. A versatile performer on the field and a gentleman off it, whose lack of international recognition throughout a long and distinguished club career exceeding 400 games still mystifies the Spurs manager.

When Clive made his first major move, from Manchester City to Chelsea in 1987 for £250,000, there were no agents involved. 'It was just between me, John Hollins [then Chelsea manager] and the vice-chairman at Man. City. I got bits of advice from various players, but to be honest I was totally green going in. I'd always played for my home town and been fairly settled, so I hadn't accumulated any knowledge of what a transfer entailed; what you ask for, what you get and what you don't get. It opened my eyes. When I signed for Chelsea, I thought it was a reasonable deal. But when I got to hear what all the other players were earning, then no, it wasn't a reasonable deal.

'My first culture shock was the price of houses. Nobody told me! I knew London was a lot more expensive, I just

Dream On

didn't realise how much more. I'd lived in a three–bed semi in Manchester worth £35,000. When I came to London I don't think I could have bought a shoe-box for £35,000. I thought I might have to double what I'd expected to pay, but even at £70,000, even at £100,000, there was no way I could buy a semi in London. If I then moved out to the suburbs, where a lot of the players were, then I could perhaps have afforded one. But I wanted to see a bit of London. I ended up buying a flat in Southfields in 1988. That was probably the worst time I could have picked to buy a property, because prices crashed shortly after. But it was a learning process.

'In 1990, I moved to QPR for £450,000. I never got a percentage of the fee because I was out of contract at the time.'

It was Don Howe who took Clive to Loftus Road, but it was only when Howe was replaced by Gerry Francis that Clive's career took off and he became a bedrock in the side.

Clive's contract was up for renewal while Gerry was still boss at QPR. 'Gerry knew that I was trying to hold out for a free transfer, which would give me not only a move, but also the chance to get more money from the deal than I would normally get if a fee was involved. In that last year at QPR, I asked Gerry for just a one-year contract. If he had stayed on at Loftus Road, he would probably have persuaded me to stay, but then Gerry resigned in November '94 and got the Tottenham job.

'Nobody could have suspected this development, because for years Gerry had been saying that he may pack it in and that he doesn't need football. But he goes to Tottenham, and I suppose I was secretly hoping he would come in for me. At the end of the 1995 season, he phones me. He said he knew my situation – my year's contract was up – and he said he was interested in me. Now it was a case of deciding if I really wanted to go to Tottenham.

'In all honesty, the temptation to stay at QPR was Ray Wilkins. I really like Ray as a man, as a player and as a manager. I have an awful lot of respect for him. But if I did anything wrong, it was when Ray asked me what it would take to keep me at Rangers. I told him the amount. He ummed and aahed, but eventually came up with the deal. However, in the time it took them to come up with the deal, Gerry had let it be known he was interested in me at Tottenham. So then I had a re-think. What do I go for? Money, or money and a chance to win something? Because throughout my career I've won nothing major, and with the greatest respect to QPR, I couldn't see them doing anything above Tottenham, particularly as they were just about to lose Les Ferdinand.

'So when I weighed up the pros and cons, there were too many pros in Tottenham's favour. And Tottenham gave me a three-year contract as against the two years at Rangers. There is security in the extra year, plus the chance to end my career winning something.'

Once more the deal was brief and private. 'The deal was settled between me and Gerry, because I trust Gerry. After my move from Chelsea to QPR, I had become very wary of agents because all I could see was that they'd do the contract, then you wouldn't hear from them until it needed renewing again. I decided not to use them again, plus by then I had more self-confidence to negotiate on my own.

'I went to Gerry's house in Bagshot. We didn't talk figures, he just attempted to sell the club to me. He highlighted the differences between a so-called big club like Spurs and a so-called small club like QPR.

'He had to refer back to Alan Sugar over what deal he

Dream On

could offer me, but in the end he said yes. I got a basic three-year contract. There are payments made for each appearance, and bonuses for reaching Europe or doing well in a cup. It came down to having Gerry on one phone and Richard Thompson [QPR's owner] on the other. QPR had backed me into a corner saying they wanted an answer, which was fair enough. They wanted me to go and visit the chairman. What they meant was that if you go in with the chairman, you ain't leaving that room until you sign a contract. I knew that if I went to that meeting it meant I would be staying at Rangers. So I faced the daunting task of having to phone Ray Wilkins and tell him that I was going to sign for Tottenham.

'He wasn't too pleased about it. I think the feeling was that it had been Gerry who had put me in a position where I could move on a free transfer, but then it was also Gerry who came and took me. But, with the best will in the world, Gerry wasn't to know when he gave me that single-year contract that he was going to leave. That was never on the cards. It was just coincidental.'

There is nothing wrong, commercially or ethically, with agents representing the interests of players. In the Ruddock example, there is no question that the decision to leave Tottenham came from the player, with no prompting or pressure from the agent. The deal achieved for the player by his agent was far superior to anything the player could have negotiated for himself. A couple of pre-emptive phone calls, a little bluster and a lot of chutzpah netted an un-capped centre-half a fantastic financial package with one of the country's most successful clubs. Perhaps even with Clive Wilson, who was among friends, an experienced agent could have improved on whatever terms the player was able to

Wholesale/Retail/Import/Export . . . ish

secure from Tottenham. After all, who would you back to win a financial showdown: Clive Wilson or Alan Sugar?

What agents like Eric Hall must ensure if they wish their business to remain free from restrictions, is that they are seen to be as clean as the self-regulated solicitors and accountants who are after their business. The International Association of Football Agents (IAFA), mentioned by Dennis Roach, may be a start in the right direction, but there are complications. At the moment there are twice as many unlicensed agents operating in the UK as there are licensed agents, excluding the PFA who would have a fit if they were accused of going after the same dollar as Eric Hall. Yet they undoubtedly are. Certainly their cut from helping one of their members move clubs is likely to be less than an agent's commission or solicitor's fee. But what they lose on the transfer roundabout they gain on the pension swings, as the player invariably ends up with a PFA financial scheme.

According to clubs, the PFA have a conflict of interest. David Dein puts it succinctly when he says, 'I don't believe the PFA should be the player's agent. That is morally wrong. They know all of the players' contracts'. As a strong union with practically 100% membership, how can they, with inside knowledge, represent some players and not others? Collective bargaining it ain't. It may be a case of the PFA having their cake and eating it, but at least the money stays within the game to the benefit of the players. This possible conflict of interest wouldn't have arisen in American sports where there is an open playing field as all parties, through full disclosure, are aware of players' contracts.

Mel Goldberg is alarmed by an apparent trend that sees clubs overpaying for players, a euphemism for siphoning off funds to people and places who shouldn't be receiving them.

Dream On

'There was an example this season where a player coming from the Continent had an asking price – the price the selling club would have accepted – of £700,000. I was acting for an agent in France for the sale of this player. The deal was on the point of being concluded, when the buying club stopped taking calls. It was a signal I had seen before. Twenty-four hours later the club bought that player, not for £700,000, but for £950,000. So that transaction was extremely suspicious, because I know that the price was wrong.

'On a similar subject, and not unconnected, I know for example a player coming from a European club whose asking price was £550,000. He was eventually bought by an English club, not for the price his club was asking, but for £1.55 million. There was a one million pound discrepancy. This sale took place within the past five months [during the 95/96 season]. I am sure it is known by managers who have been in the game for a long time, that there is only one reason why you pay more than you are asked to pay, and that is so there is a "pot" which can be shared.

'There's an even worse example, of a club who bought an international player after telling him they were "a top team" playing in "the first division". They were indeed a First Division club, but the player thought he would be playing in the top division and landed up signing for this club without realising he would not be playing in the Premier League. The player has complained to his home soccer federation who are now taking steps to ensure that when future players from that country come to England, they are well informed as to which club they are joining. In this case the player was clearly misled. (In a related matter, it was alleged that Reading's Bulgarian international, Boris Mikhailov, was shown a video of Reading's play-off game with Bolton at Wembley, leading to some disappointment when the player arrived at Elm Park and discovered the video he had seen hadn't in fact been a home fixture.)

'At least when you are dealing with a club like Spurs, who now have high standards, everyone knows where they are and respects it. I find Alan Sugar a straight shooter who tells you what he thinks. If he likes you he'll tell you. If he doesn't he'll tell you that as well. He barks a lot but he doesn't waste his words.

'The clubs I do not like are those that pretend to be honest and noble. For example, I recently telephoned a director of a Premier League club and told him that a certain player in the Italian league was available. I knew this because the selling club had their eyes on another player to replace the one on their books. When I mentioned the name of the player, the club director said the player was too young and too inexperienced. Both of which claims were patently untrue. Furthermore the club said the player was "a bad character". They weren't interested. Now I happen to know that immediately after putting the phone down, the director to whom I had been speaking then phoned Italy and made enquiries directly with the selling club. I think that is thoroughly dishonest and disgraceful conduct. And this from a director who will happily criticise agents and middlemen when his own behaviour is far worse.'

Just because the clubs are paranoid it doesn't mean nobody is out to get them. With the PFA anathema to the clubs, the agents anathema to the PFA and the authorities attempting to legislate from the sidelines, what is required is a coming together. David Dein again: 'There is more money in transfers swishing about than ever before, and it's all up for renegotiation. We're in a different world now.' One possible solution could be implemented without recourse to drastic action. All it requires is for a player to inform his employer pre-season as to who his representative is; whether himself, his union or his licensed/unlicensed agent (remembering that in the latter case the agent can do everything short of face-to-face contact). Then there is no reason why the clubs should not be honour bound to negotiate with that representative. At least everyone would know where they stood.

Ilie Dumitrescu's season sparked back to life at Christmas, when another injury crisis brought him back into the first team. He started the match away to Blackburn, but even with the fans willing him on, it was still the same old Dumitrescu – running the ball into blind alleys, losing possession and finding himself way out of position for defensive duties. Nevertheless he kept his place for the subsequent home game against Manchester United, but his performance was just as fitful and he was withdrawn. His career at Tottenham seemed over. It was time for a move.

'I stayed in touch with Dumitrescu,' recalls Dennis Roach. 'He likes me, I like him. He trusts me and knows that everything I have said would be paid was actually paid. After returning from the loan period at Seville, he was very unhappy. And when he's unhappy, he phones friends who he thinks can help. I happened to be playing golf with Harry Redknapp of West Ham, and mentioned to him about Dumitrescu's plight. Harry felt he would be wonderful for his team. I said that I had spoken to Mr Sugar's son, Daniel, and knew that Spurs were now looking at a price of around £1.5 million, which was substantially less than the one they were hoping for originally.'

The West Ham manager followed up the chance conversation, talking with Daniel Sugar to confirm the details, before the deal was eventually done between Peter Storrie,

Wholesale/Retail/Import/Export . . . ish

managing director at Upton Park, and Alan Sugar. So in January 1996, Ilie Dumitrescu became a West Ham player. Or he would have done if this sad saga hadn't taken a further twist, one that again showed Tottenham in a poor light, and gave a further insight into the politics of the PFA.

When Spurs originally signed Dumitrescu from Steaua Bucharest, it had been on a four-year contact, subject to a medical and, as he came from outside the EC, a work permit being granted. At that time, because of his outstanding international career, the work permit was a formality and was granted by the Home Office. However, Dumitrescu's agent had the foresight to insert a clause in that initial contract, stipulating that Tottenham were responsible for maintaining that work permit and thus obliged to pay the player, even if no work permit was granted. Initially, this was no problem. But when the permit fell due for renewal, the PFA, acting they felt in the best interests of all their members, made representations to the government that the renewal should be opposed on the grounds that the player had not played in 75% of Tottenham's first team games since his arrival. The Department of Employment, taking its lead from the PFA, as it does in these matters, acquiesced and the work permit was not renewed.

The implications for Tottenham were irksome. They had a player, on a contract with two-and-a-half years to run, probably earning in excess of £6,000 per week, whom they couldn't play, and now they couldn't sell. Or could they? During the transfer negotiations with West Ham, the issue of the work permit had somehow been fudged. The player posed in West Ham colours and was paraded before the Upton Park fans, but when West Ham applied for the clearance they thought would be a formality, they received an unpleasant shock and the deal stalled. The countdown to deportation had begun.

The PFA's chief executive, Gordon Taylor, attempted to justify his stance. 'It's not the PFA that decides whether a player should have a work permit. That's the responsibility of the Employment Department. All we do is offer observations along with the FA and the Premier League. Criteria have been laid down and there has been a certain amount of flexibility in the past. But with the recent influx of foreign players the department has tightened up, and is insisting that the criteria have to be met. Dumitrescu clearly doesn't meet them.'

Dumitrescu saw things differently. 'I am an international player who has played 52 times for his country and scored twenty goals. I understand it is right for Mr Gordon Taylor to protect English football, but I am a member of his union and he should support me. When I first came to Spurs I played twelve, thirteen games and scored six goals. When Gerry Francis came he wanted a different way of playing and I respect that. It was not my fault I was out of the team. West Ham gave me this chance of making another career and I want to take it.'

It is interesting to contrast Ilie Dumitrescu's plight with that of Ronny Rosenthal who, following the purchase of Klinsmann and the return to fitness of Sheringham, couldn't get a place in the forward line at Tottenham. 'Maybe it was a mistake,' recalled Ronny, 'but I regret not going to see Ossie and telling him I can play in midfield. But when Gerry arrived, I made a point of going to see him and saying how I could play in midfield, I even play for my national side in that position. I knew I wouldn't get the glory that a striker does, but when I realised that Ilie Dumitrescu wasn't part of Gerry's plans, that allowed me to get back into the team.'

Wholesale/Retail/Import/Export . . . ish

Gordon Taylor was determined that his union should not be the fall-guys when perhaps others had a case to answer. 'I don't believe West Ham have been fully informed of the background to this case by Tottenham,' he argued. 'Spurs knew the situation. The PFA approved Dumitrescu to stay at Tottenham to give him a chance to meet the criteria. At the end of last season he had not made the criteria. We were sympathetic then, and there was another review after three months and another in December. We were sympathetic on both occasions, provided he stayed at Tottenham. Then Tottenham tried to sell him. There could have been no certainty if he left that an application would be accepted, given the criteria.'

Dennis Roach felt strongly that Dumitrescu was an innocent victim. 'It's not the player's fault that the manager who signed him got the sack, and that the new manager didn't feel he was the right man for the job.'

And when the situation was made public, it was generally felt that the players (Swiss international Marc Hottiger had also fallen foul of the same ruling while trying to move from Newcastle to Everton) were victims of a bad bureaucratic ruling and a bias by the PFA on behalf of their 'home' members. If players like Dumitrescu and Hottiger were good enough to warrant a work permit when they entered the country, then they hadn't suddenly become bad players overnight. Their permits ought to have been extended.

Mel Goldberg had no doubts who were the villains of the piece. 'I think the rule is ridiculous. I understand the thinking behind the PFA's stance in that they don't want to put British footballers out of work. But there has got to be a degree of common sense. If we have a world class player who has proved his ability beyond doubt, but doesn't happen to get into the club's side because he doesn't fit the manager's pattern, the PFA should use a bit of discretion.

'I feel the PFA have behaved very poorly here. Spurs are stuck with a player who doesn't fit into their team. West Ham have been relying on Dumitrescu and now they can't have him. Spurs have spent the money they would have got from the player, and the British game has suffered badly. Unless the appeal is successful the player will be forced to return to Romania.

'I put the blame wholly on the PFA for that. I have done a lot of work on permit applications. The Premier League are consulted. The FA are consulted. But the bottom line is that the PFA give a nod and a wink to the Department of Employment as to whether a player should get a work permit. In Dumitrescu's case, they appear to have said, "Don't give him one". So no marks out of ten for the PFA on this issue.'

The PFA, the Professional Footballers' Association, purports to represent all players working in England, including foreign imports. They have apparently taken the view that while the likes of Klinsmann, Gullit, Bergkamp and Cantona are no problem, too many imports, particularly mediocre players who are attractively priced, hinder the progress of homegrown talent. It was for this reason they vetoed their own member, Ilie Dumitrescu. A first in TUC annals? Ironically, although Tottenham aren't a club known for promoting from within their youth system, both Darren Caskey and Gerry McMahon made more appearances than Dumitrescu, so he obviously wasn't preventing their selection.

'We shall be saying that Ilie's application is not for a renewal,' explained Peter Storrie of his club's appeal, 'it is a new application. What happened at Spurs is an irrelevance in our view.'

'Dumitrescu has played at the highest level,' pleaded

Wholesale/Retail/Import/Export . . . ish

Harry Redknapp. 'The reports to the Employment Department from the FA and the Premier League were positive. I don't know about the PFA. I hope what I hear isn't true.'

In the middle of all this turmoil, on 17 February, Spurs played West Ham at White Hart Lane. Afterwards, the euphoria of a 1–0 win for West Ham – 'My best result since taking over the club' – was tempered when Redknapp was again asked to comment on the Dumitrescu situation. 'The decision has absolutely slaughtered the boy. I'm more concerned now about Ilie Dumitrescu than I am West Ham, Tottenham or money. The boy lives here, his family is here, he pays his taxes. I mean, the boy wants to play football. He wants to play in the European Championships this summer, and if he gets kicked out of the country all of that goes by the wayside. He said he hasn't slept for four nights. I'll be honest with you: I've had the fellah crying his eyes out, and it's not fair. He's a member of the PFA; he pays his subs. Surely if you belong to a union, that union will back you to the hilt, that's why you belong. If not, then don't take his subs. Don't let him join the union if you're saying "No, you're a foreigner, we don't want you," when it goes boss-eyed.

'I put the TV on Saturday night, and saw a fellow, Asprilla, who has only been in the country three days, and he's playing for Newcastle. We've been 30 days waiting for a work permit for Bilic [a Croatian international]. It's like everything in life – it's who you know.

'All right, it hasn't worked out for him at Tottenham, but that still doesn't stop him being a world class player. We don't even kick illegal immigrants out of the country do we? To be honest, we are willing to pay the money and take him on a short term permit. That's how big a gamble we're prepared to take. We'll pay the money and play him on a permit to the end of the season. We stand to lose everything, but I'm willing to gamble because I know the player will be in my team. I've seen him train for the last three weeks, I know what he can do.'

Redknapp was asked, if the appeal failed, how far West Ham would take the matter.

'Well, the point is that he belongs to Tottenham Hotspur. He doesn't belong to us. They pay his wages, not us.'

Gerry Francis, too, made the point that a change of club shouldn't affect the basic right to continue playing. 'It's like penalising Andy Sinton, who couldn't get into the Sheffield Wednesday team, or Ruel Fox, who couldn't get a game at Newcastle.'

Perhaps mindful of the fact that he had already spent the Dumitrescu income on acquiring Andy Sinton, Gerry was keen for a compromise solution that would at last see money change hands. 'I think they should at least give him a work permit to play until the end of the season. And if he plays 75% of the games at West Ham, then extend it. That would be a fair way of doing it.'

There was a final dig from Gerry at the PFA, who were not emerging from this issue with too many friends. 'I think both Dumitrescu and Hottiger have had backing from the FA and the Premier League. The only backing they haven't got is from the PFA. You have to look beyond the present situation. I can play eleven Europeans now as a manager, that is the law. We have to ask ourselves how we can learn from the foreigners and make our players a little bit better.'

Gerry had struck a point with that phrase 'You have to look beyond the present situation'. For just as the British Government was beginning to realise the implications of belonging to a united Europe, so were football clubs and authorities waking up and smelling the same coffee.

*   *   *

Wholesale/Retail/Import/Export . . . ish

The so-called 'Bosman Affair' was a watershed issue for football that meandered through the European legal system, making the Venables/Sugar episode look like a quickie divorce. It was the culmination of a five-year legal battle by Jean Marc Bosman, initiated when he was refused a move from his Belgian club, FC Liege, to the French second division club Dunkerque, and offered an inferior contract to his previous one. A halt was eventually called and a ruling made in December 1995. The world of football lost no time in jumping to a number of wrong conclusions. Depending upon whom you listened to, football was either finished or saved.

The first point to remember is that the ruling was made by the European Court of Justice and therefore only applies to EC and EFA (Lichtenstein, Norway and Iceland) countries. So although the football federations in these countries must abide by the judgement, the rest of UEFA and FIFA's members can happily ignore it.

The second point is that the ruling is just that, a ruling on the particular case that was brought before the court, and it may take further test cases to complete the process of reform. For the time being, English clubs, along with their counterparts in the EC, must come to grips with some new facts of life. Two changes are definite and take place with immediate effect.

If a player comes to the end of his contract, and wants a move to a club in another EC country, then he can do so and his previous club have no right to charge a transfer fee. He is a free agent. In addition, there is no limit on the number of 'foreign' EC players a team can field. What hasn't, as yet, changed, at least in England, is the right of clubs to charge a transfer fee when an out-of-contract player moves clubs within the same country. The same stipulation applies when a player wants to move abroad to a country outside the EC.

A major source of confusion at the time of the ruling – Article 48 dealing with freedom of movement was invoked to support it – was whether all transfer fees would be outlawed as there is a second Article, 85, which deals with competition, and as such has implications for internal transfers within an EC country. As yet there has been no definitive ruling on Article 85. However, ominously, another Belgian footballer, Jean Marie Houben, is currently trawling his case through the courts on just this issue.

Ironically, under the English system, though not Scotland which is analogous to Belgium, Jean Marc Bosman would have qualified for the free transfer he spent so long pursuing, and the whole episode could have been avoided. As an out-of-contract player, offered inferior terms to those he had previously enjoyed, he would have been free to move to another club. And even if the terms offered by his club were an improvement on his old contract, he could still choose to walk and allow a tribunal to set a fee if the clubs themselves could not agree on one.

UEFA, the game's governing body in Europe, found itself in an awkward position. Backed by FIFA, the governing body of world football. ('Because Bosman has put the transfer system in doubt in the EC, is it necessary to change the rules?' queried Sepp Blatter, general secretary at FIFA, 'Because 21 associations have to proceed differently to 193 who comprise FIFA?') UEFA contested why the ruling should be applicable to all their 49 members. It didn't want to introduce double standards regarding transfers or have the onerous task of policing the variances by country.

There could be no such excuses regarding foreign quotas, and in February UEFA accepted that restrictions would go but 'asked' the clubs still in their three European club competitions to adhere to the 3+2 rule for this season.

Here in England, Irishmen, Welshmen and Scotsmen are not regarded as foreigners at home, but they were pre-Bosman when English clubs played abroad. No more than three foreigners and two assimilated players – those like Welshman Ryan Giggs, who had affiliated to a 'foreign' club for more than five years – could be picked in a squad for European competition. This put top English clubs at a severe disadvantage; they could rarely field the same side that had got them into Europe in the first place. For once, the Premier League led the way with firm and decisive action. 'We were advised by our lawyers,' said Rick Parry, 'that the judgment took immediate effect and notified the clubs that the three foreigners rule could no longer be imposed, and similarly that clubs could not demand a transfer fee for a player out of contract.' It is now accepted in France, Spain and Italy that this applies to internal transfers as well.

Gut reaction was that a lot of small clubs would go to the wall if they were to lose the right to sell players to big clubs. If they go bust however, this will only be a contributory cause, as, since the formation of the Premier League, transfer income for these small clubs, as a percentage of revenue, has been declining. The majority of transfers (£100m in 1995), are now conducted chiefly between the top two divisions and overseas clubs.

Everyone must now learn to 'grow their own', utilising the assistance they receive from the government's two-year YTS scheme for sixteen–eighteen year-olds. If players of sufficient quality continue to be produced, then such prospects will help ensure the future of the clubs, either by retaining those players or by selling them while they are

Dream On

still within contract. In France, a player is compelled to sign
his first contract with the club that developed him, so that
he doesn't become a free agent until he is 24. As football
outside divisions one and two is regional and part-time, the
provision of such a lengthy contract doesn't entail a huge
financial risk.

In England, however, lower division clubs could not afford
to give an eighteen-year-old a comparable contract. Perhaps
if all parties – FA, Premier League, Football League and
the PFA – accepted a limited extension of three years to
the YTS scheme, centrally funded by a transfer levy, to
subsidise a selected number of boys, say five per club, for
clubs outside the top two divisions, then at 21 the player
would be free to leave or re-sign as the case may be. The
best prospects would be snapped up for nothing, although
it is possible that a mandatory residual financial scheme
could award certain payments to the developing club, if
the player attained Premier League and/or international
status. Many more however could be re-signed and, as the
majority of transfers happen after the age of 21, a fee could
then be charged for a contractual sale. Moreover, with the
rapacious demand for immediate success by the leading
clubs, an experienced foreign player is going to appear a
more attractive proposition than a potentially good young
native player.

With an element of funding and concentration on local
roots, it should be possible for the smaller clubs to survive and flourish – even if they have to go regional and
part-time – as an integral part of the system in their
own right. To regard them merely as grooming fodder
or nursery clubs for the Premiership is as insulting as it is
short-sighted.

Meanwhile, in the 'real' world, David Dein is convinced

that the Bosman ruling is going to change football's transfers. 'Clubs will want now to give longer contracts to their
better players,' he says. 'The players, through their agents,
will no doubt try to negotiate shorter contracts, which
puts them in a better bargaining position at the end of
their contracts when ostensibly they become a free agent
should they wish to move abroad. Whether that will extend
to England as well is the next situation that is going to have
to be confronted. So my view is that transfer fees will have
to come down because of the risk element to a club. Salaries
will go up because one will compensate the other.

'Arsenal have to write the Bergkamp money off. Our view
on Bergkamp was that the guy was 26 when we bought him,
we got him on a four-year contract. Effectively we paid
£7.5 million. We write that off over four years, hoping
that, during those four years, if he does well, we try and
extend his contract. So he runs on for another two or three
years afterwards. As it happens, in his case he will be an
ideal person, because of his attitude, his professionalism, to
be a person who we cultivate for the future. For the next
generation, within our system.

'But there will be a lot of players, at the end of their contract, looking to go abroad to other EU countries because
they realise they are going to capitalise on that move. We
are in a transformation period, and we are approaching it
with caution.'

The abolition of the foreign player quota must surely
prove a boon for English sides in the long term. Those
home clubs which dominated European competition in the
'70s and '80s did so with the aid of UK foreigners. The
Bosman ruling now allows clubs to revert to the days when
such a line-up was permissible, in European competition,
as well as at home. In fact, it is now theoretically possible

for eleven Italians as opposed to eleven Celts to represent Liverpool. But it shouldn't happen, providing youth policies are prioritised by all clubs in England. For the big clubs it is a money-saving option, and for the smaller clubs to ensure their very survival.

An inevitable result will be a greater fluidity of movement as players flit between clubs and countries on short contracts and high salaries. For clubs, the fluctuations in fortune will be dramatic as successful teams come together and break up within a couple of seasons. A fresh onus will be placed not just on how clubs attract players, but on how they intend to keep them. Again a look to France is instructive. There, prior to the '95–'96 season, twice as many players changed clubs within their top division as compared to the Premier League. As a result it is not unusual to see small clubs from small towns reaching the French first division, through growing their own and mixing them with the increased availability of experienced players.

On 7 March, Ilie Dumitrescu got his work permit. The Department for Education and Employment (DfEE), bowing to pressure from all quarters, executed a U-turn after a meeting with the football authorities and the PFA. A new criterion now permits one move between British clubs for non-EU players. Providing those players have appeared in 75% of their country's international matches for the two years prior to the move, then it no longer matters how few games they may have played for their club. PFA representative, Brendon Batson, reported the news in a manner that suggested a certain amount of arm twisting had accompanied the negotiations: 'It is a compromise that meets the needs, at the moment, of the people involved in football. All we said was that if there is a criterion, it should be adhered to. We were party to the agreed change and are happy with it.'

The failure by Tottenham to utilise Dumitrescu's fragile skills echoed the experience of Nico Claesen almost a decade earlier. Similar players in style and temperament, there was widespread feeling among fans that the loss in both cases was Tottenham's. Dumitrescu was even denied the bit part that Claesen played in what has become Tottenham's only enduring flirtation with success, the FA Cup. However, even if he'd stayed, Dumitrescu would have been unlikely to have changed the outcome of this year's competition, Tottenham being just one of the fall guys as expediency replaced tradition in the undermining of the greatest club cup competition in the world.

Chapter 11

Yesterdays Gone

The great thing about the FA Cup, as anyone will tell you, is that on the day, David can still beat Goliath.

We should be grateful that particular biblical tussle took place 3,000 years ago, otherwise history may now record how David, fighting his third giant in eight days, and forced to concede home advantage after fears of Philistines travelling without tickets, triumphed in a sudden-death stone-out (the fatal sling-shot being timed at 91mph) in a BC Cup (sponsored by Toga-Toga) tie, switched to a Sunday afternoon for live coverage on *Mis-Match of the Day – The Road To Jerusalem*.

For the 1995–96 season, the Cup took its now customary battering from the elements: snow, wind, rain and Sky. Although the eccentricities of the British climate have to be tolerated, the increasingly rapacious demands of satellite TV do not. The decision of Sky Sports to begin their live Cup coverage as early as the First Round proper is commendable, but as the competition progresses, the station's appetite for live action can affect a club's season as much as any freak gale, blizzard or thunderstorm.

Dream On

The irony of the FA Cup is that by the time the big boys make their much heralded entrance at the Third Round stage, the bulk of the competition is over. With 500 ties already decided, there remain only 63 in which to crown a winner. But it is at the Third Round stage that the competition really comes alive, as the non-league minnows from football's backwaters, having survived the tortuous journey through qualifying and preliminary rounds, finally get a chance to swim with the sharks.

The entry of First Division and Premiership sides at the Third Round stage is traditionally one of the key moments in the English football calendar. Once upon a time there was a nationally focused FA Cup Saturday when all that round's ties were played. Now, interruptions fostered by Mother Nature, Auntie Beeb and Uncle Rupert serve only to dilute the event. With two of the most attractive ties shifted to Sunday and Monday for live transmission, the Cup is frequently left with no focal point, swamped in a weekend of league fixtures. This was particularly acute at the Sixth Round stage, when the four ties were staged over a Saturday, Sunday, Monday and Wednesday. The Cup, as Henry Winter pointed out in the *Daily Telegraph*, 'Really does have a magic of its own: it has made itself disappear'.

In efforts to appease television, but also to be seen to move with the times, the Cup draws were first moved from their quirky Monday lunchtime Radio 2 slot, to wider exposure on television. The radio slot may have been an anachronism, but at least it united the football world by focusing attention on one spot at one time. In school playgrounds and offices across the country, ears strained to catch the whispered reverential tones of the BBC's football correspondent, Bryon Butler, as he invited us to come with him into the FA Council chamber where the

draw for the next round was about to take place. There, four
FA dignitaries – one to draw the home team, one to draw
the away team, one to read out the team names and one to
have a coughing fit in the background – would command
the nation's attention for the ensuing five minutes.

It was a scenario reminiscent of Chamberlain's declara-
tion of war with Germany, and not surprisingly the BBC and
the FA sought to capitalise on its audience potential while
taking the opportunity to add a little televised pizazz. To
some extent this was achieved with the move to television,
although the lack of a regular slot – it eventually ended up
an appendage to whatever live match the BBC would be
screening – left many fans nostalgic for the inconvenient,
but dependable radio slot.

Regretfully, the pizazz reached a nadir this season as
the FA sought to import some of the National Lottery's
controlled hysteria, coupled with the living room mateyness
of *Fantasy Football League*. The extended draw ceremonies
(25 minutes for the Third Round) were performed by guests
who ranged from Terry Venables and Denis Law to Tony
Adams and Peter Beardsley. An invited audience of football
fans was encouraged to whoop its pleasure as the balls were
expelled from the perspex hamster obstacle course that had
replaced the traditional velvet drawstring bag.

The revised format was a bold step, but a bad one,
miscalculating the reverence placed on such an occasion,
and totally failing to reproduce the solemnity that should
accompany a pivotal point in any club's season. The
smothering presence of Graham Kelly was needed to
keep guests in check as they joshed and quipped their
way through the proceedings. For one round, Adams and
Beardsley started the proceedings by drawing the unlikely
ball number one. When ball number two followed to

complete the pairing, much hilarity ensued. As the third ball was ejected, Adams jokingly announced a pre-emptive 'Number three' before the ball's true identity could be known, at which a horrified Kelly reprimanded the pair for a crime he rightly felt akin to sniggering at a funeral.

The FA would do well to mark their flirtation with light entertainment down as a home defeat, and give the razzmatazz back to Camelot and the draw back to football. It is all too easy to be disparaging of the FA's efforts to cash in on the FA Cup's charisma and money-making appeal, although there are people at Lancaster Gate paid sufficiently well to get these things right. The slapstick Cup draws must take their place alongside the same muddled thinking that has seen semi-final weekend sold out to television, ties switched and kick-offs staggered, with little apparent consideration for travelling fans, exorbitant ticket prices for showpiece matches, a failure to challenge the police over their ten-day replay rules, the switch to a penalty shoot-out in preference to a second replay, and, in particular, the sponsorship of the Cup competition itself.

The Football Association apparently think it acceptable to add the suffix 'sponsored by Littlewoods', thereby keeping faith with their *Blueprint for the Future of Football*, which drew the line at title sponsorship, because they didn't allow the sponsor's name to be employed as a prefix as with the FA Carling Premiership. Semantic nonsense. It still amounts to a sell-out, when value could have been maintained – as with the Champions League – by selling exclusive rights to a select number of sponsors. It could have been left to television to bring in their broadcast sponsorship (as Sky have done with their Ford Escort Monday Night Football package), while the event itself remained uncontaminated. With ITV supplanting the BBC as Sky's terrestrial partner from 1997, it may be time for the FA to lay down a few ground rules, particularly given the pyrotechnics that have accompanied the Coca-Cola League Cup final these past few seasons. Few fans would argue that the showpiece Wembley finals need shaking up, but events at the national stadium have become increasingly tarty; an uneasy blend of rock concert and political rally. It has now become 'traditional' for hundreds of placard carrying youngsters to swarm the pitch spelling out a sponsor's message that is hidden from all but those watching on television. Gymnasts cavort across the sacred turf twirling ribbons and turning somersaults. Scantily clad cheerleaders titillate the crowd, encouraging nothing more than lewd remarks and pneumonia. Top Ten hits blast from the PA and trophies are presented and paraded to the accompaniment of whatever Tina Turner song best sums up the sponsor's product. Inane DJs encourage the crowd to take sides in daft competitions. Above this din, the forgotten fans on their big day out, struggle to make themselves heard, blasted away by anthems chosen for them, to which no one knows the words, but for which they are chastised when failing to render a suitably passionate version on cue. In a final sop to tradition, for the FA Cup final, the band of the Grenadier Guards is marched on to lead the bewildered congregation through *Abide With Me*.

By this time the two teams, having spent the previous ten minutes holed up in the players' tunnel waiting for a signal that *Abide With Me* has at last run out of verses, decide to make their entrance and catch everyone on the hop. More nonsense ensues as the teams are compelled to line up and be inspected by minor royals and junior ministers who, after a cursory verse of the national anthem, retire to take all the best seats and watch a game between two sides they know nothing about and in which they have no interest. Once under way, the TV commentators will remark how both sides look unsettled and how quiet the fans are. Is it really any wonder?

A Wembley final, particularly an FA Cup final, deserves better. It's the fans' day out, and the event – a football event – should be left to its own devices, to generate once again an atmosphere of its own. If the FA must meddle, then sort out the food and drink concessions so that money is spent in the stadium rather than lost to the game through the pubs and off-licences of the High Street. Sort out the crazy programme prices. Sort out the crazy car-parking prices. Sort out the tickets and stop the touts making more money from one ticket than the FA make from ten.

It may be that soon the only remaining magic inherent in the competition will be its ability to remain alive, despite grievous wounds at the hands of television, sponsors and the governing body itself. The FA in particular is guilty for allowing its competition – begun in 1871 and pre-dating the formation of the Football League by almost twenty years – to slip to secondary status, behind a Premier League in existence for a mere four years. The situation draws an unkind parallel with that in Italy, where the national cup competition, decided over a two-legged final before an apathetic paying public, is reduced to no more than a spurious sideshow alongside the prestigious Serie A. With the English Premier League apparently happy to throw up cliffhanger run-ins and nail-biter finales season after season, the Football Association must take swift and decisive action if a new generation of football supporters are not to emerge sceptical of the Cup's supposed importance, unimpressed by its heritage and indifferent to its survival.

The first thing that must be done is to restore its day of

Yesterdays Gone

focus so that from the Third Round onwards the Premier League steps aside and the FA Cup tops the bill. This means that there can be no televised games (Premiership or Football League) and only one Cup game taken out for live transmission on the Sunday, so Monday night Cup football must go. With ITV taking over in 1997 the temptation to broadcast live games on a regional basis must also be resisted (although the return of the regional highlights package would be welcomed). Moving the semis back to Saturday would proscribe live television so the Sunday timing should remain, with the proviso that both games kick off at 3pm, one being broadcast terrestrially and one by satellite; less television would facilitate the restoration of the special event status reflecting the scarcity value of the event.

The sponsorship clock, on the other hand, cannot be wound back so easily, though the price for maintaining the status quo should be the realisation that it is to the mutual benefit of both fans and sponsors that games are not played in half-empty stadia with no atmosphere. So for the semis and final, more tickets for the fans, not forgetting that it is no good increasing the allocation if the vast majority cost £30 plus. Lastly, the civil authorities must be challenged on the 'ten-day rule' for replays. If international demands for club and country alike make a provision for a second replay impractical, then at least the first could be played before the league programme moves back to the top of the bill the following weekend. Contemporary logistics should make it a doddle to organise a replay within three or four days.

For Spurs, the Cup once again represented the sole chance of honours and the best route to lucrative European competition, having refused to take the Intertoto competition seriously and, initially, along with Wimbledon, being banned and fined for fielding an under-strength team. Though the ban was rescinded on appeal, the number of English representatives in the 1996/97 UEFA Cup was reduced from four to three, jeopardising Tottenham's chance of qualifying from a high league position. Far too frequently, an early Cup exit has effectively ended the club's season prematurely. In the previous two years, a dogged battle against relegation, and then an extended Cup run to the semi-final, had maintained interest through to April. This year, despite a top five league position, there was never going to be a sustained challenge for championship honours. The Cup once again loomed large, without ever invoking the kind of optimism in the fans that a year ending in '1' instills.

Drawn to play away at third division Hereford, the tie seemed as close to a formality as a Premiership side could reasonably expect at the Third Round stage, although older fans will know that it is from such supposed formalities that the great Cup shocks are born. The scarcity of tickets – Hereford's Edgar Street ground holds barely 9,000 – caused supply problems at the Tottenham end, compounded by the White Hart Lane ticket office reserving a number of seats for those prepared to stump up for an executive travel package. The outrage from supporters who had risen pre-dawn and queued in vain (and in the rain), when sufficiently well-heeled fans could secure a match-ticket with the lifting of a telephone and the flourish of a credit card, was understandable, but drew little sympathy from the club.

For the press, the tie was sufficiently intriguing to winkle out the Number Ones from their cosseted enclosures and into wellies and windcheaters. It also brought forth some apposite reflections on the fate of clubs like Hereford, best summed up by Glenn Moore in the *Independent* when he wrote, 'Oh the loneliness of a small town club. In this age of glossy football magazines, sports supplements and Sky TV, supporters can follow the over-hyped Carling darlings more easily than their local team. They rarely get to see them in the flesh, but it is a Premiership shirt they wear in the playground or the pub, not an Endsleigh one. Whether this is regarded as pathetic or undesirable it has serious consequences for a club such as Hereford. While the top clubs find it increasingly difficult to provide enough seats for their supporters there is plenty of space on most terraces in the lower divisions. Thus, when the miracle happens and Hereford draw Tottenham in the Cup, hard decisions have to be taken. Does the club take the money or take the gamble?'

For the hosts, the draw indeed highlighted the conflict between Cup romance and Cup reality.

'We'll come out of the game about £35,000 richer,' said Robin Fry, managing director at Hereford, 'but it has probably cost us around £100,000 coming out of the bag first against Spurs. We reckon if we had gone to White Hart Lane we would have picked up a cheque for £140,000 [each club takes 45% of gate receipts] and that would have secured us for the rest of the season. If we get a draw, and have to replay at Spurs, you'll hear champagne corks popping in the boardroom as loud as if we had won.'

The current disparity between the haves and the have-nots in English football was brought home to Spurs fans by the culture shock of the amenities at Edgar Street. Fanzine *Cock-a-Doodle-Doo* mocked the Cup romantics: '*They* don't have to find Hereford itself, or avoid the roadworks on the

M4, or stand in a shed for two hours with next to no hot drinks facilities and toilets that are as bad as any you've ever seen'. On the field, the eye-opener was perpetuated by a Spurs team who never appeared to come to terms with the tenacity of the opposition, nor the unpredictability of a quagmire pitch. A fortunate first-half header from Ronny Rosenthal was cancelled out by Hereford after 62 minutes, but not before the home side had won – and missed – a penalty. After the 1–1 draw, they must have suspected that their best chance of winning the tie had passed.

'There was a terrible mood of anticlimax after the game,' conceded Hereford captain Dean Smith. 'I honestly felt we were the better side. We didn't quite know how to feel; happy, sad or what. In missing the penalty, I've actually made the club a lot of money.'

Goal-scorer John Brough, a free transfer central defender who had stifled the threat of Sheringham, was less than complimentary about the Spurs threat: 'I've had harder games in the Third Division,' he noted afterwards. A telling comment on how Gerry's rigid 4–4–2 had been strangled by Hereford's 3–5–2. The Third Division side were so keen to win the game that their two full-backs frequently joined the attack in a versatile formation that outflanked and out-fought the city slickers from north London.

'We wondered about changing the game to White Hart Lane,' admitted Hereford chairman Peter Hill, 'but Graham Turner [the Hereford manager who has the grand title 'Director of Football'] felt we needed a lift to give the club some impetus, to give something to the fans and recreate the atmosphere that used to be here. It was a massive gamble, but it has paid off. Now we can get the transfer embargo lifted to help Graham strengthen the squad. We are solvent, but only just. You cannot get by on 2,000 fans a week.'

Yesterdays Gone

For Gary Mabbutt, a draw was blessed relief. Before the match, he had expressed the dread that such ties instil in supposedly superior opposition, recalling one of Hereford's previous giant-killing acts when they defeated First Division Newcastle in 1972. 'My recurring nightmare is to be in a Ronnie Radford situation. The Newcastle players must despair: every time the Cup comes around, they turn on the television and there they are, watching him score. I do not want to be seeing it happen to me on *Match of the Day* in 25 years' time.'

Teddy Sheringham, too, felt relief and no shame in survival: 'We were up for it and we knew it was going to be a very difficult game. The pitch was atrocious and it was all about effort, because superior skill and talent doesn't come out on a pitch like that. You couldn't fault one of our players for effort. It was a very good result, no matter what anybody thinks.'

For Tottenham fans, players, manager and board alike, it had been an afternoon of jitters in the Third World.

For the replay ten days later, the footballing status quo was reinstated, and Spurs ran out comfortable 5–1 winners. The heroes this time were not Hereford's journeymen players, but their fans who injected some passion and colour into a White Hart Lane traditionally devoid of both. Determined to extract every last minute of enjoyment from an evening that had given them so little, their reward came in the 89th minute when a speculative twenty-yarder from Hereford substitute Gareth Stoker crossed the line via the Spurs crossbar and the back of 'keeper Ian Walker's head. North London would be as close to Wembley as Hereford would get this year. But the players, who returned to the pitch to applaud their fans, still buoyant despite being detained inside White Hart Lane 'for security reasons',

Dream On

would know just how close they had come to a major Cup upset in the first game.

Outside, the Spurs fans went home happy after Teddy Sheringham's first hat-trick for thirteen months, surely not begrudging their country cousins their fifteen minutes of fame. Hereford's share of a handsome 31,534 gate will have done much to secure the club's existence for a further year, and if in that time the club is able to groom another star like Darren Peacock, then their place in the system will not only be secured, but eminently worthwhile for the big clubs as well.

The uncertainty over Tottenham's progress into the next round had compelled the TV companies to play their hand sooner than they would have wished in choosing their live games. Now that it was confirmed that Spurs would play at home to Wolves in the Fourth Round, Sky decided the tie was sufficiently attractive to screen extended highlights early that same Saturday evening. It was a prudent decision, for a day when heavy snow was to wipe out all but three Fourth Round ties, but probably owed more to both clubs' traditions than their current abilities. Tottenham, fourth in the Premiership, were favourites to overcome a Wolves side struggling to haul themselves clear of the First Division relegation zone. But Gerry Francis was taking no chances, and fielded a cautious starting line-up that set out more to contain the opposition than actually go hell-for-leather for a home win.

Wolves themselves played Hereford's 5–3–2, but lacked the conviction to push their full-backs into the attack. Thus Tottenham spent a frustrating afternoon trying to get behind a defence that lacked any ambition beyond keeping a clean sheet.

'Maybe,' ventured Clive Wilson in defence of the home

tactics, 'Gerry thought if we got a corner, got a goal like we normally do, we could hold on, keep them out'. Which is just what happened when Wilson himself nicked a goal from a sloppy Wolves clearance. 'That should have been game, set and match for us,' added Gerry afterwards. But equally sloppy play from Dean Austin gifted Wolves' Don Goodman an equaliser, so bang went the strategy.

The cat and mouse tactics from Spurs weren't what the home crowd had paid to see, and they made their feelings known as the teams trudged off at half-time. On a pitch dusted with snow and rapidly icing up, the second half saw further Spurs pressure but no real reward. Sheringham and Armstrong had scored more goals for Spurs this season than the entire Wolves team had managed in Division One, but both players were peripheral to the action. As the mercury plummeted, and the teams slogged towards a replay, the Spurs crowd howled for Ronny Rosenthal to be introduced, but Gerry, cautious as ever, saw no reason to shuffle the pack. Clive Wilson acknowledges the manager's conservative use of substitutes: 'He has always been like that. He doesn't put them on unless he feels there's a real reason to do so. He only ever puts them on if he is trying to stop the opposition winning, when he will put on an extra centre-half or another midfield player. The one time he has thrown caution to the wind was in the FA Cup Fifth Round at Southampton last year, but then Spurs were already two down.' Ronny was introduced after 42 minutes and was the catalyst, with three goals, behind a 6–2 victory.

Post match, Gerry lost no time in fingering Dean Austin for gifting Wolves their goal, remarking how, 'It gave their fans a major lift and deflated us,' before rounding on his team as a whole. 'In the last twenty minutes, they just sat back and let us have the ball and try and break them down.

I felt we could have done a lot better. We tried to keep the ball and pull them out; unfortunately they weren't coming out. It's something we need to learn from.'

Wolves manager, Mark McGhee, admitted that his side's modest ambitions had much to do with the scant time he and assistant Colin Lee had been afforded to work with the players since their recent appointment. 'We thought we would come here and make life as difficult as we could for them. Colin and I preach all the time that the best form of defence is possession.' He also paid generous tribute to Sheringham. 'We concentrated on stifling the dangers – Sheringham and Armstrong. Because Sheringham, for me, is the most complete centre-forward in England. He's a centre-forward I would take if I could afford him.'

'I remember,' recalled Sheringham of that afternoon, 'Wolves played very defensively, and they only had a couple of shots throughout the game. They made it very difficult for us. They did very well and they were quite happy with the draw. But, secretly, so were we. We could so easily have thrown caution to the wind and tried to win the game 2–1 only to get done by a sucker punch and lose. We were a very composed, very professional unit that day. We could hear them in the dressing room after the game cheering and laughing that they'd got a draw at our place. But we were happy with that. We knew once they got in front of their own fans, they would be forced to come out and try to beat us. And we knew we were the superior team, and on a good pitch we would have every chance of beating them. Which is exactly the way it turned out. In the second game, we tore them apart.'

Before many at Molineux had even brushed the snow from their seats, Spurs were a goal up. Ronny Rosenthal, reinstated into the starting line-up, finishing off a glorious counter attack that had swept the length of the pitch from a Wolves corner. Within ten minutes, Teddy had seized on a sloppy back pass and at 2–0 Wolves were out of the Cup. The home fans were stunned, perhaps now realising, as Hereford had before them, the gulf between the Premiership and everyone else. As the raucous Spurs fans celebrated in anticipation of a repeat of the Hereford hatful, their team instead played a controlled patient game, holding what they had and not risking a thing. The domination was total, but no more goals came. Wolves managed just the one effort on target throughout the 90 minutes. Their fans, tiring of applauding the visitors' elegant football and, like most in the capacity crowd, frozen to the marrow on an arctic night, were drifting home long before the final whistle. Gerry was understandably pleased: 'We've shown consistency, and have talented players who work hard for each other,' he beamed.

After such a spectacular opening, it was all mildly anti-climactic for the Spurs supporters, who had again endured nightmare conditions, both in buying tickets and travelling through a Midlands deep in midwinter snow. In truth, those unable to get tickets, and watching at home or in the pub on Sky Sports, were probably better off. There is an undeniable magic about an away Cup win that does somehow justify most suffering and discomfort, but the treacherous drive home must have caused many to reconsider their priorities. For those who didn't, far worse was yet to come.

On the road to Wembley (rather than at Wembley itself), Nottingham Forest are Tottenham's perennial highway-men. Year after year they gallop from behind the bushes and rob Spurs of all their remaining ambitions. At least Dick Turpin wore a mask. But Forest feel no need to hide their intentions. Indeed, it often appears, to Spurs fans at least, that Forest's sole reason for existing is to spike Tottenham's season. Having done so, they can then cheerfully crumple to lesser opposition in subsequent rounds, safe in the knowledge that their season hasn't been totally without satisfaction. From a Spurs point of view, the Fifth Round draw that paired the two sides had an ominous ring about it, although when originally made, there were still many either/ors to separate the adversaries. But as Spurs eventually overcame Wolves, and Forest, too, needed a replay before disposing of Oxford, the two clubs inexorably converged like iceberg and *Titanic*.

As the country enjoyed a brief respite from the foul weather that had disrupted earlier rounds, Sky Sports exercised their right to delay the tie by 48 hours and switched it to the Monday night for live transmission. There was no denying the potential attractiveness of the fixture, but once more the Spurs fans would be asked to travel north on a working day.

Bernie Kingsley, writing in the Spurs fanzine *Cock-a-Doodle-Doo*, describes his trip: 'I was surprised when a friend who wasn't going rang on the morning of the match to ask "Is it on?"

'"Why shouldn't it be?" I replied.

'"They're predicting heavy snow later."

'"Nah," said I, "it's bound to be okay, they've got undersoil heating and anyway, Sky will want it on."

'Leaving London at 3pm, it was cold but clear. A straightforward run saw us tucking into fish and chips in the Bridgford Restaurant well before six. When we came out it was even colder, possibly sleeting a little. Entered pub 6.40, weather still OK. Exit pub 7.25 to find an inch of snow on the ground and more falling.

Yesterdays Gone

'As we entered the ground it was still snowing, but the pitch looked all right and we were glad to be right at the back out of the snow. "It'd be funny if they played in all white again like at Wolves, with a white ball," I'd joked along the way. They did.

'After five minutes, I say to Dave, "No way is this lasting 90 minutes". The snow was getting heavier. On eight minutes the ref calls for the orange ball, but it makes little difference. Walker at the far end is virtually invisible. A linesman is consulted and we carry on, but when we win another corner, as Fox shapes to take it the ref takes the players off. Within a few minutes the abandonment is confirmed, to choruses of "We hate Sky Sports and we hate Sky Sports . . ."

'There is no word of another date, or what happens about tickets, so everyone troops out. And the nightmare starts.

'I won't bore you with all the details. Two-and-three-quarter hours to reach the M1, about ten miles, including one spell of doing 100 yards at the Clifton Bridge inter-section in an hour gives the flavour. Once on the M1, for maybe fifteen–twenty miles it was single file traffic on sheet ice, at times moving at barely 5mph. By Leicester, gritting had eased things a little, but in all it took some six-and-a-half hours to get home: no doubt many others took much longer. I was at Munich in the fog in '83, I've seen games abandoned for snow and rain, I've driven regularly in snow in the Alps, but this was by far the worst journey ever.'

Indeed Tottenham folklore is now littered with 'How I got back from Nottingham' stories, many of which make the above account seem like a picnic. The fixture was rescheduled for the following week.

'Nine days later,' reported Bernie, 'we were back. Tickets were still valid, refunds were available for those who couldn't make it, and Forest produced a flimsy supplementary programme for 50p. Has football finally realised consumers can't be totally ripped off? Would Tottenham have applied the same standard had it been at home?'

In the first brief encounter, it had been Spurs who started the more positive, taking the game to Forest before the elements intervened. In the re-match, it was Forest who took the early initiative, scoring within four minutes. But once again, Gerry's team held firm where their predecessors might have folded. The remainder of the first half saw Spurs in sparkling form, scoring two and squandering more.

'We approached the game very well,' remembers Teddy Sheringham. 'Even though we were 1–0 down in the first ten minutes, we had approached the game so well that we were back on level terms very quickly. We went on to take the lead and could have gone further in front, 3–1 or 4–1, at a crucial time before half-time. But we didn't.

'It is said so many times that players don't want the half-time break to come. And this was the case here. We were feeling good and had them on the rack. We went in and all Gerry Francis could say to us was to keep on doing what we were doing.'

But would that be enough? Teddy had his doubts.

'In the other dressing room, you've got characters like Stuart Pearce. Now he doesn't want to go out of the FA Cup, and so he, along with the manager, would be getting hold of his side, and they'd be geeing themselves up to pull the game around.'

Which is exactly what happened, as Spurs appeared to take their foot off the accelerator and allow Forest to pulverise them. Despite heroics in defence from Mabbutt and Calderwood, it couldn't last, and Ian Woan thundered in a glorious equaliser direct from a free kick. With seventeen minutes still to play, the smart money would have been on Forest. But, seeming to lack the conviction to settle the affair, or else determined to further toy with their prey, the game ended 2–2 and it was back to White Hart Lane for the deciding encounter.

'They were really up for it in the second half,' reflects Sheringham. 'That's not to say that we weren't, but they had the bit between the teeth. Perhaps it is wrong of us. That's when you need a good captain or strong minded players in a team, to say at half-time, "Hey, come on, you know what is going to be going on in their dressing room. Let's keep going!"'

But do Tottenham have such players?

'We have one or two, but when you are talking about that type of player, you are talking about the very top players; people like Stuart Pearce, Roy Keane, Tony Adams and Steve Bruce. They're the players that win things. They're the ones who are up there. I wouldn't say we've got any one player who is really like that. We've got a lot who are very strong characters, which is why we've done so well. But no one player who will really . . .'

Teddy trails off as he, like the fans, laments the absence of the type of player epitomised by Graham Roberts, Steve Perryman, Alan Mullery and Dave Mackay.

'Anyway, they upped the tempo a little more. And maybe we dropped it a little, or even stayed where we were. Certainly there was no reason to sit back and cruise and stay at 2–1. We wanted to go out there and get 3–1 and be comfortable. Or get 4–1 and really enjoy the game.'

In the end it was neither comfortable nor convenient. Chris Armstrong, scorer of both Spurs goals, and Teddy Sheringham had both picked up minor injuries, and Spurs

Dream On

had again failed to kill off opposition when the opportunity had presented itself. It was a trait that had cost them dearly in the league, and had now almost cost them their sole remaining chance for honours this season. They were still in the Cup, but a home tie against Forest – who had won five of their previous seven visits to White Hart Lane – was little cause for optimism.

Because of Forest's continued involvement in the UEFA Cup via a pressing appointment with Jurgen Klinsmann's Bayern Munich, the FA Cup Fifth Round replay could not be played until the day of the Sixth Round. The Spurs-Forest game drew the limelight away from the Chelsea-Wimbledon Sixth Round clash across London. With Aston Villa patiently awaiting the winners of the Spurs-Forest tie, and the demands of television taking the remaining ties to Sunday and Monday slots, the Cup once again found itself competing with Premiership action for attention.

The sight, in an otherwise packed White Hart Lane, of so many empty seats in the visitors' section was instructive. Despite the fact that Tottenham had twice found no problem in taking a large following to Nottingham for midweek fixtures, Forest was apparently unable to reciprocate for a Saturday afternoon game. True, the replay came only days after Forest's trip to Munich, but with a place in the last eight at stake, perhaps 2,000 fans had made the trip south. The FA Cup was apparently not the be all and end all for Forest fans.

This was Tottenham's sixth match in the competition – normally enough to secure a Wembley place, but still trying this time around to take them to the last eight. For Forest, this would be their fifteenth cup tie of the season, and their second in four days. After an arduous round trip that had seen them defeated 2–1 in Munich, Spurs were expected to punish their presumably jaded opposition. Not so. Forest began by looking much the brighter and it was no surprise that their superior football earned them a lead after only nine minutes. Spurs tried to raise their game, but it simply wasn't happening on the day. With Sinton cup-tied, Anderton still injured, Dozzell suspended, Armstrong looking distinctly unfit and only Stuart Nethercott and Steve Slade, a regular scorer in the reserves but still to start a match for the first team, on the bench, the limitations of Gerry's threadbare squad were all too apparent. Once more it appeared that Forest were unwilling to press home their advantage, and a needless free kick conceded deep in their own half allowed Spurs back in the game.

When Sheringham shaped up to let fly, White Hart Lane was hardly a-buzz with anticipation. 'Gerry had seen me take free kicks before,' recalled Teddy. 'He looks at them, and studies them, and he'd probably seen something I hadn't. He mentioned it to me the day before the game so we tried it out in training. I took them exactly as I was to against Forest, and one out of three or four went in.'

Teddy's modesty belies a beautiful strike that sailed past wall and 'keeper but was to be the highlight of the game for Tottenham. At 1–1, a flat second half stretched to extra time, where caution shaded ambition. After 120 minutes of classic if not cultured Cup football, the 31,055 crowd rose as one to applaud the two teams. From the home crowd, there was a distinct feeling that things were about to take a dramatic turn for the worse. The highwayman had just emerged from the bushes. It was time to stand and deliver.

The penalty shoot-out appears to be a means of settling a match favoured by tournament organisers and television

Dream On

companies with schedules to keep. There is no denying the inherent drama, but for fans, players and managers the spectacle can be traumatic. Forest manager Frank Clark was later to admit that, 'It's a shame that any team has to go out in this way, but we certainly wouldn't have liked another replay. We could have been playing until August Bank Holiday.'

As attention focused on the Paxton Road end of the ground, the skies darkened, the snow closed in once more and Tottenham's season died.

By the time Sheringham stepped up for his kick, he knew he had to score to keep Spurs in the Cup. By then his side were 1–3 down after two correct guesses by Forest 'keeper Mark Crossley had denied both Wilson and Rosenthal. 'Teddy used to put them on the left when he played at Forest,' confessed the Forest 'keeper later, 'so I decided in advance and went for it. I got lucky.'

Teddy's shot was well struck, but to the left as Crossley had anticipated. Another transitional season was confirmed.

In the week following that game, somewhat perversely, penalty taking appeared on the curriculum at Chase Lodge. A little late, some may have felt, but a chance nevertheless for Gerry to make a point he strongly felt, that even if a 'keeper knew which way a kick was going, it should still prove impossible to save, if struck with assurance. To prove his argument, Gerry pre-warned Erik Thorstvedt, placed the ball, lined up his shot, and then promptly had his kicks saved.

With a quarter of the season still remaining, Gerry faced a problem in motivating his squad. The flirtation with the FA Cup had first hidden, but ultimately highlighted, the Tottenham squad's acute lack of substance. The protracted Cup run had meandered over six games but produced only two wins, surely a record for a knockout competition? To obtain the UEFA Cup place the team needed revitalising. Perhaps more importantly, so did Gerry's magic.

The players joked to themselves about Gerry's constant moaning in the press, and his fixation with the perceived season-long 'injury crisis'. Even the fans were increasingly bemused at Gerry's blue and white tinted post-match summarising, where he would appear to have watched a completely different contest to the one they had just witnessed. That most blinkered of species, the Upper West Stand season-ticket holder, would be hard pushed to see the degree of refereeing bias that Gerry perceived at some games. His trademark, the half-time pep-talk and second half revival, was but a distant memory.

The team had grown used to their manager, and perhaps his ploys were not as effective as they once were. To keep them on their toes, Gerry had traditionally varied his hard man/soft man approach. The players knew he could be pointedly critical, but by judicious use – the anticipated Forest post mortem never materialised – he hoped to restore momentum. One thing was certain: the manager was not about to let the season drift away.

Senior players were deeply disappointed with the Cup exit, acutely aware that time was running out for them to collect that Wembley winner's medal. Just how good were Gerry's tactics, given that they had contributed to the FA Cup defeats for the last two seasons, both times to inferior opposition? Everton last year, and Forest this year who, true to expectations, crumbled in the subsequent round at home to Aston Villa. There was a growing feeling that Gerry's 4–4–2 could only take the team so far; its inherent limitations placing a ceiling on the heights it could take the team. At least under Terry Venables, so the feeling went, though the magic didn't happen very often, when it did and everything clicked, it could transport the team to a higher plane beyond anywhere Gerry's tactics had yet reached.

So Teddy's penalty miss was to be Tottenham's last kick in the FA Cup for another season. With five more years to go until the year ends in '1', can he last until the year 2001 before finally getting his hands on a trophy? Gerry Francis must hope so, because his chairman has made it clear he will never sanction the kind of money it would take to replace Teddy in today's marketplace. When bidding starts at £4 million for possibles, and exceeds £7 million for probables, the clubs with definites can name their own price. Mindful of missed opportunities that saw players like Sheringham, Ian Wright and Alan Shearer move for sums that today look modest, managers will not be so cautious in future. Despite a slow start and a laboured apprenticeship, it is hard to imagine another goal-scorer of Teddy's ability languishing for seven years in a south London backwater.

That period at Millwall saw him become the greatest goal-scorer in their history, but only Brian Clough was brave enough to gamble on his talent being transferable to the highest level. The transition to Forest's passing game was almost seamless for Sheringham, who under Brian Clough honed a quickness of mind that compensated for an acknowledged lack of pace.

When Terry Venables paid £2.1 million to bring Teddy back south after a single season at Forest, thereby inadvertantly causing the word 'bung' to enter parlance, and giving rise to the game's longest running investigative farce the manager was already into overdraft on his credit account with the fans. As strikers, both Paul Stewart and Gordon Durie were big money flops, carried, as was most of the team, by Lineker's machine-gun consistency for rattling in the goals. When Lineker discovered his yen for travelling, Teddy was not the obvious replacement, despite a solid start at Forest with twenty goals in his first season. But the increasingly eccentric Clough was keen to get his money back. Venables swooped, and while Forest went down that year, Teddy scored 28 goals in his first season at White Hart Lane. Gary who?

The following season a dreadful injury at Old Trafford, belatedly diagnosed as a split cartilage, looked for a while as if it might threaten his career. It certainly threatened Tottenham's season, as the goals dried up and they plummeted to the relegation zone. But Teddy bounced back after six months, with a goal at Norwich in his comeback game, and the team survived.

Perhaps mindful of the reliance on one star for goals, manager Ossie Ardiles increased his options that summer with the signing of Klinsmann. A problem solved or a problem doubled? Klinsmann certainly wasn't about to change the habits of a lifetime, so Teddy courteously obliged with an Oscar winning performance as Best Supporting Role. 'I've always felt I am a team player. If I wanted to be a single player I would have perhaps gone into tennis or golf and tried to make it there.'

When Ossie Ardiles sought his opinion, he was pleasantly surprised as it had never happened with any previous manager. When Gerry Francis arrived, rather than anticipating star treatment, which he undoubtedly deserved, he was looking for reassurance. 'Gerry talks to me, consults me about things. He took me into his office early on and told me what he thought. Whatever people may think, when a new manager comes to a club, it doesn't matter who you are, you fear for your own place because different managers have different ideas and if you don't fit in with those plans then you are on your way.

'I thought to myself "Maybe that's the end for me". But he took me aside, explained what he wanted, and made me fully aware of how much he appreciated me. And that made me feel at ease.'

Reassured, the goals came, but everyone else went; first Ossie, then Jurgen. Even Plan B was scuppered when Nicky Barmby went north. When Teddy's name was linked with Manchester United, you could just imagine the temptation: recent Double winners, in Europe, with three times the turnover of Tottenham, but a football club first and a plc second. But Spurs, to their credit, moved swiftly, and just a few weeks into this current season Teddy signed a new four-year deal that will see him contracted to White Hart Lane until well past his theoretical sell-by date.

For the fans, Teddy is probably the most popular player at the club right now. He won Spurs fanzine *Cock-a-Doodle-Doo* 'Best Player' poll by a landslide, and his name, more than any other, appears on replica shirts. When interviewed, he says all the right things about Arsenal, always wanting to play for Spurs and being happy at the club. 'I was a West Ham fan as a young kid, but once Glenn Hoddle came on the scene at Tottenham, I came down to watch him. I even got here early enough to watch his skills in the warm-up.' For an interview with *Cock-a-Doodle-Doo*, he was charming, courteous and game for a laugh, donning tuxedo to pose with cocktails for a spoof *Hello!* photospread (despite, or because of, appearing in *Hello!* itself with his girlfriend Nicola Smith?).

However, it wasn't always smooth sailing. Despite his spectacular debut season, the reception afforded Teddy was restrained. A lost second season through injury did his cause no good at all, allowing Darren Anderton to take pole position in the popularity stakes. Like Lineker, Sheringham made goal-scoring look easy, and it was difficult for fans to fathom why each and every chance wasn't tucked away. The lack of pace, and therefore an understandable reluctance to chase lost causes, riled some fans who branded him lazy and a moody git.

When Klinsmann arrived, Teddy's deeper supporting role saw him with much more time on the ball, beginning moves as well as finishing them. Unsympathetic to this new, deeper role, fans bellowed at Teddy to 'Get your arse up there' and hooted derision when his distribution failed to find the ghosting Klinsmann. For one season at least, Jurgen was most definitely the King of White Hart Lane.

Luckily, Teddy is not short of confidence. No matter what critics may find to snipe about, Teddy knows that his record stands comparison with anyone. He scores Premiership goals at the rate of one every two games, and even if some fans are slow to appreciate his abilities, he must have an impressive collection of press cuttings where opposing managers (including Alex Ferguson) have singled him out as the one player they would like to add to their side. Even Klinsmann has gone on record to affirm how much Teddy's play contributed to his one sensational season in London. 'Teddy is not only an exceptional individual player,' he remarked, 'but exceptional also in his teamwork. That's why it was so easy for me to play my kind of football there and score so many goals. I know Teddy to be a striker of the highest order.'

Such praise has led to speculation, and a cute tabloid headline: 'Jurgen: I Want My Teddy', that Sheringham may be tempted overseas for a spell with Bayern. 'The chance has never come about, so I've never had to seriously think about it,' is his response, which will not completely relax his fans or his manager. He is equally disarming when questioned about his contribution to Jurgen's success. 'It's just a question of knowledge; working with someone, understanding what they like doing, what they are good at, where they like going, how they like to receive the ball, where they like to give it. Learning what another striker is like.' He was under no false illusions about Jurgen, realising that his equable temperament was a strong counterpoint to Jurgen's volatility. 'Jurgen was a very temperamental man. His mentality was on an edge, he could go one way or the other. He was highly strung. He would snap very easily some days about the way he was treated by referees.'

As with most Tottenham players, Teddy was initially an unpopular choice when selected for England, viewed as a beneficiary of Terry Venables' residual bias towards his former signings. With Shearer clearly first choice to lead his country's attack, Sheringham became just one of a number of bridesmaids who, along with Ian Wright, Andy Cole and Les Ferdinand, enjoyed their allotted fifteen minutes of fame as the tabloids' champion. With just the one goal in his first six starts, the fickle Wembley crowd had taken to hooting their derision when his name was announced. Certainly, he was not the instant hit that Darren Anderton became for his country. Fortunately, Venables persisted with him whenever he deemed a second striker was needed. The manager knew what he wanted, and that Sheringham, throughout his career, had operated in tandem both as main man and as second on the bill, to a variety of partners from Tony Cascarino at Millwall via Nigel Clough at Forest to Jurgen Klinsmann, Nicky Barmby and now Chris Armstrong at Tottenham.

Confidence in his own ability and a laid-back manner

encourage him not to overcomplicate matters. 'I don't think there is an actual main man or a back-up. It's a partnership. I feel I could play with anyone in any situation, because I can adapt, because I want to adapt, really. If I had to go back to playing up front as the main man, then I could do it. But it's not just about me playing up front. It's not just me playing against their centre-half, it's my team playing against someone else's team.'

Playing alongside Jurgen had taught him the invaluable lesson for international football, namely that chances are few and far between and can only be maximised with one hundred per cent concentration. Added to his intelligent reading of the play, his versatility was a godsend to the Venables system, even compensating for that vital yard of pace which is supposed to be the prerequisite of the world class attacker.

'Ted is genuinely two footed,' concedes Venables, 'as good as anyone in the air, the best around at bringing others into the game, and he scores goals'.

In the space of a second he became the tabloids' favourite, the result of a spectacularly headed goal against Switzerland in November. Looking beyond the flavour-of-the-moment headlines, he was realistic enough to admit that his overall performance left something to be desired and that, 'If the ball hadn't gone in the net my night would have been remembered differently.' The goal, he felt, 'Bought me time.' Time to play the game he was selected for.

'Stop Sheringham and you stop England,' was the compliment paid by Croatia's manager when he brought his side to Wembley. At age 30, perhaps Teddy isn't the answer to his country's long term needs, which may be a problem when Glenn Hoddle takes over from Venables. But for the immediate future, and in particular the European

Dream On

Championships, his place as an automatic selection seems assured.

But it is at White Hart Lane that there are more pressing problems for Sheringham. There is little doubt the player is unhappy, although he is too tactful to announce this publicly. The desire to end his career with some silverware in his trophy cabinet may yet override the loyalty he feels towards his manager. A Division Two championship medal, a Zenith blah blah blah medal and a Rumbelows Cup runners-up medal are poor reward for such a prolific career. His recent contract extension would appear to preclude a big money move, but, as was shown with the Andy Cole swoop, there are some bids that it is very hard to refuse, and he may yet see out his days wearing a red shirt of one hue or another. Certainly, the Bosman judgment has come too late for Teddy. Why should a major club pay a huge transfer fee for a 30–year-old when it can pick up a 22–year-old from Ajax for a signing-on fee?

'I've said that Tottenham have a very good team. But if you want to win championships you have to have a very good squad. With all due respect to the players we have at the club, we haven't got that at the moment. If you looked at Liverpool's bench the other day, there was Redknapp and Rush and Ruddock, three quality internationals. And we can't do that at Tottenham, so at the moment we can't expect to be winning championships.' And unless there is a change in policy it will be even more difficult in the future, with Premiership matchday squads increased to sixteen next season, with clubs able to choose three from five named subs.

His partnership with Chris Armstrong has been spectacularly successful in its first season, although he hides well his frustrations at Armstrong's lack of awareness that so often sees Teddy's astute running unrewarded with the return ball he is screaming for.

'We're like chalk and cheese,' says Teddy. 'You couldn't find two strikers less alike. Chris is very strong, very quick, and can score goals. He is very good in the air as well. But he has different attributes to Jurgen. Jurgen was more of the finished article, whereas Chris is a raw talent at the moment and he needs to be worked on. Which he knows, which Gerry knows, and which is what is happening.'

Armstrong's speed of learning and adaptation to Sheringham's preferences may well be a factor in determining the direction both players' careers take. Similarly, a case of less business and more football at White Hart Lane would suit him. 'If I was in charge I'd do things differently. But I'm not,' is all he'll say on the matter, although he concedes, 'I think the club is being run very much as a business now rather than a football club. A football club is all about people and mentalities and comradeship. All footballers talk about tea ladies and the staff at the ground. If you get on with them it makes for a nice atmosphere. It's homely. When I was at Millwall, John Docherty always tried to create a homely atmosphere; the club as a unit, everyone knowing one another and getting on with one another.

'At Tottenham I don't feel it's all about having a laugh with the tea lady, or getting on with the laundry girls. It is more of a business. You go to work and that is it. But a football club is not like other industries. It's not about computers or machines or making things work. It's about making people tick, and you have to feel at home. You have to feel relaxed. You have to feel wanted to be playing your best football. If people are happy then you feel at home. You relax and enjoy yourself, you save all your energies for the pitch.'

Dream On

The pitch, in fact, is a source of much concern to Sheringham, although apparently not to those who run the club. From Christmas onwards the surface has been a disgrace, with poor drainage trapping surface water. Several matches have nearly been postponed following a heavy downpour close to kick-off time. Against West Ham in February, it was widely felt that it was only the presence of Sky Sports' cameras that saw the fixture take place. The ensuing mudlark may have made for good television, but the 0–1 defeat emphasised Teddy's argument.

'The pitch does have a lot to do with the way I play. I love to play on a good pitch and our pitch is like playing in a field at times. And that takes the gloss off quality players. There is no reason to have quality players on the pitch – and we do have quality players at Tottenham – because the bad pitch brings us down to the level of ordinary players.

'I find it very hard to see how people can fail to look at Manchester United and Blackburn and Newcastle, who have been top teams for the past few years, and not appreciate the efforts made at those clubs to make their pitches right. To give their players every help they can. And that's just not the case at Tottenham. In my opinion it's a secondary thought. The thinking seems to be along the lines of: "They are good players – they can play on anything".

'That's not the case. Good players need the help of a good pitch. We have to watch every bounce of the ball. If you take your eyes off for a moment it'll bobble over your foot and slip away from you. A good pitch is like an extra £5 million player on your side.'

After that West Ham game, an indiscreet comment from a director brought forth a volley from Sheringham on the state of the pitch and the club's supposed priorities. Teddy, ever the diplomat, won't comment on such speculation, nor the postscript that Gerry asked him to apologise. The outburst was born of frustration – a case of a good workman justifiably blaming his tools.

A bad case of misrepresentation by the media over his 'wonder' boot deal with Adidas and his supposed resentment over the arrival of Chris Armstrong and the impending departure of Nicky Barmby has made him wary of outsiders. He resolved to keep his thoughts to himself and get on with his game.

But he is grateful for his good fortune: 'I love the life I've got and I don't need to be doing anything else. It is a luxurious life but it's hard making things work. But it's a great life, you are only on this earth once and so I'm enjoying it the way I want to enjoy it.'

If Alan Sugar thinks that money can't buy success then he is deliberately ignoring the far-reaching influence stars can have. Stars like Sheringham (and Klinsmann) who, in George Graham's description, 'are prepared to get their hands dirty', are that most precious asset, providing inspiration without causing resentment among their team-mates, while setting standards that permeate right through the club. Youth team coach Des Bulpin pays Sheringham the obvious compliments: 'He is exceptionally intelligent and technically good,' but stresses, 'He is a very good trainer'. In terms of Tottenham's tomorrows, as aspirational model – to put it in a way Alan Sugar will understand – he can provide exceptionally good value for money.

'In the present Spurs side, although he is not in my position,' says youth team midfielder Stephen Clemence, son of former England goalkeeper Ray, 'I like watching Teddy Sheringham. He's a brilliant player. His vision, his finishing, he knits the team together and when he isn't playing, then you see how much he is missed.' If Stephen Clemence goes all the way, then Teddy Sheringham will have played a not inconsequential part in the process.

Chapter 12

Survival of the Fittest

If Spurs have truly abdicated their position as the loose cannons of the transfer market, and if Alan Sugar is to be believed when he states, 'I have no compunction in saying we're going to win the championship and I'm going to demonstrate how to do it without irrational cheque-book madness', then Des Bulpin, Tottenham youth team coach, has perhaps the most important job at the club. The softly spoken 44-year-old with the West Country burr is an unlikely figure to carry the future hopes of Tottenham Hotspur, its continued multi-million-pound turnover, its responsibility to shareholders and its uncompromising chairman.

As is often the case with youth coaches, Des never made it to the top as a player. However, this meant he was able to begin coaching at Bristol City working alongside Roy Hodgson – who was later to become the Swiss national coach and is now in charge of Internazionale of Milan. In 1985 Des moved down the road to Bristol Rovers and the turning point in his career followed in 1987, when Gerry

Francis replaced Bobby Gould and made Des the youth and reserve team manager. Thus began a relationship that was to see Des follow Gerry through successive moves, first to QPR and then on to Tottenham.

Des displays a fierce loyalty towards Gerry Francis. So much so that when Gerry resigned from QPR in 1994, he also felt obliged to quit. 'Gerry resigned over a principle,' recalls Des, 'and I felt it was my place to resign with him. Gerry Francis has treated me well. I find him a very straight person. Loyalty is important, and if I expect it from him, I should give it also.'

When Gerry landed the Tottenham job, he brought with him both his former backroom staff from Loftus Road – Des Bulpin to take charge of the youth setup and Roger Cross to be the assistant manager. Although most clubs run youth schemes along similar lines, the size of the operation at Tottenham underlined the size of Des Bulpin's task. With a large squad of 22 YTS apprentices and young pros on their books, Spurs are the only club in the South East Counties League (under-18s) to operate two youth teams. The junior side plays in Division Two, with the team made up from first-year apprentices and associated schoolboys and run by Bobby Arber. The senior side is run by Des and largely comprises the second-year players, some of whom will already have signed professional forms.

'I think a lot of the things they do here are very good,' says Des. 'I work with Bobby Arber, who was at West Ham as a kid, and through him and through people like Bill Nicholson, a lot of the coaching and the practices have been passed down through the years emphasising a passing game.

'I think that the club has been clever in the way that we use Division One and Division Two. I pick what I feel is my strongest side, while Bobby has the apprentices that are left over plus the best of the schoolboys to make up the numbers. I feel it is a good blooding for the schoolboys to play against another club's apprentices at a young age. I think it is something that favours us when we are looking to sign young boys.'

Des is a modest man, who, in his short time at QPR, achieved considerable success with their youth sides winning a league championship and league cup. He puts much of this success down to the presence of several key players, who have since gone on to the first team. But QPR had undoubtedly produced promising youngsters before, yet they had never won their youth league. So what was the secret?

'We looked at the players we had and planned how we would play with those resources. Kevin Gallen was exceptional at youth level, a very strong lad who scored a lot of goals. So what I did was, within the pattern of play, to get a lot of balls and lots of crosses up front. And he thrived on that, and was therefore a big influence on the team. But we also worked a lot on free kicks, corners, throw-ins and set plays.

'We also highlighted the importance of fitness. I remember taking the QPR lads to Leeds, and we got absolutely hammered. They were physically too strong for us. I found out that Leeds were working with weights three times a week, so I took that on, and at QPR we became physically stronger. Since we've been here at Tottenham, I have introduced weights two or three times a week, and I think the boys are stronger for it.'

In his first season with Spurs, Des repeated his success at Loftus Road by winning the South East Counties title and taking Spurs to the final of the FA Youth Cup. 'I don't think everything is down to the coach by a long way. We had some good players. Gary Brady, Stephen Carr, are two outstanding players. Neil Fenn, Simon Spencer, and the goalkeeper Simon Brown were also outstanding. Of the first-year boys, Mark Arber and Ross Darcy and Stephen Clemence all did well. Overall I feel last year we had an abundance of good players.'

The speed at which most youth games are played makes it difficult to assess the skills of many youngsters, particularly when trying to decide if a player has that special ingredient that makes him worth retaining.

'I think the exceptional ones hit you,' says Des. 'By the way they move, by their feet, by their alertness, and the speed with which they pick up things when you are coaching them. With some, if you tell them something basic in training, the next time the opportunity comes to use that information you see they have already cottoned on to it. Whereas some boys, you will tell them something and it doesn't happen, and you must tell them again and again. Their learning process is slow. I find exceptional players learn quickly.

'I also think that where today's game has got so quick, a player needs to have a special attribute. You need to be either exceptionally quick, or exceptionally strong, or exceptionally good in the air, or exceptionally good at scoring goals. I also think attitude is very important. You get some boys who really want to be a footballer, while other boys may have all the ability in the world but it's not important to them. We have quite a few boys here with excellent attitudes, but we have one or two with attitudes that are a little bit . . . You need to keep on at them. But that's life and I think that nowadays you need to be a social worker as well as a coach.'

If asked to define 'having a good attitude', Des has no doubt about the qualities needed: 'To learn, to want to work, to accept discipline, to watch good pros like Gary Mabbutt and take on board that sort of attitude. I think Gary is a superb person for them to look up to.

'That's another thing, I think that sometimes our boys don't study the game enough. When they watch the first team they should be watching whoever plays in their position, even to the extent of watching players on the other side from whom they can learn.'

Des is committed to a pattern of play that supports Gerry's collective responsibility, whereby the team attacks as a unit and defends as a unit. 'We normally play 4-4-2 and we work on playing similarly to Gerry's first team. The manager feels that if we play basically the same way, when people come through they understand what their role is within the team. We have a way we want to play, we want the ball passed quickly, we want crosses and we want the ball forward so we work on that. We work a lot on defending. We train a lot in the afternoons here. A lot of clubs don't. I believe in working hard, so we normally work both mornings and afternoons on Tuesday, Wednesday and Thursday. The lads complain about being tired but that doesn't particularly worry me.

'Gerry Francis likes running. Lots of managers say it isn't important, but Gerry thinks that it is once a lad passes eighteen, and I agree. Because at the end of the day if they are going to be professionals, all that matters is winning. Whether we like it or not, that is what matters. Because if you are not successful and winning, then you haven't got a job. So you've got to breed into players an aggression and a will to win.'

Given the yearly intake at Tottenham and the limited opportunities at first team level, most players must sooner or later realise the odds are against them making Premiership football at White Hart Lane. But they will at least learn good

Dream On

footballing habits to take with them if they must move on elsewhere.

As former Tottenham juniors Steve Robinson, Neil Young and Owen Coll have discovered, life can begin again at Bournemouth, but perhaps they are fortunate that their experienced manager, Mel Machin, has always favoured a passing game. More typical though is the view of a lower division coach who says, somewhat scathingly, 'You can always tell a former Tottenham player. Good skills, but they find it difficult to come to terms with the need to battle.'

Although initially painful, an early release at seventeen or eighteen can sometimes be a blessing in disguise. With such a large playing staff at White Hart Lane, first team, and sometimes even reserve team, chances are limited. And the situation is likely to deteriorate, as from next season the Avon Combination League will drastically cut back on its fixtures. Already some young pros are playing only a dozen games in a season and are reduced to going on loan simply to get a game. So even if they are retained, they are more than likely to be released at 22 or 23 with very limited experience of playing regularly for Tottenham at a level any higher than the South East Counties.

'The trouble is,' says Des, 'that some boys get sour if they think they are not going to be taken on as professionals. But what they should do is have the right attitude to take away what they learn here, to perhaps play at Barnet or Doncaster or even non-league. And perhaps when they get stronger or bigger, someone else may spot them and they can come back to the highest level. Too many of them get disappointed and get their head down instead of getting on with it. I mean, I could be out of work tomorrow, Gerry could, we all could. It's no good being bitter or twisted. You have to

Survival of the Fittest

get on with your life, it's the same for everybody. Nobody's job is guaranteed.'

'Letting the second-year apprentices go is not nice, and I don't enjoy it. Unfortunately the world is not a pleasant place and you have to do it. If you've worked with a boy for two years you may well like the boy. But you must take the right decision, not let your heart rule your head. Last year we did well, we only had eight second-years, and of that eight we took seven on as pros.' This was an exceptionally high ratio as most clubs will see a take-up of less than 50%.

And the one boy who wasn't retained?

'He had a good attitude, but just wasn't good enough quality for what we wanted at this football club at that time. We could be wrong, we all make mistakes – even Gerry Francis occasionally. I lined the lad up with a club in Sweden, but he didn't want to go, which amazed me. He would have got quite a good financial deal out there. I've coached in Sweden and it may be part-time football but they train every evening, and play on a Sunday. It was an eight-month contract and I told him it would be a good experience and he could then return to England and go for more trials. The club would probably have given the player a flat and a car and a little bit of money. It's a different country, a new experience. I personally think it is a good idea for a lad. Again, Les Ferdinand went to Turkey when things weren't working out for him. Teddy Sheringham went abroad during his spell at Millwall to get some experience, and now look at him. But anyway, the lad decided against it. It was his decision, but I was disappointed.

'Today, he isn't playing at all. Bobby Arber actually got him fixed up with a non-league side but he didn't want that either. I think the boy had just had enough. It happens sometimes, perhaps in six months' times he'll pick himself up and take something.'

Listening to Des enthuse about his young charges, and watching the transformation from Mild Mannered Mr Bulpin into Touchline Lunatic Man on matchdays, shouting for every ball, sliding every tackle and anticipating every pass, there is no doubting his fierce commitment to the game – and that of hundreds of ex-players like him, who had the burning desire to go all the way but only the talent to take them part way there. At this level, away from the media spotlight, there is little of the glory that is endemic at senior level – achievements are measured in human rather than financial terms.

'I enjoy my work. I get a kick out of seeing kids get through. It's little thanks that sometimes mean the most. The phone went in my flat six months ago, and it was a young lad from Bristol Rovers, who I had found at the age of twelve and he'd signed for me. The phone call was from the lad telling me he'd been taken on as a professional. Now when I'd left the lad he was still at the centre of excellence, and I'd worked with him a lot. The call was to say "thanks a lot" for everything I'd done. You don't often get that, people forget you quickly and it's nice when somebody takes the trouble to say thanks.'

Alan Sugar, perhaps, should make a note to take such trouble when one of Des's young starlets again saves the club a multi-million-pound fee. Sugar's commitment to youth is certainly genuine, but the day when Spurs can challenge for the Premiership with a team of homegrown Kevin Kickaballs is a long way down the road. In answer to the charge that spending is the only way to success, Sugar says, 'We tried that approach' and dismisses it with bitter irony. 'Two-and-a-half games until we started leaking goals

or £9 million – that's not bad to keep everyone happy.'
He adds, 'We haven't bought big [in 1995]. You mean we
haven't been irrational.' Initially an admirer of Wimbledon's
ability to survive against the odds by unearthing raw talent,
developing it and then profitably selling it, he has now found
a more relevant example for his rational approach. 'Don't
know how Manchester United do it,' he remarks sarcas-
tically, 'something to do with a youth policy, something
like that'.

In the meantime, however, as with the commercial
operation at Old Trafford, it would be unwise to take a
glance at the surface gloss and misunderstand the degree
of hard work and commitment that has gone on behind the
scenes. The emergence of Butt, Scholes, Beckham and the
Neville brothers is but the current manifestation of a youth
policy that has long had the full backing of everyone at Old
Trafford. Indeed, without such backing, in particular from
manager Alex Ferguson, many of the club's best prospects
would never have found their way into a red shirt. It
was certainly one of the factors that persuaded chairman
Martin Edwards to stick with Ferguson after disappointing
performances from the first team.

Time and again, parents of boys who have signed for
Manchester United testify to the degree of warmth, enthusiasm and passion conveyed by Alex Ferguson in what sometimes amounts to a personal crusade to entice prospects to
Old Trafford.

'Manchester United are a massive club, but in terms of
warmth and depth they were magnificent.' These were the
words of one father, former Chelsea and QPR player Steve
Wicks, whose son was swayed away from north London to
join up with United. 'There was a warmth and a passion
about Alex Ferguson I never knew existed. He was the major

Dream On

reason we decided to sign for United. He talked passionately about his youngsters, how they were the club's lifeblood, how he hoped to bring more into the first team. He spent time with us, sold the club to us, had dinner with Matthew, showed him around the ground. He is a man I would totally trust with my son's future.'

Old Trafford press officer Ken Ramsden confirms the club's enthusiasm: 'Alex Ferguson is the manager who has come closest to Busby in the way he has set up the youth coaching. The manager will travel the length and breadth of the country to talk to a kid and his parents, rather than send someone else. It is important to him.'

Almost inevitably, the success reaped by such a passionate approach will attract criticism that maybe more than just promises are being offered. Until such time as a player actually signs a professional contract with his club, usually aged eighteen at the end of the two-year YTS scheme, he is free to move and join whichever other club may catch his fancy, *providing no financial inducement is offered*. This is why some clubs are keen to offer particularly attractive prospects a pro contract only halfway through their apprenticeship, to secure their services in the face of potential competition from other clubs, and provide them with more than menial YTS subsistence, a £20,000 salary at the age of seventeen being gratefully received.

In January 1996 United were twice found guilty of 'poaching', one of the cases involving Matthew Wicks. Indeed it was the cordial relations at board level that saw Arsenal satisfied with a guilty verdict from the FA and the boy returned. United got off lightly. They weren't so lucky with Oldham, when they were fined £20,000 and ordered to pay compensation, which may well amount

Survival of the Fittest

to over £100,000, for 'illegally' securing the services of seventeen-year-old David Brown.

Elsewhere, stories abound of many famous prospects whose signature had been secured at schoolboy level through clandestine payments to parents, or the oft-quoted ruse of employing a father as a 'scout', thus being able to put him on a club's payroll. With such a high failure rate for promising youngsters, it is not surprising that some fathers, and sons, may be tempted by cash inducements, only too aware that this may prove an all too rare opportunity to make a little money from the game before they fall by the wayside. The clubs themselves will know that tomorrow's generation of stars are already out there playing schools football, waiting to be discovered. More than ever the pressure is on for scouts to spot such prospects at an earlier age and begin the process whereby they feel an allegiance to one particular club, gradually being weaned away from the schools to the club's own centre of excellence to which kids can go from the age of nine. But although they can sign associate schoolboy forms at the age of fourteen, if the kid is any good, the English Schools Football Association (ESFA) will have first call on his services as they run the first national side at under-fifteen level. The FA do not step in until the under-sixteen level, which has only recently been introduced.

The clubs are highly critical of the way in which talented young boys can be cajoled by the school system into playing too many matches. Clubs like Tottenham try to use their centre of excellence to get the lad away from just playing competitive matches, concentrating instead on honing basic skills and techniques that may not otherwise be given time in the school environment.

But even when netted, it isn't always the case that a club

Dream On

will know what they have under their nose. Ryan Giggs trained regularly at Manchester City's centre of excellence, and even after Alex Ferguson had been to the home of the fourteen-year-old prodigy to ask for his signature, City did not show sufficient interest, even though Ryan's mother offered them first refusal out of loyalty.

With the stakes so high and the clubs having access to kids at such a young age, the FA and the Premier League must move quickly to draft precise and effective ground rules. With the spectre of Bosman 2, free transfers within England, the small clubs may no longer feel it worth pursuing any form of youth development unless there is stricter policing and harsher penalties. Nominal fines are no deterrent when one illegal approach can net a player potentially worth millions. The sale by Spurs of 21-year-old Nicky Barmby for £5.25 million is a graphic example of the value of one astute signing at schoolboy level.

When Tottenham's youngsters lost the FA Youth Cup final in May 1995, it was perhaps instructive that their opponents were Manchester United. For those Tottenham directors who may have taken the trouble to attend both legs (a 2–1 home win but a 0–1 and penalties defeat at Old Trafford), the ties will have exposed the chasm, not on the playing field, but in the attitudes of each club to such occasions.

On the same day that Jurgen Klinsmann had earlier announced his intention to quit Tottenham, the first leg of the final took place on a warm May evening at White Hart Lane. While Alex Ferguson set the tone for Manchester United by standing on the West Stand forecourt to meet and greet the parents he had invited down as his guests, fewer than 4,000 fans struggled to gain admittance to a game where the cost of employing extra turnstile operators

Survival of the Fittest

had obviously been vetoed by the bean counters. With scant advance publicity and only the West Stand open, the undignified crush to gain admission was a prelude to an evening that showed the London club in a very shabby light indeed. The club shop was closed, missing a great opportunity to benefit from the high percentage of families in attendance. Pre-match and at half time, crowds milled about the concourses desperately searching in vain for somewhere serving a snack or a drink. There were no stewards on view and no obvious sign of representatives from the club being on duty. There was no programme and the players had no names on their shirts, so nobody had a clue who they were watching. God only knows what impression had been created on parents who were trying to weigh up the merits of their son joining either of the two clubs. The 20,190 attendance for the return leg at Old Trafford told its own story.

For players earmarked by Spurs as 'potentials', there are clearly defined stages of progression leading to that elusive professional contract. At every stage, more fall by the wayside as the club refines its selection criteria. Those who actually make it to professional status at White Hart Lane have every right to feel that they are the cream from their generation.

For the aspiring youngster, the first step on the ladder is to get himself noticed by head scout John Moncur (who presumably hired his own son, now at West Ham), or one of his team, who comb the UK looking for promising talent. Once spotted, he will be invited to White Hart Lane to attend the club's centre of excellence. This is where juniors aged between nine and sixteen come to the club for a couple of evenings a week to receive training and coaching.

Dream On

Most clubs now operate their own centre of excellence, taking advantage of a recent relaxation of regulations that previously restricted access to the under-fifteens.

At age fourteen, if he is still showing promise, a lad may then be signed by Tottenham on 'schoolboy' terms. If he is exceptional, he may win a scholarship to Lilleshall. From the many thousands of talented fourteen-year-olds playing football across England, just sixteen are selected each year for a two-year stint at the FA's national school. Tottenham's Stephen Clemence recalls the selection process that brought him to Lilleshall: 'I started off with about 80 boys from the south-east, on trial at Bisham Abbey, and I got through that one. Then it went to the first of three national trials up at Lilleshall. The first trial started off with 80 finalists from all over the country. This was whittled down to 50, and then the final trial was for 30, of which sixteen boys were selected for a scholarship. Luckily enough I was selected.

'My mum and dad left it to me as to whether I went or not. I weighed up the reasons for staying put or going. I'd always wanted to be a professional footballer, and came to the conclusion that it would be best for my football if I accepted.'

The idea of the national school is to remove the chosen few from their home environment, with its inherent distractions that may range from delinquent classmates to poor family diet, to one where they can spend two years honing their football skills under expert tutelage, whilst still maintaining their academic studies as a Plan B insurance policy for later life.

For a youngster barely into his teens and plucked from the inner-city war zones, the 300-acre estate in Shropshire that houses Lilleshall must seem as alien as the fresh fruit and pasta diet they will subsequently encounter. The school

Survival of the Fittest

does its best to settle the lads for their two-year stay but suffers, as would any boarding school, with its fair share of homesickness and culture shocks. It is a credit to the selection process that so few entrants have actually failed to complete the course.

Given the low success rate normally associated with youth football, the record of Lilleshall is certainly better than average. Kevin Gallen, Daniele Dichio, Andy Cole, Nicky Barmby, Sol Campbell and Ian Walker all became established Premiership players after graduating from Lilleshall. But even if every one of each year's sixteen graduates was to go on to a successful pro career, that would still be but a fraction of the number needed.

At the age of sixteen, the next stage is reached, selection for the club's Youth Training Scheme (YTS). This government sponsored initiative is intended to give youngsters the chance to gain work experience while earning a nominal wage. Intended originally to fill the nation's factories with willing apprentices, football clubs have taken advantage of the scheme as a means of further retaining young prospects, while sharing the costs with the government. Around 1,400 lads nationwide are enrolled, including the Lilleshall graduates.

At any time during the two-year duration of this scheme, the club can offer a professional contract. What usually happens, however, is that the club wait and then decide which of the eighteen-year-olds they want to retain on professional terms, and which they are happy to let go. If a boy makes it this far with Spurs, then he will sign his first contract and be looking to leave Des and his youth setup behind and progress to the reserve and under-21 teams run by Chris Hughton.

If any of the current crop personify Alan Sugar's faith in the value of a youth policy, it would be Stephen Clemence,

son of Barnet manager Ray, who played eleven seasons for
Liverpool before moving south, and playing a further 330
games in goal for Spurs between 1981 and 1987. A lack
of ability has never been a problem for Stephen; an unfair
accusation of favouritism perhaps, but that will always
be the handicap of sons saddled with famous fathers. If
anything, his father's fame has made things tougher for
Stephen because of the high expectations fostered upon
those from footballing families. But despite this, Stephen's
progress through the youth ranks has been spectacular.

He began his playing career with an under-eight side
playing Saturday mornings. From there, Stephen moved
to Broxbourne Saints with whom he stayed, despite signing
for Tottenham as a schoolboy at age thirteen, until selection
for the national school at Lilleshall at the age of fourteen.
There was in fact an earlier opportunity for Stephen to
have been coached by Spurs: 'I wanted to go when I was
younger, but my dad wouldn't let me go. He didn't want me
to get involved with Tottenham too early because he wanted
me to continue enjoying my football without pressures.' In
fact Ray and Veronica Clemence are the antithesis of pushy
parents. The proximity of Chase Lodge to Underhill, the
respective home grounds of Tottenham youth and Barnet
FC, enables Ray to go to the first half of Stephen's game
when Barnet are at home. His mother goes home and away,
and Stephen in turn goes to Barnet whenever Tottenham
are away. 'We support each other,' he says. Although he
takes an active interest in his son's career – he negotiated
Stephen's contract with John Moncur – Ray stays firmly
on the right side of the line. As Des Bulpin appreciatively
acknowledges, 'Ray has achieved much more in the game
than I've ever achieved but he never comes and pushes his
way in on what I do'.

Survival of the Fittest

'When I was a youngster,' recalls Stephen, 'I used to play centre-forward, and it was only when I came to Tottenham that Bob Arber decided to play me at the centre of midfield. I've played there ever since. It's my favourite position now, although for England schoolboys I played on the left side of midfield.' So far, Stephen has played for every England team for which he is qualified. Indeed, he played for the under-eighteens in his first year as an apprentice. Not that this recognition has caused him to lose his down-to-earth approach, and he was surprised to go straight into Tottenham's 'senior' youth team. 'It was great getting straight into that team. I didn't expect it, I just tried to keep my place. I felt I was holding my own but this year I've noticed the difference: I'm stronger, I feel more confident in my ability.'

'Stephen is a prolific goal-scorer for a midfield player,' enthuses Des Bulpin. 'He's very athletic and he's keen to learn. We are expecting him to do well at this football club.'

Indeed everyone at White Hart Lane has high hopes for Stephen Clemence, currently in his first year as a professional. But even tomorrow's superstar isn't excused club chores. In return for a basic wage and coaching tuition, the under-eighteen lads are given menial tasks to earn their keep. 'I have to collect the kit at the training ground and pack it up to be laundered. I also have to do the staff teas and rolls and take the lunches up to the coach's room after training. We have to pump up the first team's footballs, clean them and look after the bibs and cones. And we all get allocated two pros' boots to clean – I've got Ronny Rosenthal and Robert Simpson [a reserve]. If Spurs are at home on a Saturday afternoon, all the youth players are obliged to watch the match. Afterwards, we have to clean out the dressing rooms, the under-seventeens and under-eighteens taking turns on alternate weeks.'

Dream On

But it's not all drudgery.

'Monday we have college. Tuesday we will train at Mill Hill, running and fitness work. Tuesday afternoon we return to White Hart Lane for more running and some work with weights. Wednesday can be either at Mill Hill or at White Hart Lane, playing five-a-side games, doing sprints, or working on particular techniques. Thursday we train again at Mill Hill in the morning, and back at the ground in the afternoon. It is then that we start to prepare for Saturday's game. On a Friday we work on how we are going to play: the set pieces, with perhaps some shooting practice. Saturday is match day, and Sunday we have off.'

And on such days off, those apprentices like young Stephen Clemence – himself with the July finals of the European Under-18 Championships in France to look forward to – may seek comfort from precedent and look to Sol Campbell, dreaming that they too will emulate his meteoric rise to full international status. While those of a nervous disposition will recall the case of Ollie Morah.

Ollie joined Spurs straight from school in the late 1980s, and soon gained a reputation as a big powerful centre-forward who was destined for a big future in the game. His rise was spectacular: FA national school, international honours for England at schoolboy and youth levels and an FA Youth Cup win with Spurs in 1990. Ollie's career was marked with all the right ingredients, except luck – the one that every player needs to make that final transition to first team stardom. For Ollie, niggling injuries and limited first team opportunities – he was after all competing for Gary Lineker's position – saw him drift away from Tottenham for a loan spell at Hereford, before eventually signing full-time for Swindon Town in 1992. Subsequent moves and further injury problems saw further drifting out to Sutton

Survival of the Fittest

United, Cambridge United and eventually to Conference side Welling. Now, at 23, he must really wonder what went wrong. In his Spurs days, Ollie played in the same side as Ian Walker, another homegrown player who has gone all the way to Terry Venables' squad, and is best remembered for his performance in a South East Counties League Cup final when his two goals in the away leg at Highbury won the trophy for Tottenham and completely eclipsed Arsenal's hotshot striker, a certain Andy Cole. On that day, few would have tipped the Spurs man to be playing non-league football at 23, or ventured that Andy Cole would cost Manchester United £7 million in 1995.

To be fair to Ollie, the odds were always stacked against him, as they are for any Tottenham homegrown talent short of the highest class. In 1984, Gary O'Reilly, nowadays a presenter and reporter with Sky Sports, felt compelled to leave Tottenham for Brighton with two years still to run on his contract, 'because when I signed I knew that the club would always buy. I got into the first team squad, but they bought players in my position. Although this spurred me on to improve, and sometimes I was played in preference to them, eventually I had enough of playing in the reserves. I tried that path and it came to a natural end. Because I had confidence in my own ability, I took a salary cut and dropped a division. When Brighton just missed promotion in my first season, I felt my decision to move was justified.'

Other contemporaries like Mark Bowen, Ian Crook and Ian Culverhouse, who all moved to Norwich, could tell a similar story. Those that stayed and gave Tottenham their best years, like Paul Miller and Mark Falco, were never accepted by the crowd in the way their more glamorous and costly colleagues were, despite both playing around 200 games apiece, and, in Falco's case, scoring at the excellent rate of almost a goal every two games.

Perhaps it's incumbent for those who rise through the ranks to go one more step and challenge for international honours. For example, unless he achieves this status, David Howells, although appreciated, will never rival Sol Campbell or Ian Walker in the popularity stakes.

Moreover, it is arguable that today, young pros like Stephen Clemence face an additional obstacle, with the reserve team being used as a shop window in an attempt to offload big money buys like Jason Cundy, who have no place in Gerry's plans. But the players on long, high-salaried contracts are content to sit tight. The reverse is true for the young starlets. First team squad members like Gerry McMahon and Steve Slade will be free to move at the end of this season (post Bosman 2 they will be able to move for nothing). Failure to make their first pro contract a long one means that, like Gary O'Reilly, they may see better opportunities elsewhere. Unlike him, they won't be financially penalised for doing something about it.

While changing circumstances make it difficult for Tottenham at this level, choice has determined their strategy regarding stars. Quite simply, they aren't going to play the money game and they resent those that do.

Newcastle are now the Premiership's biggest spenders, thereby incurring Alan Sugar's wrath. 'We'll see when their accounts are published at Companies House whether the company is solvent or insolvent . . . If you want five clubs run by the chequebook then let's all give up.' The Sugar solution is a long-term one: 'I've strong views about this. We could easily go out and spend £7 million on Carlos Kickaball, my famous football player who's not worth buying. It occurs to me I would rather spend £5 million on a school. A proper

Survival of the Fittest

state run school that teaches the three Rs and that, but is also a football academy for youth players. The most important thing is security of ownership of students or graduates or whatever you want to call them. Because you cannot invest a lot of time, effort, money and teaching into a young player and then he can just clear off. So we're hoping to reform the whole situation.'

So are Newcastle, but they are prepared to raid the transfer market in the meantime. They have announced plans for their own £20 million footballing academy, no doubt tiring of seeing the best North-East talent come to fruition with other clubs. With Blackburn also having invested heavily in a new youth complex, there can be little doubt that other clubs will follow suit. 'We would aim to produce gentlemen, whether they succeed as footballers or not,' says Kevin Keegan. 'Clubs have got to take over the whole coaching system and do it right. There is a problem with the role of schoolteachers; they don't want us and sometimes we don't want them. We don't work hard enough on it at the moment, and clubs like Ajax and Bayern Munich do.'

For Dario Gradi, the highly respected manager of second division Crewe and one of the leading candidates for the post of the FA technical director, although the situation is improving, there is a lot of ground to make up. 'Our system at the moment produces knackered, or even worse, injured schoolboys, because the schools murder them. They've got to be lacking in technique because they don't practise, they only play, and you don't improve your skills in matches because you don't get that many touches of the ball. In schools' football, all you are trying to do is win the game for your school. You run around the pitch like a blue-arsed fly, trying to do everything because your mates aren't so good.

Dream On

The schools have always been a nightmare. Overcoming their power was a major advance.' Enabling the professional clubs to have kids for unlimited coaching, school commitments permitting.

For England this may seem a bold initiative. But it is only what they have been doing across the Channel for many years. In Italy, Holland or France there is no schools football as we know it. Instead, promising youngsters are affiliated to their local club at an early age, and receive expert tuition from professional coaches. At Ajax, young Dutch players are taught the values of technique (basic skills and tricks), of intelligence (knowing when to pass, when to dribble, and when to move into position or ask for the ball), of personality (self-confidence to use individual flair) and of speed (of both mind and feet).

For these countries, success is not judged by the tournaments their youth teams may win, but by the quality of the youngsters filtering into their professional clubs.

'When England schoolboys play the Germans at Wembley,' notes Dario Gradi, 'it's the England school teachers' XI versus the German FA team, selected from their clubs. The England boys do all right, because they're big, strong, competitive lads, picked by teachers interested only in winning games. The others are picked by the German FA who are interested in producing players.'

The much maligned Charles Hughes, the FA's director of coaching, fought long and hard to break the stranglehold of the ESFA and get the national school at Lilleshall established. Perhaps his insistence on the virtues of direct play have obscured the fact that building blocks are now in place for his successor to exploit. Under the aegis of the technical director the elitist principle of Lilleshall should be extended to the professional clubs where, say, a maximum of sixteen

Survival of the Fittest

boys per club from the age of fourteen can be relieved of the obligations to their school team and be given full time to the clubs. This would enable the clubs to run under-fifteen and under-sixteen teams for the first time.

For the clubs, this will mean a quantum change in the quantity and quality of coaches with, it is to be hoped, the introduction of a new FA coaching badge specifically tailored to the needs of the youngsters. So the right coaches are coaching the right things. In the mutual interests of both parties. Technique not tactics must be the be-all and end-all at this stage in a young player's development.

The schools feel differently. They strongly resent their sports masters, who voluntarily give up a great deal of their time, being branded as well-meaning amateurs, prepared to sacrifice a child's footballing future for the sake of a few inter-school trophies. They are understandably wary of how clubs would handle such a precious resource. Given that the clubs hardly have a blemish-free record with their adult players, this seems a reasonable enough concern. In addition, most professional clubs still operate a mornings-only training schedule, which is hardly the pioneering spirit to coaching they ought to be displaying. You can't help but sympathise with the ESFA if they feel that the clubs' new found interest in youth is simply a cynical reaction to the escalating transfer market.

As far as Tottenham is concerned, Des Bulpin's work notwithstanding, it is a case of succeeding in spite of the current system, not because of it. Nevertheless, there is much to be pleased with. Of a first team squad of 28, twelve have come up through the ranks with David Howells, Ian Walker and Sol Campbell being undisputed first choices for their positions. And every now and again a jewel is unearthed. To find two in quick succession is surely no accident, and the international recognition earned by both Walker and Campbell is testament to how talent will emerge. But of course it is crazy that Sol Campbell's versatility is the result of having to play in defence, midfield and attack in the Premiership. If he'd been Dutch all would have been worked out at an earlier age; skill and technique honed by tutorials over the years, the hurly-burly of league action merely adding the final gloss with experience.

Chapter 13

The End of the Beginning

Alan Sugar wasn't used to being lectured, but he was taking this one well.

'You want some advice?' ventured Alex Fynn somewhat rhetorically.

'Okay, let's hear it,' sighed Sugar, momentarily thrown by Alex's departure from his usual 'Why do you always look so miserable?' opening.

'You've got to speculate to accumulate. You haven't heard that before have you?'

'Nah, never,' replied Sugar, humouring the intruder who had the annoying habit of turning up in boardrooms around the Premiership – as here at Highbury – and telling the Spurs chairman how to run his club.

'What I mean,' continued Alex, 'is that your promise to Bill Nicholson about winning a championship won't be fulfilled in your children's lifetime unless you have a deficit in the transfer market.'

Sugar said nothing, no doubt making a mental note to double the boardroom security at home games.

Dream On

'I don't mean you should go into the red on the bottom line, but by the time your youth policy bears fruit, Tottenham will be off the pace. It took Manchester United years of commitment to reach where they are today. You've got to spend more if you want success.'

Sugar was too relaxed to rise to the bait. The occasion of the Arsenal-Spurs derby transformed Highbury's boardroom, its wood-panelled innermost sanctum, into part show-business function, part establishment gathering. Directors, families, friends and guests enjoyed plentiful food and an open bar; both sides of the north London divide brought together in a boisterous atmosphere. Here is one of the few venues away from White Hart Lane where the Tottenham chairman feels relaxed enough to hold court.

'Watch out,' warned Jeremy Beadle, the court jester, 'he's doing a book you know.'

'I know,' grinned Sugar. 'I'm going to get one to stick under my computer.'

Son Daniel Sugar, operations manager at White Hart Lane, was more expansive and less flippant in response to the same challenge. But he would not acquiesce to Alex's argument that Gerry Francis mistrusted skill, nor that a transfer surplus and mid-table mediocrity was considered a satisfactory result by Tottenham's pragmatic regime.

Indeed Sugar Jnr. defended Francis, citing Monaco's Belgian international Enzo Scifo as the kind of skilled midfielder the manager had recently considered bringing to Tottenham, but nevertheless implying that money, and reservations about adaptability, had prevented what would have been a risky purchase. When Darren Anderton was once again fit for selection, Daniel Sugar strongly envisaged a more flexible tactical approach. He also acknowledged a

The End of the Beginning

need to strengthen Tottenham's shallow first team squad, hinting at a greater financial commitment to challenge for trophies than his father was letting on. The intimation was that the fans could expect renewed forays into the transfer market until the first batch of Sugar's Saplings were ready to burst forth from the nursery.

For someone who first came into football only five years ago, Alan Sugar has made up for lost time in offending people, making enemies and formulating some pretty radical opinions on how the game should be run. In other words, carrying on in much the same manner that reflected his dealing with the City.

Sugar's tenure at Tottenham has been a crash course in crisis management, giving him first hand experience of problems many of his boardroom contemporaries have yet to face up to. He is not daunted by convention or precedent. He is not a wannabe fan who is in awe of star players. He is not embarrassed about making a profit, or criticising what he sees as wrong. And he has the rock-solid conviction that comes from being a self-made multi-millionaire for whom most decisions have proved correct.

To his credit, in those five years at Tottenham, he appears to have made few mistakes, aside from his acceptance that Terry Venables should be the chief executive. There are few issues that are clear-cut black or white, right or wrong. Instead there are shades of grey, degrees of pleasure, a spectrum of passions and opinions. For someone like Alan Sugar to come along and apply cold, clinical businesslike logic to his decision making is bound to make him unpopular with football's purists. A rational brain in an irrational industry. Where once, in the autobiography of Len Shackleton – a maverick forward of the '50s whose skills were spurned by the England selectors – a blank page famously encapsulated 'what the average club director knows about football' – the same might now be written about the average fan regarding the business of football.

But so far as Tottenham Hotspur is concerned, the club is in a better shape now than when he arrived, perhaps better than it has been for a very long time. The only dispute would be over the definition of 'better shape'. If the phrase refers to the book-keeping and the bottom line, the day-to-day control and the accountability of employees, then it is unquestionably true. But when applied to the playing side of the club, there is a general feeling among the fans that something crucial has been sacrificed to make the books balance; the club has misplaced its heart and its soul. The chairman would rubbish this assessment, and argue that the club could no longer continue to operate in its former guise and expect to survive. With the new Sky TV deal about to substantially increase the cash payments to clubs, and the Bosman era about to force clubs to write down the value of their playing assets, Sugar could no longer afford the luxury of his predecessor's 'We will see what comes round the corner, then we will decide what to do' Micawberesque attitude.

For Spurs fans, loving him or hating him is an option, but getting rid of him is not. Since the firing of Terry Venables, Alan Sugar has come to the forefront in the running of the club, and has undoubtedly acquired a taste and an aptitude for the task. Having seen his investment quadruple as Tottenham's share price soars to record levels, there are few, if any, willing or able to buy the man out. With one son gaining a firm grounding in what is becoming another part of the family business, it would appear that we are witnessing the start, not so much of a Sugar reign, but of a Sugar dynasty.

The End of the Beginning

'Well, it's both passion and a business really,' he responds when asked to comment on his involvement. 'It has become a passion, but it is a business whether people like it or not. And it has become much bigger since I took over. Transfer fees have gone up, television money has gone up, sponsorship deals have gone up. Costs have gone up out of all proportion.

'I have to focus on the fact that it is a commercial enterprise. I don't call it a business – normally that word means something that is going to be profitable, something you are in to buy and sell and make a load of money. The fact is, that football is an institution that has to be run properly and have tight financial controls.'

And those tight controls extend to making sure money coming in doesn't go straight out again.

'I can't ever see us spending £7 million on a player, I really can't. The reason I say this is because at the end of the day the punters are the ones who have to pay. If a guy comes to our games with his two kids, the day is going to cost him at least 60 or 70 quid. Now if that's what it takes for the club to be able to afford a player at £4.5 million, could I ask that guy to stump up 150 quid to watch a game on a Saturday? I think the answer is no.'

Which is all fine and dandy as a moral stance, but what if the other nineteen Premiership clubs decide to continue with their immoral ways? Newcastle's £43 million outlay on players appals Sugar, and he warns of a super-elite emerging from within the Premiership.

'Now whether that money has come from Sir John Hall's coffers, or whether he is paying for loans, that's none of my business. All I do know is, if you work out how much they're getting from TV, from sell-out gates and from replica shirts, and put all that into a computer and run the spreadsheet, you'll come out with a big red figure. And that you can't deny. Now maybe there's some secret I don't know about, but even if you won every trophy going, you'd never recoup that amount. And pay the players wages? And run the stadium? Never in a million years.

'If you want five clubs all run by the chequebook, then let's all give up because the other fifteen will just be cannon fodder to make up the numbers. But those five clubs will end up having to subsidise the other fifteen, because the paying public will soon stop turning up to support the cannon-fodder teams.'

With most leading clubs being run as someone's personal fiefdom, that kind of criticism is never welcome. Particularly coming from a club like Tottenham who have, in the past, sought to spend their way to success. But his new found faith in the power of youth football is as genuine as his desire to see his club's glories restored.

'I promised Bill Nicholson that we'd win the league again. And he can hold me to that if he wants to. There is no question of a doubt in my mind. When I set my mind to do something, there aren't many things I don't achieve. And I set a target of Tottenham becoming league champions. If it's anything to do with me, I'm pretty damn sure we are going to do it. And I'm going to demonstrate how to do it without irrational chequebook madness, by demonstrating skills in man management, team selection and squad building.'

Nor will he see new-found wealth from TV and sponsorship go straight into the players' bank accounts. 'What we've got to be careful of, is that this money doesn't go through us like a dose of salts. Which is exactly what happened to the money last time. It's a bit like a laxative. We, the clubs, didn't see the benefit. It just got passed on in higher wages and higher transfer fees.'

The End of the Beginning

Sugar has great faith in the abilities of manager Gerry Francis. Both men appear to share a distrust for a team full of stars, although whether Francis, despite cultivating a strong youth policy throughout his managerial career, privately shares his chairman's faith that a championship can be won by concentrating on homegrown players, is debatable.

'You can see the difference between the Fab Five and a solid eleven,' he enthuses in reference to the respective teams of his previous two managers. 'You can't have three Sheringhams and four Armstrongs. You've got to have youth players who are chomping at the bit. Put it this way: if I had two Darren Andertons, the one that sits on the bench and doesn't get a game isn't going to be very happy. So he's going to bugger off. Look at Manchester United, they got rid of their star players, but they had a group of enthusiastic youngsters who *will* sit around, and *will* wait, and *will* be patient to get into the first team.'

But will the fans be patient? Although most would see the logic in homegrown starlets to supplement the occasional big money buy, few supporters would be enthusiastic about an extended transitional period, where the club was hopelessly uncompetitive. Times change. Post-Premiership, expectations are higher. For Manchester United this means winning something and being in Europe every year. Conditioned by success, the 25-year wait for the title has probably been replaced by a limit of 25 months without one. For Tottenham, it means nothing less than being a viable challenger. However the chairman is adamant that his fans must learn the value of good housekeeping. Clubs, he feels, have two choices: 'Either go out and find their own Alan Sugar, or Sir John Hall, and there aren't too many of them around, or create a level playing field that can only come from homegrown players.

'If you take your Barclaycard, go out for the night and spend beyond your means, your partner is going to love you. But you are going to hate yourself the following morning. Because you're going to have to pay for it. Sensible people know they can't do that.

'I look at some of our fans as children. They are always asking their dad for new toys and you have to explain you can't afford them. I'm hoping that our fans will grow up with me, and understand that my medicine is good medicine. It's not a case of me wanting to stick the money in my pocket, it's good medicine for the household. You can buy anything if you throw enough money at it, but what you are really looking for is consistency. I personally don't think you can buy consistency with a chequebook.'

Most children, or supporters as they used to be called, are actually very much on Sugar's side. The man has done as much for the club as any chairman could be expected to do. Appointing Ossie Ardiles, the new South Stand, Klinsmann, Gerry Francis, the six-points and FA Cup victory over the FA, the overturning of UEFA's ban (Spurs, along with Wimbledon, were initially banned from European competition for fielding weakened teams in their Intertoto Cup matches. On appeal the ban was reduced to a hefty fine, with the tab being shared by all the Premier League clubs.) If only he had a coaching badge and could play at left back. Even the hiccups – losing Ruddock, the Klinsmann/shirt outburst, the lambasting of Arsenal over Bergkamp and the 'I'm selling!' tantrum – can be excused as the kind of overreaction to coming second that most fans would be familiar with. He has even been prepared to learn from his mistakes. Contrary to the anticipated defensive

The End of the Beginning

rhetoric, when asked at the AGM, 'Weren't you a little naïve regarding Klinsmann?' he said, 'Naïve, stupid, bloody fool, call me what you like. I was. But let's give thanks to Klinsmann. He was a boost to the club when it was out of the FA Cup and for that he was a valuable member of the setup. The fact that he didn't last was by the by, but I've learned now to dot the I's and cross the T's.'

Even the Venables episode is no longer held as a black mark against him, after subsequent newspaper revelations showed that maybe Sugar did have a point after all. 'Having been the backroom boy for two years while Mr Venables was running the show, I only came to the forefront when Mr Venables, er, left. Unfortunately the media hype about what I was supposed to be like tended to percolate down to people in the industry. So before I even met them they had a preconceived view of me. But I'm not bothered about my public perception,' he confirms. 'If anything, I think it has given me great credibility for standing up for what I think is right.'

Not that he is completely home and dry yet; he may need to rein Claude in a little, and cut Gerry Francis a little more slack. The alienation of many long-time fans can't be good for the club, even though his intentions may be honourable. Season ticket prices at White Hart Lane continue to escalate and, as Rick Parry has warned, 'It does seem the limit is not far away.' The 'Oak Room Cleansing Exercise', as Sugar tastelessly called it, saw many long-time fans ousted from their traditional enclave in the West Stand. Sugar is unrepentant, and his thinking is typical of the lack of sentiment displayed on occasions by the current regime: 'Certain people like to be seen, to be associated. They don't pay to get in – they want to be treated like royalty. And when they get slung out they get the hump. I must admit

Tottenham had their fair share of them. They think they are celebs. When it comes to parting with money, they're gone, quicker than Asprilla down the wing, if you know what I mean.'

There is also an element of taking the fans for granted, perhaps not appreciating that it is the popularity of the Premier League that is pulling Tottenham along in its wake rather than the guarantee of excellent value for money at White Hart Lane. 'When I took over,' he told a critic, 'we had an empty ground. Now we get 33,000 people. We are being forced into building the North Stand to accommodate even more people who want to watch this dross you're referring to. This demoralised group going nowhere. I dunno, maybe they're all masochists. I'm very happy with the situation at the moment.'

He may be, but despite their current support, the fans aren't. Gerry's first team squad is looking increasingly threadbare. Both manager and fans know the club isn't up to mounting a credible title challenge. On the plus side, the chairman is at least thinking long-term, but a quick fix is badly needed in the short term. It may be time for the son to put an arm around his dad and go for a quiet stroll in the garden.

For Gerry, too, it's make-your-mind-up time. The summer would be an honourable time to step down if he felt he no longer wanted to continue as manager. But there was no indication that might be the case. Quite the contrary, there had even been talk of a contract. Indeed, if anything, Gerry, like his chairman, appeared to have immersed himself even deeper in the club. Was he too becoming a Spurs man?

At Arsenal, particularly within their fanzines, the Spurs manager was known as 'Moaner Francis' and it must be

said they do have a point. Gerry has yet to learn the art
of the dignified silence. Although he stops short of the
Joe Kinnear fuse-blowing tantrums that bring with them
a disrepute charge, you can be sure that every disallowed
goal or defeat or failed penalty appeal will be attributed
to some global refereeing conspiracy. He even berates his
players in public, but gets away with it because they realise
he cares. When Ronny Rosenthal gave away a goal against
Manchester United through failing to do what he usually
does so well, blocking off the attacking options, Gerry
expressed his dismay to the media. Given that Ronny
had previously both saved and made a goal, and that
Tottenham subsequently won 4–1, the criticism appeared
harsh and niggardly. Not to Ronny though.

'Gerry is not the type of manager who will talk about his
players. It was done spontaneously because we didn't keep
the lead and it started from my fault. He made a point of
it at half-time. It isn't done maliciously. It's more a way of
how to concentrate, how to fix things. He tries to tell you
so it won't happen again.'

But is it such a disaster that Tottenham have a bad
loser for a manager? For fans it must be a comfort
to know that the manager feels every bit as awful as
they do about a cup exit or three dropped points. They
certainly don't want to switch on the radio to hear
their manager mouthing platitudes about the opposition's
brilliance and how football's a funny game and tomorrow's another day.

And there is some justification to what he says. Maybe
not his harping on refereeing decisions, but the dramatic
turnaround in the club's fortune since his arrival has, rather
than highlight his exceptional talents, simply convinced
people that things could never have been that bad in the

Dream On

first place. But they were, and it is understandable if Gerry thinks people need regular reminders.

'When we finished last summer, I was really looking forward to adding to the squad and thinking we might realistically be in with a chance of competing this year. Unfortunately, Teddy got injured, Darren Anderton got injured. We lost Klinsmann, Popescu and Barmby. Bang! just like that. You tell me any team that can recover from that? And so I've had to try to build two teams, in a very short space of time.

'At the same time we had the media pressure in response to all the things that were going on. Which can only happen at this place, so I've learnt. So the pre-season with the injuries was a very hard and difficult time. And then of course we went into the first three league games with half a team in many ways. We got a point at Man. City then lost at home to Villa and Liverpool. And a lot of teams could have gone under – we were a relegation outfit evidently.

'I was under pressure every day to spend the money we had. But you had to keep cool, you had to keep believing in what you were doing. And I had to transmit that to my players; that was vital. And having said that, after that third game against Liverpool, we went 21 league games with only three defeats, which is a remarkable recovery and a remarkable achievement by the players concerned.'

As Gerry swiftly found, not only do fans have short memories, they can also be extremely fickle. It wasn't good enough that the team was putting on a brave face and actually doing quite well. The Spurs fans were impatient for a little more panache and a little less hoof.

'Well, I don't know what this "traditional Tottenham football" is,' he fumed, at accusations that his team were becoming Route One merchants. 'But I find that kind of

The End of the Beginning

talk very disappointing. I don't think there is a "mould". If you are only playing football one way, you are going to win nothing. Certainly not the league. In modern day football, you've got teams who will stop you doing what you are good at. And tactics that stop you doing what you are good at. So if you are going to just play a certain way, people are going to stop you. So maybe that is the reason why, in 35 years, Spurs haven't won the league.'

One of Gerry's first buys was expected to be a big-money defender. He saved the money and made a very creditable defence from the players he had inherited. But again he doesn't feel he or the players received the praise due to them.

'Last year, we not only out-scored the team that had played under Ossie, we also kept ten clean sheets. To do both is absolutely incredible. And it was done with virtually the same players. [David Howells, who had been cast aside by Ossie, was recalled to add his defensive qualities to the midfield. Indeed, Paul Allen's scrapping ability would also have been appreciated by Gerry if he hadn't already been offloaded to Southampton.] No money, no buys, no nothing from November to May. So we could have played a different system, one that maybe didn't score so many goals, but didn't concede so many either. But to actually out-score them and keep ten clean sheets, that takes some doing.'

Maybe Gerry's self-defence mechanism was honed during leaner spells earlier in his career.

'At Bristol Rovers, I had to lend them my own money to buy players that won the league and took them to Wembley. So I'm used to working under adverse conditions. However, when Alan said to me whatever money I could make, I could use, it was like music to my ears. I know what I am good at; I knew I could turn things around with the players I had.

Dream On

And I knew if I did generate money in whatever way, I could utilise it, which had never been the case in my career before. At QPR I had to sell £10 million worth of players and could only spend £2 million. So I was quite happy to accept the position here. But I reckon I must be the only manager in history to come to Tottenham and not have any money to spend.'

But in his mind, Gerry will know that sooner rather than later, the excuses must stop. In his first season, anything other than relegation would have been acceptable. As it was, seventh place and an FA Cup semi-final did more than whet appetites – it created expectations. Last season an earlier Cup exit and poorer league form hardly fulfilled them. For the coming season, everyone may be a little less tolerant.

Gerry has cautiously claimed that he will remain at Tottenham 'as long as the club is in a position to win things', and so his continued tenure suggests that Alan Sugar had indicated, to Francis if not to everyone else, that funds will be made available for new players. But any spending needs to be completed pre-season; if a serious challenge is to be mounted the club can ill afford another stutter through autumn. And in return, the chairman may now start setting some targets of his own, the least of which will be qualification for Europe, if not some actual silverware.

Not that that will worry Francis. He is hugely confident in his own abilities, and in the merits of a playing system he may tweak and tune but will not abandon. The house style at Tottenham is one of collective responsibility. But there have been signs that good old 4–4–2 may be compromised. The 3–5–2 played against Chelsea at the end of the season left Chelsea manager Glenn Hoddle 'dumbstruck'. He had watched Spurs at Arsenal a few days before and never

The End of the Beginning

envisaged that Gerry would make, for him, such a radical tactical change.

'From London's point of view,' reasons Gerry, 'ourselves, Chelsea, Arsenal, we've got to put things together in the future and try to challenge some of the northern dominance. Other than Arsenal, it has been 35 years since any London side won the league championship, which is a long time. For Tottenham, we need to move up a step, we need those twelve or fifteen points that will put us among the big boys. I seriously think that if we'd had a fit Darren Anderton we might have had those ten extra points, which would have put us a lot closer.'

With Anderton fit once more 96–97 may see Gerry forced to evolve his system to accommodate the players he has and the demands of the fans. Daily exposure to Bill Nicholson, a man for whom Gerry has frequently expressed the utmost admiration, must influence his thinking even if only subliminally. Despite the changing face of White Hart Lane, there are still enough ghosts prowling the corridors to leave any manager in no doubt as to what the expectations are at the club. But his start will have encouraged him, being the most successful by any new Spurs manager.

'I didn't know anything about the record. Tottenham have this thing whereby every fifty games they have an enquiry into the performance of the manager over that period. I think Arthur Rowe held the record back in 1949 for only eleven defeats in the first 50 games. We've beaten that – by one actually. When I was first told of that, I thought well, nice. Like the defensive record [602 minutes without conceding a goal up until the Bolton game] or other records we have achieved or broken. But it wasn't until I sat down and thought about the words, that in the whole history of Tottenham Hotspur Football Club – of Bill Nick,

Dream On

or Arthur Rowe and Terry Venables and Keith Burkinshaw, all the managers – we actually had the best record from all that history, going back pre-war. Well, I had a meeting with the players the next day and told them. Obviously, we haven't gone on like Bill Nick or Arthur Rowe did, and actually achieved anything yet in terms of winning things. But it certainly wasn't a bad start.'

Despite his bullishness about the current squad – 'If every player on our books was fit, we'd be a match for any team' – Gerry will undoubtedly be scouting at the European Championships this summer for fresh blood. And if he goes cap in hand to his chairman, Alan Sugar is going to find it hard to plead poverty. A rights issue, reducing Sugar's ownership from 50% to 40%, ostensibly to raise £11.5 million for the redevelopment of the North Stand, should ensure there is enough money in the bank for players as well as bricks and mortar. The new Sky TV deal will, for the first time, put real money in the club's bank accounts. When the deal kicks in, Spurs can expect around £9 million a season, almost four times the current level.

A new accounting procedure, taking heed of the Bosman ruling, will see players 'written down' on the books. Like fixtures and fittings, their value will be gradually reduced over a period of years, so that should they exercise their option to walk at the end of their contract, the impact on the club's balance sheet is minimised. It is a sign that Sugar is looking and thinking long term, and can only augur well for the club.

So change is in the air, but it's a shame it has come so late in the day. Arsenal are not blind to the obligations they hold, but never lose sight of the fact they are first and foremost a football club. Although even their most famous supporter doubts the club can maintain the hype generated

The End of the Beginning

by the chequebook frenzy of last summer. 'The place went crazy,' recalls Nick Hornby. 'But what are they going to do this year? If you've got to spend £11 million on players every season to keep the interest going, you're in trouble.'

Unlike some previous end-of-season clashes between Spurs and Arsenal, this encounter promised anything but a quiet stroll, for it carried a significance beyond the usual north London pride and prejudice. Both sides had long since conceded any interest in the title race; their remaining involvement being limited to games against the top sides which could help push the trophy one way or another. The two FA Cup finalists were decided and the Coca-Cola Cup rested at Villa Park. The only issue outstanding at the top of the table, and one that could be greatly clarified tonight, was who would claim the remaining UEFA Cup place, awarded to whichever team could finish fifth in the Premiership.

Arsenal were favourites – indeed they currently held that fifth spot – but a win for Spurs would see them leapfrog above their neighbours with three games remaining. Since the FA Cup defeat by Forest, Gerry Francis had focused his attention on that remaining place in Europe. With almost a quarter of the season remaining after the Cup exit in early March, a UEFA Cup place had seemed a realistic aim. But indifferent results since then had brought in just seven points from a possible eighteen. Most recently, an insipid 1–1 draw at home to Middlesbrough, where Spurs had taken the lead with five minutes remaining yet still were unable to hold on to it, had apparently signalled the end of any lingering UEFA hopes. But for once, the cry of 'how did *they* get on?' had brought forth favourable news – Arsenal were surprisingly beaten at Hillsborough that same afternoon.

Dream On

And so, as decreed by Sky Sports, the two teams faced
one another on an April evening to decide the unofficial
championship of north London. Yet despite the presence of
Sheringham, Armstrong, Bergkamp and Wright, with over
80 goals between them this season, the player who made the
headlines was one who had yet to score during the current
campaign. When Darren Anderton left the subs' bench to
play the final thirteen minutes, the heartfelt cheer from the
Spurs fans was no doubt echoed by his manager, his chairman
and the watching Terry Venables. Out since September with
a persistent groin injury, Darren's presence had been sorely
missed by both Spurs and England. His introduction here was
too late to influence a poor game that finished 0–0, a result that
suited Arsenal as it maintained their two-point advantage with
now only three games remaining.

As Anderton came on, David Platt shook his hand, much
to the amazement of his colleagues and fans alike. It was
reported that Platt was later rebuked by a team-mate who
told him, 'You don't do that to a Tottenham player'.
As it was Platt's first north London derby perhaps he
could be excused his naïvety. Or perhaps he was merely
demonstrating good manners. Either way, he would have
been left in no doubt about the inappropriateness of his
sporting gesture if he had seen the ripped out seats at the
Clock End. Or passed through Highbury Fields on his way
home, where fans were asked to reveal their colours as a
prelude to unpleasant skirmishes.

For Spurs, the season appeared to hold no further interest, but with seven weeks until the start of the European
Championships, there was at last a glimmer of hope for
Anderton that he might still play a part in the biggest
tournament in England for 30 years.

*   *   *

The End of the Beginning

In a team which has shed most of its stars, Darren Anderton remains as possibly the club's greatest current asset and most coveted player. Should Alan Sugar ever be daft enough to sell him, and assuming his objection to crazy transfer fees doesn't extend to receiving as well as paying, then Alex Ferguson would be favourite to head the queue of Premiership managers keen to break the current record to acquire the much-prized 24-year-old.

Four years earlier, the player had starred in Portsmouth's extended 1992 FA Cup run. In particular his semi-final goal against Liverpool brought him to national attention. The similarities in style and appearance to Chris Waddle were enough to draw a flattering comparison, and Terry Venables, acutely missing the player he had sold to Marseille, used his good links with Pompey owner Jim Gregory, his ex-boss at QPR, to secure a deal at just under £2 million.

For an uncapped, almost unknown, youngster who had played only 62 league games for Portsmouth, the purchase of Anderton contained a huge element of risk. Darren stayed in a rented flat in north London, away from home for the first time, and very obviously missing family and friends on the south coast. And for a while in that first season, it looked as if the gamble by Venables had backfired. The player looked out of his depth in the Premier League, pale, undernourished and sadly lacking in pace and confidence. He hovered out on the wing, almost hiding from the ball. When it found him, he was easily dispossessed; head and shoulders would drop and the crowd began to jeer in a further parallel to Waddle, who endured a nightmare first season at Tottenham. But in many ways this was just Darren conforming to the stereotype of a typical Tottenham big money signing.

Dream On

A hernia operation midway through that first season restored the zing to his play, and when he returned in the New Year, alongside the blossoming Barmby and new signing Teddy Sheringham, the team enjoyed a purple patch that took them to an FA Cup semi-final and saw some truly exhilarating home performances.

Two further seasons of steady progress saw Anderton emerge as a key figure in the Spurs team. With Terry Venables by then coach of the national side, it was no surprise when Darren was picked to make his international debut against Denmark in 1994, but few would have expected such a confident performance on his first outing. 'As good an international debut as I've seen,' commented Venables afterwards.

At Tottenham, under Gerry Francis, a further transformation took place, as Anderton was switched from the wing to midfield. It was an odd move given the player's undoubted abilities as a wide player. But it was in midfield that Gerry had most problems, and so Darren had to adapt to a more responsible role, no longer allowed the luxury of peripheral involvement. 'It has developed my game,' he admits, 'things like tackling and reading of the game. When I was a kid, I always played central midfield anyway. Glenn Hoddle was one of my favourite players. I like to think of myself as more of a playmaker than an out and out winger. Gerry advised me to play in a more central position where I can be more involved.'

An automatic choice for club and country, the current season held much promise. But another hernia operation and a long convalescence wiped out virtually the whole season.

'It definitely has not been easy,' he recalls of his long comeback trail. 'All along people were saying it would be

The End of the Beginning

three weeks, maybe four, until I was back. So I kept thinking I was going to be playing again in a few weeks, but it just hasn't happened on so many occasions. I never knew I'd be out for seven months.'

Those seven months saw Darren detached from first team circles, routines and the comforts of player camaraderie. As with Paul Gascoigne a few years earlier, while his team-mates were busy at Chase Lodge preparing for matches, Darren was running lonely laps of the White Hart Lane pitch, followed by muscle building work with weights, swimming, physiotherapy and gentle ball work. The routine of easing himself back to match fitness wasn't helped by persistent media stories that his career might be over – one even putting into headlines a mystery 'hip crumbling' condition that was straight from an episode of *The X-Files*.

'I hate watching the Tottenham games,' he said of the time when match days would see him spectating from the shadows of the players' tunnel. 'That's the hardest part. It's so frustrating because I want to be out there playing. To be honest, I'd rather be at home not watching at all. I'm obviously pleased if we win, and it would be great if we could qualify for Europe next season, but I just get this empty feeling. All I want is my place back.'

For Gerry Francis, too, the long wait was acutely frustrating. As the layoff stretched from weeks to months, his team selection was one long compromise, as short term arrangements began to take on an air of permanence. For Terry Venables, trying to settle on a nucleus of players for the summer's major tournament, the prolonged injury was an added complication.

'I have no doubts about his ability,' said Venables. 'He's a bright player, adaptable and alert. The way he adapted

to international football before his injury was a real plus
for us. He made goals, he scored goals, and his all-round
contribution was excellent. It might have surprised people
who weren't that familiar with him, but I always knew. From
the first time I saw Darren I thought he had the potential to
be an international footballer.'

Even Alan Sugar, with one eye on the pitch and the other
on the club's share price, was moved to praise his most
prized 'livestock': 'Let me tell you,' he said, during the
convalescence period, 'we've got one of the world's best
players joining us soon. He's definitely a £10–15 million
player, no question. His name? Darren Anderton. Now that
may bring people down to earth, for he is worth that much
in this crazy market. Because if I was to fritter away £15
million in today's transfer market, I would only get myself,
if lucky, another Darren Anderton. But we've got him.'

A fortnight after that thirteen-minute run-out at Highbury, Darren started his first Premiership game for 215
days, in Tottenham's final home fixture against Chelsea.
Not surprisingly, he looked tired and a little out of sorts, but
he lasted the full 90 minutes of a 1–1 draw with no obvious
discomfort other than a lack of match practice. It was good
to see him back in the starting line-up after so long, and the
welcome he received from the home fans will have left him
in no doubt as to how much they appreciate his skills. When
fans come to question the justification for paying over £400
each for their season ticket, it is players like Darren who
make signing the cheque a little easier. But on that day the
whole Spurs side looked as if they were coming back from
a seven-month lay-off. Truly the end of the season couldn't
come quick enough.

But five days later, the season once again flickered into
life for Spurs. Arsenal were held 0–0 at home to Liverpool,

while Spurs enjoyed a classy 3–1 win away to Leeds, with Darren Anderton capping a masterful display with his first two goals of the season. The calculators were out again, as fans deduced that it was still possible for Spurs to get into Europe, providing things went their way on the final day of the season. That was the good news. The bad news was that Arsenal had to lose at home to Bolton, while Spurs had to win away at Newcastle.

Sometimes it's hard not to feel that the English Premier League exists solely to provide Sky Sports with seemingly limitless prime-time drama. Once more, nine months of toil would be decided on the final Sunday of the season, with Sky again exercising their right to have the entire Premiership programme put back a day, to enable their cameras to cover all the crucial games. Newcastle needed to beat Spurs to clinch their first championship since 1927. But they also needed rivals Manchester United to lose at Middlesbrough for the equation to be complete. Spurs, too, knew their own fate rested outside their control. Even an unlikely win at Newcastle wouldn't automatically see them into Europe; they had to hope that already-relegated Bolton would also win at Highbury. It made for a wonderful finale, whether viewing on Sky's two channels, or actually at a game with eyes on pitch and ear to radio.

When Jason Dozzell put Spurs 1–0 ahead after 57 minutes at St James' Park it certainly made things interesting. By then, Manchester United were already two goals up at Middlesbrough and the title was decided. The battle for the remaining UEFA place became the focus of attention. Ferdinand equalised for Newcastle, so the pendulum swung back in Arsenal's favour. But then news filtered out of north London that Bolton had taken a 76th-minute lead. At the same time, Blackburn were winning at Chelsea, so the deposed champions had come from nowhere to claim the valued fifth spot. Within two minutes it had all changed, as Everton took a late lead over Aston Villa, which propelled them to the head of the pack, and for six minutes they were in Europe. Until, that is, Arsenal did what Arsenal do best.

'I was at Highbury,' recalls Arsenal season-ticket holder Harry Lansdown, 'and with half-an-hour to go we heard that Tottenham were winning at St James' Park. And then Bolton went and scored. So, it looked as if Spurs would have the last laugh. Arsenal fans started screaming at their team. One lone voice shouted, "Resign Rioch!" Then it turned again. Newcastle scored, but Everton took the lead in their match. So Arsenal were still out. Though slightly less galling, it was still painful. Then with eight minutes to go, David Platt pulled a goal back. But a draw wasn't good enough. So that was it: £11 million spent on new players last summer and a season of nothingness. Who would want to sign for Arsenal this year if they weren't in Europe for a second year running?

'Then Bergkamp suddenly found some space, looked up, and 25 yards out, struck the ball into the roof of the net, beyond the diving 'keeper's left hand. The ground erupted. We were back in Europe. It felt as good as winning a cup. And I couldn't help remembering Alan Sugar's line all those months ago about the "madness of paying so much for Bergkamp". He's probably right. It was crazy, especially with the Bosman ruling around the corner. That's at the business level. But then again, we've got a wonderful star who is committed to the club. And when he shot us back into Europe with just five minutes left – a goal that could be worth millions – the feeling was, yes Mr Sugar, one of

The End of the Beginning

madness. That's what football is about. Going mad. Maybe
he'll learn one day.'

So Arsenal spent £11 million on two players and were
rewarded with a UEFA Cup place. To get even half their
money back they will have to reach the final. It begs the
question of how much more they will have to spend to
be consistently successful. Alan Sugar's sensible spending,
on the other hand, consigned Tottenham to the status of
also rans, flattering to deceive only through Gerry Francis'
ability to make the whole greater than the sum of the parts.
So it wasn't fifth, but eighth that Spurs finished. One place
down on last season, with one point fewer. At least Gerry
had instilled consistency of one kind to the team. Perhaps
Alan Sugar had Hobson's choice and can't spend freely as
his first duty is to his shareholders. In which case forget
honours, except next time around the stakes will be even
higher and life outside the Premier league is unthinkable.
Following BSkyB/BBC's £693 million contract for the
Premier League from 1997, 'The Football League clubs
are left with a major problem,' according to Geoffrey
Richmond, chairman of newly promoted Division One
Bradford City. 'The gap, already vast, comes close to being
unbridgeable.'

Unfortunately, this is another contagious English disease about to be exported. The major Continental clubs
look enviously at the commercial riches of their English
counterparts and want to establish their own greed-is-good
oligarchies, to the detriment of the pyramid system, which
has served them well from the national team at the top to
the small clubs at the bottom. No matter, a commonality of
purpose has been decreed, the establishment of a Premier
League at home, a European Super League abroad. Either

Dream On

way the principle is the same: more big event games at home and abroad. For clubs like Manchester United, Newcastle and Arsenal the die is cast. Indeed, Arsenal probably see themselves as having more in common with Sampdoria than with Tottenham. And Tottenham? Well, the words kitchen and heat come to mind.

Postscript

June saw England become football's shop window. The country paraded its footballing heritage while Europe's finest players came to flaunt their skills and audition for prospective purchasers. Overseas stars now needed little coaxing to come to England for high salaries. For the first time, football will be getting real money from television as the latest Sky/BBC TV contract promised the top clubs around £9 million a season when the £743 million deal is fully operative. Unfortunately, and in keeping with Alan Sugar's expressed fears, most of this would seem to be heading straight for the pockets of players and their representatives. As fast as money was poured into the game, it was being syphoned off by opportunists who are more than happy to take advantage of the current English financial profligacy.

It went generally unremarked that Premiership clubs were buying up everyone else's stars, and yet there was no stampede for native talent. For the winners, huge signing-on fees and wages in excess of £20,000 per week were becoming

Dream On

commonplace. For the losers, fate was unforgiving. Erik Thostvedt, out of contract after seven-and-a-half years at White Hart Lane, qualified at last for his free transfer and lined up a move to Wolves on a three-year deal. Sadly, the legacy of his accumulated back injuries put the deal on ice and, in July, Erik, at 33, was forced to contemplate retirement. His former captain Gary Mabbutt was eventually offered the contract extension he sought, but the protracted negotiations and persistent press stories linking Tottenham with central defenders will have done little for his morale. In the present climate, who would bet on any of the Premiership's current attractions going on to match Mabbutt's fifteen-year innings?

Darren Anderton's late fitness was rewarded not just with a place in England's Euro '96 squad – alongside his team mates Messrs. Campbell and Walker – but indeed in England's every starting line-up for those Championships. Sadly, his performance was peripheral. Still, he should at least be in contention when next the tournament comes around, which may not be the fate of Teddy Sheringham. He too was an ever-present for England (as was Colin Calderwood for Scotland), but his form was fitful, pretty much as he ended the season. Despite two goals against Holland, Teddy must now hope that new England coach Glenn Hoddle – one Tottenham man replacing another – shares his predecessor's predilection for intelligence over pace.

Another ex-Tottenham man, Jurgen Klinsmann, found his first season back in Germany hadn't gone quite to plan, but still provided a more fruitful twelve months than north London would have done. Bayern Munich failed in their primary task to win the Bundesliga, but disappointment was tempered by lifting the UEFA Cup, thanks in no small measure to Jurgen's fourteen goals – a record for any individual in a European competition. For an encore, he captained his country to victory in the final of the European Championships at Wembley.

Alan Sugar announced his intention to walk away from Amstrad – a company that now seemingly brought him grief, while Tottenham made him money and gave him pleasure. If all went to plan he would now have the time to increase his involvement with the club. Certainly he was thinking long term, with a schedule set for the North Stand development, and plans afoot for the rebuilding of the East Stand. There was even a surprise move to win election as a Premier League representative on the FA Council, but failure to win sufficient votes hinted that his fellow club chairmen still harboured reservations about the born-again football evangelist.

One success for Sugar, however, was when manager Gerry Francis, offered a four-year contract, eventually compromised on a two-year deal worth a reported £350,000 a year before bonuses.

Over at Highbury, Bruce Rioch still had not signed a contract of any sort, as rumour persisted that the manager was unhappy over vice-chairman David Dein's insistence on having an active role in player purchases. With no big signings since David Platt a year earlier, Arsenal fans saw the likes of Middlesbrough and Coventry out-manoeuvering them in the transfer market while Tottenham stood on the sidelines. The trend of the summer echoed the previous year as money passed between Premiership clubs, or out of the country altogether. The Football League was receiving less media coverage than beach volleyball, and was left to pray that Sky's magic could eventually do for them what it had done for the Premiership.

Dream On

The Intertoto Cup came around again, but the fact that Bordeaux had shown how Intertoto qualification could lead to the UEFA Cup final did not impress its Premiership counterparts, and this year there were no English clubs taking part in the competition.

For Manchester United, two Doubles in three years placed the club at the pinnacle of English football. Their priority now was to repeat that success on a European stage, and five major signings by Alex Ferguson clearly showed no intention of resting on laurels.

But 35 years on from their own Double, what hopes for the forthcoming season can Spurs fans realistically hold? Gerry is once more apparently shopping for journeymen players who will dirty their hands for the good of the team. The availability of Darren Anderton for the start of the season will be a boost, and the removal of many question marks over Chris Armstrong's abilities will strengthen Gerry's attacking options. But in midfield and defence, the squad remains threadbare and looks far from championship material.

Already, Alan Sugar's bold proclamation of the future resting with home produced youth stars appears to be empty rhetoric as two of the club's brightest hopes – striker Steve Slade and goalkeeper Chris Day – have signed for non-Premiership sides rather than remain at Tottenham. To lose young players of such quality is a stark reminder of the gulf between ambition and commitment.

With Gerry Francis only pencilled in for another couple of years, the worry for fans is twofold: just how far behind Manchester United will the club fall, and is Alan Sugar the problem or the solution?

Chapter 14

1996–97:
What's Glory Got To Do With It?

One consolation to be taken from season 1996/97 – a season for Spurs fans more drab, frustrating and achingly tedious than any other in living memory – is that the spectre of relegation no longer holds any fear. Where once the 'dreaded drop' was viewed as the ultimate footballing humiliation, there was now an infinitely more depressing (and immediate) scenario to haunt their Saturday afternoons – mediocrity.

The legacy of the Sugar/Littner/Francis triumvirate may indeed be a company whose bookkeeping practices could win an accounting Oscar; whose share performance has City investors high-fiving in their pinstripes, and whose marketing gurus have turned White Hart Lane into north London's biggest corporate hospitality venue. But those crucial ninety minutes when all eyes are focused on the pitch and not the balance sheet only serves to highlight that the glitz of one is countered by the drabness of the other.

Dream On

For fans to whom plc may as well stand for 'permanent lost cause' things have come to such a sorry state that the headless chicken era of Ossie Ardiles' management is now nostalgically viewed as the good old days. White Hart Lane regulars, numbed almost comatose by the safety-first tactics of Gerry Francis which have wrung all remaining life from what was once the glory game, can only look back in wonder at how they dared complain when Ardiles fielded a five-man forward line and neglected defensive responsibilities. The new 'Spurs way' of playing was far too reminiscent of the old Wimbledon way. 'If a team is squeezing the space and you have Chris Armstrong, why not put it over the top and he might score', despite, in the next breath, Gerry's protestations to the contrary – 'I have been here for two years and I have never asked the players to knock the ball long.'

A miserly 19 goals at home – only Nottingham Forest and Leeds scored fewer – and a paltry eight home wins, and 18 defeats from 38 games is an awful record. Never higher than sixth, never lower than fourteenth, never in danger, never threatening a challenge, it is an indictment on the rest of the Premiership that Spurs should still finish tenth. 'The team is playing the worst football I have seen since we went down [in 1977],' confirmed lifelong Spurs fan, journalist and TV presenter Richard Littlejohn. 'Actually it's worse than that, because that side had Hoddle in it.'

An FA Cup third round draw away to Manchester United was cruel luck when a decent cup run would have been a welcome diversion from a league season already dead on its feet by January. Defeat at Old Trafford, following the Coca-Cola Cup exit at Bolton, left Spurs with nothing to play for and four months of the season to spin out. For Spurs this season, there was no glorious failure, just failure. As the

1996–97: What's Glory Got To Do With It?

fanzine *Cock-a-Doodle-Doo* wrote in April when explaining its lack of a traditional end of season poll, '. . . just how do you vote for worst game of the season?'

Supporters looked in vain for signs that the club shared their concerns. The goodwill engendered by Gerry's initial ship-steadying has been replaced by a suspicion that the man is no more than a competent captain whose purpose has been served. A farcical season-long injury crisis is the manager's excuse for an inglorious showing in the league and both cup competitions, but sympathy is in short supply from fans. They cannot understand why Gerry dithered so long before adding to a squad woefully short of Premiership class and depth. The only significant pre-season arrival was Danish international Allan Nielsen for £1.65 million. Mid-season swoops for Steffen Iversen (£2.7 million), John Scales (£2.6 million) and Ramon Vega (£3.75 million) were seen as too little, too late. All three signings were captured in the face of stiff competition and as such were major triumphs for the club's enduring ability to sell itself. However, with all three suffering chronic injury problems their impact on Tottenham's season was marginal and once more the manager was left asking for patience as another season of transition was endured.

If the fans have had enough, it comes as no surprise to hear that many of the players have too. Of the entire Spurs squad, excluding the most recent acquisitions, only the England quartet of Sheringham, Anderton, Campbell and Walker would generate interest at the top end of the market. All must be seriously scrutinising their contracts for any potential get-out clauses that could free them from a club where ambition is seemingly absent from the agenda.

'It's been a poor season for Spurs, disastrous in fact,'

Dream On

Teddy Sheringham was reported as saying. 'As a player with international ambitions you do worry about being in a struggling team for too long. You can't carry on playing in a struggling team – as Spurs have been.' It can only be hoped that the long-term contracts signed by the three newcomers prove considerably more watertight than Jurgen Klinsmann's.

At the end of 1996 Spurs announced a doubling of their profit to nearly £12 million. Rarely can a set of healthy figures have been so poorly received by a club's fans. Most are now familiar enough with the workings of a plc to understand where that money will go, but if there is a lesson to be learnt from Tottenham's situation, then other clubs are not listening. For if there was one underlying trend amongst football clubs in the 1996/97 season, it was the headlong rush towards the perceived holy grail of a stockmarket flotation.

In the short term, such flotations bring millions into a club, which can dramatically transform fortunes by wiping out debts at a stroke and providing a war chest for player purchases. However, once a club becomes a plc, then its obligations change dramatically. *The main purpose of a plc is to generate a dividend for its shareholders.* As Spurs fans are finding out, success on the pitch is not necessary to make investors happy. In fact the drive for 'conventional' success (i.e. trophies, Europe, glory) can be detrimental to a shareholder's investment. When one star signing could wipe out a club's multi-million pound profit, which chief executive would forsake a juicy dividend to appease the fans? Indeed selling the odd two-legged asset is a sure-fire way to generate a few million in profits. And if that sale harms the football club's prospects? Which now takes priority? In plc-land, head will overrule heart every time.

1996–97: What's Glory Got To Do With It?

Spurs fan Stephen Altman summed up the conflict of interest when writing to *Cock-a-Doodle-Doo*; 'The likes of Edinburgh, Dozzell, Ronny and Fox may embarrass us fans, but to Sugar they are money in the bank. How? Well [Alan Sugar] needs just eleven clinically alive bodies each Saturday to advertise the Hewlett Packard logo ... He needs at least eleven able-bodied mannequins to wear the shirts so the turnstiles will click around 32,000 times every other Saturday. Even if our line-up included Weah, Ronaldo, Suker and Maldini he couldn't fit any more in: that's money in the bank. Although these players earn in a week what you and I see every decade, that's nothing to what he'd have to pay true soccer talent.'

As Manchester United approached their Champions League semi-final clash with Borussia Dortmund in April, chairman Martin Edwards – announcing record half-year profits of more than £19 million – found time to joke that his company would be better off if the team reached the final but lost, as there wouldn't be such huge bonuses to pay.

Nevertheless, in its wisdom, and despite a patchy record to date, the City now views football as a fashionable investment. Sexy even. Awash with money from TV deals, sponsorship, merchandising and, increasingly, the capitalisation on the Premiership's appeal to overseas audiences, the opportunity to get a snout in the Premiership trough is proving irresistible to many. Clubs too are being swept along, seduced by the vibrant figures coming out of Old Trafford. The me-too desire is trickling down to the likes of Sheffield United and Charlton who are cashing in on the City's insatiable appetite for football club shares. Even clubs like Arsenal, Aston Villa and Liverpool where individuals holding massive share interests must surely, reluctantly and purely for the benefit of the club of course, succumb to the lure of a one-off cash windfall that going public would bring. The trend has eased the way in for a new breed of owner – Caspian plc at Leeds and the Scholar/Wray consortium at Forest – who have no emotional, geographical or historical links with their new empire but simply a desire to capitalise on a perceived business opportunity in football.

With successful Premiership clubs now anticipating around £10 million a season each from Sky/BBC, and with pay-per-view on the horizon, it is no wonder that investors are queuing up to take shares in clubs. When they see how Alan Sugar, in the space of just six undistinguished seasons, has been able to turn an investment of less than £10 million into a shareholding worth nearer £60 million then it's no wonder that City eyes light up with flashing pound signs. Even Martin Edwards, despite his best efforts to give away Manchester United to Michael Knighton in the late 1980s for around £10 million, has since managed to make his stake in the club worth a cool £50 million, even allowing for his recent share sale that netted him literally millions without diluting his control.

But the worries that every investor must confront are those unique factors that can set a football club's price tumbling. Injuries to star players, general loss of form and bad refereeing decisions are all impervious to City rules and able to confound the best management teams. Within weeks of Newcastle's much hyped flotation, their share price had dipped below the launch price, despite the replacement of Kevin Keegan with Kenny Dalglish – a choice seen by many as a pre-flotation appeasement to the City. Sunderland's share price slumped as relegation loomed, Charlton's shares lost 25% over a matter of weeks and trading in Millwall was suspended after the share price nose-dived to just four pence.

1996–97: What's Glory Got To Do With It?

For fans at Tottenham, pioneers of the stock market flotation, the conflict between the demands of the plc and the needs of the football club have never been resolved satisfactorily. Under Irving Scholar – the Man from Del Monte-Carlo who liked to say 'Yes!' – there was never any doubt where the club's priorities lay. Diversification off the field was intended to fund success on the field. Alan Sugar however, has traditionally taken a different line; 'We do not exist just to produce funds for a manager,' he confirmed when distancing himself from the role George Graham had enjoyed at Highbury. 'Everyone knows I'm right – they just won't stand up and say so.' Thus does Alan Sugar defend his pioneering policy on bucking the transfer spiral, explained in no uncertain terms as a desire ' . . . to demonstrate that this club can reach a great status without irresponsible dealings in the transfer market.'

His dogged adherence to running Tottenham as a business has a logic the City investors appreciate, but few fans do. Justification for this policy flew in the face of some appalling results. 'No chequebook in the world is big enough to buy team spirit,' he remarked after the 6–1 Coca-Cola Cup hammering at First Division Bolton. Indeed, results such as this (and the 7–1 humiliation at Newcastle) merely confirmed his doctrine for 'success through youth', a mission to succeed by assembling a squad of players who have progressed through the club's youth policy and laced only with the odd experienced (read 'expensive') outsider. It wouldn't take much of a cynic to view Sugar's concurrent passion for the introduction of legislation that would prevent the poaching of such committed, socialist, non-materialistic, unambitious, virginal, charitable prodigies, as an acknowledgement that the Tottenham Hotspur of three years hence could in fact be the last place such talent would want to stay. Continuing to cite Manchester United as a role model for a 'kids before cash' society fails to acknowledge the uniqueness of United's current youth crop, or to understand that the likes of Beckham, Scholes, Butt and the Neville brothers might actually be tempted to remain at Old Trafford not through any sense of loyalty or contractual handcuffs, but by generous wages and bonus payments, lucrative product endorsement contracts, four titles in five years and the constant high profile that comes from playing in the country's most glamorous side.

Perhaps most worrying has always been the conviction by Sugar that not only has he got it right, but that he carries with him, by virtue of the club's healthy home attendances, the bulk of the Spurs support. Not so. An average home attendance of 31,000 is testimony to the snowballing ascendency of the Premier League *despite* the grim fare served up, and serves to hint at what potential there could be should any Spurs team ever deliver what is so often only promised. The true feelings of the fans is surely reflected within the pages of the club's three fanzines and countless callers to radio phone-ins, where a picture emerges of a club increasingly detached from its support. Thus in late January, when there was little to play for, could Gerry Francis delude himself; 'The one thing as a manager that I have never been accused of is "not playing football". The supporters have been fantastic, they know what the situation [injuries] has been. They think we are going along the right lines.' Quite which fans Gerry had been talking to wasn't made clear, but it certainly wasn't those flooding the fanzines with opinions best summarised by Stafford Green in *Cock-a-Doodle-Doo*, typical of many, who wrote simply that, 'Francis must go, condemned for lack of style, lack

1996–97: What's Glory Got To Do With It?

of results, lack of intelligence and destroying the traditions and heritage of a once famous and admired club'.

When confronted by hostility at the club's AGM in November 1996, Alan Sugar preferred to believe that criticism came from a 'minority of publicity seekers', and tried patronisingly to explain to such dissidents his perception of the 'real' world. It is a world where the Bosman ruling is 'the most devastating' decision against which all else 'falls into insignificance. We have not seen the worst of it yet.' A world in which foreigners are off home 'if they don't like the softness of the spaghetti or the smell of the coffee,' and one where the club's investment in its proposed Chigwell school needs to be protected lest a homegrown Beckham be lured away by the gift of a car to Dad. 'If we were to do things other clubs do, we would have 6 points deducted.'

Returning to a favoured analogy, Sugar 'reminded' shareholders how he had 'taken over Del Boy's stall and turned it into Marks & Spencer', conveniently ignoring the fact that Tottenham were never, ever the equivalent of Del Boy's stall, but a big club with a proud history and a special tradition of playing 'the Spurs way'. Ajax, a club which shares similarities to Spurs both on and off the field, once woke up to headlines describing their winning of the European Cup as 'a miserable triumph'. The players and staff were embarrassed, feeling victory had not been achieved in 'the Ajax way'. Spurs – Alan Sugar would think – should be so lucky.

By allowing Gerry Francis – in the words of Simon Barnes of *The Times* – to 'seek the low road of consistent competence', Alan Sugar fuels fan dissatisfaction in the short term as well as making a bad business decision in the long term. Tottenham's 'brand value' cannot be maintained by the board's current lack of ambition, neither punters nor sponsors will be queuing up to be associated with mediocrity. Worse still, why should future generations follow the family tradition when they can be entertained by stars at a cheaper price at Highbury. This was the thrust of the argument of a group of 'business' fans [the Tottenham Action Group] who called for a boycott of club merchandise saying, 'To make Sugar think, you must hit him in his wallet, – that's where it hurts him.'

'Wimbledon with fans' was the withering description famously used by Jimmy Greaves to sum up his old club's new status. But how long will those fans stay loyal? Even within London, the club has clearly lost out in the swagger stakes to Chelsea, while Wimbledon have put together significant cup runs and Arsenal entertain the bigger crowds. Moreover, all three have better playing records. To qualify as a big club demands consistent success, or in Tottenham's case, the chance of occasional success and at least glorious failure.

Thankfully, the second half of the season at last brought indicators that Sugar's stance was shifting. Bold rhetoric was now tempered by his cautionary qualification that you '. . . have to expect to fall at the first hurdle, but by three years time we shall be going for the title and a cup win will be a realistic ambition'. By mid April he was more specific. He told BBC's *Football Focus*; 'I would truthfully be really shocked if we did not get into Europe next time. There is no industry in which I have been where I have not become a market leader and I want to do the same in football.' Announcing £7 million half-year profits for the period to January 1997, the penny had finally dropped that you cannot maximise the opportunities for the plc if you have an unsuccessful football club.

1996–97: What's Glory Got To Do With It?

'This season has so far been disappointing to everyone connected with the club,' wrote Sugar in the club's interim report. 'No one should doubt our ambition for this club. Football is the core activity of our business as a provider of entertainment and brand leader and it is only when we get this right that we can fully maximise associated business opportunities.' At last, Sugar the businessman seems to have grasped what the fans have been telling him all along: there is more potential for a successful club than for a stagnant one. The vibes are unmistakable, another season has been written off, but next year would not be so disposable. If Arsenal can sack a manager who got them into Europe for not being up to scratch, then bring in a replacement and immediately challenge for the title, it's no wonder that Spurs fans ask why their club seems to cherish lower standards and expectations. Constant talk of aiming for a UEFA place assumes a pitifully low ambition for a club that once set the agenda for English clubs in Europe. While Arsenal are broadening their horizons, Tottenham are deliberately limiting theirs. Maybe the chairman is now asking the same questions the fans are.

Gerry Francis's record shows him to be an excellent manager at small clubs but unsatisfactory at a big club. There must be a change, because if Gerry Francis continues in the same vein he will get the chance to reinforce the accuracy of that assessment – Spurs having been reduced to the status of QPR!

The coming season will be the time for Gerry to deliver in spades. And he must realise what 'deliver' means; to a chairman whose price rise on season tickets for 1997-98 clearly leaves him a hostage to fortune and to fans who are paying those astronomical admission prices and want success now. Record profits give a hint to the funds that may be available next season, but even Alan Sugar must wonder whether Gerry is the man to spend it. He appears to be still singing the same old song. After a rare home win against Wimbledon in early April, Joe Kinnear's brutally honest summary of his team's apathetic performance was X-rated stuff – '. . . too bad to be true . . . one player decides f--- it and bang you're dead and the rest of the team suffer, so I've had to iron out one or two players in no uncertain manner' – but a welcome contrast to those familiar with Gerry's traditional litany of excuses; '. . . the eighteenth time we've hit the bar or post and not one of them has gone in . . . I've never known anything like it [injuries]. Any other team in the country would have had a real problem this year with what we've had to put up with.'

Looking ahead to season 1997-98, the decks have been cleared to smooth Gerry's path. A separation of powers early in the new year saw the manager relieved of financial and contractual obligations peripheral to coaching duties. In a move mimicking the setup at many continental clubs, Gerry can now concentrate on the skills that have historically been his forte. But although Alan Sugar continues to dominate the headlines and dictate the strategy, there has been a tactical shift in the corridors of power behind the West Stand as an attempt is being made to grapple with reality lower down the hierarchy.

Daniel Sugar, a comparative youngster who skipped school to watch the 1987 Cup final, describes his new role at Tottenham as 'football operations manager'. Conversations with Daniel reveal a man clearly on a mission with only the best interests of the club at heart, and one who appears to have got his priorities right: 'It's no good winning the FA Cup every time the year ends in one and not winning the league for another 36 years, is it?' Privy to all that happens behind closed doors, Daniel Sugar is under no

1996–97: What's Glory Got To Do With It?

illusions about the size of his task. Overseeing the scouting system, schoolboy and the youth development, the football in the community scheme, now comes within his orbit. As well as this, once manager Gerry has earmarked a potential signing and Sugar senior has rubberstamped the transaction, transfer and contract negotiations are now led by Sugar junior with chief executive Claude Littner. Daniel Sugar certainly feels he has the manager's support. 'As long as Gerry can concentrate on the eleven players who will represent him on a Saturday afternoon, he doesn't care how the medical setup is organised or how the scouting system is run as long as he is continually provided with the right players. His attitude to us is; "If you are going to make my life easier, then go and do it". I think other managers [at Tottenham] up until now have wanted involvement in those peripheral matters and have not wanted interference. But with Gerry I think we are very fortunate that he takes the attitude he does.'

In contrast to the sudden swoop when it became known that Liverpool would release John Scales, the securing of Steffen Iversen and Ramon Vega both involved protracted negotiations long after Gerry had expressed his desire to bring the two to White Hart Lane. Indeed, Gerry and assistant Roger Cross dined with Vega post Euro '96, but it would be another six months of hard work by Daniel and Claude before Cagliari could be coaxed into releasing their Swiss international. Similarly Steffen Iversen was persuaded to relinquish a chance to play in the Champions League quarter-finals with Rosenborg, surprise victors over AC Milan.

'In both of those cases,' confirmed Daniel, 'my father told Claude and myself to go and get the best deal we could for this club. And both of those transfers were completed within the boundaries of our wage structure and our budget.

We've always had a budget and we won't spend what we haven't got.'

Unfortunately, those two transfers came too far into the season to influence its course for Tottenham, a fact acknowledged by Daniel but justified by a new realism about transfer dealings. 'We can't rush into things – the way the game is going one has to plan transfers probably a season in advance now. That's the way it has been in Spain and Italy for a long time and the Bosman ruling will now force Premiership clubs into such thinking. I think from Tottenham's point of view, it means a situation where we are perpetually renegotiating the salaries of our players. It will cost us more money.'

This obsession with money is endemic amongst Premier League clubs but in Tottenham's case there is at least the mitigating factor of a genuine desire to grow their own. 'I'm obsessed with youth development. In the past we have brought through the likes of Hoddle, Souness, Jamie Redknapp, Sol Campbell, Ian Walker and Nicky Barmby. Clearly we cannot continue to afford the transfer fees and salaries for the likes of Iversen and Vega, so we have to start bringing more kids through. We have to start removing obstacles to make that happen, even if we have to build a school and dormitories at our training ground. I have spent a hell of a lot of time with Ajax in Amsterdam, and we are perhaps looking to form some kind of alliance with them. We could learn a lot from them – although I'm sure they're not going to learn too much from us about youth teams. We've got so far to go at Tottenham Hotspur Football Club, there are a lot of things we could be doing, and things we could be doing better.'

Despite growing criticism, support for Gerry Francis – according to Daniel Sugar – remains strong within the

1996–97: What's Glory Got To Do With It?

club. 'Gerry Francis is a man unlike others I have seen here [at Tottenham] in the past. I would honestly say he is one of the best coaches I have seen. He has a great attention to detail and he is a real hard working guy. I speak with Gerry frequently and I think he has some fantastic ideas. I think that if you give someone the tools to work with and the opportunity, only then is the time to judge them. I think Gerry has been incredibly unlucky with the injury problems, people are sick and tired of hearing about Gary Mabbutt's broken leg [the great man's season lasted 18 minutes] and Jurgen Klinsmann clearing off back to Germany and Popescu pissing off to Barcelona. But they are facts, you can't take those players out of a team and try to replace them in a season. I think you have to look at the team the manager has assembled today, and the price for which he has assembled that team. Now let's see that team in action and check he has the balance right. If that team is not successful then he will be judged on his results, as he would expect. But I am convinced that Gerry Francis will be a successful manager for Tottenham Hotspur. I do think that there have been mistakes made, and my opinion is that he may have been a little slow at looking at the European situation. But now when you look at the players he has since brought in, they have been mainly foreigners.'

Still, there have been many overseas stars linked to Spurs but snapped up by others. 'That's an area I'll be working at. I want to see the club improve its knowledge of the European scene. I would like to think that over the next few months the club could establish a European scouting network both for this and future managers. We need structure – a structure at the training ground and a football structure so that when the next manager comes in – please God it's in a few years after we've won the league and the

Dream On

Champions League and Gerry has retired to the Seychelles and dyed his grey hair – we can say to that manager, "If you come to Tottenham Hotspur then these are the guidelines you will work within and this is our system". That has got to be the way.'

So where does Gerry Francis sit amongst all this revolution? Apparently, very comfortably. The club's policy of thrift is not a million miles away from Gerry's own feelings. He is given a budget, reasonable but not lavish, with which to achieve his aims. He also receives the full backing of his board – 'Gerry Francis doesn't need challenging,' confirms Sugar. But for how long? In his two-and-a-half seasons at Tottenham, there has been little sign of real progress. If we are to ignore plc responsibilities and judge Gerry purely on his team's playing performance, then he has underachieved. His first season, one where he inherited a mess and could reasonably be excused for not coming up to expectations has proved to be his most successful by far. Since then, two full seasons have seen a slide into turgid mediocrity. Caution in the transfer market ('In Gerry we have a manager who likes to know what a player had for breakfast,' admits Daniel Sugar) saw the club lose out as others snapped up Euro-bargains. It was a financial loss as well. It must still rankle with Alan Sugar that had Gerry bought Messrs. Iversen and Vega in the club's previous financial year, then he could have saved substantially on his tax bill as transfer fees are one of the few 100% tax-allowable expenses. Instead, money that could have bought a quality addition to the squad went straight to the Exchequer, and Gerry paid the price for dithering when injuries ravaged his team leaving him with only rookie cover for key positions. As he juggled his line-up between 4-4-2 and 3-5-2 (or

1996–97: What's Glory Got To Do With It?

5-3-2 as it really was) the lack of true wing-backs was an embarrassment. Darren Anderton's absence for virtually the whole season (again) seemed to surprise only the manager, leaving him without a midfield playmaker and highlighting the absence of cover in such a key position.

For fans who were solidly behind their new manager back in November 1994, the 1996-97 season has been trying indeed. Gerry's matchday programme notes qualify him for a degree in revisionist history. Commenting on the home victory against Blackburn in January, Gerry wrote that [Andy Sinton's goal] 'was in fact our seventh goal scored this season from one of Allan's [Nielsen] throws and is in keeping with the tradition established here by the likes of Dave Mackay and Martin Chivers in the past'. Well it is certainly true that Messrs Mackay and Chivers could take a long throw in, but it was only a sideshow. The 'tradition' they perpetuated was helping to win trophies by playing in the Spurs way. They were not long throw merchants, Gerry, they were stars in pursuit of glory. More disturbing for a club committed to 'grow your own' talent is his reluctance, with the notable exception of Stephen Carr, to give youngsters an extended run in the first team.

As with others at the club, criticism is unwelcome and seen as unconstructive. From being the most English of players, Gerry has evolved into the most English of managers. Old-pros disease (chronic belly-ache leading to foot-in mouth) comes as second nature; 'Nobody knows what it is like to be a manager,' he opines in best caps-on-the-table manner. 'The only people worth listening to about management are managers, because they are the only people who know what it's like. When you have failed or have been successful, then you can talk from experience.

Dream On

Anyone else doesn't know a thing about it . . . It is always a lonely job . . . I don't think anyone really knows what it is like to do it, or how lonely the job can be.'

Gerry may well discover exactly how lonely in the near future, as fate and market forces are brought to play against his squad. Spurs will do well to resist the temptation to cash in on Teddy Sheringham as he fast approaches zero value at the end of his contract. The £10 million valuation slapped on the England striker after another glowing performance against Georgia would not necessarily deter some clubs, while Sol Campbell has been linked with a move to Anfield too often for the comfort of most Spurs fans. 'Campbell can go to Liverpool,' retorted Sugar after more newspaper gossip, 'on the team bus this weekend. It will be the only time he goes there with our permission. He has got two years on his contract and I am convinced that he will eventually sign a new deal.' He did, the week after the season finished. Goalkeeper Ian Walker missed the last couple of games through injury and faced a two-month layoff that ruled him out of England's hectic summer itinerary. After a long absence, Darren Anderton returned prematurely, failed to complete the season and was also given two months to rest and recuperate. Chris Armstrong hasn't played since December, Colin Calderwood was booked for a date with the surgeon's knife and Steffen Iversen was last seen in March. All will do well to be back in training by the time pre-season comes around.

But Alan Sugar is in no mood for an injury-ridden *déjà-vu*. Reminded of his 'we'll win the title within three years' boast, by Richard Littlejohn, the chairman conceded in May that he had now just two years left to fulfil that ambition. Further cajoling even brought forth a willingness to quit, 'I'll do my best for the next couple of years. If I can't crack it,

1996–97: What's Glory Got To Do With It?

I'll let some other brain surgeon come and have a go. I'll clear off.'

For Spurs fans, the signs that Alan Sugar may have at last woken from his slumber and seen the light might have come just in time. While no permanent damage has been inflicted and bruised north London pride can still heal, there remains an opportunity to regain ground lost to other 'big' clubs. The Premier League, free from the FA/Football League ties that hindered the English game for so long, is moving forward with great momentum. Premiership TV rights seem destined for pay-per-view sooner rather than later, but the experience of Sky's counterparts in France and in Italy indicates that only the biggest of clubs will be able to earn more than they currently can from subscription channels like Sky Sports. Thus Spurs must regain their former position within the English game or it will cost them dearly. A European Super League (ESL) is inevitable, most likely with clubs playing domestic action at weekends and ESL games midweek. This is the way forward, but with such a league dependent on television and sponsorship, admission could be by invitation only and extended only to those clubs able to win trophies and fulfil financial criteria. If introduced today, Alan Sugar would do well not to waste too much time sitting by the phone waiting for Silvio Berlusconi to call.